A DEATH IN CALIFORNIA

JOAN BARTHEL

CONGDON & LATTÈS, INC.
NEW YORK

Library of Congress Cataloging in Publication Data

Barthel, Joan.
A death in California.

1. Masters. Hope, 1941- . 2. Murder—California.
3. Criminal psychology. 4. Victims of crimes—Psychology.
I. Title.
HV6533.C2B37   364.1'523'0924   [B]   81-5431   AACR2

ISBN 0-312-92130-6 (Distributor)
ISBN 0-86553-026-2

The portions of the lyric to "A Tramp Shining"
by Jimmy Webb are Copyright © 1968
Canopy Music, Inc., all rights reserved, and
are used by permission of Warner Bros. Music.

Published by Congdon & Lattès, Inc.
Distributed by St. Martin's Press
Published simultaneously in Canada by Thomas Nelson & Sons Limited

Printed in the United States of America by the Haddon Craftsmen,
Scranton, Pennsylvania

Designed by Irving Perkins

First Edition

For James E. Cronin,
my teacher,
founder of
The Writers Institute,
Saint Louis University

List of Characters

LOS ANGELES

Hope Masters, a Beverly Hills socialite
Tom Masters, Hope's estranged husband
Bill Ashlock, advertising writer, Hope's lover
Fran Ashlock, Bill's estranged wife
Keith, Hope Masters's oldest child, age 12
Hope Elizabeth, Hope Masters's daughter, age 10
K.C., Hope Masters's youngest child, age 3
Honey, Hope Masters's mother
Van, Hope Masters's stepfather, member of a prominent Los Angeles
    law firm
Michael Abbott, young lawyer, a friend of Hope Masters
Lionel, screenwriter, a friend of Hope Masters
Sandi, a friend of Bill Ashlock
Nadine, a friend of Tom Masters
Martha Padilla, Hope Masters's weekday maid
Licha Mancha, Hope Masters's weekend maid
Reverend Kermit Castellanos, rector of All Saints Episcopal Church,
    Beverly Hills
Cliff Einstein, Bill Ashlock's boss at the advertising agency

Helen Linley, Bill Ashlock's secretary
Sara Monaco, receptionist at the advertising agency
Richard Miller, Bill Ashlock's partner in a filmmaking company
Ned Nelsen, Hope Masters's defense attorney
Tom Breslin, Hope Masters's defense attorney and Ned Nelsen's partner
Gene Tinch, a private detective
Fillmore Crank, manager of the Howard Johnson's Motor Lodge in North Hollywood
Gary LePon, assistant manager of the Sheraton–Universal Hotel in Hollywood
Robert McRae, desk clerk at the Holiday Inn in Hollywood
Paul Luther, agent, Federal Bureau of Investigation
Robert Sage, agent, Federal Bureau of Investigation
Beverly Hills police
   Billy Ray Smith
   William Clyde Stien
   Philip DeMond
Los Angeles investigators
   Kenneth Pollock
   Paul O'Steen
   Arthur Stoyanoff

CHICAGO

Robert Pietrusiak, a patient at Illinois Research Hospital
Catherine Pietrusiak, his wife
Armond Lee, a guard at Illinois Research Hospital
Marthe Purmal, an attorney with Legal Services
Mort Friedman, chief prosecutor, Cook County State's Attorney's Office
Robert Baucom, agent, Federal Bureau of Investigation
Illinois State Police
   Robert Swalwell
   Sven (Gus) Ljuggren

Williard Rowe
Frank Waldrup
Illinois Department of Corrections
Ronald Tonsel
Willis Stephans
Ray Clark
Ron Hepner
Pete Lane

TULARE COUNTY

Jim Webb, caretaker at the ranch
Teresa Webb, his wife
Gerald Webb, Jim Webb's brother, a part-time Baptist minister
Dorothy Anderson, former housekeeper at the ranch

Tulare County investigators
  Gene Parker
  Jim Brown
  Forrest Barnes
  Henry Babcock
  Ralph Tucker
  Jack Flores
  Vern Hensley
  Doyle Hoppert
  Donald Landers
  Michael Scott
  Joseph Teller
  Butch Coley
  Ollie Farris
George Carter, judge, Porterville Justice Court
Virginia Anderson, clerk, Porterville Justice Court
William Thompson, bailiff, Porterville Justice Court
James Heusdens, prosecutor, deputy district attorney, Tulare County
Joseph Haley, prosecutor, deputy district attorney, Tulare County

Jay Powell, public defender, Tulare County
Jay Ballantyne, judge, Superior Court, Tulare County
Leonard M. Ginsburg, judge, Superior Court, Tulare County

OTHER PLACES

Taylor Wright, a jewelry salesman from Benton Harbor, Michigan
Larry Burbage, an electronics equipment salesman from Atlanta,
    Georgia
Richard Crane, an engineer from the state of Washington, found
    murdered in a motel on Sunset Strip

G. Daniel Walker, a man of many identities

AUTHOR'S NOTE

THIS BOOK HAS been written from the memories of many people. The core of the story, which is a weekend at a ranch in northern California, is based on Hope Masters's remembrance of that time. Certain scenes in this story have been composed in a literary rather than a journalistic manner, using a variety of sources, including police reports and notes, court transcripts and other legal documents, tape recordings, letters, and diaries, as well as dozens of interviews, some of them conducted at that time, some recently, as I was writing this book. One person's memory sometimes collides with another's; but what is important about memory, it seems to me, is not its indisputability, but its texture.

For her openness in discussing with me, not only the events of 1973 but her life and thoughts, in an unconditional, wholehearted way, I am grateful to Hope Masters. I am grateful to members of her family, especially her mother, and to her friends who, in talking with me, helped me come to know her.

Special thanks to the people who spent many hours with me—sometimes days—talking about the case and about themselves: Detective Robert Swalwell of the Illinois State Police; Detectives James Brown and Gene Parker in Tulare County, California; former Deputy District Attorney James Heusdens; former District Attorney Jay Powell; George Carter of the Porterville Justice Court; Judge Leonard M. Ginsburg; Thomas P.

Breslin and Ned R. Nelson, attorneys; and Gene Tinch, private investigator.

My thanks to jurors Ruthe Snelling and Lois Bollinger for sharing their insights into the trial. I appreciate the friendly cooperation of Taylor Wright and Marthe Purmal and the courtesy of Tom Masters.

For their help with research, I am grateful to Jenny Vogt and her staff in the Tulare County Clerk's Office in Visalia, California, and to Shirley Askins at the Criminal Court, and to Kevin A. Swanson and Velda J. Poe at the Appellate Court in Fresno, California.

For their editorial help, I thank Ellie Kossack and Deborah Lyons. I am obliged to friends whose help was sustaining: Elizabeth Pace, Linda Berman, Girlie Persad, and Zita Drake in New York, and Janine Coyle in Los Angeles. My loving thanks to Jim and Anne, who helped as only a husband and a daughter can.

Joan Barthel
May 1981

PART I

PROLOGUE

So MANY PRETTY girls were swirling through the lobby that the desk clerk didn't pay much attention to the man who was checking in. He didn't notice the slight heave of relief from the tired-looking, middle-aged man when the clerk said yes, they had a single for one night, and the pool was open. The man set his briefcase down on the floor beside the desk and reached for the registration pad. "T. O. Wright, Benton Harbor, Michigan." Under FIRM NAME: "T. O. Wright and Sons." The clerk, Patrick Rye, wrenched his attention from the girls in the lobby back to the desk and reached for a key. "Room one-ten," he told T. O. Wright. "First floor."

The man picked up his briefcase and went back out through the revolving door to his car, parked at the entrance. He drove around the long rectangle of the Marriott to a parking space and sat at the wheel for a moment. He was exhausted from his week on the road, this long day's driving from Cleveland through Toledo and now into Ann Arbor, and he longed for the bliss of a heated pool. Before he'd left home Monday morning, he'd made sure his brown swimming trunks were packed. Swimming was a Wright family passion—maybe it came with the territory—and swimming was the reason he wasn't heading home to Benton Harbor this Friday evening. His sons, Taylor and Jamie, were swimming in an A.A.U. meet tomorrow in Jackson; he planned to meet them and the rest

3

of the family there. As tired as he was, he'd passed up the Howard Johnson's when they told him their pool was closed for repairs.

He took out his suitcase and his briefcase, then locked the car and turned on the alarm. No use taking out the sample cases just for one night; he'd have to leave early to get to Jackson by nine. He wasn't carrying diamonds anyway, nothing precious; T. O. Wright and Sons handled costume jewelry. Nice things, though—bracelets and chains, gold-filled brooches and pins, stone rings; he was wearing one of the rings himself. Nice jewelry, a nice business, and Room 110 was a nice room, like all the other nice, nondescript motel rooms he lived in on the road: green and gold tones, with a dark green carpet, a green and gold landscape print hanging above the bed. He turned on the light at the door, set down the briefcase and the suitcase, and sat on the edge of the bed. He glanced at his watch—a nice watch, a Seiko. Still early; time for the evening news on TV before drinks and dinner, and a swim before bed.

Before he turned on the news, though, he picked up the phone. Taylor Ortho Wright III was forty-two years old, but he was very much one of the "Sons" in the firm and his dad would be waiting for a report. He had followed his dad into the family business, just as he'd followed the family educational tradition. Like his father and his uncle, he'd enrolled at the University of Missouri to study economics; in his freshman year, 1950, he'd pledged their fraternity, Phi Psi. The conversation with his father was long, half an hour, and when he hung up, he decided to skip the news and concentrate on drinks and dinner.

The hostess at the door of the restaurant in the lobby, just down from the desk, smiled at him. "There's a wait tonight," she murmured with a sweet, sympathetic smile.

Taylor Wright looked past her at the packed tables and nodded. "About how long?"

Her smile became more sympathetic. "About an hour and a half. May I have your name, and wouldn't you like to have a drink at the bar?"

He signed his name on her list: T. O. Wright. But the bar was jammed, too. He squeezed between the barstools, got a Scotch and water, and wandered back into the lobby, down the hall toward the banquet room, following the sounds of the party.

Near the entrance to the party room, a hatcheck girl smiled at him. She was young—eighteen, maybe twenty, he thought—black and pretty. Her smile was so glittering that, tired and hungry as he was, Taylor Wright smiled back.

"Hi there," she said. "Are you going to the party?"

Taylor shook his head. "I'm not a member of that group."

"Oh, you're not? What do you do?"

He sipped his Scotch and looked at her over the rim of the glass. "I'm a salesman. I'm a jewelry salesman."

She hadn't stopped smiling. "Oh, that's nice." She seemed about to say more, but a man came out of the banquet room and handed her the check stub for his coat. When she handed the man his coat, he handed her the stick-on WELCOME badge he'd been wearing, and she stuck it lightly up on the wall beside her. Taylor moved closer.

"You're a jewelry salesman," she said, and suddenly Taylor found himself talking to her about himself, about his business. She seemed interested, but then another man came out of the party, then another, and she was busy with their coats. Taylor was just about to walk back down the lobby when she called to him. "Oh, don't go away. Why don't you go in to the party? They need men in there, and it's a good party."

He shook his head, almost shyly. "I can't go in. I'm not a member."

Her smile flashed again as she tore the WELCOME badge off the wall and stuck it on his lapel. "Now you're a member," she announced. "Have fun."

She was right; it was a good party, and Taylor felt right at home as he moved through groups of laughing people to the bar, where he set down his empty glass and asked for a Scotch. He felt more relaxed than he had all day. Still hungry, though, he picked up a plate and moved along the buffet table, which was loaded with all sorts of good things—tiny shrimp, hot meatballs in sauce, little hot pastries with a spicy meat filling.

After another Scotch, he began to mingle. Most of the girls he talked with seemed to work for the Marriott, and he met their boss, the motel manager, John West. A man with John West, Wynn Schueller, had been in the navy with Taylor's uncle. *Small world, nice party,* Taylor thought, as he had another plate of food, a couple more Scotches. It was about ten when John West announced the party was over. Some of the girls clustered around their boss. "Oh, don't close it yet, don't close it yet," they squealed. John West smiled. "Okay," he said, and everybody had one more drink.

When the party was finally over, the restaurant had plenty of room, but Taylor wasn't hungry. He'd had a pretty good dinner on the hors d'oeuvres, so he walked into the bar, where the party seemed to have spilled over. John West was there for a little while, and some of the same girls. Everyone seemed to know everyone else, including the bartenders.

People kept calling their names, Mark and Clark. It seemed very funny that their names rhymed.

When the woman approached him, he noticed right away that she was older than the other women in the bar—at least thirty-five, maybe forty, a little on the heavy side. But she was very nice too, very friendly. She had long, dark brown hair and she was wearing a long party dress in some pale color—light pink or light blue. In the dimness of the bar, it was hard to tell.

"Hello," she said, easing up onto the barstool beside him, which he hadn't even noticed was empty. They began to talk. Taylor wasn't looking for a woman; although a traveling salesman could hardly be called a homebody, he was certainly a family man, with a great wife and kids, and he wasn't interested in any pickup. Still, he was lonesome, a little bored, and he enjoyed talking to her, just as he'd enjoyed talking to people at the party. You couldn't be a good salesman without liking to talk to people, and when a man on the stool on the other side of him started talking, Taylor enjoyed that too.

"What are you here for?" the woman asked. "I mean, what do you do?"

"I'm in the jewelry business," Taylor said. "I sell jewelry. My whole family sells jewelry."

The woman smiled. "Ah, you sell diamonds." It didn't sound like a question, more like a statement, and Taylor quickly corrected her.

"No, we don't have anything to do with diamonds. We carry costume jewelry. Chains, primarily. We sell to wholesalers. Nothing to do with diamonds."

"What territory do you cover?" the man next to him asked, and Taylor turned slightly to answer. "The whole Midwest," he replied. "Our factories are in Providence, Rhode Island, but I cover the Midwest. That's my territory."

"I cover the Midwest too," the man said. He laughed, and Taylor turned in order to see him better. He was a little older than the woman, maybe forty-five, partly bald, short and heavyset, wearing glasses. "Are you a salesman too?" Taylor asked, and the man laughed again. "No, I'm a reporter," he said. "I'm the police reporter for the *Ann Arbor News.*"

Taylor had another drink and didn't notice the man and the woman leave, but when Mark and Clark said the bar was closing, Taylor didn't see them. Even though they'd talked a lot, mostly about Taylor's business, he realized he hadn't asked their names.

Only four or five people were left in the bar, finishing their last drinks, as Taylor wandered out. Too late for a swim now. He wasn't drunk, but he was glad his room was on the first floor. Still, it seemed a very long way, down one long, carpeted aisle, around a corner, past an ice machine, down another hall, another corner. The walk seemed endless, as though he would never reach his room.

But there it was, 110. He fished in his pocket for the key, found it, and placed it in the lock. Just as he was turning the key, he heard her.

"Hello," she said softly.

Taylor looked back over his shoulder and saw her standing in the open doorway of the room across the hall. He thought she smiled at him.

"Didn't we meet in the bar?" she asked, still softly, and Taylor remembered, foggily, that they had.

"Would you like to have another drink with us?" she asked. As he turned to answer her, he was struck from behind.

Afterward, Taylor could not remember whether he had been hit in the hall or whether the man who'd hit him had been waiting in the doorway of Taylor's room. But he remembered being dragged across the hall, into the room where the woman had been standing in the doorway. He heard somebody close the door. The room was dark, but the door to the bathroom was partly open; by the bathroom light he could see the outline of twin beds and a man sitting on the edge of one bed, leaning over him as he lay on the floor.

It was not the man he had met in the bar. He recognized the man who had hit him as the man he'd talked with in the bar, the man who'd said he was a reporter. Taylor had never seen this other man, this second man, though it was a man he would never, after that night, forget.

The man leaned over him and clutched him by the front of his shirt. His long dark hair fell across his face and almost into Taylor's face. "Mr. Wright," the man said in a low voice, "I guess you know you're in trouble."

Taylor Wright peered up at him. His head was throbbing. "Yes, I guess I am," he said. "I guess I better go home now."

The man on the bed got very angry at that. "No, you are not," he said, jerking Taylor Wright to his feet. "Okay, Mr. Big Deal, now we are going to find out all about you." He began tearing Taylor's clothes off; the other man joined in. Taylor Wright said the first thing that came into his head, which was a mistake. "What are you, some kind of a queer?" he asked the man with the long hair, the man who seemed to be in charge. Taylor was hit again then, so hard that he blacked out. When he came to, he saw that he was naked except for his T-shirt and socks.

The room was quiet, and for a moment Taylor thought it was all over. Then somebody was hitting him again, shaking him, talking in a harsh, fierce tone. "Where is your jewelry? Where are your samples?"

As bloody and beaten as he was, Taylor Wright was stubborn, too. "I'm not going to tell you a damn thing," he said. "You'll have to kill me first."

The man who was standing over him stuck a gun into his mouth. In the light coming from the bathroom, Taylor saw that it was a blue steel revolver. It felt cold and hard in his throat.

The man with the gun cocked the trigger, and Taylor heard voices in the darkness beyond the bed, away from the lighted space where he was half-sitting, half-lying.

"No, no, oh, no, don't," the voices were saying. The woman's voice rose above the voice of the other man. "Please don't shoot him. Don't do that, don't kill him."

The man suddenly jerked the gun from Taylor Wright's mouth and slammed him on the head with it. Taylor lost consciousness again, and when he came to, he could hear a mix of voices in the dark part of the room. Someone picked up his arm and took off his ring and his Seiko watch; it was done almost gently. Someone pulled his hands behind his back and tied his hands and feet with a necktie. Then the room was still.

In Room 107, Andrew J. Vollink and his wife were awakened, a little before three in the morning, by the sound of voices and loud thumping in the room next door. They thought of calling the desk to complain, but then the sounds died down, and the Vollinks went back to sleep.

At the desk, Patrick Rye had been relieved by the night clerk, Clifford Gregory, working the 11:00 P.M. to 7:00 A.M. shift. When Cliff Gregory answered the desk phone around 5:00 in the morning, he heard someone complaining about a car alarm ringing somewhere on the west side of the Marriott. Cliff called the police and when a police car arrived, very quickly, Cliff and one of the policemen went out into the parking lot and found the car with the alarm ringing. Cliff checked the license against the registration slips and found that the car belonged to T. O. Wright in Room 110. He and the policeman went to Room 110 and knocked. When there was no answer, Cliff used the master key to open the door. Although the room was empty, nothing seemed wrong, so the policeman left and Cliff Gregory went back to his desk. The alarm kept ringing.

It was nearly 6:30 in the morning when Taylor Wright got his feet untied and stumbled out of Room 109, bloody and battered, his hands still tied behind him, still wearing only a T-shirt and socks. He limped along the hallway until he found a maid, who helped him into a linen supply room and sat him down while she called the desk. Cliff Gregory phoned the police again and by 7:30 a policeman and a detective had taken over.

Room 109 was a mess: blood all over the carpet and on the walls, two feet up from the floor. There were bloodspots on the bed and on the pile of clothing on the floor near the bed. Taylor Wright's trousers were lying there, turned inside out, with the pockets pulled out, with his Jockey shorts still hanging on the trouser leg. His brown briefcase was lying on the bed, but nearly all his things were gone, including most of his clothing, his shaving kit, and his billfold with his driver's license, VFW and yacht club cards, a Sears Roebuck card, MasterCharge and American Express cards, and an identification bracelet engraved T. O. W. III that he had had for more than twenty years, since his high school graduation.

His room key was on top of the pile of his clothing. Detective Bunten of the Ann Arbor Police used it to get into 110. The room looked unused and the bed was made, although it looked as though someone had lain on it, ruffling the spread. A copy of a Cleveland newspaper from the day before was lying on the TV set, and a nearly full tube of Close-up toothpaste and a pink toothbrush were lying in the bathroom.

Detective Bunten found only four latent fingerprints: two from a glass on the floor near the door, one on top of the TV set, and one in the bathroom on the counter in front of the sink. He noticed towels strewn about, and he assumed that the towels had been used to wipe fingerprints away. Taylor's 1973 cream-colored Chevy had not been stolen; it was still there in the lot, with its trunk open and its alarm rung out.

The police reached Taylor's wife, Patricia, at Parkside High School in Jackson, at the swimming meet. He was carried out of the Marriott on a stretcher and taken by ambulance to St. Joseph's Hospital. His cheek-bone was broken in four places, his nose in two; he was treated, and advised to see a plastic surgeon.

When Taylor left the hospital, he went home to recuperate. He was still at home twelve days later, on Wednesday, February 21, 1973, the day a well-dressed man checked into the Beverly Hilton Hotel on Wilshire Boulevard in Beverly Hills, California, and used his room telephone to call Grant-U-Drive at 6270 Yucca Street in Hollywood to reserve a car. He told the car rental clerk that he was with an advertising agency in Detroit and had come to Los Angeles to work on the General Motors account and to negotiate a deal with Metro-Goldwyn-Mayer. He said he needed a car for one week. A little later that afternoon, around 4:30, he appeared at

Grant-U-Drive and rented a brand-new Lincoln Continental two-door, white with a black top, only 155 miles on the odometer, California license 984GVQ. He presented an American Express card, number 040-106-8895-200AX, and signed for the car with the name on the card: T. O. Wright III.

CHAPTER
ONE

HOPE OPENED HER eyes, closed them, opened them again, yawned, and stretched. She raised her head slightly from the pillow and peered down to the end of the bed where Bill was jogging in place.

"What time is it?" she asked, yawning again.

Bill turned his head toward her and kept jogging. "Nearly seven," he answered. "Hi, sweetheart."

Hope groaned and fell back onto the pillow, pulling the covers partly over her head. Waking up never seemed to get any easier. Bill was a morning person, always up at 6:00 to exercise in the darkened bedroom, with an educational program on TV to keep him company. Sometimes he jogged outdoors, in the dawn fog shrouding the hills above the house, but whether he went out or stayed in, he made three miles every morning before he showered and shaved, woke the children, and got their breakfast —he bought granola by the sack. He took the older children, Keith and Hope Elizabeth, to school on his way to work, so that Hope had only three-year-old K.C. to contend with. This morning K.C. was no problem; Hope's new maid would keep him in her small room off the kitchen, so Hope could go back for her morning nap, then wake up slowly with coffee and cigarettes and a handful of vitamins to get her going by noon.

Bill leaned over and kissed her on the forehead. "Bye, sweetheart." She

11

groped to hug him, then her eyes flew open, and she propped herself up on one elbow.

"Hey, wait a minute," she protested. "We have to talk about the weekend."

"I'll call you from the office," Bill said cheerfully. "And I'll be back early, by three or three-thirty. Go back to sleep."

Hope heard the bedroom door close, and as she slid back under the blanket and bunched the pillow into a comfortable place under her head, she could hear Bill talking to Keith in his room across the hall. Just before she drifted back to sleep, she heard Keith laughing.

Hope Masters was thirty-one years old. She was five feet two and weighed ninety pounds. With smoky green eyes in a small-boned, oval face and champagne-colored hair streaming past her shoulder blades, she looked more like a sultry teen-ager than the mother of three children. Her oldest child, Keith, was twelve, and when Hope ran out of clean clothes, as she often did, she wore his jeans. She was very pretty, in an almost childlike, fragile, vulnerable way. Most of her friends were men.

Hope had lived in Beverly Hills, or nearby, all her life, and she seemed to have merged into her landscape, a genuine California girl. Not because she was robust or sun-kissed, brimming with vitality—she was, in fact, too thin, with a chronic back problem and a poor appetite—but because she had somehow absorbed all the concentrated expectations of her environment. When Hope said, "If I had my druthers, I'd live in a small town in Connecticut," she was not taken seriously. People who knew her found it impossible to imagine her living anywhere but amid primary contradictions. Her life of apparent status and privilege was as uncertain as the very earth under her feet, which might loosen and shift, after a surging rain, and lurch down the hillside.

She was flirty and frivolous and intensely practical. She was a worrier and excessively optimistic. She almost never cried. She could be impulsive and generous, or a bitch on wheels; sometimes brittle with anxiety, hard-edged, sometimes compassionate and earthy, not an easy person to decipher. A man who knew her well called her "opaque." Sophisticated and cynical, she watched religious programs on television because, she said, "I need some input," and she clung to her scrapbook of maxims, begun when she was a schoolgirl and repeated and added to as she grew older:

EVERYONE OVER FORTY IS RESPONSIBLE FOR HIS FACE.

LIFE IS THE ART OF DRAWING WITHOUT AN ERASER.

CHARACTER IS WHAT YOU ARE IN THE DARK.
IT IS BETTER TO HAVE LOVED AND LOST THAN NEVER
TO HAVE LOVED AT ALL.

She was born on October 21, 1941, in a Jewish hospital. "Good Sa-
maritan was full," Hope explained, "so I was born at Cedars of Leba-
non. My mother will never live it down." She was christened Hope
Elise, but soon after her parents were divorced, when Hope was two, her
mother drove down to city hall and deleted "Elise" from the original
birth certificate.

Her childhood, too, was subject to alteration. She remembered her
father, James Stagliano, a musician, whom she came to call "my wild
Italian father," as a merry man. When he moved back East—he played
French horn for the Boston Symphony—they more or less lost touch,
though he seemed never to have lost his merry bent: for her sixteenth
birthday, when she flew to New York for a visit with him, he took her
to the Stork Club where they were thrown out for "fancy dancing."

For the next dozen years of her life, Hope was in and out of various
schools, various houses and hotel rooms, although she spent long spans of
time with her mother's parents in Holmby Hills, in an enormous white
Spanish-style mansion with a sweeping lawn and a living room so vast it
seemed like a ballroom, with velvet draperies and crystal chandeliers,
usually empty and echoing. Hope's mother, also named Hope but called
"Honey" by her family, was often away—dating, playing tennis, traveling
—so Hope became very attached to her grandmother. They would lie on
the floor, side by side, stretching and doing exercises, while her grandmother told stories and explained to Hope that Honey needed to be taken
care of, and how Hope was to do it. Hope saw her mother as soft and
fluttery; she remembered, when she was about nine, choosing Honey's
dresses when they went shopping.

Hope had a big bedroom upstairs at the Holmby Hills house where she
and her friend Phyllis spent a lot of time playing with Hope's collection
of dolls, when they weren't downstairs, in the big oak bar off the living
room, playing bartender and customer, with grape juice. They were often
alone in the house, with no adults around, although Phyllis remembered
vividly when one adult, a male relative of Hope's, appeared at the door
one day and called Hope in from the lawn where the girls were playing.
Phyllis soon heard screaming and crying and a loud whack, and, soon after,
Hope came running out of the house, "a battered mess," Phyllis recalled,
"with her nose bleeding, blood smeared all over her face." The girls ran

to the empty apartment above the garage, where they hid the rest of the day.

At Westlake, a very proper girls' school, Hope wore a blue cotton uniform with short sleeves and a sash tied in back, white anklets, and black shoes. She hated the school, but she was living with her grandmother and was generally content. When she was eleven, her grandmother died, and Hope was transferred to Warner Avenue Elementary School, a public school. Around that time, Hope lost track of Phyllis, too. Although Hope's mother was dating Phyllis's stepfather, when each was between marriages, each parent eventually married someone else, and the girls were taken, or sent, in different directions.

Hope loved Warner Avenue Elementary, but after two years, her mother placed her at Marlborough, an even more proper girls' school, which Hope disliked even more than Westlake. There was a lot of clique-ishness, grouping up and picking on people. She used to come home crying nearly every day. By tenth grade she was miserable. She stayed away from school a lot, pretending to be sick; she threatened to flunk out deliberately, and by eleventh grade had maneuvered her way back to public school, to Los Angeles High. Again she loved it; again she came into conflict with her mother's long-range vision. She remembered her mother saying that nobody who went to L.A. High would amount to anything, that the nice people went elsewhere. "I see people who are a whole lot nicer at Los Angeles High," Hope informed Honey. "I can't figure out what 'nice' means." Honey won, at least temporarily; Hope transferred back to Westlake to repeat eleventh grade. Her mother's plan was to have Hope finish at Westlake, make her debut at the Los Madrinas Ball, and go on to Stanford.

Hope had another plan. When she was sixteen, she drove down to Mexico with the boy next door and came back married. They didn't tell their parents for fear the marriage would be annulled; the nineteen-year-old groom went back to his classes at USC. Hope enrolled there, too. She hadn't finished high school, but when her test came back showing an I.Q. of 183, USC took her on conditionally. The newlyweds continued to live at their respective homes, but they were together often during the day on campus and at a friend's nearby apartment. Hope wanted to become pregnant, largely so that she could have a home of her own; Honey had married again, to a rich, very prominent lawyer with whom Hope didn't get along well at all.

When Hope became pregnant, she and her husband felt it was safe to tell their families they were married. Hope's mother approved of the groom, who was heir to a biscuit fortune and whose family displayed a legitimate ancestral crest, but his mother cried for hours. Then both mothers arranged a large, formal wedding at All Saints Episcopal Church in Beverly Hills. The groom's mother wore black.

Hope's first place of her own was a studio apartment downtown, where she and her husband slept on a mattress on the floor. When she was eight months pregnant, the landlord said he didn't allow children. Hope and her husband moved to a slightly larger place—two rooms. They were living on three hundred dollars a month, half provided by each family. When their son was eighteen months old, Hope decided to have another baby, so Keith wouldn't grow up alone. She wanted a girl, to be named Lisa Marie, after her Italian grandmother, Maria Teresa Stagliano, but during labor, Hope's mother stayed with her and insisted a girl should be named Hope, too. Her mother-in-law wanted Elizabeth because it was an English name, so the new baby girl was named Hope Elizabeth.

By then Hope and her husband and the children were living in a pretty little house in Benedict Canyon, largely paid for by Hope's mother, although Hope had chipped in with the ten thousand dollars that her Holmby Hills grandmother had set aside, years earlier, for Hope's wedding. But Hope was bored and dissatisfied. Her husband seemed to spend a lot of time watering the macadamia nut trees in his garden, and their social life consisted largely of bridge games with Honey and her husband. Hope came to hate these evenings because Van would become enraged at his partner, usually Hope, for the smallest mistake. Sometimes she would rush from the game table in tears, and she liked to point out, afterward, that "a well-adjusted person is one who can play bridge and golf as though they were games."

When Hope was twenty-three years old, she filed for divorce. Her husband cried, and Hope felt bad, but she reveled in her new freedom. She double-dated with her friend Phyllis, whose life was running parallel to Hope's, on the same erratic track: by the age of nineteen, Phyllis had been married and divorced and had an infant son. Hope and Phyllis often shared baby-sitters to cut down on costs when they went out together; those were the days of the go-go dancers, and Phyllis remembered how they'd loved it. "We never had a chance to play like that when we were kids, so we did it later," Phyllis explained. In a restaurant one night, Hope met a dashing young public relations man, Tom Masters. They dated for four months. She had one last date with another man the night before she and Tom were married in a rented chapel in Las Vegas. Hope wore a white miniskirt and pink roses entwined in her hair; she carried flowers brought up from Los Angeles by another close friend, who kept them fresh in the refrigerator of her father's private plane. Just before the ceremony, Tom paid an extra five dollars, and someone lighted candles. They spent a five-day honeymoon in Las Vegas, with the temperature at 120 degrees throughout. Their son, Kirk Craig, whom they nicknamed K.C., was born in January 1970; Hope and Tom separated six weeks later —just for a week, that time, and later for good.

Thus, by 1973, when she was thirty-one, Hope Masters had lived an assortment of lives and had collected within herself a set of contradictions that seemed to manifest them all. Although she was often referred to as "the heiress" and "the socialite," she had spent, for an heiress, unusual amounts of time changing diapers and cleaning ovens. Large sums of money, legally hers, rested in trust funds, but, without access to it, she and her children ate a lot of frankfurters, sliced and scrambled in eggs. Once they lived for a week on potatoes and milk. She had no health insurance, no credit cards. She was listed in the Blue Book, the social register, while her children qualified for free lunches at their public school. She felt deprived without a live-in maid, and when she didn't have one was looking for one, although her income of $435 a month—some from each husband, some from her mother—entitled her to food stamps. She was living in Beverly Hills, California, one of the most expensive residential areas in the United States, where there are no streets, just "Drives" —living there even while, to piece out her income, she was working at a series of odd jobs, some of them odder than others. For a while she was a cocktail waitress at a bar downtown, where the customers enjoyed throwing chairs around and where she was obliged to sweep up a good deal of broken glass. She sold clothes at a boutique for fat women. She worked, briefly, for a doctor who specialized in giving injections. Once she held, also briefly, a telephone sales job, which involved calling Catholic priests all over the country on a WATS line. Another girl in the office would get the priest on the line by posing as a person with a problem, but Hope felt that was dishonest; she preferred to just ask for the priest, then begin to talk. Usually she ended up just having a long talk without selling a magazine subscription, so that job didn't last.

Talking was Hope's strongest point. She loved to talk, and when she wasn't talking, she loved to listen. It was in these compulsions that the contradictions of her life seemed summed up. She had discarded one husband because she considered him a boring stay-at-home, another because she considered him uninterested in children and domesticity. She wanted to spend time with her children, to befriend them, be involved with them, but she also wanted to have fun for herself, the kind of fun that her beauty and sparkle and personality made accessible. When Keith and Hope Elizabeth were old enough to understand, she promised them she'd never go out on a date two nights in a row, and she almost never did, but on the nights she did go out, she usually arranged two or three dates in one evening, two or three nightclubs in one evening, especially during a period when she and Phyllis were dating nightclub bouncers. Often she and Phyllis and their dates would end up at a Chinese restaurant on Sunset eating pea pods and partying until 4:00 A.M., when the place closed. Behaviors that were either expressed or implied in her upbringing had taken obvious hold—she could be naturally arrogant to a waiter in a restaurant, and often was—but other behavior came naturally, too. She was softhearted toward loners and troubled creatures; over the years she'd taken in dozens of stray cats and a handful of runaway children. A friend called Hope's house "early Crash Pad." If the waiter she treated imperiously had broken down and cried and told her his troubles, she'd have soothed him, advised him, and maybe taken him in, too. When one of her former maids turned up pregnant, Hope took her in, and when the baby was due, took her to the hospital. When the hospital said only a family member could go into the labor room, Hope signed the form in the space for FATHER.

She may have been generous, even extravagant, with her emotions and her love because she herself felt such an intense need to be loved without qualms or qualification, simply for herself. She wanted to love a man in that same way, and when she met Bill Ashlock in December 1972, at a Christmas party, she felt almost right away that he was that man. She found him quiet but not boring, successful but not flashy. He seemed able to express his feelings for her as readily as she did hers for him. That ability meant a great deal to Hope. "People have such a hard time saying 'I love you' or 'I appreciate you,'" Hope said. "That's one area where I don't suffer at all. I *do* tell them. If they're just going across the street, I tell them! I always give the people I love lots of attention, lots of appreciation. I always try to let them know they're important to me; then if something happens to either of you, you won't have any regrets about anything left unsaid. I'm a big believer in, if you feel something good and positive about somebody, for God's sake, *tell* them! Because you never know what's going to happen. You never know what tomorrow's going to bring."

At 10:30 that Friday morning, February 23, 1973, Hope's new maid, Martha Padilla, knocked on the bedroom door and told Hope that Mr.

Ashlock was calling and had asked Martha to wake Hope to talk to him.

Hope came awake quickly. Bill called her every day from his office—usually they talked for at least an hour—and she'd expected his call today, but it was odd for him to call so early and ask that she be awakened. She half-sat up in bed and reached for the bedside phone, propping herself up on her right elbow.

"Hi," she said. "Bill?"

"Hopie," Bill said, "listen to this. You want to have the biggest laugh of your life?"

"Sure," she said.

"Well, for some crazy reason, I'm going to be interviewed. A guy called me and said he's doing a story for the *L.A. Times* on the ten most eligible bachelors in town, and he wants to interview me."

Hope laughed. "Tell him you're not a bachelor."

Bill laughed too, then he sounded serious. "Hopie, the thing is, I don't want to do this if it's going to affect our relationship, where you're going to think I'm interested in meeting other girls, because I'm not."

"I know you're not," Hope said.

"And another thing," Bill went on. "Do you think it could be a problem for you, with your divorce coming up or anything? Because if you think it could be a problem, I won't do it."

"No, no," Hope said. "That won't be a problem. Go ahead, have your little ego trip and do it. It sounds like fun."

"Well, if you think it's okay," Bill said, "I'll go ahead and do it. I'm supposed to meet him for lunch. And I'll call you after lunch."

"Wait a minute," Hope said. "I've got an idea." She sat up straighter in bed and shifted the phone around, brushing her long hair back from her face. "Bill, maybe if you mention certain places when you talk to this guy, and they get printed in the story, maybe later we could get a free dinner at those places or something. I could find out from Tom what he thinks."

"Well, okay," Bill said. "But find out right away, because the guy is coming over. I'm going to meet him at noon."

"I will," Hope said. "I'll call you right back."

Bill hung up, and Hope quickly dialed Tom Masters. Although she and Tom had been separated for two years, she saw him often, and they kept in touch by phone; she had called him just a few days earlier to tell him about one of Bill's commercials being on a "ten-best" list. She had filed initial divorce papers on Tom only a few weeks before. Their marriage had been over for a long, long time, but she deliberately delayed filing.

"I knew that would have been out of the frying pan into the fire," Hope explained. "So I waited a long time, and didn't file papers, because if I'd been divorced right away, someone might have come along and I might, in an emotional burst of enthusiasm, have gone off and gotten married again." Even early in her marriage to Tom, several men had continued to call her, telling her they were waiting for her. Now that she felt her relationship with Bill Ashlock was sound and right and destined for marriage, she had finally filed papers on Tom.

She had mixed feelings about Tom Masters. On the one hand, she considered him unsympathetic to people, not at all compassionate, even cold-blooded. "When I look in your eyes," she had once told him, "no one's home." Although Keith and Hope Elizabeth had been only eight and ten years old when she married Tom, it was her feeling that he resented the time she spent with them, time when she could have been going out on the town with him, and he once suggested sending them to boarding school. Remembering her own misery at Westlake, especially the times when she'd boarded there while her mother was traveling abroad, Hope had instantly and firmly refused to consider it, and she and Tom had had a major battle. They'd fought about their own child, K.C., too, when Tom's parents, who lived in Massachusetts, were flying to Las Vegas for a holiday. To save them coming the rest of the way to Los Angeles to see their grandson, Tom wanted to take K.C. and get a room at Caesar's Palace, where his parents could play with K.C. between shows. When Hope declared that such a plan was ridiculous for a two-year-old, she and Tom had another big row. Hope didn't like Las Vegas anyway. She'd gone there a couple of times with Tom, who liked the place and seemed to know a lot of people there.

On the other hand, she had to admit that Tom was a pretty good father to K.C. Besides paying his $185 a month in child support faithfully, he paid for a lot of extras: K.C.'s jackets and shoes, haircuts, the dentist. Hope estimated the extras came to about $3,000 a year. Tom came by every Saturday to take K.C. someplace—if only to the car wash or to get a hamburger. He always brought him back Saturday evening. Tom played golf on Sundays, so he never took K.C. on Sunday. Besides his Saturday visits, Tom sometimes stopped in during the week to see K.C. and chat with Hope. That week, just a few days earlier, he'd come by after work and shared their bucket of Kentucky Fried Chicken, though he hadn't stayed long because he'd said he had to meet a client for a drink at the Beverly Hilton Hotel. Hope remembered it clearly because she knew Tom hated the Hilton and she'd never known him to go there, at least not for just a drink. Usually when he met someone after work, he went to the Cock & Bull or to the Playboy Club, near his office, at the end of Sunset Strip. Once in a while, for someone special, he'd go to the Polo Lounge at the Beverly Hills Hotel, the most celebrated bar in town, but never to the Beverly Hilton. "Why in the world are you going to the Hilton?" she remembered asking Tom. "You know it takes forever to park there." She didn't remember what Tom had replied, or whether he had replied at all.

Although her marriage to Tom had been a disaster, Hope had often told him she wished him well, both in his personal life and in his business. She knew how important it was to Tom that he succeed in his work, which was a blend of the media business and show business, what Hope called, when she was feeling kindly toward Tom, "the image business," and "flesh peddling," when she was not. Even as a kid growing up in New England, Tom had been stagestruck. When Richard Burton came to a town nearby to film *Who's Afraid of Virginia Woolf?*, Tom, a teen-ager then, had worked for the movie company as, in Hope's words, a "go-fer." Richard Burton had given Tom a pair of boots and when Tom came to California after high school, to seek his fortune, he'd brought the boots with him.

Tom was only twenty-four when he and Hope were married, but he'd been seeking that fortune most aggressively. He'd already changed his name, from Omasta to Masters, and now, at twenty-seven, he'd already set up his own P.R. firm. He still had a long way to go—he drove a five-year-old Chevy, and in 1972 he'd grossed only about twenty-five thousand dollars, which had to cover a lot of expenses, including office staff. For a while Hope's friend Phyllis had worked for Tom part-time, three mornings a week. She found Tom demanding but not really difficult; when he saw what a good speller she was, he seemed surprised and pleased, and Phyllis never had any complaints about the way he treated her. She was a little surprised, too, because she and Hope had agreed that Tom was very cold, very macho, and Phyllis had not gotten along especially well with him outside the office. Phyllis and her boyfriend had sometimes gone with Hope and Tom to a restaurant or to a nightclub, and she was often annoyed because, she said, "you could be in the middle of your drink, or not even have put your fork down on your plate, and Tom would announce that it was time to leave." She thought that maybe because they'd gone to these places free—as a press agent, Tom got a lot of passes—Tom must have felt he could call the shots, just as he tried to do at home. Phyllis had gone to dinner at Tom and Hope's only once, and she recalled how, after dinner, when she and Hope were sitting in the living room talking,

Tom had suddenly said, "I'm ready for bed. You can leave now." Besides being resentful of her children by her first husband, Tom, in Hope's view, had seemed antagonistic to Hope's friends and had tried to arrange Hope's life, which mostly meant staying home all day and going out with him all night. As much as she liked going out, Hope didn't like Tom's attitude. He told her what to wear and how to set her hair; he liked a lot of dramatic makeup. "I was simply a prop," Hope decided. "He wanted a real flashy broad on his arm, so that's what I was."

Still, she'd always felt that if she could help Tom get ahead in his struggling new business, she would. She had loaned him money from the thousand-dollar emergency fund she tried to keep on hand, because she knew he owed people money, and now, when she telephoned him, she told Tom that if the article about Bill mentioned a restaurant or a club that Tom was connected with, not only might she and Bill get a free meal but Tom might, in some way, get something out of it.

Tom didn't seem interested. "There's very little publicity value in a story like this," he said on the phone. "If the story is about ten guys, a lot of places will be mentioned—and anyway, it's only a one-time thing."

Hope reminded him, then, that she was going away for the weekend with Bill and that Martha would be expecting Tom to pick up K.C. on Saturday morning and keep him all day. Tom said he remembered and hung up abruptly. Hope wasn't taken aback; she'd always thought Tom to be basically cold to people, except to people who could do him some good. She thought maybe he was that way because of his business. "I think Tom doesn't get emotionally involved," she said, "because in his business there comes a time when the person he represents goes downhill and can't make it anymore."

Besides, she thought Tom might have hung up rudely because she sensed he was jealous of Bill. Not because of Hope, but because of K.C., who was very fond of Bill. Before dinner, when Bill sat before the gas-jet fireplace with his customary gin and tonic, K.C. would sit either next to him or on his lap, with a glass of tonic and lime Bill fixed for him.

Hope called Gary then, a lawyer who was a neighbor and a close friend. Gary had sometimes taken Hope out, not because they were romantically involved, but because he felt she should get out more, meet people, have fun. The night she'd met Bill at the Christmas party, she'd gone with Gary. About two months earlier, Hope had broken up with the man she'd been living with, a screenwriter named Lionel. Lionel had left town, and Hope had been sitting home alone, mostly, when Gary called to insist she go to the party with him. "This is ridiculous," Gary told Hope. "Lionel's been gone for two months, and it's time you started circulating." Hope had conceded she was lonely, so she'd gone to dinner with Gary at a place in Century City, then to a party at the Century House where the banquet room was set up with fifty small round tables and what seemed like hundreds of people sitting and standing around. Gary squeezed through the crush at the bar, got drinks, and found two places at a table with people he knew.

"Then I looked up, and there were those eyes looking at me from way across the room," Hope told Phyllis. "At first I thought it was Tom, because of the big dark eyes and the mustache, and I couldn't think of anyone else who would be staring at me like that. I was a little drunk, I guess, acting kind of silly, so I pointed and said, 'Look at that guy over there. I think that's my ex-husband.'" Later, she told Phyllis, when she was out in the foyer, the man came up to her. "I want to apologize for staring at you," he had said. "And I want to apologize for pointing at you," Hope said. They both laughed. He told her his name—William Ashlock —and she told him hers. "I feel uncomfortable here," he said. "I'm too old." Hope laughed again. "I'm too old, Gary's too old, we're all too old," she replied. Gary walked over then, and Hope introduced the men. Gary suggested they all go to another party he knew about, a smaller party at the Beverly Hilton, and they agreed to meet at the entrance to the Hilton party room, by some pillars. Bill drove his own car; Hope drove to the Hilton with Gary. "I think this guy is one of the nicest people we've met in a long time," Gary said. "If he wants to drive you home, it's okay, go ahead, let him drive you home."

"Bill was standing by the pillars, exactly where I'd told him to wait," Hope told Phyllis, and almost right away they'd said good night to Gary and gone to a Roaring Twenties place in the hotel, where they had a drink and listened to the music. Then they wandered around the Hilton for a while, looking at the shops. When Bill drove Hope home, he came in for only a few minutes, but the next day he telephoned and said he'd like to come by after work. "Oh, my God," Hope said, "the house is a disaster, I have no help, and anyway I can't go out again tonight." Bill said it didn't matter about the house and that they didn't have to go out, he'd bring a pizza.

He came by with a large pizza and met the children, who seemed to take to him at once. He didn't stay over that night—in fact, he and Hope didn't sleep together until they'd known each other a month, when they went to Lake Arrowhead for a weekend, one of the two weekends they ever had together out of town. Even before that first weekend away, Bill had been moving in, piece by piece; he'd bring a sweater or a jacket and leave it, then his guitar. By the end of January he'd pretty much moved in altogether, and they were tentatively planning to be married in about six months, when the final divorce papers came through, in late spring or early summer.

But Bill still kept his apartment on Lafayette Park Place downtown, not far from his office. Once in a while he and Hope spent the night there, when they wanted to talk without the children running around. Just the previous Friday evening, after dinner, they'd gone to Bill's place for the night. They'd been feeling a little reckless and had gone to the Brown Derby for dinner, which they couldn't afford; it was already the middle of the month and, as usual, they'd had little money left. Martha Padilla was living in then, and although Hope didn't like to leave K.C. with the new maid very long—Martha was only seventeen years old and inclined to spend much of the time with her boyfriend in his car, parked in Hope's driveway—she'd assumed K.C. had gone to sleep by then, and she knew Tom would pick him up on Saturday. The older children would be all right with Martha, and would probably play around with friends in the neighborhood on Saturday. So Hope and Bill had gone back to his apartment, where she'd phoned Martha to say she wouldn't be home till Saturday afternoon.

Besides a cozy getaway spot for the two of them, Bill's apartment was also a place for him to work. Often, at noon, instead of going out to lunch, he'd go to his apartment and compose music or write copy for television commercials. Bill had been creative supervisor at Dailey & Associates, an advertising agency, for three years. Many of his commercials and print ads had won awards, twenty-eight altogether, including the International Broadcasting Award and one from the American Advertising Federation. Recently, one of his ads had appeared on a "ten-best" list, the one Hope had called Tom about, an ad for Santa Anita Racetrack, with surging classical music in the background and a collage of morning shots—dogs waking up in the hayloft, horses stretching in their stalls and loping around the paddock, chefs in the kitchen smiling as they wielded glossy knives over piles of fresh vegetables and fruits. The narrator had only one simple line: "Today is our day at Santa Anita. Tomorrow may be your day." But the first prize had gone to a competing ad, with the tag line "Try it, you'll like it."

Bill enjoyed his work. One night he brought home a can of 16 mm. film, a selection of his commercials. Martha Padilla had called her twin sister Mary, who worked for the Smiths, next door to Hope, and the two maids and Hope and the children had watched Bill's show in the living room, applauding vigorously after each spot. The children especially liked the commercial set in an elegant dining room with a crystal chandelier, a table set with china and flowers and fine linen, and twelve formally dressed people sitting around it. A maid carried in a big, beautiful roast on a platter and set it in front of the host, who stood up and began to slice it. At least, he tried to slice it. Then everything began to shake: knives and forks, wineglasses, the table itself. He grunted and groaned as he stabbed at the meat, but the more he stabbed, the more things shook, until all the glasses and dishes were pitching off the table and the chandelier was swinging wildly. The scene shifted to the kitchen, where the maid was shaking Adolph's meat tenderizer over another roast. "A little of this kind of shaking beforehand can save that kind of shaking after."

Hope was even prouder of Bill's work than he was, and had even been somewhat involved in it. In a layout Bill had just finished for Occidental Life, an ad for insurance policies for wives, he had used Hope as his model. Hope's picture was placed right in the center of the page. She wore a black dress and held a long-stemmed rose. Her eyes were grave, her expression sweet but serious above the bold caption: WHAT IF SHE DIES FIRST?

Bill had been born in St. Louis in 1932. He'd enrolled at the University of Missouri to study journalism; in his freshman year, 1951, he'd pledged a fraternity, Phi Psi. After graduation he joined the air force as a jet pilot. Back in St. Louis, he'd worked for an advertising agency until 1966, when he and his wife Frances and their two little girls had moved to southern California. Bill loved California. He adapted to its casual life-style as perhaps only a man whose birthright was the sleet and slush of the Midwest could—without reservation, wholeheartedly. He became passionate about physical fitness, and grew tanner and leaner, lunching on cottage cheese and yogurt and never, ever, skipping his daily exercise. His new trimness pleased him so much that he no longer carried his wallet in his pants pocket, not even a matchbook, nothing that might cause the slightest ripple in the silhouette; he usually had the pants pockets sewn shut so he wouldn't be tempted to put anything in them. He carried his wallet and credit cards in the glove compartment of his car, or in his briefcase. He was so zealous about weight that, even though most of Hope's friends thought she was too thin, Bill urged her to stay the way she was. "Whenever I get involved with someone, she gains thirty pounds," Bill told Hope.

Since slimming down, Bill had become very careful about his clothes. He liked tweedy jackets and well-cut slacks, perhaps beige, with a blue and beige tie and a maroon shirt. He owned eight blazers in eight colors. Hope had seen his clothing chart, showing which jacket would go well with which pants and shirt and tie. At one time, he told Hope, he had been unconcerned about clothes, but when he got some settlement money from the sale of the house he and Fran had bought when they came to California, a girl he was seeing had urged him to buy new clothes, and he'd bought a whole new wardrobe costing about three thousand dollars. Hope had never met that girl, but she knew her name was Sandi and, as far as Hope was aware, Sandi was the only other woman, besides Bill's wife, he'd been serious about. Bill was separated from Fran, and Sandi was separated from her husband, Fred, and he had moved in with her and her four children. He told Hope that he and Sandi had talked about marriage, but when his final divorce papers came through and Sandi announced they would then be married in two weeks, Bill had apparently changed his mind. He'd moved out of Sandi's, into his own apartment on Lafayette Park Place, and he hadn't yet signed his final papers.

Bill's daughters got along beautifully with Hope's children. They were six and eight years old, fitting like stepping stones into Hope's family, a combination of five children from three to twelve. Bill took his girls on alternate weekends, and often he and Hope went off somewhere with all five children. Before he'd met Hope, Bill sometimes had asked Fran along on outings when he took the girls, which Hope later interpreted as Bill's gesture of appeasement to Fran, who didn't like Sandi. But after meeting Hope, he took her instead of Fran. Once Hope had heard him talking to Fran on the phone, from her house, to make arrangements to take the girls to Lion Country Safari. Fran had been expecting to go along, but Bill told her he was taking Hope and her children, too, so there wouldn't be room for Fran in Hope's Vega. When Bill went to pick up the girls, he wanted Hope to come in and meet Fran, but Hope felt it would be better for her to wait in the car. Later, at other times when Bill went to get the girls, Hope always waited in the car, reading a book, because she sensed Fran was still hurt about being left out of the Lion Country trip. "I would have taken her along, because that's the kind of person I am," Hope explained, "but it would have been uncomfortable for her. She knew exactly what was going on." Another reason Hope always stayed in the car and never met Fran was that, when Bill asked Hope to marry him, Hope knew that Fran was always going to be left out. Bill had told Hope a great deal about both Fran and Sandi, and it sounded to Hope as though "each of them wanted Bill to come back to her in the worst way," and she sensed that each of them felt that Bill would leave Hope and come back to her, sooner or later. And still another reason that Hope tried to lay back, when it came to Fran, was that the Ashlock girls got along so

famously with Hope's three, and with Hope herself. Hope had shown his
girls how to make him laugh, demonstrating by burying her face in his
neck and growling, and she heard later that, when they got home, the girls
couldn't wait to tell Fran. "Hopie's the only person in the world who can
make Daddy laugh," they told their mother.

Hope was thinking that if Bill's interview couldn't help Tom in some
way, maybe it could help her neighbor Gary, who had a financial interest
in a restaurant chain. When she got Gary on the phone, she told him
about Bill's story. "Is there any company, or any place that you own, that
it would do you some good to have mentioned?" she asked. "What about
the restaurants?"

"Not really," Gary said. "I really don't want my name in the paper. But
Bill is more than welcome to say he's a member of one of my companies."

"No, that isn't the point," Hope said. "I just wanted to know if there's
anything that would help you if it got mentioned in the paper."

"Not really," Gary said again. "Thanks anyway, Hopie."

As Hope and Gary were talking, about ten minutes before noon, a
neatly dressed man in a three-piece suit, wearing wire-rimmed glasses and
carrying a pipe, stepped off the elevator on the ninth floor of the tall,
modern building on Wilshire Boulevard where Dailey & Associates had
its offices.

He told the receptionist, Sara Monaco, that he had a lunch appointment with Bill Ashlock, and he gave Sara his name. Sara nodded, jotted
the name down on a slip of paper, and disappeared into Bill's office. "He'll
be just a few minutes," she told the man who was waiting. "He's on the
telephone, talking to his girlfriend."

The man laughed. "That's a little ironic," he said, "because I'm here
to interview him on his bachelorhood." He told Sara he was from the
Los Angeles Times. After a few minutes, Sara went in again to remind
Bill there was a man waiting. Bill was putting on his jacket. "I'm ready,"
Bill told Sara, "but I've forgotten the guy's name." Sara laughed, and
repeated it for him.

Bill was right behind Sara as she returned to the reception room. The
man with the pipe stood up and smiled. He and Bill shook hands, and they
left together.

Hope got out of bed and made her way down the long hallway to the
kitchen for a cup of coffee. She took the coffee and her cigarettes into
the living room and curled up for a few minutes on the sofa, her feet

tucked under her. K.C. was lying on the rug, playing with miniature cars. The living room was big and comfortable, cluttered with pillows and books, including one whole shelf of Nancy Drew books that Hope had kept for twenty years, and meaningful odds and ends, including an ashtray she'd taken from the Stork Club the night she and her father had been asked to leave. One wall was brick, with a gas-jet fireplace in the center and a long ledge for sitting, running along the wall. A long, plump sofa faced the fireplace, and a smaller sofa was placed at an angle, forming a cozy, L-shaped sitting space. The wall behind the small sofa was all glass, with a sliding door that opened onto a narrow balcony overlooking the street below and the treetops across the street. Across the room, a big round table and chairs made a dining area, near a door opening onto a tiny flagstone patio. Beyond the patio, a rocky hillside covered with thick, thorny bushes rose steeply, almost straight up.

Hope had lived on the Drive for four years. She had stayed on in the Benedict Canyon house for five years after her divorce, but when she married Tom and was expecting another child, that house was far too small. Her mother had bought this house for them, transferring Hope's ten thousand dollars' interest from one place to the other. The house was almost hidden from the street by shrubs and trees. On rainy winter days, shrouded on all sides by foliage, it seemed to perch in a ghostly, gray-green, dripping forest.

Hope pulled on blue jeans and a shirt, ran a comb through her hair, found a sweater, and told Martha she was going out for a little while. The pale winter sunshine felt marvelous as she got into her car, a '71 apple-green Vega, and backed carefully down the short, sharply inclined driveway. She backed up again, but less carefully, because the Drive was a cul-de-sac and ended, a few houses below hers, in a small paved turn-around circle where the neighborhood children often played. With all the children in school, the street was now deserted. At the top of the hill, she turned right and began the twisting descent to the shopping section in Beverly Hills. She drove past Sammy Davis's house, anonymous and scarcely visible behind tall, clipped hedges and an even taller iron gate; she knew whose house it was from Tom, who had pointed out to her one night how Sammy Davis kept all the lights on, all night, his house safely ablaze with electricity to scare off intruders. Tom seemed to know where everyone lived, in the villas and mansions and thirty-five-room bungalows tucked away along these hills; it was his business to know. Hope said that when Sharon Tate was murdered in just such a house, Tom had been excited by the case—Hope called it obsessed.

Passing the pale pink Beverly Hills Hotel, Hope crossed Sunset

Boulevard and continued south, past royal palm trees edging the curbs and vaguely shading the houses on either side, including her mother's. Honey's house was appraised at over a million dollars. It had no front lawn at all, just a semicircular driveway; the front door was only ten yards or so from the street. Although there was a small, lovely lawn in back of the house, that, too, backed right onto an alley, and the house itself was scarcely an arm's length from the house next door. When a window in Honey's den or kitchen was open, a person in one of these rooms could hear conversations going on inside the house next door. Honey's living room and her bedroom were huge, but there was only one other bedroom, a small den, a double dining room, and a kitchen. There was no pool.

But Honey's house, along with the other houses on Rodeo and Beverly and Bedford and a few other special streets that stretched the few blocks between Sunset and Wilshire boulevards, was not just a place to live. Houses in "The Flats" stood for all the things money could buy and a few things money couldn't, such as membership in the Los Angeles Country Club, where Honey met her friends for lunch and bridge two or three times a week. "It's not so much what you are that gets you in, but what you aren't," Hope said, explaining that you couldn't join the L.A. Country Club if you were new to California (unless you were from the East Coast 400), or Jewish, or Roman Catholic, or a journalist, or in show business. She often repeated the story she'd heard about Victor Mature applying for club membership and being told, "We don't accept actors." "I'm no actor," Victor Mature is supposed to have said, "and I have sixty-four pictures to prove it."

Hope pulled into the parking lot behind the bank and went in to cash a check. Her checking account was down to about two hundred dollars, which was not unusual and didn't particularly bother her; it had been lower. But her shaky financial status seemed to bother Bill and, three weeks earlier, he'd put her name on his checking account, making it a joint account. Hope had written only one check on that account, for groceries, because Bill told her he gave Fran eight hundred dollars a month, exactly half of his monthly take-home after taxes, and the other eight hundred dollars got stretched pretty thin. But Bill insisted that he wanted to help Hope out a little, just as he insisted on continuing to split his salary with Fran, which Hope personally considered excessive, in view of the fact that Fran was working full time. But when Hope suggested to Bill that he ask Fran if she could manage with somewhat less from him, Bill didn't want to. Hope was sure it was because he felt guilty about Fran, not so much about the separation and pending divorce as about some other things, including his feeling that he hadn't been very considerate of Fran at least part of the ten years they'd been married. One morning, when Hope was barely awake and Bill was just about to get up, he had said suddenly, "You know, if Fran ever hadn't gotten out of bed to fix my breakfast, I would have complained. But now I won't even let you get up. It was terrible what I expected of Fran."

Hope agreed with him. She'd never met Fran, but from what Bill said, Fran sounded like a model wife who kept an immaculate house with well-scrubbed floors and meals on time. "Let's face it, Fran did a lot of plain old miserable housework, of which I do as little as possible," Hope said. She didn't feel guilty about Fran, though, because Bill and Fran were already separated when Bill met Hope, and eventually Bill agreed that he simply had to cut down on the amount of money he was sending Fran. He said he would call Fran to discuss it, which Hope told him was ridiculous and absolutely the wrong thing to do. "It's silly to forewarn her," Hope pointed out. "If you tell her in advance, she'll just change her circumstances and then she can prove she needs that much. Just go to court; just *do* it." Bill didn't want to handle it that way. "I just can't hit her with a court order," he told Hope, so one night he telephoned Fran from Hope's bedroom phone and told her that money was becoming a hassle for him and Hope. He asked Fran whether she would accept a couple of hundred dollars less each month. Fran said she wouldn't. Bill told Hope that Fran said no. "Look, I'm only getting one hundred eighty-five dollars a month from Tom," Hope told him. "You're just paying her eight hundred dollars a month to make yourself feel better." Hope told Bill to talk to his lawyer about it, and when he didn't, she talked to one herself.

From the bank, Hope crossed the street to the market. She walked up and down the aisles briskly, tossing things in her cart. She wanted to get back soon so that when Bill came home early, as he had promised, they could leave right away. If they didn't get away by midafternoon, traffic would be a mess. Hope loved weekends at the ranch, even though it wasn't hers; Honey and her husband had a quarter interest, along with three other couples, and the four families rotated the weekends. This weekend, especially, Hope couldn't wait to get there. Her back had been acting up for days, with her pain pills not helping much, and she had a busy week coming up. She had to go to court for the divorce hearing and, on Wednesday, she was to be hostess at a Chips luncheon.

Chips meant Colleagues' Helpers in Philanthropic Service. The Colleagues were rich women who met periodically to raise money for worthy causes; the Chips, by and large, were their daughters. The Chips' two main functions were to help at the Colleagues' annual sale at the Santa Monica Auditorium, where the women brought their used furs and clothing and jewelry to sell, and to make an annual Christmas trip downtown to a home for unwed mothers, where the Chips decorated a tree and served punch and cookies. Membership in both the Colleagues and the Chips was strictly limited; it was by birth or, rarely, by invitation. Through her mother's social connections, Hope was a charter member and, although it was unusual for a Chips member to live in a house with a leaky roof and to qualify for food stamps, her status, as Honey's daughter, was always secure.

Besides the court date and the luncheon, she had an appointment for some lab tests her doctor had ordered. For a while now, Hope had been troubled by a strange feeling of fright and weakness, and she had called her doctor about it. "It's like a feeling of death coming closer," Hope told the doctor, "and I just had to tell somebody about it. I can see death." The doctor listened carefully. "What does it look like?" "It's like a fog surrounding me, around my whole day," Hope replied. "I know it's not just psychological because I'm real happy. But I'm becoming less alive, and I don't know why."

When she got back up to the house, Bill wasn't home yet, and Martha said he hadn't called. Hope asked her to put away the groceries and went to the telephone.

Bill's secretary, Helen Linley, said Bill wasn't back from lunch. Hope had never met Helen Linley but they knew each other somewhat, since Hope and Bill talked on the phone so much. Helen Linley had a soft, motherly voice; she had worked at Dailey & Associates longer than anyone else there, and she had a grown son, Sgt. Frank Linley of the Los Angeles Police Department, Homicide Division.

"He said something about doing an interview with somebody, but I can't believe he'd be gone so long," Hope told Mrs. Linley. "Do you know where he went?" Mrs. Linley said she didn't know. "Well, I hope he can get away early," Hope said, "because we're going to the ranch." Helen Linley said she thought he could, judging from the things she'd seen on his desk.

Bill's boss, Cliff Einstein, had been looking for Bill around the office too, starting around 1:30. Cliff wasn't annoyed that Bill was taking a long lunch, only a little surprised, partly because Bill was so careful about telling people where he was and when he'd be back, partly because Cliff knew Bill shunned long, fattening lunches. Once in a while, if Cliff and

Bill had something to discuss, they'd go to lunch together, usually at Ma Ma Lion's on the corner of Western and Sixth or at Blarney's Castle next door; if they wanted something fancier, they'd go to the Windsor on Seventh Street. Most of the time, though, Bill's habit was to have just yogurt and cottage cheese either at his desk or at his apartment, or maybe skip lunch altogether. Obviously Bill's regime paid off: most people thought Bill was younger than Cliff, though Cliff was just thirty-three, seven years younger. Cliff Einstein was the senior vice-president and creative director at Dailey & Associates, but he and Bill worked as equals. Cliff considered Bill Ashlock a very, very good copywriter, as good as any copywriter in Los Angeles, in fact, one of the best in advertising anywhere. Cliff liked Bill, too, though he wasn't really close to him. He didn't think anyone was really close to Bill, but sometimes, on a business trip, the two men would share a hotel room and talk.

When Bill came back from lunch, a little before three o'clock, Cliff noticed he seemed excited, almost elated.

"I have to tell you about something that's happened to me," Bill said to Cliff. "I'm being interviewed by a reporter from the *Times* for an article on the town's most eligible bachelors."

Cliff was taken aback, because of Bill's quiet style; he also wondered if Bill could be called eligible, since he wasn't divorced yet. Cliff knew about Hope, too; he'd never met her, but Bill had shown him her picture soon after they met, and Cliff thought the life insurance ad with her picture was beautiful. He knew that if anyone asked Bill about his bachelorhood, in five seconds Bill would have been showing off Hope's picture, in the black dress with the long-stemmed rose.

"Tell me about it," Cliff said. "How did they find you?"

"Well, you won't believe this," Bill said, "but he called the girls over at J. Walter Thompson, because J. Walter Thompson has the best-looking girls, and he asked them to suggest somebody, and the girls said, 'Call Bill Ashlock.' " He told Cliff that the reporter was very interesting, very nice, just back from Vietnam, and that he'd told Bill about another bachelor being interviewed for the article, a pilot for Air New Zealand.

"Air New Zealand—one of our accounts," Cliff said.

"I know. It's a coincidence," Bill said. "I'll get the agency some publicity, too." He asked Cliff some questions about the agency's size, its billings and growth, and Cliff told him to use anything he wanted to use in the interview.

Once or twice that afternoon, Cliff teased Bill a little about being a famous guy, but he continued to be a little puzzled about Bill's being chosen and about Air New Zealand. He knew that Air New Zealand had only two or three planes, maybe half a dozen pilots, and he knew those pilots didn't live in Los Angeles. They lived in Auckland. And another thing didn't really puzzle Cliff, but it intrigued him: Bill had said the man didn't take notes, that he could remember everything in his head.

After Bill had talked with Cliff, he called Hope. "I just got back," he told her. "I had a great free lunch at the Brown Derby."

"Well, I couldn't imagine where you were so long," Hope said. "How did it go?"

"Fine," Bill said. "Great. He asked me a lot of questions, and I asked him a lot of questions, and we just talked. We talked about the advertising business and about England and all kinds of things. He's a very pleasant guy. I told him about you, and about going up to the ranch. And Hopie"—Bill paused—"Hopie, he wants to come up to the ranch and take some pictures."

Hope groaned. "Oh, *no.*"

"I tried to talk him out of it. I told him, 'Look, I am a very dull person, I go with a girl who has three kids, and we take the kids around, we watch TV, and it's just not that interesting, let's forget it.' "

"What did he say then?"

"He said, 'Oh, no, no, that's what makes it interesting.' "

Hope said nothing.

"Well, what do you think, Hopie?" Bill asked, finally. "Is it all right with you if he comes? He said it would make a great photographic layout, and he really wants to come so much that I hate to say no, but if you say no, I'll tell him no."

Hope sighed. "No, it's okay. But I'll have to ask my mother."

"Okay," Bill said. "I told him I'd ask you, and he's going to call me at five-thirty. I'll be there by then. I'm leaving now."

Hope telephoned her mother.

"As long as you don't use the name of the ranch in the papers, I don't see why there would be any problem," Honey said. "It's certainly all right with me if he just wants pictures of horses and trees or whatever."

"Okay," Hope said. "I'll tell him not to use the name of the ranch."

"And Hopie," her mother continued, "I really don't care for the idea of you being photographed with Bill when you're up there with him for the weekend. With your divorce coming up, Hopie, that doesn't look very good."

"Well, he wants to take pictures," Hope said.

"I don't want him to make it look as though you're doing anything wrong," her mother said.

"Okay," Hope said. She knew if she said anything more, she and her mother would probably get into an argument, as they often did, about Hope's relationships with men.

"I haven't been able to reach Jim Webb," Honey said. "I tried on Wednesday and all day yesterday, and today, but no one answers."

"I'll try him now," Hope said. "See you next week."

Jim Webb, the caretaker at the ranch, lived in a small house near the main house with his wife Teresa and their children. Honey liked to let Jim Webb know when someone was coming up so he could turn on the lights and heat. But when Hope tried again, there was no answer.

Hope felt tired and cross. The house would be cold and dark when she and Bill got there, whenever that was, with Bill running so late. The plans for this weekend had been arranged and rearranged so much that, for a moment, Hope thought about calling the whole thing off. Early in the week they'd planned to take all the children, Bill's and hers, with Hope's friend Evy going along to help with the kids and the cooking. Then Evy backed out so she could go to a party Friday night. Hope had lined up Licha, her weekend maid, but Licha had gotten a last-minute singing job Friday night. Meantime, Fran Ashlock was getting cross, too, not knowing if her girls would be going away for the weekend or not. Bill had kept saying he'd phone her when he knew, and later Hope had heard him telling one of the girls that she and her sister couldn't go this time because Hope didn't have help, but they could go another time. And now a total stranger was coming.

When he heard the doorbell, K.C. ran to the door, with Hope right behind him. Bill picked up K.C. and reached around him to kiss Hope.

"My mother says it's okay," Hope said, "as long as he doesn't use the name of the ranch, and as long as he doesn't make it look like we're having an affair."

"I know," Bill said. "I called her too. And I got directions."

At exactly 5:30 the phone rang. Bill answered the phone on the dining table, with Hope standing alongside.

"It's all right if you come," Bill said, "but we don't want the name of the ranch used, and it—well, for Hopie and me, it should just look like a day's outing at the ranch. I mean . . ." He stopped talking and listened for a moment.

"Fine," Bill said then. "Around one o'clock tomorrow. Now let me tell you how to get there." Reading from his notes, Bill said to take the main highway north to Bakersfield, but from Springville to the ranch it began to get complicated, and Hope began to get impatient.

"Just tell him to go to Springville," she began saying to Bill, who nodded. "Just a minute," he told the caller, then he turned and listened to Hope. "Just tell him to go to Springville and when he hits a gas station, to call us and we can direct him from there." Bill repeated this into the phone and gave the ranch phone number. "Fine," Bill said. "We'll expect to hear from you around one."

He hung up and turned to Hope. "Let's go," he said. "All ready?"

"No," Hope said. "You were late, so we're running late. What did he say about the pictures?"

"It's okay," Bill said. "He said he won't use the name of the ranch and he'll certainly make sure nothing looks improper." He leered at her and twirled the ends of his mustache, and even though she was feeling tense and uptight about the way things were turning out, Hope had to laugh. She started down the hall to the bedroom to pick up her things, then she stopped and turned back toward Bill.

"I don't even know this guy's name."

"Taylor Wright," Bill said.

CHAPTER
TWO

Martha carried the luggage and groceries to the car while Hope and Bill said good-bye to the children, all of them clustered in the doorway. Bill swung K.C. up into his arms one more time as Hope repeated the instructions to Martha, reminding her that K.C.'s father would pick him up on Saturday morning, and that Martha was not to leave until Licha came to take over Saturday evening. She made sure Martha had the ranch phone number, then she slid into the front seat of the Vega, beside Bill, leaned back, and closed her eyes.

"We're going," Hope sighed, as Bill turned up the Drive, then headed down the mountainside. "I can't believe we're finally going." She felt as though she could fall asleep right there in the car. But by the time they were out of the city, heading north on the freeway, she felt fresher, and she sat up straight. The traffic was thick but moving well along the divided highway, four lanes in each direction. Bill turned slightly toward her and smiled. "Feeling better?"

"Lots," Hope said, digging in her bag for her comb. She turned toward Bill and tucked her knees under her, curled up on the seat. "I'm so glad we're not going to a party tonight. I'm so glad we're together. Just us."

"Me too," Bill said. Then Hope frowned a little. "Well, it's not really just us. Bill, why is this guy coming all this way just to take pictures?

We could have put on some jeans and stood by a tree back in L.A."

"Oh, Hopie," Bill said, "you're always worried about everybody else. If the guy wants to make the drive, let him do it."

"Well, I still wish he wasn't coming," Hope said. "And with him coming all this way, we're going to at least have to take him to lunch or something."

"I liked him a lot," Bill said, "and I think you will, too. He's very entertaining. We had a good time at lunch."

"What did you talk about?"

"Oh, we talked about our war experiences, and about Vietnam. He told me he just got back from three years in Vietnam and he's just kind of filling up time now before he gets another assignment."

"Well, I hope he enjoys this assignment," Hope said. "Did you tell him that one of his ten most eligible bachelors ate warmed-over meatloaf last night and then watched TV?"

Bill laughed. "Speaking of meatloaf, are you hungry?"

"Yes," Hope said. "I just remembered I didn't eat anything today. But let's go a little farther before we stop."

Below Bakersfield, Bill left the freeway and drove north on Highway 99, straight up through the vast San Joaquin Valley, the center of California farming, with its flat fields of cotton and potatoes, not far from the town of Delano where, only a few years before, Cesar Chavez and his farmworkers had caught national attention. Oranges and almonds, grapes and olives poured abundantly from these irrigated fields, onto the piggyback trucks that thundered along Highway 99 all night long, on their way to morning markets. Past a restaurant with a big, lighted parking lot —The Ranch House—Hope saw a flashing neon sign that said EAT. "I know that place," she told Bill. "Let's stop there." The diner was plain, but the food was good. Hope had a hamburger and two cups of coffee and felt better than she had all day.

The highway narrowed to three lanes, with oleander bushes running down the center strip. They passed the Golden Hills Trailer Park, with a few lights on in some of the trailers. "I wonder how anybody can live there," Hope said.

"You mean you don't want to live in a trailer?" Bill teased. "Funny, I had you figured for the kind of girl who would want to live in a trailer someday."

"Oh, Bill," Hope said, "won't it be wonderful when we can get a place somewhere out in the country? You could work there and only go into the city two or three times a week. And the kids would love it."

"We'll do it, Hopie," Bill said, instantly serious. "We're going to do it."

"I just can't have my mother involved," Hope said. "I don't want her to be making house payments for us because then she feels she can run our lives. I've been through that with my mother before, and it's a real hassle."

"We'll do it ourselves," Bill said. "When I get this deal going with Checkmate, it'll help a lot." Checkmate was the name of a partnership Bill had formed with a filmmaker named Richard Miller. Bill had shown Hope the business cards he and Miller had had done up, all hand-lettering, and he had shown her one of their short films, a scenic mix of sunset and camels, the Sphinx and desert sands, with the caption: *A New Person Is Born Every Day. It Could Be You.*

"Well, I hope it gets going soon," Hope said briskly. "Meantime, Bill, what about using the children in some commercials? I mean, something that wouldn't be emotionally disturbing to them, something fun, like going on rides at an amusement park or something."

"Maybe," Bill said. "But first I'm really going to push on this ad for Occidental and try to get them to use your picture. They're coming in next week to see it."

"Good," Hope said. "And I wish you could see this." She gestured toward the window, at the darkness. "It's really too bad we're coming up at night, on your first trip. These mountains are covered with wildflowers."

"I'll see them tomorrow," Bill said. "I'm so glad to be here, I don't care how dark it is, or how late."

The ranch was a three-hour drive from Los Angeles, about midway between Bakersfield and Fresno but off the highway in a picture-book world of its own. Past Porterville, the nearest town of any size, with a Wells Fargo Bank, an Elks club, a courthouse, and a jail, they headed east into the foothills of the Sierra Nevadas, past the black depths of Lake Success, onto a two-lane road. The town of Springville lay ahead, a hamlet with the bare necessities for mountain-country living: a small grocery, a hardware store and gas station, a bar or two, a store that sold ice and beer and bait and tackle. "Go slow on this road," Hope told Bill. "If we get into Springville, we've gone too far. It's easy to miss the turnoff, even in the daytime."

There were no other cars on the road, no lights anywhere. The dark shape of the mountain above them blended into the blackness. Hope peered out her window, searching for the road. "Here it is. Turn right."

Bill turned onto the dirt road. In the glare of the headlights, he could see that the gate, part way up the bumpy road, around the curve, was open, so he drove a little faster, past a big white frame house with a porch. "Make a left," Hope directed, "and park here, alongside the house."

Bill turned and parked in the open space between the house and the orange grove. The foreman's house beyond the trees was dark. "I guess the Webbs are gone, because the gate was open," Hope said. "Or maybe they're in bed. But if they're in bed they should have closed the gate." She fished out a flashlight from the glove compartment and swung the light around as she got out of the car. "At least I hope my mother called them and had them turn the heat on."

But the house was chilly when she opened the side door into the little storage and entrance room that opened into the kitchen. She switched on the lights and walked through the kitchen into the living room, where she flicked on the thermostat. When she turned on the lamp on the table between two rocking chairs, the room was suddenly welcoming and mellow. Bill came in and stood in the middle of the room, looking around. "I love it," he said. "It's just the way I thought it would be."

It was a comfortable room, pleasant and unpretentious, like a room in a midwestern farmhouse. Indeed, in the Midwest the whole place would have been called a farm, rather than a ranch, though it probably fit somewhere in between. Jim Webb's title of "foreman" was largely honorary—he had no ranch hands to boss; he worked a regular job at the state hospital in Porterville. But he kept some cattle on the property, looked after a handful of horses, and watered the orange trees, so it qualified as a ranch or, at least, a spread, more than five hundred mountainous acres, with two deep lakes and a rushing river. Hope's mother had paid seventy thousand dollars for her quarter interest.

It was a good hideaway for a man and woman in love. Bill sat at the end of the sofa, near the fireplace, taking it all in. A long coffee table separated the sofa from two big rocking chairs, with brass lamps on tables at each end of the sofa. Behind the sofa was a large dining area, with an oval table that could seat eight people. Above the sideboard along the far wall were two carved wooden mallard ducks. On a knickknack shelf on the living room wall was a china cup with a painted caption: *Your Father's Mustache*, and, below that shelf, a row of *Reader's Digest Condensed Books*. Two hurricane lamps stood at either end of the mantel over the fireplace.

Bill grinned. "At least a person wouldn't have any trouble getting out of here." Five doors led out of the living room. Hope opened the main door, the front door, which led out onto the front porch, and Bill came to stand beside her. "Let's take a walk," they said at the same time, and laughed.

Two mulberry trees stood like benign sentinels in the golden glow from the house lights. Bill stopped under one of them and turned back to look at the house, lighted and cheerful and homey-looking now, with wooden benches on the porch, a dinner bell hung over the porch steps, a pile of firewood neatly stacked. "I love it," he said again. "I never want to go back to L.A."

"There's a river down here," Hope said, walking past him. He caught up with her and they walked down the road they'd driven up, through the gate, where they left the road and stood at the edge of a hill dipping down to the river. In the distance, below them, they could hear the rush of the water. "It's the Tule River," Hope said. "It's not real big, but it's nice and clean, and there's a nice little sandy beach down there, great for swimming."

She took out a cigarette and Bill lighted it for her. He didn't smoke, but he had never complained about her smoking; he never complained about anything she did. They stood for a while in the moonlight, in no rush to get anything said. They walked slowly back up the road, past the house, around to the side where the car was parked, facing the dark mountain. Hope held the back door open for Bill as he carried in the grocery bags. "Let's have a drink," Bill said. "And how about a fire?"

"There's wood by the fireplace," Hope said. "At least there should be. Jim Webb is supposed to keep wood ready. Anyway, there's some on the porch. I'm going to change."

She carried her small suitcase through the living room and into the corner bedroom at the front of the house, which looked out onto the front lawn. The two twin beds in the room were pushed together, making one bed, but with separate twin-sized bedspreads. Hope opened her suitcase and took out a long, light pink brushed-cotton gown. Then she walked from the bedroom into the small hall, around the corner to the bathroom.

When she came out, Bill was kneeling by the fireplace, with the fire already leaping. "One more log," he said, and heaved a small one onto the fire. He drew the screen shut and stood up. Hope walked back into the kitchen, turned off the light, then she turned off the living room lamps. Bill settled at the end of the sofa nearer the fire, with his drink on the coffee table. Hope sat on the floor at his feet, right up close to the fire, with a glass of white wine.

"It's after midnight and I'm not the least bit tired," she said.

Bill reached out and touched her hair. "You look nice," he said. She reached up and took his hand, still gazing into the fire. She did look nice, with her long hair falling softly past her shoulders, her soft, little-girl gown; she looked nice and fragile and very innocent.

"Bill," she murmured, "I feel so lucky. I mean, it's extremely lucky that we really, really like each other's children, isn't it? We're so lucky that we can treat them all the same and really, really mean it."

"I know," Bill said. "And it'll be great when we have a place of our own, like this, and they can all play together." They sat silently for a while, watching the fire. Then Bill shifted a little, on the sofa.

"Hopie," he said, "what do you think I should do about Sandi?"

Hope looked at the fire, not at Bill. "I think probably you should see her again and see how you feel," she said.

"I don't want to see her again," Bill said. "I knew six months before I met you that it was over between Sandi and me. But she keeps calling me. She called me at the office nine times yesterday. Four times she called to say she was never going to call again."

"Well, I just think you're going to have to see her in person and look her straight in the eye and tell her you don't want to see her again," Hope said. "I think you have to do that because you've only talked to her on the phone and she probably thinks that if she can just see you once more, you'll feel differently. And I've told you before that I don't want to get six months down the road with you and then find out that you still love Sandi."

"God, Hopie," Bill said, "I don't want to see her, just the way I don't want you to see Lionel."

Hope sighed a little. This was not a new conversation, this talk of Sandi and of Lionel. The discussion about Sandi had been going on as long as she'd known Bill, and she had urged him again and again to see Sandi, preferably at lunch, and have it over with. Whenever Hope had a problem with a man, she tried to arrange a lunch date. "It's neutral territory," she explained, "and nobody is likely to freak out in a restaurant." She had asked Tom Masters to meet her for lunch and she'd told him then that it wasn't going to work out, two weeks after they were married.

As for Lionel, she knew Bill was still jealous, worried that Lionel might reenter Hope's life. Her relationship with Lionel had been the more recent, and the more serious, of the two affairs she'd had between the time she split with Tom and the time she met Bill. The first was with Michael Abbott, a young law student—quiet, good-looking, earnest—who had lived with her on the Drive for a few months. They had shared a bedroom but also financial problems, and she'd sewn many patches on Michael's jeans. After a while, Michael needed more quiet time to himself than Hope's boisterous household, with three young children, assorted maids, cats and kittens and guinea pigs, was able to provide, and he'd moved out. He introduced Hope to a friend of his, Lionel, the screenwriter. Hope's children took to him instantly and noisily. In fact, they clamored around Lionel so relentlessly that sometimes he and Hope would take their drinks and disappear into the walk-in closet in the bedroom, where they would close the door, sit on the floor, and talk privately.

Lionel was debonair, handsome, and charming, a wonderful raconteur and cook. But he had a habit of saying to her, sometimes in the middle of the night, "I'm going to Europe," and then he would be gone, never a phone call or even a postcard, leaving Hope feeling abandoned. Sometimes he didn't even tell her; she would just wake up in the morning and find him gone, leaving her and the children to wonder where he had gone and when he would be back, if ever.

He'd always come back, to cry on Hope's shoulder and to tell her he'd never do that again, though he always did. She would ask Michael's advice. "I can't figure it out," she'd tell him.

"You don't have to figure it out, Hopie," Michael would say. "You're getting hurt."

When Lionel went to London to work on a television version of *Dr. Jekyll and Mr. Hyde,* he didn't write or phone, which confirmed Hope's feeling that Lionel was basically inconsiderate and not truly her friend. In fact, she had told him so. "You may or may not be my lover, but you'll never be my friend."

Being friends with a man was important to Hope, perhaps even more important than being lovers, though if the two could be combined, as she had done with Bill, that was the best of all possible romantic worlds. Michael Abbott remained a close friend; he often came by the house, bringing a bottle of wine, when Lionel was away. He and Hope would sit by the gas fire, sip wine, play chess, and give each other advice. Even after Bill moved in with her, Hope stayed in close touch with Michael; she had called him to tell him about Bill's commercial making the "ten-best" list, and she had told him she and Bill were coming up to the ranch. She thought Michael and Bill were very much alike, and she had repeated to Bill Michael's theory about why a relationship fails.

"Michael says there are three kinds of needs," Hope explained. "Number one needs are essential. Number two needs are important, but not all of them are essential. And number three needs are adjustable. My number one need is to be important to somebody, to a cuddly warm person I can communicate with. Number two is sex; that's pretty important. Number three needs, like, what kind of movies do you like? and, what time do you like to get up in the morning? can be worked out." Hope and Bill had discussed their needs and had agreed that their number one needs were all covered, their number two needs were pretty well balanced, and their number three needs, though very different, were easily worked out.

Hope had brought other men to the ranch, but none of them had seemed to enjoy it as much as Bill was enjoying it now, on his very first visit. Even Michael, easygoing as he was, had grumbled a bit the last time he'd come for a weekend, because Hope had asked him to help her with the children, and Michael hadn't been able to take a horse and ride by himself and do the things he'd have done without all the children underfoot. Later Hope had tried to make it up to Michael by asking him again, just for the day, with his friend Billy. Billy had called a friend of his who lived in Porterville, and Hope remembered how the three men had spent a good day together, riding and swimming.

Hope glanced up at Bill and marveled at how contented he looked. He smiled down at her. "Someday we'll have our own fireplace, Hopie, with a house to go around it."

"We have to figure out how to make some more money first," Hope reminded him, and they talked again about TV commercials. Hope felt that, besides the print ad for the insurance company, she might be able to model in a few commercials, considering Bill's contacts. She was young and beautiful enough and she had some acting experience. She'd never taken a regular acting job, though she'd had offers, because it required too much of a time commitment—getting up at five in the morning—but she'd worked as an extra on a few films. She'd worn pale makeup and a Depression outfit in *They Shoot Horses, Don't They?* In *The Great Bank Robbery* she wore a prostitute's costume, a purple dress with lots of feathers and ribbons, but that didn't work out well. "Kim Novak took one look at me and I was banished to the other end of town," Hope recalled. She'd worked fairly regularly on the TV series "The Virginian" because she knew the producer. She had a bit part in another series, "It Takes a Thief," until she met the star, Robert Wagner. "I guess I didn't flatter him enough," Hope decided. "He came up to me one day and said hello, and I said hello and went back to reading my book. Next thing I knew, I was banished from the main set." When she was getting nothing but "boring bits," she concluded that "pretty people don't make good extras," and she more or less got out of that line of work, although she made a sales film for Franciscan china. Not long after that, she had a call from a woman who'd gotten her name from the photographer on that film, inviting her to appear on "The Dating Game." "How much does it pay?" Hope asked, and the woman sounded shocked. "Pay?" she exclaimed. "People are dying to appear on this show. And you'll meet a lot of guys." Hope turned it down, saying she had enough guys already.

Bill made more drinks, and they kept talking about the future, about the house in the country they would have someday, how good it was that they had found each other. "I used to think I was happy," Bill said, "but now, every day, I look forward to coming home at night to you, and if I ever thought I couldn't come home to you, I'd rather be dead."

"You'll always come home to me," Hope declared. "And don't worry for a while about dying. You're forty, remember."

"I'm not worried about actually dying," Bill said. "When you're dead, you're dead, and that's it. What really bothers me is the thought of getting old and sick." Hope knew about his fear; he had told her how he had watched his father die slowly of cancer when Bill was seven years old. She had tried to talk him into believing in God and in an afterlife, but he was hard to sway. Hope's attempts to bring him around to her way of thinking were somewhat complicated by the vagaries of her own thinking. She did not question the existence of God, or a life hereafter, but she had spent years questioning the earthly means to that divine end. One of her friends had taught Hope the Hail Mary when they were little girls, and for a while Hope collected rosaries to hang on her wall. But as she grew up, Hope came to know so many Catholics whom she considered guilt-ridden that she was leery of getting more involved with that faith. Technically, she was an Episcopalian, by baptism and through her mother's church membership, but she had never felt comfortable at All Saints because of the social aspect. She remembered one lonely stretch of time when she had attended church regularly. "No one spoke to me," she recalled. "No one ever made me feel that I belonged to the family of God." So she had stopped going, although she was very fond of the pastor there, the Reverend Kermit Castellanos. He had visited her in the hospital when K.C. was born, bringing her a handful of flowers from the altar, and she had chosen her baby's initials, K.C., in his honor. But she had refused to have K.C. baptized. "It's basically a casting out of the devil, isn't it?" she asked Reverend Castellanos. "Well, we prefer to think of it as a kind of initiation," he said, but he had agreed with her that, according to the words of the rite, it was indeed designed to cast out the devil. "I refuse to believe that there's evil in a tiny baby," Hope said. She didn't think anyone was truly evil, actually, only that people fell into two categories: good, and not so good. She felt she had always tried to be good to other people, especially to those who needed friends. When a classmate of hers at L.A. High, named Posie, was excluded from certain groups because her mother was Catholic and her father Jewish, Hope had made a special effort to befriend her. A few years later, when Posie was nineteen, she was killed in an air crash, and, not long after, Hope said she heard Posie talking to her in the night, asking Hope to talk to Posie's father. So Hope wrote him a five-page letter, telling him that Posie had told her to tell him not to worry about Posie and not to feel bad and that Posie knew her father had had a hard time understanding the Catholic service that had been held for Posie, but that was okay. Later, Hope heard that her letter had stopped Posie's father from committing suicide, which made her feel very good, because she felt that was the whole point of religion, to help others. She looked for guidance herself from various sources, including religious programs on television, books on astrology, and assorted churches and spiritual self-help groups around town. Once, just to please her, Bill had gone with her to one of the churches, the Self-Realization Garden, and afterward had sounded less skeptical. "I have to admit, maybe these people have something," he told her, which made Hope think she was making some headway.

"You won't get real sick," Hope told him now. "You're in great condition; you're at the absolute peak moment of your life. And when we do get old, we'll do it very slowly and gracefully. We won't even bother to dye our hair when it turns gray."

"Okay," Bill said, laughing. "In the meantime, we'd better get some sleep. It's five o'clock."

Hope didn't want to go to bed at all. She wanted to sit by the fire until daybreak, then make coffee and walk up the back of the property, past the lower lake and the upper lake and part way up the mountain, which she knew would be covered with budding wildflowers now. But she knew Bill was right. With the reporter due at one o'clock, they had to get some sleep. She got up from the floor, feeling a bit stiff, and stood for a moment, looking down at the dying fire. Bill put his arm around her and snuggled his face in her hair.

"I love you," he murmured. "And I'm so lucky."

Hope didn't sleep well. Sometime during the morning she heard cars passing the house; she dozed again, but then she heard a noise on the roof, as though someone were walking across the roof. She woke Bill and told him; he said there was no one.

When she heard Bill moving around the house, she got up and wandered out to the kitchen, where Bill had made coffee. "It's ten-thirty," he said, "so I thought I better shower and shave and get the place in order."

Hope poured herself a cup of coffee. "The place is okay," she said, yawning. She set her coffee on the table by the phone and dialed Jim Webb, but there was no answer.

"I took a little walk," Bill said. "God, it's beautiful up here. Those trees are loaded with oranges."

"You can make a terrific screwdriver with those oranges," Hope said.

"And that mountain," Bill continued, standing at the sink, looking out the window above it. "How high is it?"

"I don't know," Hope said. "It's called Snailhead Mountain, I know that." She lighted a cigarette and wandered back into the bedroom. She opened the curtains and sat on the edge of the bed for a while, in her usual morning daze, then she got back into bed. She drifted in and out of sleep, but she was awake when the phone rang. When she got out to the living room, Bill was telling the man to wait in Springville, and Hope shook her head. "It's silly for you to go all the way there," she said. "Give me the phone and I'll give him directions."

Bill handed her the phone.

"Just come back out of Springville, the way you came," Hope said to the man on the phone, "for about a mile. Watch for a dirt road, and make a left. You come across a little bridge and you stop at the first gate on the left. Then wait there for Bill to come down and open the gate."

"How will I know my left?" the man asked. "Oh, I know. That's the hand with the rock in it."

Hope laughed at the old joke, and hung up. She turned to Bill. "Wait about ten minutes and then go down to the gate and let him in." She went into the bathroom, rinsed her face, brushed her teeth, and rolled half a dozen curlers loosely into her hair. Back in the bedroom, she pulled out a pair of brown pants, and a matching vest and a pink silk blouse from her bag and dressed quickly.

In the kitchen, she took a liter of chilled Almaden Chablis from the refrigerator, opened it, and poured out one glassful. She had a theory that guests felt uncomfortable when they saw you opening a new bottle of wine just for them, so she always tried to pour out a little before someone came. She put the glass of wine into the refrigerator, then she carried the bottle and some glasses into the living room and set them on the coffee table. She made another trip, carrying cheese and crackers, then she went back into the bathroom and studied herself in the mirror, wondering whether she should put on makeup. When she had been with Tom she'd worn a lot of makeup, but Bill preferred her plain, and she'd pretty much gotten out of the habit except when they went to a party. She was thinking about it when she heard the car alongside the house, followed by the sound of men's voices. She opened the bathroom window.

Then she saw him.

He was tall and very handsome, with dark wavy hair and a deep tan. He was wearing dark slacks, a dark turtleneck sweater with a white shirt over it, and a leather jacket. He was facing Bill, gesturing toward the mountain with a large carved pipe, the other hand thrust into his pocket, the very image of male ease and casual elegance.

Hope looked at him for at least a minute before she spoke. *My God,* she thought, *this guy's a real number. He looks like Robert Wagner. If I were single I could get involved with him and it would be trouble for years and years. He's a ladykiller.*

"Come on in," she called, and both men turned to the window. "Come on in the house."

As she passed the bathroom mirror on the way out, Hope glanced at herself once more and smiled. That settles it, she thought. No makeup. For this guy, better to be El Frumpo.

Bill and the visitor were sitting in the living room when Hope came in. Both men stood up. "Hopie, this is Taylor Wright," Bill said.

The man smiled. "Hello," he said.

"Hi, Taylor," Hope said. "Where did you get that terrific tan?"

"I've been skiing," Taylor said.

Hope sat on the sofa. Bill poured wine for each of them and sat in a chair by the picture window. Taylor took the rocking chair nearest the fireplace.

"Where are you from, Taylor?" Hope asked.

"I'm from the Midwest," he said. "Let's say Middle America."

"So am I," Bill said.

Taylor smiled. "I know."

Hope felt nervous. She got up from the sofa and puttered around the room a little, passing cheese and crackers, sitting down for a while, then getting up again. But Taylor seemed very much at home.

"In fact, I was married in Middle America," he went on. "I have two daughters, and I have a granddaughter."

"You don't look old enough to be a grandfather," Hope said.

"I'm fifty-one," Taylor said.

Hope and Bill were amazed. "That's incredible," Hope said. "You look about thirty-five. Are you sure you're fifty-one?" Everybody laughed.

"I'm sure," he said.

"Well, why not?" Hope said. "Bill's forty, and he's the youngest-looking forty I've ever seen. But if you're fifty-one, you've got him beat."

"Well, you don't look thirty-one, Hopie," Bill said. "I'd say we all have at least a ten-year margin."

Hope laughed. "We must be the oldest group of young-looking people in town."

"One of my daughters just had a baby," Taylor said. "They all live in the Midwest. Now I'm divorced, and I also have another child, a little boy, who's three years old. He lives just outside Paris with his mother."

"I have a three-year-old boy, too," Hope said. "Tell me about yours. What's his name?"

"Christian," Taylor said. "Christian, or Chris."

"What's your wife's name?" Hope asked.

"Well, we're not married," Taylor said.

"Well, I'm not saying marriage is always the answer," Hope said, "and maybe I shouldn't have gotten married, but when there are children involved, you know, it's nice to get married, because of the children." She talked a little about Tom Masters, then she got up and poured more wine. "It's nice for children when they know you're married, or that you're going to get married. My little boy, K.C., always comes into the bedroom and climbs into bed with Bill and me."

"Yes, that's nice," Taylor agreed. "When I'm there, Chris sleeps with us, too."

"Are you there a lot?" Hope asked.

"Every winter. I live there in the winter, which is why I always keep my pipe tobacco in a tin, because of the dampness. And I travel a lot. As I told Bill, I haven't been in the United States for the past three years. I just came back, and I'm not up on what's going on."

Hope lighted another cigarette. "You haven't missed much," she said coolly. She was acting less nervous now, enjoying the conversation.

"I haven't seen any movies, for instance, for three years," Taylor said. "What's worth seeing?"

"Hardly anything," Hope declared. "Bill and I hardly ever go to a movie because they're so filthy and violent. Once I had to go to one of those miserable movies with my husband because he had two clients appearing in it, and I haven't forgotten it."

"What movie was that?" Taylor asked, looking interested.

Beyond the Valley of the Dolls," Hope said. "The sex part was just kind of stupid, and I could have stood that, but what was really awful was the scene of the woman lying in bed, and a man sticks a gun in her mouth and fired. It just made me sick."

Taylor smiled slightly. "Well, something for everybody," he said.

They talked for two hours, drinking wine. Taylor was a wonderful conversationalist; he reminded Hope very much of Lionel. He was a good listener, too, as Hope talked on. She talked about fluoridation of the water, which she didn't like, and free school lunches, which she liked as long as the children eating free didn't have to stand in a separate line. "If they stand in a separate line, everyone else knows they're not paying for their lunch and it sets them apart. It embarrasses them," Hope pointed out. She talked about her children, her life, all kinds of things, in such an easy, amiable fashion with Taylor that later she couldn't remember what all she'd said.

The wine bottle was nearly empty when Taylor looked at his watch, a handsome Seiko. "We'd better take some pictures of you and this distinguished bachelor," he said, "before it gets too dark."

"How did you happen to pick Bill as a distinguished bachelor?" Hope asked.

"Well, he drives a sports car, and he has a pilot's license, and"—Taylor paused, keeping his eyes on Hope—"he dates attractive women."

"Well, I'd rather not be in the pictures," Hope said, a little nervously. "Just take pictures of Bill."

Bill shook his head. "Oh, no. You have to be in the pictures, too. That's the whole point."

Hope gave in. *It's Bill's big day,* Hope thought, *and as long as Taylor's here, I may as well go along with it.* "Okay," she said. "Do you want me to change?"

Taylor looked at her again with that long, steady gaze. "No, your clothes are fine. But I'd like you to put on some makeup."

"Okay," Hope said. "Bill, call Jim Webb again and see if he can get a horse ready for us."

In the bathroom she put on makeup carefully: Max Factor Technicolor pale pancake, blusher, a smudge of eyeshadow, mascara, and cinnamon-colored lip gloss. She took the curlers out of her hair and brushed it, letting it cascade in bright waves down her back. Taylor was still sitting in the rocking chair when she came back into the living room; Bill stood in the kitchen doorway. "I can't get Jim Webb," Bill said.

"Well, let's go walk around a little," Hope said. "We'll get him later."

"Just a minute," Taylor said, getting up from his chair and coming close to Hope. He looked steadily at her, deeply into her eyes. "You look beautiful," he said. "But I'd like more eyeshadow."

By this time Hope had decided to take the whole thing as a photographic assignment and enjoy it, even though she wasn't being paid. Back in the bathroom, she put on more gray eyeshadow until her eyes looked very dusky and very wide. She pulled on shiny boots, which she wasn't supposed to wear because of her back but they looked terrific with her tight pants.

Bill had poured the rest of the wine into a yellow plastic glass, and the three of them went out the back door. Bill looked casual and nice in his jeans and boots and a white shirt with the word LOVE in black letters. Taylor was wearing his leather jacket; all afternoon, sitting in the warm living room, he'd kept his jacket on.

The early winter dusk was beginning to close in as they walked up the road, past the orange grove and the foreman's cottage. Beyond the gate that led up past the lake, they left the road and headed for the river. Bill was walking ahead, and when Hope began sliding a little on the damp grass, Taylor reached out and grasped her hand.

They walked and slid down the muddy hill to the river. "It's too dark down here for pictures, but it's beautiful," Taylor said. They sat on the slippery boulders at the edge of the river and sipped the rest of the wine, sharing the glass. Bill had climbed a little beyond them, to an old waterwheel by the river's edge. "You didn't tell me your birthday," Hope said to Taylor, "but I know exactly what you are. You're a Leo. You're Leo, the lion." Taylor smiled and didn't answer, but Hope felt sure she was right. From her study of astrology, she had found that people conformed amazingly well to their signs. Bill was Virgo: neat, organized, a perfectionist in his work. With her October 21 birthday, she was Libra, but almost Scorpio. "Scorpio moon people tend to be psychic," Hope said. "Almost witchy. They're great at parties: flirty, charming, weak, and wonderful."

She didn't think she was actually flirting with Taylor, but she was joking with him, kidding around, letting him know she knew he had a million girls on his string. When they left the river and Hope slipped on the way back up the hill, it was Taylor who caught her around the waist, helped her up, and held her hand as they crossed the meadow, back to the road.

When they got to the main house, Hope telephoned. "Someone's here taking pictures for a newspaper story," she told Jim Webb. "We need a nice gentle horse, maybe Bonnie, so would you get her and clean her up and brush up her mane so she looks presentable and saddle her up." Jim Webb said he would, but in a few minutes he knocked at the door. Hope introduced him to Bill and to Taylor; all the men shook hands. "I can't find the key to the tack room," Jim Webb told Hope. "So I can't get a saddle."

Bill looked uncertainly at Hope, but Taylor waved his hand in an easy, graceful gesture. "Can you get a rope and make a halter so we can lead the horse?" he asked.

"Sure," Jim Webb said. "I've got a rope around here."

"Then just go ahead and get the horse and put a rope around it," Taylor directed. Listening, Hope was more convinced than ever that Taylor was a Leo: arrogant and capable. In fact, a Leo was usually the most capable of the bunch.

When they went outside again, Bill stayed in the background, leaning against the fence that bordered the road, while Taylor talked with Jim Webb about ropes and various kinds of halters and whether they would need a second horse. Hope talked a little, but there were other people around in the yard—she assumed they were Jim Webb's family and friends—and she didn't want to sound bossy to Jim in front of them. She didn't know any of his family except his young wife, Teresa, and the two children, and she didn't see any of them in the group, so she spoke only to Jim and to Taylor. "Bonnie is a real gentle horse," Hope said. "The kids all ride Bonnie, she's so gentle, so maybe Bill can just sit on Bonnie bareback."

Taylor took the horse, leading her by the rope, down the road past the main house. Bill fell into step with him, Hope following. When she saw a car coming up the road, around the curve, she waved and yelled, thinking it was one of Jim Webb's buddies, driving too fast. "Hey, stop, cut it out! Take it easy or you'll hit the horse." The car stopped suddenly and Hope recognized Jim Webb's wife, Terry. "Oh, my God," Hope muttered to herself. "I yelled at Terry, of all people." The car window was rolled up, but Hope could tell from the expression on Terry's face that she'd heard Hope yell in that nasty tone. Hope thought she saw children in the back seat, but she felt bad about screaming at Terry, so she turned away, toward the orange grove, and scooped up some oranges lying under the trees. When she passed the main house, she tossed the oranges onto the lawn. "We can have fresh screwdrivers later," she called to the men, catching up with them. "Let me take the horse," she said. "She likes women. Go ahead, go on down to the beach, and take some pictures without the horse. I'll bring her along."

Bill and Taylor turned off the road at the place where she and Bill had stood Friday night in the darkness, listening to the river. When they went down the hill, Hope lost sight of them. She tried to follow, with Bonnie, but when the horse got about six feet down the sloping path, she yanked her head down and began munching grass. She wouldn't budge, and Hope got really mad. "Goddamn you, Bonnie!" The horse still balked. *I can't believe that I can't even control this ridiculous horse,* Hope thought, angrily. *My ten-year-old daughter can make this horse do whatever she wants her to do, and I can't.* She was angry at herself and at everyone else, and she kept yelling as she tugged at the horse. "Come on, that's what you're here for!" She yelled so loudly that Jim Webb and the people around his house heard her.

Eventually Bill heard, too, and came back up the muddy path to take the horse. Down on the beach, Hope and Taylor shared the wine in the yellow glass as Bill led the horse down. Hope was joking with Taylor again in a teasing, flirting way, just as she did with other men she knew who were so good-looking and charming and, in her judgment, spoiled. The river valley was in shadow, and both Bill and Taylor agreed that there wasn't nearly enough light for good pictures, but Taylor kept clicking away with his Yashica camera, taking pictures of Bill and the horse, Bill and Hope, Bill and Hope and the horse. The way Taylor was looking at her with the camera made Hope feel uncomfortable, and she was glad when he said, "That's enough. I'll get some more tomorrow."

Taylor led Bonnie back up the hill. Bill put his arm around Hope. "Hey, I think you're laying it on a little thick with this guy," he said. "I think he's getting the wrong idea."

"Okay," Hope said. "Is this better?" She put her arms around Bill and kissed him hard.

He smiled. "Much, much better."

They walked up the hill and up the road to the house with their arms around each other. "Just take the horse over to Jim's and give it to anyone who'll take it," Hope called to Taylor, who was disappearing around the bend, past the orange grove.

In the bedroom, Hope took off her boots and changed into navy blue cords. She went out on the front porch where Bill was sitting on the rail and put her arms around him. "I guess we're stuck with this guy for a while," Bill said.

"It's okay," Hope murmured. She was feeling lightheaded and hazy from the wine and maybe from her pain pill. She took Robaxin for her back, sometimes Valium, or Empirin with codeine and, occasionally, a sleeping pill.

Taylor came around to the front porch. "We were just talking about you," Bill said, as Hope still nestled against his neck. "We'd like you to stay for dinner."

"And you might as well stay overnight," Hope said. "We have plenty of room."

"I can't stay overnight," Taylor said. "A friend of mine is flying in from a ski resort tonight and I'm meeting her in Bakersfield."

"Well, you can at least stay a while," Hope said, and Taylor smiled. "Yes, I can stay a while."

They made screwdrivers with the vodka Bill had brought from the city and the big oranges Hope had picked up in the grove. Bill had a gin and tonic afterward, which Hope shared. When Bill said he would make a fire, Hope reminded him that they needed a few things from the market. "We can take my car," Taylor offered, so the three of them got into the front seat of the Lincoln, Taylor driving, Hope in the middle. "I have meat, but I need milk and butter," she told Bill. "And charcoal," he added.

At the small grocery next to the gas station in Springville, Hope played with two young children wandering around the aisles. One child, near the cashier, not more than three years old, was crying, so Hope picked up the toddler and wiped his runny nose with a tissue from her pocket. Bill was gathering groceries, and Taylor was watching Hope.

At the liquor store, a little farther down the short main street, Bill and Taylor bought more vodka, gin, and beer, then they piled the bags into the back seat and drove the mile back to the ranch. The gate was still open and, when they had driven through, Bill asked Hope whether he should lock it. "No, Jim will lock it later," she said.

Bill made more drinks and went around the back of the house, facing the mountain, to start the charcoal grill. Taylor went with him while Hope set out chicken liver spread and crackers, but in a few minutes he came back inside. "Bill told me you worry about his drinking," Taylor told Hope.

"Well, I've known people who are alcoholics, so I guess I'm touchy about it," she said.

"Don't worry about it," Taylor said. "I drink a fifth a day."

Hope and Taylor went into the living room, where they sat drinking and chatting. When Bill came in, Taylor took out a notebook and asked Bill where he was born and the names of his parents. It was the first time since he arrived that Taylor had used a notebook. Bill went out again, and came back to announce that the steaks were ready. Hope jumped up. "Oh, shoot, why didn't you tell me sooner? The wild rice isn't done and I haven't made the salad." Bill wrapped the meat in foil and put it in a warm oven while Hope dashed around the kitchen. "Let me help," Taylor insisted, so Hope told him where the plates and silver were, and he set the table.

By the time they sat down to eat, with Hope at the head of the dining table and the men on either side of her, it was nearly nine o'clock. Hope felt too tired to eat, and a little sick. She picked at her salad and rice, then she took her steak and placed it on Bill's plate. "I can't eat any more," she said. "I'm going to lie down for just a minute."

She got a pillow from the bedroom and lay down on the sofa, dozing lightly. She could hear Bill and Taylor talking like old friends, laughing and joking as they cleared the table. Bill was unusually talkative because he'd been drinking and because he seemed to be having such a good time. He came over to the sofa, while Taylor was in the kitchen, stacking dishes, and bent down to nuzzle her. "I love you," he said, and Hope reached up to put her arms around his neck and give him a long, warm kiss. "It's awfully quiet in there," Taylor called from the kitchen in a funny, teasing voice. When he came back into the living room, he sat in the rocking chair near the fireplace where he'd sat all afternoon. Bill stirred up the fire as Hope raised her head from the pillow. "I don't mean to rush you," she told Taylor, "but what about your friend who's coming into Bakersfield tonight?"

"Oh, no problem," Taylor said lightly. "If I'm not at the airport, she'll just go on to the motel."

"You could pick her up and bring her back here," Hope offered, but Taylor shook his head. "No, I'll come back tomorrow."

Still, he showed no signs of leaving, and Hope decided that if she went into the bedroom for a nap, he might take the hint. "What time is it?" she asked Bill.

"About ten," he said.

Hope got up from the sofa. "I am really beat," she told Taylor, "and please excuse me, but I have to go to sleep now. I'll see you tomorrow." Taylor smiled and stood up as she left the living room and walked through the short hall into the corner bedroom, with Bill following.

"I'm not going to bed for the night," she told Bill. "I'm just going to take a nap. Wake me when he's gone."

She unbuttoned her pink silk blouse, but she kept her clothes on as she lay down on the bed nearest the window. Bill had pulled back the bed-spread, and he placed it over her. He leaned over and kissed her. "I love you," he said. He walked around the end of the bed, turned out the light with the wall switch, and left the room, closing the door behind him. Hope fell at once into a deep, heavy, oblivious sleep.

She came awake suddenly. The room was pitch black, but she sensed a large shape looming over her. Then something was jabbing at her mouth, trying to force her mouth open. It was cold, heavy, hard. She knew it was a gun.

CHAPTER
THREE

HALFWAY ACROSS THE country, a man who had never heard of Hope Masters or Bill Ashlock was working hard for them that weekend. He spent all Friday evening, when Hope and Bill were driving up to the ranch, pacing around a gym in downtown Chicago, watching a volleyball game.

At times like that, it helped to have a sense of humor and an understanding wife, and Robert Swalwell of the Illinois State Police had both. Patricia had never complained about his work, about putting the kids to bed alone and making a pot of coffee and waiting for Bob to come home, whenever. When he was on a special case like this one, his hours were as impossible as his salary, which sometimes was stretched so thin, with a big family and a mortgage to match, that Pat had to go back to work temporarily to tide them over. Pat had been a nurse when they were first married, but she had stopped working when the babies came, five in eight years: four boys and a girl. Now that the kids were a little older, from seven to fourteen, they could manage on their own at least part of the time, with the older ones taking charge.

Besides his sense of humor and his even-tempered wife, Bob Swalwell had two other advantages. He looked like a cop—that is, he looked the way people wanted cops to look, like Richard Boone: tall and craggy, with very light, very clear blue eyes that could turn icy cold or could crinkle quickly into a marvelous smile. Not that there was much to smile about this weekend. Bob Swalwell was involved in the very serious business of tracking a man he considered truly evil, the only truly evil person he had ever known.

His other advantage was that he loved his work. Sometimes he was a little surprised at how much he loved being a cop, considering that it had never been his life's ambition, not something he'd dreamed about as a boy, not a case of following in a father's footsteps. He'd never even known his father, who'd died when Bob was six months old. Bob grew up in his grandparents' house on the South Side of Chicago, and although his mother later married a nice man who liked the boy, Bob was restless and didn't finish high school. He worked here and there, a little of this and a little of that, until one day, when he was working on a construction job as a pile driver, he looked around and saw men who were sixty, sixty-five years old still slugging, still sweating, still getting hurt. He decided he'd better think ahead, so he filed an application with the State Police and, a year later, got a call from them. When he reported to the Police Academy on January 1, 1959, he had a hangover, and he always was amused by the timing of a career that began the morning after New Year's Eve.

But it was a fine career, an honorable career, even when the work was routine. "The first year, you get a shine on that star, and you're going to set the world right," he recalled wryly. He worked out of a small barracks in suburban Elgin, only four men patrolling the maze of highways in and out of Chicago. Drunk drivers, speeders, a few hit-and-runs, but mostly stopping people to write a ticket or issue a warning or just give someone a hand—like the woman he saw parked in a roadside pull-off area, near a tollbooth, speaking into one of the deflector rods (a metal rod with a glistening red center) along the edge of the highway. She was bending over the rod, shouting into it: "Radar! Radar!" When Swalwell walked up to her and asked if he could help, she turned around and beamed at him. "My, you got here quickly," she said, pleased. "I was just calling you on the radar."

He wanted very much to join the detective unit, but there never seemed to be an opening, so he stayed on the road, keeping regular hours, catching up with his family and with the reading he'd missed as a boy: *Les Miserables, Crime and Punishment,* and so forth. Sometimes when he found himself on the night shift, checking out a country gas station at two in the morning, he also found himself hoping he'd get lucky and catch someone trying to break in. "After a while, the challenge in writing a ticket is gone," he said. But he kept his sense of humor, his sense of compassion. After a decade on the force, he was no longer starry eyed, but he wasn't cynical, either. He still cared about people. "If a police officer doesn't care, who the hell is going to care?" he used to say. "Life is so damned short—what do you gain by being cynical? A little compassion goes a long way, and it doesn't cost a nickel." He cared a lot about the men he worked with, especially one of the youngest troopers, a Swede named Sven Ljuggren, "Gus" for short. They became exceptionally close friends and sometimes rode together, although Gus was patrolling alone at 9:10 A.M. on May 26, 1969, when he stopped a car southbound on U.S. 12, because the 1968 Chevy had only one license plate.

Ordinarily Gus would not have stopped a car for such a minor infraction, but his car had a new radio that he wanted to check out. So he waved the Chevy over to the side of the highway, pulled his car ahead of it, got out, and walked up to the driver.

The man at the wheel was dark haired, somewhere in his thirties, very well dressed in a dark business suit, white shirt, and tie. Gus told him he was missing one license plate and that he was going to report it. The man was so pleasant and cooperative that Gus invited him to sit in the front seat of the patrol car while he called in. The man accepted Gus's invitation.

Gus placed the call on his radio at 9:14 A.M., giving the Chevy's license number. Gus had no suspicion that the car was stolen; he merely wanted to see how long it would take for the call to go through and be answered. While they waited, Gus and the man chatted. The man said he was in advertising, and gave Gus his business card. Gus told the man he had just bought an interest in a marina; the man said maybe he could help advertise the new facility. When the man said he needed to get something from the Chevy, Gus thought nothing of it and remained in the police car. The man returned, opened the car door on the passenger side, and shot Gus in the head with a small, blue steel .25 caliber revolver.

Bob Swalwell was working that day, for the first time, with the detective unit. Even on a temporary assignment, a fill-in job, he felt good in plainclothes, a dark blue suit with a vest and a small gold lapel pin, the size of a dime, that said STATE POLICE. He was just about to go out for morning coffee at 9:18 A.M. when the radio call came. "I've been shot," Gus said. He was just able to give his location on the road before his voice died away.

When Bob Swalwell reached the scene, he was stiff with rage. Even though Gus miraculously survived—the bullet had passed through his head, entering slightly below his right ear and lodging just a half-inch under the skin by his left ear—the man had obviously shot to kill, and Swalwell took that very personally. Gus had a wife and kids, Bob had a wife and kids, so did most of the troopers—it could have been any of them. When he visited Gus in the hospital, neither of them got emotional about it; in fact, they talked very breezily. "You were lucky," Bob told Gus. "Lucky, your ass," Gus shot back. "If I'd been lucky he'd have missed me." Back at the barracks, Bob Swalwell asked, urgently, to be assigned to the job of tracking down the gunman. He was so passionate in his pleading that his lieutenant agreed.

When Gus had blacked out and lurched over sidways in the front seat, the business card the man had given him had lodged under his right leg. Swalwell started with the card:

G. Daniel Walker
Ad-Biz Ink.

From the two addresses printed on the card—740 North Rush Street, Chicago, and 803 Main Street, Geneva, Wisconsin—he worked backward, piecing together a profile of a man he'd never seen.

G. Daniel Walker was thirty-eight years old, married, with a three-year-old son. He owned a house on Lake Geneva and he sounded like, looked like, dressed and acted like a successful advertising man, which he apparently was. He had worked for two ad agencies in Toledo, another in Chicago. Although the first agency he'd started on his own in 1965 had failed, his second venture—Ad-Biz Ink—seemed to be thriving. Yet the green Chevy he'd been driving when Gus stopped him had been stolen. Why would such a man be driving a stolen car?

Bob Swalwell probed more, learned more, and the answer amazed him more than the question. Gerald Daniel Walker, also known as Daniel Wayne Walker and Daniel Wynne Walker, was born in Toledo, Ohio, on August 10, 1931, the only child of Virgil Walker and Irene Massie Walker. Virgil was an antiques dealer, Irene a housewife, and the boy seemed to have had a stable upbringing. He went to school and church regularly—Swalwell even came across a nun Walker had known, Sister Mavis. He served with the army in Korea. By the time he shot Gus, he had been arrested eight times, starting when he was twenty-two years old with a charge of armed robbery in Toledo. Later he was convicted of armed robbery in Miami and sentenced to ten years at the Florida State

Penitentiary. He escaped, was caught, later paroled. Within two years he was convicted again of armed robbery, this time in Columbus, Ohio, and sentenced to ten to twenty-five years at the Ohio State Penitentiary.

Everyone Swalwell questioned about Walker said the same thing: the man was a real charmer, personable and clever, a very good talker and an even better listener—a man who could charm the birds right out of the trees. The record seemed to bear this out: when he was an inmate at Ohio State, Walker had courted and married the warden's private secretary. He was paroled in 1963 and given his final release on May 1, 1966, the year his son Drew was born, the year he started Ad-Biz Ink and began to make quite a lot of money. His income was about forty-five thousand a year when he was stealing such items as a small helicopter and a neighbor's tent; he pitched the tent in his own back yard.

Swalwell could only conclude that Walker robbed people and some-times shot people for one reason: the fun of it. The thrill of it all. Some of Walker's acquaintances said Walker had told them he'd committed the Florida robberies "for a lark" and had given the loot to charity. A camera shop owner in Arlington Heights, whom Walker had robbed, said Walker had recited poetry to him. "He just needs that little extra something to make life interesting," Swalwell concluded. "He uses people. He could shoot you, then sit down and have lunch right beside your body and it wouldn't faze him. He's just a bad seed. An amoral human being." Along with the quirky little crimes—stealing the helicopter and the tent—Swalwell found darker suggestions. A young woman living in a high-rise apartment at the Lake Point Towers in Chicago related in terror how Walker had come in unexpectedly one night, found her with another man, pulled out a gun—his favorite was the little blue steel .25—and shot the man in the head. He wrapped a towel around the man's head to catch some of the blood, got him into his car, and drove him to O'Hare Airport, where he pushed him out of the car. "Get out of Chicago," Walker warned the man, "and don't ever come back." Walker then returned to the woman's apartment, pulled the gun again, and held it to her head. "If I ever find you with another man," he told her, "this is what will happen."

Walker was married at the time, but his charm had apparently begun to fade for his wife, Edna, who worked with Swalwell and the other men on the case as they tracked Walker around Chicago. Edna was an espe-cially good lead, because Walker wanted the child—he had a father-son passport ready, with pictures of Drew and himself. A police car followed Edna everywhere, and on at least one occasion, Walker was spotted following the police car that was following Edna. Swalwell was surer than ever that Walker was playing the game for thrills and laughter when Walker telephoned the police to tell them where he'd been and where he might be later. Cat-and-mouse. There were other bizarre moments in the three weeks Walker was loose, such as the night Swalwell and another cop drove to a house on Division Street where a friend of Walker's lived. They searched the place, including a crawl space in the attic, where the second cop, who weighed over 250 pounds, got wedged in. All the while they struggled to get him out, they learned later, Walker was indeed hidden in that dark cranny, just an arm's length away.

The search for G. Daniel Walker ended on June 12, 1969, after a wild, high-speed chase through the streets of Chicago, with the Illinois State Police, the Chicago city police, the FBI, and a little old lady with a cane all taking part; she stood on the sidewalk as the sirens screamed past, gesturing with her cane—he went that-a-way! At LaBagh Woods, a forest preserve at the edge of the city, Walker ran from the car and into the woods, peeling off his clothes as he ran. The helicopter lost him then, but a swarm of policemen found him stretched out behind a log, with the gun he had shot Gus with nearby. He was arrested and charged with Attempt to Commit Murder and Aggravated Battery and, later that year, brought to trial.

The court appointed an attorney to defend him, but Walker preferred to defend himself, which he did with such verve and skill that, for a while, the verdict seemed in serious doubt. Walker put a doctor on the stand to testify that a small round wound in Walker's leg—a wound that Swalwell was convinced Walker had scraped and gouged himself—might have been a gunshot wound. Walker pleaded that he had shot Gus accidentally and that, in the confusion, he himself had been shot in the leg. In his summation to the jury, he stressed his heartbreak, as a father. "If you believe me, you will let me go home tonight and be with my son." His plea was so poignant that the jury was out seven hours. But the verdict was Guilty, and on December 5, 1969, Walker was sentenced to sixteen to twenty years on the first charge, eight to ten on the second. Even though the sentences were concurrent, and even though Walker promptly filed an appeal, it was assumed that Walker would be shut up for quite a spell in the Illinois State Penitentiary at Joliet, a grim, old-time prison with high cement walls, not noted for its escape rate.

Bob Swalwell went back to uniform, back to patrolling the roads and reading Dostoevski, but he kept hearing about Walker. Even at Joliet, the sort of place that tends to swallow men forever, Walker's visibility was high. He was parading around the place in his customary flamboyant style, demanding that his cell be repainted, doing legal work for other inmates, filing law suits of his own against prison officials, getting himself taken back to court time after time on one pretext or another, and, in general, as Swalwell summed it up, "driving everybody absolutely nuts." The list of transgressions on his record grew longer and weirder, from "Lying" to "Attempting to intimidate three lieutenants" to "Having black pepper in his cell." One of Walker's suits charged harassment; he claimed he had been beaten, and a retinue of lawyers and reform-minded citizens began dropping in on him. One of the Legal Aid attorneys was a tall, slender young woman with long dark hair and big round glasses: Marthe Purmal, nicknamed "Marcy."

Swalwell considered himself a reasonably progressive cop—he approved of the Miranda law, for instance, because "it makes you do your home-work"—and he agreed that prisons could surely use reforming. But he also felt that Walker was using these people, as he had used people all his life. He knew Walker's abundance of charm and cunning, so he was not really surprised to hear on his car radio on the morning of January 31, 1973, as he was driving to work, that Walker had escaped.

Swalwell knew that the state supreme court decision on Walker's appeal was due that day; he knew the appeal had been denied, and he knew that Walker would have known that too. But although he wasn't surprised, he was still furious at what Walker had done to Gus, and he was determined to put Walker back behind bars. When he got to the barracks, he asked, as he had asked more than three years before, to be assigned to the job. "It's prison business now," Swalwell was told. "Let the Department of Corrections handle it."

"It's not just prison business," Swalwell said. "It's personal business. Gus is my friend." He said it so loudly and angrily that they gave in.

Once again Walker was on the run; once again Swalwell was running after him, in his dark blue three-piece suit with the lapel pin. But this time it was harder. Edna had gotten a divorce; she and the boy had moved. Ad-Biz was out of business. Swalwell simply started where a cop has to start, where it happened. "In our work, ninety-nine percent of our work is done after the fact," Swalwell liked to point out. "We go in and pick up the pieces, then we deal with the pieces."

Walker had not escaped directly from Joliet, but from a hospital in Chicago where he had been admitted as a patient on a ruse that even Swalwell, who was keenly aware of Walker's capabilities, considered pretty good. Walker had complained of internal bleeding, and had blood in his urine to prove it. When the prison doctors couldn't explain the blood, after a series of tests, Walker got a court order for outside medical care, and was sent to the Illinois Research Hospital on South Wood Street. Illinois Research was a regular hospital, not connected with the prison, and only a few people knew of Walker's special status. He didn't wear prison clothes, nor even hospital clothes, but soft flannel pajamas and an expensive-looking robe. Although prison guards were assigned to him on three shifts, around the clock, some of them tended to spend some time watching television in the lounge next door to Walker's room, 701. "We have a mutual understanding," Walker told his roommate in the two-bed room, Robert Pietrusiak. "I don't bother the guards and they don't bother me." Although Pietrusiak never saw Walker give a guard any money, he remembered Walker pointing out that guards at the penitentiary were notoriously underpaid, adding slyly, "Money talks."

When Walker refused to let hospital people draw his blood for tests, he was given a needle, vacuum container, and tubes and allowed to draw it himself, privately, in the bathroom. By the time somebody figured out that Walker was putting blood from his arm into his urine, it was too late. Just at seven o'clock on Wednesday morning, January 31, as the guards were changing shifts, Walker left Room 701, saying he was going down to six to take a shower. He stepped into an elevator operated by Armond Lee. He never came back.

Bob Swalwell and his partner on the case, Trooper Willard Rowe, picked up their first intriguing piece when they talked with Bob Pietrusiak and his wife, Catherine. The Pietrusiaks said that Walker had introduced them to Marcy Purmal, the Legal Aid lawyer, who visited Walker often and whose relationship with him seemed, well, different from the usual relationship between attorney and client. They said they had seen Marcy kissing Walker and rubbing his knee, although sometimes they saw nothing, when Marcy and Walker drew the curtains that encircled his bed and there would be long periods of silence. One time, though, when the curtains were closed around Walker's bed, the Pietrusiaks heard loud laughter, as Marcy and Walker read aloud from a court document. The authorities at Joliet, presumably fed up with their rambunctious inmate, had attempted to have Walker transferred to another prison, but Walker had sued to stay. He explained to Pietrusiak that at Joliet he had a private cell with a separate office where he did his legal work, and the prison officials wanted him out because of his court actions against them and because he was winning cases on behalf of other prisoners. He told

Pietrusiak that other prisoners were fond of him, accepting of him. Anyway, the judge had ruled in Walker's favor, and Marcy and Walker seemed to be celebrating. Pietrusiak caught a glimpse of a bottle; it contained either vodka or gin, which Walker was mixing with orange juice. He thought Walker kept the booze hidden most of the time, although a floor nurse, Patricia Coates, told Swalwell that one night Walker had offered her a glass of vodka. She said she had declined.

Nurse Coates and three other nurses—Mary Sheehan, Andrea Gaspar, and Carol Hitzman—told the police that they felt Walker had definitely not been properly guarded. Two of them reported seeing one of his guards asleep on a couch in the TV room on two different evenings, and all of them confirmed that Walker had been a difficult patient, not allowing them near the cabinet by his bed, constantly getting phone calls. When Walker told them he would make his own bed and that they were not to even come anywhere near his bed, they stayed away, though whenever one of them, or a female lab technician, had to come near Walker, Pietrusiak noticed that Walker would get very flirtatious and often try to grab, pat, or pinch them.

Altogether, Catherine Pietursiak, who was a social worker at a county hospital where prisoners were sometimes treated, was amazed at the freedom Walker enjoyed at Illinois Research. At the county hospital, she said, prisoners were usually handcuffed to their beds, or at least never allowed out of bed without a guard hovering close by. She thought it unusual, too, that Walker drew his own blood, and one night she mentioned it to a nurse. "Well, it's not usual hospital procedure," the nurse agreed, "but in this case it's okay." Mrs. Pietrusiak spent a lot of time in Room 701, not just during visiting hours, because her husband was scheduled for serious surgery, and she had plenty of chances to observe Walker. She noticed that he washed his hair every morning and styled it carefully, using hair spray. He always seemed meticulously neat and well groomed, always ready for company, which included, besides Marcy, a young woman he called "C.J." The Pietrusiaks heard Walker tease Marcy about C.J., and vice versa. C.J. usually brought peanut butter and fruit; Walker explained to Bob Pietrusiak that C.J. was a health nut and didn't eat meat, although once C.J. brought in a salami sandwich and Walker told Marcy all about it.

The Pietrusiaks found Walker congenial and engaging. He talked freely about his prison career, mentioning that in Florida he had worked on a chain gang. He said he had been imprisoned in that state "for trying to feed a couple of union organizers to the fish." He told them that his wife and two children lived in Switzerland because his wife had been involved in a crime here for which he had been convicted and she was thus a fugitive from the law. Walker told the Pietrusiaks that that crime was wounding an officer from the Illinois Bureau of Investigation who had come to serve him with a subpoena at his Wisconsin home, but he never said he had shot the man. "Anything could have happened," Walker said. "I could have shot the man, my wife could have shot the man, somebody else could have shot the man." He told them that he himself had once been kidnaped in Ohio by two men and shot in the head three times with a .38-caliber revolver; left for dead by the roadside, he had stumbled to help and had recovered nicely.

Even after Bob Pietrusiak's surgery, when he was taken to the intensive care unit and then to another room, he and his wife remained friendly with Walker. Once, when Catherine went with Bob for a test somewhere in the hospital, she asked Walker to watch her purse. He said he would.

On Tuesday evening, January 30, Catherine and Bob dropped in to Room 701 to visit Walker. Marcy was already there. That evening, for the first time, Walker asked the Pietrusiaks where they lived. Catherine was surprised at the question, because the three of them had already talked about the couple living in Aurora, a somewhat distant suburb, and had laughed about "the boonies." Catherine had been staying in the city while Bob was sick, and she knew Walker had heard them discussing who was taking in their mail, who was walking their dog.

"Aurora," Catherine said.

"I mean, where in Aurora?" Walker asked, smiling.

"Seven-thirty-one Talma Street," Catherine said.

"Where?" Walker asked. Catherine repeated the address.

Walker laughed. "I may come and visit you sometime," he said.

The Pietrusiaks laughed too. "Sure," Bob said. "You're welcome anytime, as soon as we put bars on the guest room windows." Everybody laughed together.

"You'll have to walk our dog," Catherine said.

"When are you getting out of here?" Walker asked Bob.

"This weekend," Pietrusiak said. "The second or third."

Marcy had said nothing. The Pietrusiaks thought she seemed agitated, oddly nervous. Catherine gestured toward a white Marshall Field box lying on Walker's bed. "Did you get another pair of pajamas?" She had seen gift boxes on his bed before, and Walker had always exhibited his gifts—pajamas, a new robe. This time Walker did not open the box.

"Oh, yes," he said, "pajamas." He quickly put his hand on the box lid, keeping it closed. "They're very nice." Then he changed the subject. "What have you done with your car, all this time?"

"Oh, it's in the garage," Bob Pietrusiak said.

Nobody knew what to say then; the atmosphere seemed strangely tense. "Well," Bob said, "I'd better get on back to my room." Walker invited Bob and Catherine to come back the next evening, so the four of them could play Monopoly.

At 6:30 P.M. that next evening, January 31, a man came around to the back door at the home of Robert and Gwen Dreyer at 707 Talma Street and asked directions to the Pietrusiak house. It was already dark, but the Dreyers' porch light was on, and they saw him clearly: steel-rimmed glasses, extremely neat and well groomed, long dark hair, carrying a gift-wrapped box. He told them he had seen Mr. Pietrusiak in the hospital and had come by to leave a package for him.

Later, Marcy Purmal received a two-part, two-page letter from Walker. The first section of the letter was dated midnight, January 31.

C'mere you pretty thing—

While this letter may not reach you for awhile, there is no need for it not to be written.

As you can see, I am safe and sound for the moment, having gone so far as to surround myself with an electric typewriter and cassette recorder. On four buck —what I had left when/ the bottom fell in and you started (Ooooooophs! Old nibble fingers of the electic is not what he once was, but given the opportunity to write to you and I shall return not only to my former form but greater heights, also). As I was saying, it did become rather tough when you started hanging around with the good guys in the white hats and having your body watched, nevertheless, I made it to a safe port and still have two bucks left—see! Thrifty I can be!

Now then to business. I shall not forget you, Marcy, anymore than I will continue to be mindful of the extreme pressures you are presently under and the impossibilities of our weekend for the present, and morover, I shall never forget you, your love, my love for you, and the fact that I cannot be whole without you —given half a chance and I will send for you forthwith.

For now . . . I am bone weary, and besides that tired. I am going to fill the tub with hot-hot water and soak the day out and then slip between my powder blue sheets and dream of you. I will call when convenient and make other arrangements just as soon as schedule provides and permits.

The second half of the letter was dated 10:00 A.M., February 1, 1973.

Good Morning, my love—

While I did not sleep in your arms, as planned, considering your absence I did sleep rather well. Something about escaping which is tiring I fear. . . .

All right, I have been up long enough to shower, run the hot comb through my locks, drink several cups of coffee, and have three eggs with a toasted onion roll—see! Already you have me eating breakfast. The day is rather dismal, where I am at, nevertheless, I am back on my jogging kick, however my legs do not seem to know it. I never realized just how much was wrong with me until I took off on a one mile jog and quit at the half-way point before I fell on my face. Oh, don't worry, I intend to do something about it, my dear.

My dreams were filled with thoughts of you stepping *out of* your pants instead of into them as you did with sleep thick and heavy in your eyes and on your tongue. Ah—yes, I do remember each and every little expression, especially where you come into play. . . .

I love you! Love you! LOVE! I am sure you will grow tired of hearing this, however, I am insane for you—so nuts I dashed over for a bit of Chapstick upon awaking, and find myself tempted to do so today. Instead, I am going to break this off and dash into town and buy some underwear, razor, toothbrush, and stuff. Mostly the makin's for some of those dishes you have been promising to make for me and instead spent all your time at my bedside—just keep it up and see where it gets you.

Love you and shall return shortly—I promise.

Want to get this off for its appointed rounds and into your hands. Remember only one thing—I love you.

> Ciao . . .
> Under Cat/ink.

An emphatic sense of déjà vu swirled around Bob Swalwell as he checked out Walker's old haunts: the high-rise apartment at Lake Point Towers; the bars and cocktail lounges of Chicago's best hotels; a lively spot on Rush Street called The Cedars; the apartment on Division Street where Swalwell's buddy had been wedged in the attic.

C.J., the other woman who had visited Walker in the hospital, turned out to be a housewife who favored prison reform. On January 27, 1972, she and G. Daniel Walker had opened a joint account at the Oak Park Savings and Trust. At 10:15 A.M. on February 2—two days after Walker's escape—she closed the account, number 479761, and received a cashier's check for the balance, $348.31. She told Mr. Ridolfi, a bank officer, that she was going to give the check to her attorney.

Some of Walker's friends and acquaintances didn't wait for the police to call. A woman called the police in Gurnee, where she lived, to report that Walker, an ex-boyfriend of hers, had just called her, simply said "I'm here," and hung up. The Gurnee police chief and one of his men drove out to the woman's house and watched it. A couple from Glenview called their local police to say they had visited Walker in the hospital and wanted to cooperate. When they visited, they said, they had met Marthe Purmal, whom they called Walker's attorney and girlfriend. Marcy's apartment on South Shore Drive was staked out by officers from the Illinois State Prison.

As time went on and the search deepened, many other authorities were involved, including—but not limited to—members of the Fox Lake Police Department, Waukegan Police Department, Park City Police Department, McHenry City Police Department, Grayslake Police Department, Lake Villa Police Department, Gurnee Police Department, North Chicago Police Department, Libertyville Police Department, Northbrook Police Department, DesPlaines Police Department, Skokie Police Department, Antioch Police Department, Glenview Police Department, Oak Park Police Department, Aurora Police Department, Melrose Park Police Department, the Lake County Sheriff's Office, Chicago Police Department, and the Federal Bureau of Investigation. But it was Swalwell who was grittily set on catching the man who'd shot his best friend. It was Swalwell who was spending every day and most nights tracking down every tip, following the wispiest lead, poring over the cartons Walker had abandoned in his cell—twenty-nine full cartons—to find a clue. It was Swalwell who was called by Detective DiSantis of the Melrose Park Police, who had just had a call from a doctor at the West Lake Hospital about a "strange-acting subject" fitting Walker's description, and it was Swalwell who drove all the way out there to verify that it wasn't Walker. It was Swalwell whom the Aurora police called after their switchboard operator, Carol Michels, had taken a call from a man who said he was a Treasury agent and had just seen Walker driving west on Galena Boulevard in Aurora in a 1968 blue Ford, 1972 Illinois license number HG 4463. Shortly after that call, Police Car 55 radioed that they had been stopped by a man on the street and given the same information. Swalwell put out an ISPERN alert—Illinois State Police Emergency Radio Network—and the blue Ford was stopped by a patrol car near Sugar Grove, at the intersection of Illinois Highway 47 and U.S. 34. When the men in the patrol car radioed back that the driver fit Walker's description and they were taking him in, Swalwell and Trooper Rowe dashed out to the Kane County Sheriff's Office, where they met a bewildered citizen named Charles P. Schopf. Mr. Schopf said the blue Ford was certainly his. So it proved. Swalwell thought of the "Treasury agent" and cursed heartily. Cat-and-mouse again.

Robert Pietrusiak was discharged from Illinois Research Hospital on schedule—Friday, February 2. Shortly after he and Catherine got home to Aurora, that evening, he called the police. "Somebody's been living in our house," Pietrusiak said, "eating here, and the bed's been slept in, and a lot of things are missing."

The main thing missing was the family car. After that came a gray Smith-Corona portable electric typewriter; a black-and-silver Panasonic cassette tape recorder; a Yashica camera; a checkbook containing ten checks from the Continental Bank in Chicago, account number 62539700255; a gray Samsonite attaché case; a man's knee-length tan coat with fur lining; eighteen credit cards, including American Express, Master Charge, Sears Roebuck, and Montgomery Ward cards, ten gasoline cards, and department store charge cards from Marshall Field and Carson, Pirie & Scott. But what really struck Catherine was that she was missing, from the bathroom, a can of hair spray, her shampoo and creme rinse, a scissors and nail clippers. In the kitchen, she found dishes had been used and washed; in the living room, a magazine she'd left lying around had been placed neatly atop a stack of mail. When Catherine went through her purse, the purse she'd asked her husband's roommate Walker to watch for her one day, she couldn't find her second set of house keys.

Officers McDonald and Beale from the Aurora station arrived at the Pietrusiak house first and searched, dusting for fingerprints. Other detectives joined them, then men from Joliet. A bed had been used in an upstairs bedroom where there was a small television set; when the Pietrusiaks had gone to the hospital, they had unplugged the set, but now it was plugged in. A TV Preview on top of the set was taken to be checked for prints. In the kitchen, a drinking glass that Catherine said was not there when they left was sitting in the sink. It had been washed, but when it was checked, two prints appeared, on the sides of the glass, near the bottom. Officer McDonald didn't lift the prints there; he took the glass to be checked at the lab.

Down the block, at 707 Talma, Gwen Dreyer identified a mug shot of G. Daniel Walker, number 67128, as the man who'd come around to her back door on Wednesday, asking directions to the Pietrusiaks'. She said, though, that when she saw him he'd been wearing gold-rimmed glasses and his hair had been combed much more neatly.

Wendy Shancer was excited but, to tell the truth, a little scared too, as she stared at the picture in the Monday morning paper. She knew there was no mistake, and as soon as she got to work at Montgomery Ward's in the Old Orchard Shopping Center, she told her boss, Mr. Hirchert. Fred Hirchert called the police.

Mrs. Shancer said that G. Daniel Walker's picture had been in the morning *Tribune* and that she definitely recognized him as the customer she'd had two days before, on Saturday, in her deli department, Swiss Colony. He picked out some sausage and cheese. He was very nicely dressed in a blue suit and a maroon striped tie, so she was a little surprised when the computer check she ran on his credit card came back "Lost or Stolen." It was store policy not to call the police when that happened, but to tell the customer directly, because of the embarrassment, so Mrs. Shancer had suggested he go upstairs to the credit office to straighten it out.

The man went willingly. When the credit manager, Lucille Milling, asked for identification, he showed her the owner's file copy—not the actual license—of Illinois driver's license number P3627743216, Pietrusiak. Mrs. Milling shook her head. "That's not sufficient identification," she said. The man smiled. "It's the only identification I have," he said. "But my wife is over at Marshall Field's. I'll go get my wallet from her, and I'll be right back."

Both Mrs. Milling and Joanne Steffeck of the credit department said yes, that was the man, when they saw Walker's mug shot. The only thing, they told Swalwell, was that he had been wearing gold-rimmed glasses and his hair was much neater.

When Swalwell got back to his office, he found a message to call Bob Pietrusiak.

"I just got a sweater," Pietrusiak reported. "It's from Carson, Pirie & Scott, but I didn't buy it."

At another shopping center then, in Mount Prospect, Swalwell talked to another sales clerk, Kenneth Heinrich. On Saturday, around 1:00 in the afternoon, Heinrich said, a man had bought a tan sweater, using a credit card. The clerk took the card, rang up the sale, and handed the card back. But before he gave the customer his sweater, he told him, almost apologetically, that he had to call up on any sale over $20.00, and the sweater came to $23.09, with tax.

The customer smiled. "I'll go look at some shoes while you do that," he said.

The credit check was okay, but after a while, Ken Heinrich was worried. "What should I do with this sweater, now that it's been rung up?" he asked the manager of his department. "Send it to his house," the manager said.

Swalwell brought out the mug shot, then, though he already knew what the clerk would say—and he did.

By the end of the week, Swalwell felt like a salesman for a cheap photo outfit, passing out free samples. He and Rowe had left Walker's mug shot at all the department store branches they could think of, with the security guards and with the clerks in likely departments—books, pipes and tobacco, men's clothing, ladies' lingerie. Still Walker eluded them. Though he'd strewn clues like walnuts in a fruitcake, he was managing to stay a day, a day and a half, ahead. He'd already been loose nine days. That ninth day, in fact, had been an especially rotten day in a rotten week for Swalwell. He had driven some distance to question an ex-jailmate of Walker's, but the man would say nothing. He had driven back downtown to see C.J.'s lawyer, but the man wasn't in.

Back at his desk, he made a lot of phone calls, trying to keep busy. He knew as well as anybody that police work involved a lot of false leads, a lot of legwork that seemed to amount to nothing, a hell of a lot of just driving around, trying to talk to people who didn't want to talk at all, and, that often, just when you thought you were getting nowhere, there'd be a break. He knew that; it had happened to him before. Still, he had to admit he was a little discouraged. He slammed the phone down on his last call, and shoved aside the papers on his desk, all the maddening pieces that weren't fitting together. *What the hell,* he thought. *I'll go home for supper, for a change.* In the days when he was patrolling the roads—which he tended, now and then, to think of as the good old days—he'd had plenty of time to eat with the kids, help with their homework, play football in the back yard on Saturdays. Now he hardly saw them.

Pat and the children were delighted to see him home early that evening, Friday, February 9, just about suppertime, just about the time a jewelry salesman, Taylor Wright, was checking into a hotel in Ann Arbor.

"Every day is different," Bob Swalwell would say, when someone asked him why he liked police work so much. "You don't have anyone leading you by the hand; you have to depend on your own initiative and energy, and you never know what the next day is going to bring." The next day, Marcy Purmal drove out to O'Hare Field.

By that time, Marcy had begun to cooperate with the authorities. Specifically, she was cooperative with the Department of Corrections; teams of Corrections men had moved into her apartment, bringing shotguns. Marcy had reported a kidnap threat from her vanished client, and she had agreed to let the officers attach a recording device to her phone. Marcy told them that before the device was attached, she'd had a call from Walker, asking her to meet him at the airport, and Marcy had agreed. "I felt the airport was a safe place for me," she later explained, "with so many people around. My thought was to meet him there and persuade him to surrender."

A little after three o'clock that afternoon, Marcy parked her little yellow car in Parking Lot B and strolled around the terminal for a while, looking into windows of the shops and restaurants. In the plastic covering on a display menu in a restaurant window, she saw state troopers following her, and she decided "to have a little fun." She ducked behind a pillar and when an airport shuttle bus came by, she hopped aboard.

A pair of Corrections men spotted her just before she got on the bus, talking with a man in a tan raincoat. They tried to chase the bus, then they ran back to get their car. When they were finally able to force the bus to the side of the roadway, it had already made one stop. Marcy was still aboard; the man in the tan raincoat was not.

Swalwell was furious that he hadn't been informed of Marcy's afternoon activity earlier, before she left her apartment. When he got to O'Hare, he had the Corrections men paged from the TWA terminal, but by the time everybody converged, it was nearly five o'clock. When they checked Parking Lot B, Marcy's car was gone.

Muttering, Swalwell radioed an ISPERN alert on Marcy's yellow convertible, 1972 Illinois license WK 8970. Trooper Frank Waldrup spotted the car leaving O'Hare, and stopped it.

Marcy rolled down the window. "What are you doing?" she asked.

"This is in reference to Gerald Daniel Walker," Waldrup said formally.

Marcy's expression did not change. "Yeah, I know who you are talking about," she snapped. "Why, no, I haven't seen him."

Frank Waldrup asked Marcy to come over to the police car and show him her driver's license. When she opened her handbag, he saw a large stack of bills, with a ten on top. While he waited for Swalwell, Waldrup struck up a conversation.

"How far would you go to protect a client?"

"Well, I wouldn't turn somebody in, if that's what you mean," Marcy said coolly.

"Well, what are you doing out here at the airport?" Waldrup asked.

"Oh, I just came out for a ride," Marcy said airily. "And it's such a nice day for taking a trip to someplace warm." She smiled, but Trooper Waldrup noticed that she seemed extremely nervous, smoking one cigarette after another, constantly looking at her watch.

Swalwell noticed her nervousness, too, when Trooper Rowe brought her into the U.S. Marshal's Office at O'Hare.

"Am I being arrested?" Marcy asked.

"No," Swalwell told her. "This is strictly an interview." He got right to the point. "Did you come out here to meet Walker?"

"Are you accusing me of something?"

"I'm not accusing you of anything," Swalwell said evenly. "I'm just stating the facts." It occurred to him that he sounded like a "Dragnet" cop as he set out the facts he'd heard about her and Walker, telling her bluntly that he knew their relationship extended beyond attorney-client.

"What are you doing out here at the airport?" he asked.

"Oh, I just came to watch the airplanes take off," Marcy said, as airily as she had answered Frank Waldrup. Then she looked at Swalwell very earnestly.

"If I knew where Walker was, I would contact him and advise him to surrender," she assured the officer. "The last time I saw him was at the hospital on the night of January 30, and I haven't seen him since then."

Swalwell was not impressed. "You're lying," he snapped. He then confronted her about the drinking in Walker's hospital room, the kissing.

"That's not true," Marcy insisted. "None of that is true."

Swalwell gave her his iciest, bluest stare for what seemed a long time, but she didn't wilt.

"Can I leave now?" she asked.

"Yes," Swalwell said.

First thing Monday morning, Bob Swalwell called Mort Friedman, chief prosecutor for the Cook County State's Attorney's office. He stated all the facts again about Walker and his friends. Swalwell told Friedman, "We need your help." Friedman helped quickly. He issued subpoenas on Marcy and C.J. and on Mark Kadish, who was lawyer for both of them now, and on the Oak Park Savings and Trust, where C.J. and Walker had had their joint account. The grand jury hearing was set for the very next morning.

The rest of the day was a hectic blur. Swalwell and Trooper Rowe met with Ronald Tonsel of Corrections to arrange for Lane and Hepner to check on parolees who had been behind bars with Walker; Swalwell knew the legal work Walker had done for his jailmates, and he'd always thought some of them could be useful. Swalwell didn't like Ronald Tonsel; he considered him arrogant and difficult to work with. But Tonsel agreed to send his men out to Lake County.

Swalwell had a call from an FBI agent named Baucom, with news of a phone call that the old girlfriend Walker had terrorized had had that morning from Walker. When Baucom called her at noon, she told him she was scared. She said she'd told Walker that if he called her again, she would call the FBI. Agent Baucom reassured her and thanked her for calling.

Lane and Hepner of Corrections called in to say they were following a tip and looking for a waitress named Leslie at a place called Melvin's, near The Cedars on Rush Street.

Mort Friedman, the prosecutor, called to tell Swalwell that Marcy had had a phone call from Walker. She had told him what time she was to appear before the grand jury, what room, what she was going to say. Friedman said Walker had told Marcy he wouldn't show up unless she was indicted.

Sometime that day, a man fitting Walker's description walked into the Legal Aid office on South Halsted Street and dropped off a black purse.

At eight o'clock the next morning, Marcy left her apartment and drove to the Hyde Park Bank. Then she drove to Legal Aid, and when she arrived, Agent Willis Stephans of the Parole Board followed her into her office. Alan Dockerman of Legal Aid held out the purse to Marcy, and Stephans intercepted it. He then rushed over to the State's Attorney's office with it.

Swalwell, who had driven into town on four hours sleep, was waiting there. He opened the purse. It contained a watch, some books, and three notes. Each note was brief, written in a bold, black hand in the center of each page.

> If I could be
> Where I hope these
> Will soon be—
> D.

> Save your snatch
> for me—but look

> pretty and flash it
> like November 30th
> D.

> God made little
> green apples—but
> God Dammit, will I
> never make you?
> D.

The notes were written on stationery from the Chicago Marriott on West Higgins Road. Swalwell and Rowe checked it out, with no results. They checked all the better hotels around the Marriott, including the International Motor Inn, the Sheraton Inn, the Holiday Inn, the Embassy, the Oriental Gardens, the Roadway Inn, the Regency Hyatt House, and Howard Johnson's. All negative. They left Walker's picture with all the desk clerks.

Later, Marcy got another letter dated that day, Monday.

Just back from dropping off your purse at Ye Olde Neighborhood Legal Services office—which believe me was a funny scene, if you can picture yours truly prancing into the office to confront two surprised secretarial types: "Hi! Do you know Marcy Purmal?" Two heads nod. "Good. I want to leave this purse here for her. I suspect it is hopeless to ask if Alan is in." Two heads shake from side to side. "Fine. Just tell Marcy that one Dan Walker dropped this off for her." While I do have other things ~~phph~~ for you, I must admit they~~xxxx~~ (this god damn typewriter has a mind of its own and besides that it is a lot like you—it don't fuck either!). As I was saying, I do have other things for you, however, they take up more room than the small purse and little things. Another day at still another place, my darling. I am sorry that the purse could not be a good one of real leather and all that sort of jazz but $ are in short supply and the only thing I could find at Dunhill's which I liked costed over two hundred beans—that shooked me, when I could just picture you carry goodies to the next guy who lands in the hospital and captures your fancy. Tell me that I meant more than just a fancy. Well, dammit, tell me!

As I mentioned, I am sick over what happened to you on Sunday or rather Saturday. I should never have asked that of you and yet, I can only say that I will trust you to the ends of the earth over the way you conducted yourself. No one, and I mean no one, slipped anywhere near where I was supposed to await. You could have saved yourself at my expense—and remember this one thing, darling, in the event they ever do arrest and charge you, I will make it possible whereby you can make a deal to arrange for the charges to be dropped. Fair enough, sweet one?

I would like to hear everything that was said to you and exactly how they treated you, etc., etc. To make their lives a bit fuller, I did today start contacting everyone I know in the area, arranging with some for meets, and with others just making my presence known—one thing about it, they cannot watch everyone, huh. Funny bit: I called Donna and she immediately started begging me not to hurt her. What the fuck kind of a reputation do I have that people who once loved me and bore me a child would start crying and begging. Some more bullshit that they have been spreading around, I am sure. (Who did you say you met with that they think was me—I may beat your ass, lady.)

One point, they are good at playing two people against each other, so let us not fall for anything that may or may not be true about the other—wherever I may go, I will keep in touch, whether it be directly or through one of your friends— so always feel free to check things you may hear about me as I will do the same concerning you. These are dangerous times, as you damn well now know, and once we are over the hump we can then laugh and joke about 'em, my lovely Laura Lawyer.

It is time that I check with you via telephone and I want to mail this to you then. By the way, I just had shrimp de jonghe. Ummmmmmm—good! As you can see, about the only thing I haven't had since being out is YOU! Ah well, you can't have everything, so they tell me. Double seriously and all that rot, you impressed the hell out of me with coming and going through the hassle and continuing to have that tone of love in your voice when I called. Suppose from now on when I call you and you wish to tell me you love me you just tell me about giving myself up. Good for the tap. Love & Stuff.

The afternoon at the airport seemed to sum up the conflicts and confusions that surrounded the Walker case. Marcy Purmal vehemently denied she had been carrying a lot of money in her purse that day.

"Bullshit! I don't have any money. I work for Legal Aid." She said that the man in the tan raincoat was an attorney she knew, a man named Fox, whom she'd bumped into accidentally. She insisted that her motive for driving out to O'Hare had been to meet Walker and persuade him to surrender.

Swalwell scoffed at that explanation. He felt Marcy's cooperation re- sulted solely from her realization that she was in over her head, involved in a situation that could lead her into professional disgrace, perhaps disbarment. He called her a "radical." (She called him and his men "the

Stormtroopers.") He was never persuaded that if Walker and Marcy met, surrender would ensue, which is why he came to be hanging around the volleyball court in the Ida Noeis Building on the University of Chicago City Campus. It was Marcy's habit to play there on Friday nights, and Swalwell thought Walker might come by, because Walker loved games.

CHAPTER
FOUR

HOPE JERKED HER head away from the cold, hard object in her mouth. She rolled across her bed, then across the other twin bed. She ran out the bedroom door and through the hall door into the living room.

"Bill!" she screamed. "Bill, help me!"

The living room was dark, but in the glow of the dying fire, she could see Bill sitting in his usual place, at the end of the sofa nearest the fireplace. His feet were stretched up on the coffee table. He was holding his drink in his left hand, resting it on the arm of the sofa. His eyes were closed. As she ran across the room, Hope saw the rocking chair was empty. *Taylor is gone,* she thought in a flash of panic, *and a maniac has come in.*

"Bill, Bill, help me!" Hope kept screaming.

She reached the sofa and grasped Bill by the shoulders. She shook him slightly, and his head wobbled and fell backward against the sofa. "Bill, Bill, wake up, help me!"

The voice came from behind the sofa, from the darkness in the dining area.

"He can't help you. He's dead."

But Hope kept shaking Bill and screaming. "Help me, wake up, help me!"

The voice came again, a deadly calm, flat monotone that Hope did not recognize.

"He can't help you. He's dead."

Someone approached Hope from behind, grabbed her by the hair, and pulled her away from the sofa. He wrapped her arms behind her back and spun her around, facing the fireplace. In that instant, when she let go of Bill's shoulders, Hope heard a heavy thud.

The man holding her arms thrust them out in front of her, "Look at all the blood. See all that blood. He's dead. He's dead." In the pale firelight, Hope could see that her arms and hands were covered with blood.

She began to vomit. She ran for the bathroom and the man ran after her, tearing at her clothes. The blouse she had unbuttoned when she lay down came off as she ran. In the bathroom, she fell to her knees and groped in the darkness for the toilet bowl, vomiting and gagging.

"Get into the bedroom," the man said, grabbing at her.

"Leave me alone," Hope gasped. "I'm going to choke to death."

She felt heavy arms around her. She grabbed a towel and jammed it up against her mouth as the man half-dragged, half-carried her into the bedroom, bumping her into the walls along the way. He hurled her onto the bed nearest the window, the bed she'd been sleeping in. "I don't need a gun to kill you," he said. "I could crack your neck with one hand." And he put his hand around her neck. She heard a thunking sound, then she felt his body pressing on hers. He was wearing some kind of sweater, nothing else. Hope lay perfectly still, very passive, as he raped her. *Bill is not dead, Bill is not dead,* she was thinking. *Bill is just unconscious. When this man is finished raping me, he'll leave, and then I can help Bill.*

The man was kissing her wildly, violently, all over her hair and neck, on her breasts and all over her body, rubbing her, grabbing at her all over, as though he had a hundred hands. "If you make this enough fun for me," he growled in a deep, rasping voice, "maybe I won't kill you." He kept kissing her, jamming his mouth against hers, forcing her mouth open.

Suddenly he got up; she could hear him thrashing around the room in the darkness.

"I heard you are a real party girl, a real swinger," he said harshly. "I heard you can do all kinds of interesting things, and that oral is your specialty."

"No, no, no," Hope moaned. "Leave me alone. I can't do anything, leave me alone."

Then he was on top of her again, kissing her, rubbing her. "And I can do anything," he said. "What would you like me to do? Do you like oral sex? Anal sex?"

"No, no, no," Hope kept moaning. "I don't want to do anything. I can't do anything. Leave me alone." Muttering and breathing hard, the man raped her again. "You're hurting me," Hope said, gasping, but that seemed to make him more ferocious. She did not know who he was, only that she felt as though she were in a cage with a gorilla.

He lay still then, heavily against her body. Hope felt cold, colder than she'd ever felt in her life. The coldness in the room was unreal, unbelievable. It flashed across her mind that evil brings a feeling of intense cold. In the icy cold blackness of the room, she felt she was in the presence of true evil, and that terrified her more than anything that might happen.

He raised his head slightly. "I can't leave you alive," he said. "You could identify me." Hope moaned again.

"I don't even know who you are."

"You know I'm about six feet tall and about twenty pounds overweight and you know that my hair is beginning to thin in the back."

"I don't know what you are talking about," Hope said. "There are millions of people who could fit that description. I don't know who you are. I would never identify you. Please go away. Take my car and go away."

The man got up. As she lay motionless, she heard what sounded like tape being ripped, then she was being rolled over on her side. He pulled her hands behind her and her feet up toward her hands, then he wrapped adhesive tape around them, binding them all together in a painful, tight roll.

"Don't scream," he warned. "If you have any ideas about screaming for the foreman, I'll just kill him and you too." He covered her with blankets. As he tucked them in around her neck, he bent over and put his face against her cheek. "I love you," he said. She heard the door close.

For a long time there was stillness, no sound anywhere. Hope felt she was hallucinating, that none of this was happening, none of this was real. Her heart was pounding so she could hear it echoing around the room. She could feel veins in her wrists throbbing and popping and, very quietly, beneath the blankets, she began to tug at the end of the tape with her right hand, no more than a quarter inch at a time, so slowly and quietly she almost felt she wasn't doing it at all.

After a long time, she heard a sound in the room. Someone was there again, sounding agitated but not wild, not violent, not like the wild animal-like man who had been there earlier.

He pulled the blankets back and felt her hands. "Oh, very clever," he said in a normal tone of voice. "You've unwrapped your hands."

"It was hurting so much," Hope said. "I'm not going to try and do anything. Is Bill dead? Oh please, please tell me Bill isn't dead. Please go see if Bill is really dead."

"I have seen him and he is dead," the man said calmly.

Hope began to moan. "Oh, my God, oh, my God, my God, why Bill?" Black pain surged through her head, pounding in her skull. She felt as though it would burst open. Images of Bill flashed through her mind in a crazy dance. Bill holding her, kissing her, saying gently, "I love you." Bill sweeping K.C. up in his arms. Bill laughing. "Did he know? Did he suffer?"

"No," the man said. "He never saw the gun."

"Oh, why, oh, why, why Bill?"

"Because he was with you."

"With me?" Hope could not grasp that. "You mean he is dead because of me?"

"That's right."

"Why me? But why me?"

"Because someone wants you dead," the man said

She could not seem to understand that. It was an impossibly difficult problem to understand.

"Why me? Why would anybody want me dead? I've never hurt anyone in my life. Why me?"

"Because you're going to court next week," the man said in a calm, explanatory, matter-of-fact tone.

"Oh, God, oh, my God," Hope said. "That's only a couple of hundred dollars a month."

There was silence. When the man spoke, he sounded confused.

"Well, I don't know, then there must be something else." She heard him pacing around the room at the foot of the bed. "I didn't want to get involved in this. This isn't my job. I got involved in this at the very last minute."

He would pace for a while, then stop and stand still, sometimes talking in an almost normal voice, sometimes muttering, sometimes talking loudly. Sometimes he would leave the room for a while. Sometimes, when he returned, he would rub her body up and down with clammy, gloved hands—they felt like surgical gloves. Sometimes he rubbed her with the gun, too. Once, when he came back in, he pushed her face to one side on the pillow. "Don't move," he warned. A flashbulb popped. He turned her face to the other side; there was another flash. He took a third flash picture full face. "If I decide to let you live, which I haven't decided, and the day ever comes when you do anything to send the authorities after me, the organization will have your picture and you will be killed," he said. He allowed her hands to remain unbound.

At some point during the long, long night—she had no idea of the time —Hope knew, from the voice and from his silhouette in the doorway, as her eyes became more accustomed to the darkness, that the man she was talking to was Taylor.

She did not call him Taylor, or say she knew who he was. He seemed to assume she knew; part of the conversation referred to Saturday afternoon.

"Oh, why did I let you come here?" Hope asked the darkness. "I didn't want you to come. I didn't invite you, but Bill wanted you to come, and I could never say no to Bill."

"It doesn't matter," Taylor said. "I would have come anyway. There's a contract out on you."

Hope could not seem to grasp that, either. "A contract. A contract," she murmured.

"Well, I have been misled," Taylor said in a precise tone. "You were supposed to be about forty-five years old, with grown-up children, and you were supposed to be a drug addict and an alcoholic and you were giving your children drugs and making them sex perverts and ruining them."

"The children," Hope repeated. "What if I had brought the children?"

"The children were supposed to come," he said, "and the two older children were supposed to be killed, but the youngest one was to be removed. I would rather not kill you but now I have to because of the contract," Taylor went on. "I should have killed you when you were asleep. If I leave you alive I will get into trouble." She heard him pacing near the window as he rambled on.

"This is not my job; I don't like it. I have only killed one woman but she was forty-five years old and she was a spy in the Arab-Israeli war. But you are a good person. You are a good mother. Anybody who would pick up an ugly child with a runny nose that isn't even hers must be a good mother. I would rather die than go back to jail. Why the hell he didn't get you last week after you left the restaurant I cannot figure out. I am pissed off about that."

Hope was trying to follow what he was saying. "Restaurant?" she asked. "Restaurant?"

"When you and Bill were at the restaurant last weekend," Taylor said impatiently. "He was supposed to follow you when you left the restaurant and get you then, when you went home."

Restaurant. The Brown Derby. She and Bill had gone back to his apartment instead of to her house. She remembered thinking it would be all right to leave K.C. with Martha overnight because K.C. would be asleep by then.

Taylor kept talking, telling her things, asking her things. He seemed to know a lot about Bill but asked whether Bill had lived with her or someplace else. He seemed to know a lot about her, too. He knew her address on the Drive, where her mother lived, and about the burglar alarm system at her mother's house. He talked about her stepfather's heart condition. Hope felt her mind shredding apart. She could not sort out, in her mind, what she had told Taylor on Saturday, or what he might have learned from Bill or someone else.

Someone else.

"Who wants me killed?" Hope forced herself to ask.

"Your husband."

"Which husband?" Hope blurted. "I have had two husbands."

"You have two husbands?" he repeated. "Well, I don't know, I don't know which husband, but your husband wants you dead." Again he sounded confused and angry. "I didn't want this job but the guy that was supposed to do it got burned and now I am here and I am supposed to do it."

Slowly, in bits and terrifying pieces, as he came and went, Taylor told a story about a contract. He told Hope that her husband had been involved with a man in the organization who had loaned him forty-two thousand dollars—Taylor called it "Family money"—and her husband had taken out a very large insurance policy on her life so that when Hope was dead and he collected on her policy, he could repay the man. Hope thought Taylor said the policy was for two hundred thousand dollars, and that he was being paid thirty-six hundred dollars to carry out the contract.

He related that he had met her husband at the Beverly Hilton and that her husband had given explicit details. He wanted a blood bath, Taylor said, a Sharon Tate kind of massacre, with butchered bodies and blood splashed all around the room, because that would be good publicity for his business.

"Did you ever have anal sex with your husband?" Taylor asked.

"No," Hope said.

"Well, did you talk about it much?"

"No. Why, in God's name, are you asking me that?"

"Well," Taylor said, "because he said to take a piece of wood from the tinderbox and stick it up you."

Hope listened in horror as he talked on. "But I never liked that plan. I like a nice clean killing. Your husband told me that you take a great deal of medication, and I would rather have taken you to a party and exchanged your pills for something else. Or I could have made it look like a stroke, or a heart attack, with a needle in your eye or an ice pick in your ear. When I was in the kitchen after dinner I laid out two ice picks I could have used. At a party or in a crowd you can stick someone in the ribs and then get away easily, because it takes the person a minute or two to slump over, and then because the wound is so small no one notices it and assumes the person had a heart attack."

Hope could not believe that either of her husbands could do this, that there had been some incredible mistake. She kept trying to make some sense of it.

"Where did you meet my husband?" she asked.

"At the Beverly Hilton Hotel."

"Well, did he just say, 'I want a bloodbath, a Sharon Tate kind of thing'?"

"Oh, no," Taylor said. "He discussed in detail what he wanted done."

"My God," Hope said. "How long did this conversation last?"

"About twenty minutes," Taylor said. "He gave a lot of details, because he said to have you die in a spectacular way would make the papers and the publicity would be valuable for his business."

The grotesque story had begun to make a kind of dreadful sense to Hope. She remembered her surprise when Tom had said he was going to meet someone at the Beverly Hilton. She knew he hated the Hilton, and she remembered asking him why the Hilton. "You know it takes forever to park there." She remembered Tom's interest—she had called it an obsession—with the Sharon Tate murders. She had seen Tom reading a book—and Tom almost never read books—about those killings. Still she could not accept it.

"Well, how did he look?" she managed to ask.

"I didn't like the way he looked," Taylor said sternly. "I didn't like him at all. He's greasy."

Oh, God, Hope thought. Tom did have a greasy look. He was very neat and well groomed but he had to wash his face five times a day, and in the morning his face would be shiny, his skin was so oily. *Oh, God,* she thought. *It must be Tom. If Taylor didn't meet Tom, how would he know that Tom has oily skin? How would he know that Tom was so interested in the Tate murders? But if it's Tom, he must have lost his mind and the children need to be protected. The baby needs to be protected.*

"The children," she said again. "I have to get back to the children. The baby needs me."

"Oh, Tom will have the baby on Sunday," Taylor explained.

"No, no," Hope said. "Tom has never had the baby on Sunday. No matter how many times I have asked him—I've been sick, I've had a hundred thousand problems—he has never taken the baby on Sunday."

"I don't care," Taylor said mildly. "He'll take the baby this Sunday."

Hope thought about K.C. hurtling toward Bill on his chubby little legs. *Oh, K.C. If I die now, he will never even remember that he had a mother who loved him.* The thought was unbearable. She began to cry.

Taylor began to shout. "Stop it, shut up, stop it!" He was kneeling on the bed, shaking her, bumping her with the gun. "I cannot stand it when a woman cries!" he yelled.

Hope stopped crying. She burrowed her face into the pillow to stop her nose from running; Taylor calmed down right away. He moved away from the bed and talked in a normal tone.

"Bill was too dull for you anyway," he said patiently. "You need someone more exciting."

"He was not too dull!" Hope cried. "He has one of the most fantastic minds in the world. Just because he's quiet you think he's dull, but you don't know what he's doing when he's quiet. He could be composing a song, or he could be thinking of some fabulous thing he's going to shoot on film. He has very creative ideas, but he just doesn't talk about them. And besides that, Bill is a very good person and he loves the children and I depend on him for everything, and—"

Taylor cut her off.

"I don't want to hear any more about Bill," he said angrily.

Hope tried to lighten her tone. "And you're wrong, I don't need someone more exciting. I've had someone more exciting"—she was thinking of Lionel—"and I can't take it, it wears me out."

Taylor sounded hurt. "But you were flexing your pelvis at me all day."

"What in God's name do you mean, flexing my pelvis?" Hope demanded.

Taylor tried to describe what he meant, but in the pitch darkness, she couldn't see his gestures.

"Do you mean the way I move around a lot when I'm sitting, always readjusting my sitting position?"

"Yes," he said.

"Oh, my God, that's my back," Hope said. "I move around to make my back more comfortable."

Taylor groaned. "I didn't know that's what it was," he said. Hope thought he sounded actually sorry at his mistake, and she tried to take advantage of his mood.

"Look, I don't mind the idea of dying so much," she told him. "I think there is something going on after we die, and I'm not afraid to die. In fact, sometimes I've wanted to die. If Bill is dead, then all my hopes for the future are pretty much dead, too, and I don't care very much. But the thing is, my children really have nobody else and they will be separated because my mother couldn't cope with all three, and being separated will destroy them."

"Well, I'm sorry," Taylor said. "I know what you are saying about your children is true, and every time I go to kill you, I think of you picking up that kid in the market and it bothers me. But I have got to kill you because you have to understand that in a contract killing there is no such thing as a witness left alive. I am really sorry that I took this contract and I really don't want to kill you. You have cute feet."

Hope had determined by now that her fear and pain enraged Taylor and made him violent. She needed to be calm, maybe even funny.

"Well, before you kill me, can the condemned person have a last cigarette?"

"No," Taylor said firmly. "It's bad for you."

"You're worried about my *health*?" she asked in amazement.

Taylor sounded surprised himself. "Gee, I guess I am." There was a long pause. "I just don't know what to do," he said finally. "I just really don't know what to do. I don't know if I can trust you. If I leave you alive, you might become vindictive later."

"You can trust me," Hope said eagerly. "And I would not become vindictive. It's against my religion to become vindictive."

"Well, I just don't know," Taylor mused. "I just don't know if I can trust you."

"Look, if hating you would bring Bill back," Hope said, "then I would hate you like you have never been hated before. But I can't bring Bill back, so there's no point in me hating you and being vindictive."

She sensed he was interested in that reasoning, so she talked on. She was still terrified, more terrified than she had thought a person could be without dying from the fear, but she remembered hearing once that if you are afraid of something, the best way to overcome your fear is to bring that something out into the open, talk about it, learn about it. A person who is afraid of snakes should study snakes and observe them and become interested in them. So Hope talked to Taylor nonstop, and she tried to get him to talk about himself. He told her that when he was nineteen he had killed someone and gone off to Europe but that the organization— he never said "Mafia"—had held it over his head afterward and forced him to do jobs for them, and he was getting a little weary of killing people and was finding it hard to keep his motivation up. "I want to get out of the killing business," he said. "I can't keep doing this forever. I'm getting pretty old, and all it takes is someone just a little bit younger, a little bit faster." Still, he said, he liked the sexual aspect of killing. "Having a gun go off is like coming ten times," he said, and Hope's heart sank. She quickly steered the conversation back to the philosophy of killing.

"Look, I don't believe anyone should ever kill anyone else," Hope said earnestly. "So you and I are definitely at odds on that, but as for the fact that you kill outside the law, or outside what is socially acceptable, while other people kill because it's socially acceptable—to me that doesn't make one bit of difference. I don't think you should kill someone because they live in another country or because they have a different kind of skin. I don't think you should kill someone because they're afraid and they're running. I don't think you should kill for a lot of the reasons that people are killing each other every day. If you were killing socially correctly, you could be a hero, but you're just killing socially incorrectly, which to me makes you no worse than the other person. You're no worse than some soldier who shoots a woman. You're no worse than a cop who shoots a kid in the back. In fact, you're probably better. You're better than Lieutenant Calley. The really evil people are the people who know me and yet sent you to kill me."

Taylor seemed pleased.

"Oh, yes, I have no particular hatred for you," Hope pressed on. "I have no desire to attack you or to get revenge on you or anything like that. I'm opposed to you, but I'm also opposed to half the men in America who have gone out and killed someone for no reason. I'm even opposed to the people who shoot animals. And now if you have to kill me, I understand your position and I am asking you to please understand my position too and let me do something to see that my children are taken care of, then you can shoot me. But first let me call my mother."

"No, you cannot call your mother," Taylor said.

"You can hold a gun to my head the whole time I'm talking," Hope suggested, "and when I have made sure that my mother will get the children and keep them safe, then you can shoot me."

"No," Taylor said.

"Well, then, just let me make out a will asking that my children be kept together as a group and go to live with a family I know, rather than being separated, and then you can shoot me."

"How would your family get the will?" Taylor asked.

"You could mail it for me," Hope said. "I will trust you to mail the will if you will trust me to let me get up and write it."

Taylor didn't reply. Hope tried another tack.

"Or I could just write a note about the children, and in the note I will say I'm responsible for killing Bill, and then you don't even have to shoot me, I will shoot myself with your gun."

"Hope, you couldn't handle this gun," Taylor said patiently. "Why, you wouldn't even be able to keep it in your hand. It would knock you over. It would blow you halfway across the room. No, that would not work."

Hope was temporarily out of ideas. Before she could speak again, Taylor spoke in a low voice.

"Yes, you are a good person," he said, "although most people are not even halfway decent, and I want to help you and your children. Now I have to think about this." Hope lay without stirring, almost without breathing, as he paced up and down alongside the bed.

"This was a stupid mistake and I wish to hell Bill was still alive," Taylor said. "I have a code of ethics, and I do not feel it is okay to kill a young mother with young children, especially when they have very little money. Maybe what I ought to do now is kill your husband and then you could collect his Social Security."

Hope was too stunned to speak.

"I could burn down the house with the body in it so that it couldn't be identified. Or with both bodies."

He left the room again but came back in a minute or two.

"If only I could trust you," he said. She heard the gun being set down on the dresser again, a heavy thunking sound, then he climbed on top of her, wrapped his arms and legs around her and put his head on her shoulder. He went to sleep. With his crushing weight and the pain inside her body and in her head, Hope blacked out.

When she awoke, she could see beyond his shoulder the clock on the dresser: six o'clock. She heard a car drive past the house. *Jim Webb is leaving*, she thought. *There goes Jim Webb*. She stirred, very, very slowly, trying to slip out from under him as he slept. But he opened his eyes instantly, wide awake and alert. "What are you doing?"

"I have to go to the bathroom," Hope said.

He nuzzled his face against hers. "Kiss first."

Hope swerved her head as far as she could turn it. "I haven't brushed my teeth."

He laughed a little and pushed himself up, off the bed. He stood at the side of the bed. "You can get up. But just remember, I can shoot you just as easily when you're running as when you're lying down, so don't get any big ideas about running anywhere."

He had taken off his sweater and he seemed to enjoy her dismay as he walked naked around the room in the faint light. Hope eased out of bed and stood up shakily, feeling harsh, cramping pains in the lower part of her body. He followed her into the bathroom and sat in the doorway, on the floor, while she used the toilet.

"I don't want to see Bill's body," Hope whispered. "Would you please close the door to the hall so I can't see Bill's body."

"Sure," Taylor said amiably. He got up, closed the door, and walked back into the bathroom where Hope stood at the sink.

"Let's wash those hands," he said briskly. He turned on the warm water and held her hands, caked with dried blood, under the tap, washing them gently, as one would wash the hands of a toddler who'd been making mudpies.

Back in the bedroom, Hope sat on the edge of the bed. "I have to get out of this house or I'll go out of my mind," she said. Taylor shook his head. "No, we can't leave the house until it appears to be a normal hour. Around noon." He rubbed his hand along her cheek gently. "I'll make breakfast. You're too thin, and I want you to gain some weight. I am going to take very good care of you. I love you."

The draperies were still closed, shutting out the winter sunrise, but the room grew brighter as the morning wore on, a crazy collage of conversation and threats. Hope kept insisting she couldn't eat. Taylor showered, making Hope sit naked on the bathroom floor. In the shower, he hummed and whistled. He showed her his scars, most particularly a slash across his stomach and a lump on his ribs that he said was a bullet. He left the gun on the bathroom windowsill, the window she had leaned from on Saturday afternoon when she heard the car drive up and Taylor and Bill talking. It seemed a lifetime ago. She knew that he knew she wouldn't try to grab the gun—he was right, she couldn't handle it—nor would she try to run. To get out of the house she'd have to go through the living room, where Bill was. She knew she couldn't do that, and even if she could, where would she go? Where would she hide in these mountainous acres? She had heard the Webbs leave; even if only Jim Webb had gone, what good would it do to run to Teresa and the children? Taylor would kill them all, and she would be responsible. She was already responsible for Bill's death; Taylor had said so. The thought made her feel crazy, so she tried to concentrate on Taylor instead, to get along with him and somehow get back home, to the children.

Taylor shaved, still humming happily, then styled his long wavy hair with a hot comb. From the middle of his neck down, where the turtleneck sweater ended, his body was very white, very pale.

Back in the bedroom, he dressed in plaid pants and boots and a white shirt. He pointed to a small bloodspot on the shirt and frowned. "Oh, dear, nasty."

Chatting and humming, he bustled in and out of the room, still trying to persuade her to eat. She refused to eat, but she tried to talk normally, to play the game as though nothing had happened, as though they were ordinary people waking up on a Sunday morning in the country.

Taylor said there was a problem: Bill's body. "You could help me put the body and the sofa into the trunk of the car, and we could drive up to the lake and dump them both," he suggested.

Hope stared at him. "I am trying to cooperate with you," she said, unsteadily, "but I can't look at Bill. If I have to see Bill, I know I'll just start screaming. I won't be responsible for what I might do."

"Okay," he said cheerfully. "We'll think of something else."

He talked, again, of burning down the house. He said perhaps they could take the body back to Los Angeles and put it in Bill's apartment, then he would kill Tom Masters and bring that body back up to the ranch and plant Tom's fingerprints all around the house. He thought, though, that Hope would tell the police. Over and over she swore she would not. "Well, if you ever do tell on me," he warned her, "everyone will have your picture, and you wouldn't live very long anyway."

"Goddamn it," Hope said, "what kind of a life is that going to be? Even if you don't kill me, how can I live, not knowing when somebody else is going to step up behind me and shoot me? Maybe the next man who gets this contract won't be so touchy about killing somebody with little kids."

"Don't worry," he said, patting her hand. "I'll fix it."

"You said you were being paid thirty-six hundred dollars to kill us," Hope said. "If I give you thirty-six hundred dollars, will you let me go?"

"How much money do you have?" he asked. "Where's your purse?" He took her handbag from the dresser and went through it. When he found her checkbook, he looked in it and laughed. "I don't steal from poor people," he said.

"There's more in Bill's account," Hope said. "There's at least six hundred dollars. Bill was saving to buy me a dress I wanted."

Taylor was very interested. "What kind of a dress, exactly?"

"A white lace dress, kind of an antique dress."

Taylor nodded. He held up a set of keys. "This looks like a burglar alarm key."

"Yes," Hope said.

He laughed. "That might stop petty thieves, but it wouldn't stop anybody who knew what he was doing," he assured her.

"Look, I know I don't have much money," Hope said, "but I'm worth a lot of money, my parents are worth a lot of money. Maybe you could hold me for ransom."

"Stop worrying," Taylor said. "I told you I would fix it." He walked to the window, drew back a corner of the curtain, and looked out. "In a little while we'll go for a walk," he said.

Hope clenched her fists. "I cannot go out through the living room with Bill's body there," she insisted. "I just can't do that."

"Oh, I understand," Taylor said. He left the room, and in a few minutes Hope heard an awful sound, a heavy, dragging sound. She felt sick; her stomach heaved as the dragging sound seemed to go on and on. Then Taylor returned, still cheerful. "All fixed," he said brightly. "And I covered the sofa so you won't see any blood. I've been wiping off my fingerprints, see?" He stretched his hands close to her face, holding a rag.

"Now you stay there," he said. "I'm going out again to tidy up the place. Wash the dinner dishes, sweep up. Can't leave the house in a mess. Tsk, tsk. Isn't nice. Isn't polite."

"Oh, my God," Hope muttered. "Leave it. Leave it. My parents will hire somebody to clean up, for God's sake."

But he went out again, leaving the hall door open. She could hear him moving around, handling dishes in the kitchen.

"Now let's get you dressed," he said when he came back. She didn't see any of her clothes from the night before, but he brought her a pair of underpants, red cord pants, and a shirt from her bag. "Just step in, now," he said gently, as he eased the underpants up her legs, stroking her skin. She stood up, and he zipped the pants and buttoned her shirt, leaning forward. "Kiss, kiss." She turned away again. "I haven't brushed my teeth." He laughed and reached for a hairbrush, then he brushed her hair carefully, pulling it back from her face. "Now let's go for a walk."

Hope kept her eyes down as she walked through the living room and through the kitchen. On the tile floor of the kitchen she saw a trail of something chalky white, like scouring cleanser. They walked through the kitchen and through the storage room, out the back door, into the sunshine.

Hope stared at the orange trees, deep green, brilliant with fruit. The Bermuda grass was spongy beneath her feet. She stared at the sky. She stared across the fence at the meadow where the horses were grazing. She stared as though she could not believe what she saw. *I'm alive. I'm alive.*

But by the time they reached the curve in the driveway, near the foreman's house, she felt sick. Her legs were about to give way. "I can't go any farther," she said. "I just don't have the strength."

"Okay," Taylor said cheerfully. "I can see there's no one around, so we'll go back and get the car and drive around for a while." They walked back to the house, but at the back door, Hope stopped. "I can't go in there," she declared.

"Just step inside the door," Taylor coaxed. She stepped into the storage room and leaned against the washing machine as he went on into the kitchen. "Would you like a beer?" he asked.

"No," Hope said, "but I'd like a soda."

He brought a beer and a lemon soda into the storage room and they stood together, drinking. He wiped off the beer can with the lining of his jacket before he threw the can away.

He held Hope's hand gently, as a lover would, as he led her to the car. He put her in the front seat, next to him. Then he drove up the road, past the ranch foreman's house, past the lower lake and the upper lake, till the road ended in a grassy meadow studded with wildflowers just coming into bloom. As he guided her out of the car onto the grass, she began to shake violently, hardly able to breathe. *This is it,* she thought. *He's going to kill me up here.* A crazy thought flashed across her mind. *At least this is a nice place to die.*

"Aren't the flowers beautiful!" Taylor exclaimed. "Isn't it a beautiful day!" Hope sat down on a small boulder, about thirty feet from the car, as Taylor walked a little higher up the mountainside to a cluster of rocks, where he turned and smiled. "As long as it's so pretty here, I'm going to take pictures," he said. He had brought the gun from the house and placed it on the front seat of the car as he drove; now he tucked it into his waistband as he took pictures, standing above Hope on a boulder. "Turn around and smile," he ordered, for Hope was trying to keep her back toward him, facing down the hillside. She felt certain he was going to shoot, and she didn't want to see it coming.

"We'll go back now," he announced after about half an hour, and they drove back down the road, through the gate, past the foreman's house with no cars around, no sign of life. He pulled up by the side of the house, parked the car, then turned to her and took her hand in his. "Did you think I was going to kill you up there?"

"Yes," Hope said.

Taylor laughed.

"Don't make me go back in the house," she begged. "Please don't make me go back in the house. I just can't."

"But we have to do something about the body," Taylor said in a reasoning voice.

"Leave him here," Hope said, sounding shrill. "Leave him here. I just have to get home and get the children safe and get my parents to help me. Let the authorities take care of it."

Taylor seemed to be considering. "Well, I have your pictures now, so if you ever tell anybody about me, everybody will know who you are and you won't live very long, anyway."

"I promise I won't tell on you," Hope said. "I swear I won't. I would never testify against you."

"Wait here," Taylor said. He went into the house, leaving Hope in the front seat, staring blankly at the mountain. Except for the soft hiss of the irrigation pumps in the orange grove, the world was silent. She thought of something she needed from her car, so she got out of the Lincoln and crossed the grass to her Vega. But when she opened the car door and looked in, she couldn't remember what it was she needed, so she closed the door and got back in the Lincoln. Taylor came running out. "What are you doing?" he demanded. When she told him, he seemed satisfied. "Stay in the car now," he said. "There are some things I need to do in the house to protect myself."

Eventually he came out again with a handful of items: Bill's briefcase, her nightgown, other pieces of her clothing. He placed the gun on the seat between them, backed the car onto the driveway, turned, and drove down the road. Hope did not look at the house as they drove past, nor at the hilly place above the river where she and Bill had stood in the moonlight with their arms around each other, in no rush to talk or to get back to the house, because they had all the time in the world.

"I'm going to make it up to you," Taylor assured her as they drove past Lake Success, brimming blue beyond the car window. "As long as you don't become a menace to me, I'll take care of everything."

"But what are we going to do?" Hope said. "My God, we have to call the police sometime."

"First we'll get back and make sure the children are safe and then you can all go to your mother's house," Taylor said. "But we have to tell a good story that will keep me in the clear."

"I'm a lousy liar," Hope said. "If you invent some story, it better not be far from the truth or I won't be able to remember it." Taylor said she had to say that she and Bill had been alone all day and evening Saturday: "I'll say that Bill and I were sitting alone by the fire Saturday night, enjoying the fire—because we *had* been sitting by the fire, that way I can remember it," Hope said—and that after she went to bed Saturday evening, an intruder had burst in, sometime during the night. She would then tell what had happened exactly as it had happened, except she would say that when the man left, he had not returned, and she had no idea who he was. Then on Sunday, she would relate, this man Taylor, whom she'd never met, but whom Bill had been expecting, had arrived, found the door open, heard Hope screaming, found Bill dead and Hope tied up in the bedroom. He had freed her and then, because of her fear for the children, had taken her back to Los Angeles before notifying the police.

Taylor kept talking about how he would fix the situation. He talked again about moving Bill's body to Bill's apartment, or maybe taking Bill's body to Tom's apartment, killing Tom and bringing Tom's body, or maybe both bodies, back up to the ranch. He said he wished he had been able to leave Bill's body in a ditch somewhere by the side of a back road where it wouldn't be found for a long time and then could be considered an accident. He kept saying he would fix it, but he came up with so many plots and plans Hope couldn't keep track. "I'll call you Mr. Fix-it," Hope told him, and he laughed heartily.

"Do you know whether Bill has a birth certificate?" he asked.

"I don't think so," Hope said. "For some reason Bill and I discussed that, I really don't remember why, and I remember Bill saying he didn't have one."

"Well, you never know," Taylor said briskly. "Bill told me that all his papers were in an old suitcase in his apartment, so we'll take a look."

"Oh, God," Hope said, "I don't want to go to Bill's apartment. I had such nice times with Bill there, I can't go there ever again."

"We have to go to Bill's apartment," Taylor said pleasantly, firmly. "We can't go back to your house until five-thirty, because if we get there before Tom comes back with the baby, he'll see us there and he'll know you've been left alive and he'll go crazy. He might even kill you right there." Hope still could not comprehend that Tom was paying to have her killed; the idea was unfathomable. Still, Taylor had known so much, so many details. And Tom never took the baby on Sunday.

Taylor seemed to enjoy the ride. He pointed out various features of the Lincoln, including a device that he set to keep the speed at fifty-five miles an hour. Hope wanted to get home faster. "Make it sixty-five," she asked him. "Oh, no," Taylor said. "The number one thing to watch out for is a traffic ticket. It's the little things that can get you, in this business, and we don't want to be stopped for a traffic violation."

He talked easily about his business, how to hide things, where to stash cars one no longer needed, how to change identities and pass unnoticed. "If you want to know more about me," he said, "read *The Day of the Jackal.* I'm the Jackal." His tone had become menacing. "Are you aware that a car is following us?" When Hope automatically turned around to look, he grabbed her arm. "Don't *ever* turn around," he told her. "If you're being followed, you never want them to know that you know."

He had brought a large tin of tobacco with him from the ranch house. "Living by the water, where I live, I have to keep my tobacco in a tin, or it would get damp and spoil," he explained.

"Where do you live?" Hope asked.

"I live in a beautiful home on a lake in a small city outside Paris," he said.

"Oh, I have a friend who comes from Paris," Hope said, and she began to talk about Lionel's background, his life and career. Taylor seemed interested, and as they talked, Hope was struck by coincidences. Taylor said he was based in France, as Lionel was; Taylor said he had two daughters, as Lionel did. Lionel had been a Marine captain in Korea; Taylor said he had been in Korea, too. Lionel had worked on the film *Exodus,* and spoke fluent Hebrew; Taylor said he had been involved in the Arab-Israeli war, on the Israeli side. "Well, you have a lot in common, going around from country to country as you both do," Hope said.

Taylor laughed. "I'd like to go back to Europe," he said, and he asked again whether Bill had a birth certificate and a passport. Hope was terrified he would ask her about her own passport; she had a valid one in a drawer at home, dating back a few months earlier, when she had considered going to Europe with Lionel.

"I've got a great idea!" he exclaimed. "We'll drive to Mexico and get married. That way you can't testify against me if I get caught."

"Oh, I can't marry you, Taylor," Hope explained, "because I'm still legally married to Tom." *Thank God,* she thought, *thank God I'm still married.* Then it struck her that if he killed Tom, or had Tom killed, she would then be legally available, and the thought that Taylor might think that way, too, made her feel dizzy. She had another fear lurking in the back of her mind, too. Bill had had a vasectomy, so Hope was not using birth control pills. She was afraid she might be pregnant now, and she said so.

Taylor was overjoyed. He reached for her hand and pressed it to his lips. "Oh, that's the greatest news in the world," he exclaimed. "Nothing could make me happier. Oh, I hope you're pregnant."

Hope was convinced, then, of what she had suspected since some time during the night, especially since Taylor had become affectionate and loving, holding her hand as he'd seen Bill hold it, rubbing her cheek. Taylor wanted to—expected to—step into her life, taking Bill's place. She realized that he was acting as he thought Bill would have acted toward her, and he wanted her to act as though she were with Bill. He hated hearing her say she was afraid, or that she was in pain; he wanted her to be happy and loving, as though she were with Bill. She felt sure—during the drive itself, and later—that Taylor wanted her to act like his wife. So she did.

Taylor stopped once on the ride back, for gas. When he reached across the front seat of the car and opened the glove compartment, she saw several wallets, but she didn't see which one he took out, which credit card.

On the road again, she talked constantly, to keep him interested. She flattered him, amused him. "All my life I've been waiting for the right man," she said. "And here you are—Mr. Wright!" She talked about her mother and about her stepfather, about how she herself had married pretty soon after her mother's marriage because she had never gotten on well with her stepfather, that everything was filtered through her mother and she felt her stepfather had a bad impression of her, that she was always being compared unfavorably to his children who had great wealth and stability in their lives. She told Taylor she felt like the black sheep in the family, and he nodded understandingly. "I'll bet if your mother met my mother," he declared, "they'd get along fine."

Hope had been to Bill's apartment only a few times, at night, with Bill driving, so she had only a vague idea of where it was on Lafayette Park Place. They got lost for a while in downtown Los Angeles, and drove up and down several streets before she recognized a Chevrolet dealer's showroom on a corner.

In the underground garage at Bill's apartment house, she directed Taylor to the right parking space and stood by as he riffled through Bill's keys. The apartment was still and dark. She went to the bathroom, then sat on the sofa as Taylor rummaged through a suitcase full of papers. "Here they are," he told her, "just like Bill said. Now where are his insurance policies?" He had asked her earlier about Bill's insurance; he seemed concerned about Bill's daughters.

"Oh, please let's go," Hope said. "I'm sure they're all at the office."

"No, here's one," Taylor said happily. He said he was glad he had found it because he was concerned about the welfare of Bill's daughters.

"Put your head down so nobody can see you," Taylor said, as they drove up the steep, sloping driveway. Hope crouched very low and, as soon as he'd parked, she jumped out and ran around to the door that led into the living room. It was already dark, the wooded hillside behind her house looking sinister and threatening. Licha was running the vacuum cleaner in Hope's bedroom.

"Where's K.C.?" Hope shouted above the noise. Licha looked up, startled, and switched off the machine. "Mr. Masters took him," she said. Hope's heart dropped. *My God, it's true,* she thought. *It's true about Tom.* She forced herself not to scream.

"Licha, what time did he say he'd bring K.C. back?"

"About five-thirty," the maid said. Hope's bedroom clock said 5:45.

"Licha, I've had a problem," Hope said, trying to keep her voice steady. "Someone is here to assist me. Would you please leave the room now, and when Tom comes back with the baby, please don't tell him I'm back. I'm quite upset over the divorce coming up. Just get K.C. and bring him back here to me as fast as you can, *please.*"

Licha wrapped the vacuum cord around the machine and left the bedroom. Hope ran after her. "Licha, where's Keith?" Licha said she hadn't seen him. "Where was he last night?" Hope asked. Licha said he'd slept over at his friend Danny's. Hope vaguely remembered, then, that Keith was supposed to go with Danny and his father to a basketball game on Sunday. Hope went back into the bedroom and called Danny's house, but no one answered.

Taylor had come in. He stood in the bedroom doorway, smiling. "Don't worry," he said. "There's no problem. Tom has to bring K.C. back because Tom is expecting a phone call at a certain number at six-thirty. That's the phone call to let him know what happened. He'll bring K.C. back before then, because he isn't going to want to blow his cover by doing anything now. He's going to spend some time talking to the maid so she is sure to remember him. He'll come soon, don't worry."

Taylor was right. In a few minutes Hope heard K.C. in the kitchen with

Licha. She wanted to run to him, but she stood, frozen, in the bedroom until K.C. came down the hall to her room. She scooped him up and hugged him as though she never wanted to let go.

Hope knew that Hope Elizabeth was next door, at a birthday party at the Pinskys'. She phoned quickly to say she was back and she told her daughter, quickly, that there had been a problem with the car and that Bill had stayed up at the ranch to take care of it. Hope said a friend of Bill's had come back to help them while Bill wasn't there. The child sounded concerned that her mother had been hurt in a car accident, so Hope told her that she should go out into the Pinskys' yard and that Hope would wave to her from the window. "When you're ready to come home from the party, call me first so I know you're coming," Hope said. She was terrified of having the children alone for a moment.

She waved to Hope Elizabeth from the bedroom window, then went down the hall to the living room, where Taylor was sitting on the small sofa.

"Can I call my mother now?" Hope ventured.

"No, I don't want you to contact your mother at this point," Taylor said.

"But I always call her when I come back from out of town," Hope protested. "If I don't call her she's going to worry."

"She isn't going to worry yet," Taylor said. "Keith isn't home yet, and even after he gets back to Danny's house, he's still going to have to wander the neighborhood to get home. Your telephone is tapped, and if you make a call now it would be very dangerous. There are people watching you."

Hope stayed away from the phone, but Taylor made some calls; at least, Hope heard him talking on the bedroom phone. Once he seemed to be telling someone what to say to Tom. "This is ridiculous," Taylor said on the phone. "We've got a real psycho on our hands. It's a bad contract and I'm going to have to discuss it with you. But he is expecting your call, so call him and say that there were too many people at the ranch but it will be taken care of on Wednesday. In the meantime, I'm going to get together with you and talk about this." Hope was convinced that she and the children were in deadly danger, not only from Tom, but from some middleman who had bought the contract. She suspected it might be a man Tom knew, whom she knew by name, a man who had lent Tom five thousand dollars that Tom had not repaid. Taylor told Hope he could not tell her who the middleman was, but when Hope mentioned that man, Taylor said yes, she was right.

At seven o'clock Taylor said he would drive Licha to the bus stop down on Santa Monica Boulevard. "You must not pick up the phone and you must not try anything while I am gone," he said. "If you leave, you will be killed by the people outside, and if you call anyone, I will have to kill you myself." Hope asked whether she could take a shower. "Yes, go in the shower and stay there till I come back," he said.

Hope took K.C. into her bedroom and went into her bathroom. She turned on the water very full so that it made a lot of noise; she stood there and cried and cried.

When Taylor returned, she was sitting on the bathroom stool, her hair wrapped in a towel. "I know you didn't do anything while I was gone," he said approvingly. "That's good." She dried her hair and wrapped herself in a long, warm robe. Back in the living room, she sat on the sofa again, with K.C. playing on the floor. Taylor looked around the room, then at Hope, and smiled. He sat down near her on the sofa and took her hand. "I could really be happy living this way," he said.

By nine o'clock Keith and Hope Elizabeth were home. "I have to go to bed," Hope told Taylor. "I am just exhausted."

"Yes, you go to bed," he said. "Take the children into your room and lock the door. I am going to sit up here in the living room all night and protect you."

It had been a long day for Hope Elizabeth, and she began having temper tantrums, throwing herself at Taylor and pounding at his legs, crying, "I hate you! You're crazy! I hate you!" Hope had told her Taylor was Bill's friend, but she thought her daughter must know, somehow, that Bill would not come back, and that Taylor was there in his place. She tried to calm the child, terrified that Taylor would become upset and violent.

But Taylor handled it beautifully, laughing, soothing her, calming her down, not getting upset at all. In fact, he was wonderful with the children, wrestling with Keith on the living room rug, talking about football. Now he led them all into Hope's room, arranged the children in the wide bed, and kissed them good night. Hope went to the door to lock it behind him, from the inside. He took her in his arms. "Kiss good night," he said.

When Hope woke up early Monday morning, she heard Taylor in the kitchen, whistling as he cooked breakfast.

She heard him telling Keith he would drive him to school, and her heart pounded. "Please don't let him go to school," she begged.

"Keith has to go to school," Taylor insisted. "Things have to appear normal."

While Taylor was gone with Keith, Hope went into the bedroom and picked up the phone. Quickly, before she could lose courage, she dialed her mother.

"I'm home," Hope told her mother, "but I have a problem, and I want to make sure you'll be around this evening." Honey said she was going to a party. "I don't care what plans you have," Hope cried, "call me tonight."

She had just hung up the phone when Taylor walked in and the phone rang. It was her mother.

"You sound terrible," Honey said. "Is something very wrong? Shall I send the police?" Taylor was standing at Hope's side. "Oh, no, no," Hope said. "It's just a personal thing, and I'm a little upset. I just want to keep in touch." She hung up the phone and faced Taylor, her heart pounding.

"I see you called your mother," he said pleasantly. "That's nice."

The phone rang constantly all day Monday. Many of the calls were from Chips members, telling her they were coming to the luncheon on Wednesday. After a few calls, Taylor seemed satisfied that Hope would not cry for help when someone called, and he left the house, telling her he had things to do. He told her he was trying to have the contract canceled, but that until he did, she was in great danger, along with the children. He said the organization had people watching her, people who would shoot her and her children on sight, but he said he had people watching, too. He said that a man who was working in a yard across the street was not really a gardener, but one of "my people." He talked about a yellow car that belonged to some of his people, and later that day, Hope saw a strange car in her driveway. It was a yellow car with brown trim.

"There's no food in the house," he said. "You're a terrible housekeeper, you know. Your room is very messy." He said it teasingly, lovingly, like an indulgent lover. He insisted that she come with him and Hope Elizabeth and K.C. to get some lunch, so they all drove down to the Hamburger Hamlet, where the children had big burgers and Taylor, too, ate heartily.

"As you can see, I have to be away from the house a good deal," Taylor said to Hope, when they were back at the house. "I think you need protection when I am away. If I get you a small gun and show you how to use it, will you use it?"

"No, no, no," Hope said. "I hate guns and I won't touch it."

"Okay then," Taylor said mildly. He didn't seem to want to talk about guns, anyway. He seemed to want to talk about the children, about their schools, their sports, their friends, the ordinary things married people talk about. He seemed relaxed and happy, whistling as he wandered around the house, the man of the house.

All day Monday he came and went. Once, when he was gone and the phone rang, it was Taylor. "Well, I see a lot of girls are coming to your luncheon," he said lightly. "You'd better order more hors d'oeuvres." Hope was sure, then, that her phone was tapped. Whenever Taylor was gone for an hour or two, he would call her a few times during that period, and when he came back, he would give her a detailed account of Tom Masters's movements. He said that Tom had had lunch at Scandia; he said that Tom had a new girlfriend. He suggested, again, that he might kill Tom, and what Hope might do then. He suggested that she get the children together, take them to her mother, then go to Europe with him and eventually settle in Rhodesia where, he said, there was no extradition law.

"If only I could trust you," he said over and over, and Hope assured him, over and over, that he could.

When Keith came home from school, Taylor seemed delighted to see him and wrestled again with him on the floor. Watching them, Hope thought again of how Taylor was playing husband and father, and doing it well, she had to admit. Around dinner time, when she protested that she couldn't eat a thing, Taylor took Keith down to the House of Pies. They were gone longer than Hope had expected, and when they returned, Keith showed his mother the new jacket Taylor had bought for him.

"Now can I call my mother and tell her we're coming?" Hope asked.

"Not yet," Taylor said. "Not tonight." Late in the afternoon he had brought in a telescopic rifle that he had set up at the sliding glass door in the living room, overlooking the street and far into the distance. "I can see anything through here," he assured her. "I can watch and make sure if anybody's coming; I can really do a good job of protecting you with this. I can take someone down across a football field with this." He kept saying he wanted to show her how to use it, but Hope kept refusing, telling him it was too heavy, that she didn't want to touch it because she was afraid of guns. Finally she went across the room and looked through the eyepiece, but she didn't put her hands on it.

He had brought in at least one other gun, too, a .38-caliber revolver that Hope found in a bottom drawer of the bathroom chest when she opened the chest looking for something. She marched back out into the living room and asked him to come into the bathroom. "How dare you leave a gun where the children can get at it?" she demanded. "Don't you realize how dangerous that is?"

Taylor looked sheepish. "Yes, you're right, I'm sorry," he said. He took the gun and said he would put it in a high place, where the children wouldn't find it.

Hope put the children to bed again in her big bed and came back into the living room to try to reason with Taylor. She sat in the big chair by the fireplace; Taylor sat on the floor at her feet, looking at the fire.

"Taylor, this can't go on," Hope said. "Time is passing—my God, Taylor, we have to call the police sometime. Someone will find the body."

"I would like to sit here by the fire with you forever," Taylor said in a gentle, almost dreamy voice. "I would be your protector and take care of you and the children forever. Put the kids to bed and sit by the fire with you."

He stood up. "But now I have to leave for a while, because I need a change of identification." He gave her the usual instructions again and left quickly. Hope wanted desperately to go to bed, so she stretched out on the floor, by the fire, and closed her eyes.

She was awakened by Taylor returning, dragging several large suitcases into the living room. One big, black suitcase had a piece of red yarn taped on it. Taylor explained that the way it was done in the organization was to leave a piece of luggage at a bus stop with a piece of red yarn or some similar marking, so that whoever was searching I.D.'s would know which suitcase to pick up. When he opened the black suitcase, he frowned, as he held up pieces of clothing. "Tacky, cheap, and the wrong size," he declared. He began going through the other bags, and Hope yawned. "Taylor, I'm going to bed," she said. He frowned at her. "No, I want you to stay up and keep me company," he said sternly. "I have been sitting up here protecting you and your children, and the least you can do now is to sit up with me a while. I am very tired, and I have a backache."

"Well, let me give you a backrub," Hope offered. She was glad when he smiled at her. He took off his shirt and lay on the rug, in front of the fire, stretching both arms over his head. Hope knelt beside him and rubbed his back, kneading his shoulders, then pressing down along the sides of his back with firm strokes. "Mmmm, nice," he murmured. Hope was glad he was pleased; she thought it would keep him happy and she knew she gave good backrubs. She was still rubbing Taylor's back when Martha Padilla came back, after her days off. Martha walked through the kitchen and into the living room, but when she saw Hope on the floor with a man with no shirt on, rubbing his back, she went back through the kitchen into her own room and went to bed.

"Better?" Hope asked Taylor.

"Oh, much better." He sighed. He sat up, put his shirt back on, and poured two glasses of wine. Hope put a record on the stereo, and a wistful song began: "This time we almost made it, didn't we, girl? . . ." Hope sat in the big chair by the fire and sipped her wine. Taylor set his wine on the coffee table and walked around to the back of the small sofa, facing her. He leaned across the sofa, resting his arms on it. "Can you ever forgive me?" he asked quietly.

"Yes, I forgive you," Hope replied. "I understand that this was all a horrible mistake, and I forgive you."

"Will you marry me?" Taylor asked.

Hope shook her head. "Oh, Taylor, I don't think I could ever get it out of my mind enough to marry you."

"I can stop doing this, you know," he went on. "I can go straight, starting right now, starting tomorrow. I can go out tomorrow and get a job as an attorney and never harm another person."

"But you told me you're so involved with the organization," Hope reminded him. "You said you could never get out."

"Well, I have thought of a way," he said, and he related his plan: he would claim to have heart trouble and get out of the organization on disability.

"If I stay out of trouble for five years and become an attorney, then will you marry me?"

"Well, I think it would be fine if you became a lawyer," Hope said, "but I honestly don't know how I'd feel in five years. I just don't know." She set her glass down and stood up. "Taylor, I really have to go to bed now."

The children were sound asleep, sprawled all across Hope's wide bed, so she closed that door softly and went across the hall into Keith's room. She crawled under the blankets in one of the twin beds; Taylor got into the other bed. "Come over into my bed," he said. "I want you to cuddle with me."

Hope did not dare to argue with him about anything. She got out of her bed and got into bed with him. Taylor took her in his arms. "Just let me hold you," he murmured. He kissed her softly all over her neck, into her hair, with a lover's gentle caresses. Hope fell asleep in his arms, as he was telling her over and over, "I love you."

PART II

CHAPTER
FIVE

HONEY WAS THE ideal nickname for Hope's mother. She was not deeply tanned—women in her position avoided bronzing. She had a beige, tawny look, with blond hair carefully and smoothly waved back from her face. Like her daughter, she was petite, though she usually wore very high-heeled shoes, either alligator or a soft, buttery leather, so that she seemed taller than Hope. Her clothes were elegant, conservative, expensive-look-ing—Chanel suits, rose-colored silks—and she wore them in an elegant, conservative, expensive-looking way. Everything about Honey was taste-ful: her looks; her clothes; her heavy, cream-colored stationery; her living room, with its expanses of pale carpeting, its lemon-velvet sofas, its bowls of perfectly fresh flowers perfectly arranged.

The relationship between Honey and Hope was never very difficult to discern. A man who knew them both and who had observed them to-gether often called it "sibling rivalry." Like siblings, they were jealous and competitive. Like siblings, they bickered and quarreled and depended on each other in an intense and perpetual emotional bonding. Honey said Hope was a difficult child; Hope said Honey was trying to run her life. Both women were right.

Honey was born in Canada, but her parents moved to southern Califor-nia when she was a young girl, so she always felt she belonged. Her father was a successful businessman, in wholesale lighting, and Honey liked to recall "the tremendous stability" of her childhood. "When I grew up in Beverly Hills," she reminisced, "it was a darling little village. All the shopowners knew the families. It was a very traditional way of life, very conservative. My family was known and respected in the community, and I was never exposed to the kind of mishmash that comes to California."

Honey disliked talking about her first marriage, to Hope's father; Hope liked to bring it up. "How about Jimmy and all his crazy pals?" Hope asked, when her mother commented on the "mishmash."

"Yes, yes, that's true," Honey said in an edgy, controlled voice. "I was exposed, in my first marriage, to the Hollywood side of life and I hated it. I hated everything about it. Not that I hated having all the great people in music come to our home. It was wonderful to have George Szell playing the piano in our living room, accompanying Jimmy on the French horn, or to have José Iturbi play 'The Fire Dance' just for you when you were little. Or to have John Barbirolli pretend he was a great brown bear and ride you around on his back."

"What about Frank Sinatra?" Hope persisted. "You liked him. You liked Nancy."

"Yes," Honey said reluctantly, "I met him when he first came to Hollywood and had a radio show. Sinatra was very pleasant."

After her divorce, Honey left Hope with her own parents in Holmby Hills, secure in the knowledge that "Hope was sheltered and protected" and would be "brought up like a little princess." Hope, she maintained, was "a very joyous child." Honey enjoyed the social life that her beauty and wealth made possible—world travel, extravagant parties—until she married Van and settled into a sedate upper-class life.

Van's family was known and respected in the community, like Honey's, only more so. He had been sent east to school, and when he returned from Yale Law School, he joined an old-line, conservative law firm and married one of the richest women in the United States, with oil money behind her and an oil scandal behind that. After three generations, the scandal had pretty much petered out, except for entries in American history books, but the money never did. Besides, Van had family money of his own. His father had discovered a copper mine and had promptly retired to play golf—at the age of thirty-five. Van had had children with his first wife, so when he married Honey, Hope acquired two older stepbrothers and a stepsister her own age, Cynthia. Even though Cynthia visited only on occasional weekends, Hope felt her mother had decorated Hope's bedroom to suit Cynthia, so Hope dressed a little sloppier, ran around a little more, and acted up in various other ways. Hope was fifteen when her mother remarried; although Van legally adopted her, the two of them got on badly from the beginning. Hope said he reminded her of the American eagle: stiff, unbending, conservative; Van said she was ungrateful. Hope felt that much of the problem was due to her mother, who complained constantly about Hope to Van, who then berated Hope for making her mother unhappy. When Honey had a period of fainting spells, Van sent her to the Scripps Clinic for a complete checkup. "My daughter is making my life miserable," Honey told the doctors, who told Van, who told Hope. Hope always felt like a third wheel in the house, unwanted and ignored; she was particularly annoyed by Van's habit of walking into the den where she was watching television and changing channels without asking her.

Even after she got out of the house by eloping with the boy next door, Hope found her life still entwined with Honey's and Van's. Besides his father's money, Van had inherited his father's love of golf, and he and Hope's husband played together often. The four of them played bridge often, at the games that sometimes reduced Hope to tears. Honey and Van had arranged to buy the first house Hope lived in, after Keith was born, the place in Benedict Canyon that Honey described as "a little dollhouse, just adorable" and that she had decorated in black and white and gray. By the time Hope was divorced and remarried, with a third child coming, the house was far too small, and Honey had arranged to buy the house on the Drive, which had less charm but more bedrooms. All along, Honey reminded Hope, she and Van had "provided for the basic essentials. We saw to it that the medical bills were paid, that your home was paid for, and, of course, we bought all the furniture. We paid for the birth of your children, all three of them: the doctors' bills, the hospital bills, the nurses. And then we set up a little income for you."

Honey disapproved of almost all the men Hope had relationships with after Hope had separated from her second husband. She liked Bill Ashlock, however. She had met him only once, about a week before he and Hope went to the ranch, when they came by her house to pick up Keith, who had been visiting his grandmother. Bill was driving Hope's station wagon, with his two girls and K.C. and Hope Elizabeth piled inside. Bill told Honey they'd all been spending the Washington's Birthday weekend at Hope's, and now he was on the way to the market to pick up things for a barbecue. "With all five children!" Honey had exclaimed, and Bill had laughed. "The more the merrier," he'd said. Honey and Van and Bill had chatted a little about the trip to the ranch the next weekend. At that time, Bill and Hope still planned to take the children, and Honey told Bill's girls what fun they would have riding Bonnie, the gentlest of the ranch horses. "We'll have a wonderful time," Bill had agreed. "We're all just one big happy family now."

When Bill and the children had gone, Honey and Van had discussed Hope's future. Honey said it didn't seem right that Bill would have to support Hope's three children, along with his own two, and that since Hope was getting so little from her first husband, Honey and Van would need to help out with Keith and Hope Elizabeth, at least. Honey had disapproved of Bill living with Hope, but she was glad Hope planned to be married. Although Bill was in advertising, Honey didn't consider him "the typical Hollywood character" at all.

Hope said her mother helped her as she did because she felt guilty about having neglected Hope as a child, and perhaps about having married so much money, while Hope hadn't; Hope pointed out that her mother's personal allowance from Van was three thousand dollars a month, which didn't have to cover maintenance on her Lincoln Continental or lunches at the Los Angeles Country Club. Honey didn't understand why, when she wanted to buy Hope a mink, Hope refused it, though she obviously expected financial help from her mother. Sometimes Honey thought she had arranged Hope's upbringing in the wrong way. "My parents brought her up like a little princess," she once told Van. "Perhaps that was wrong, because she never had to do anything for herself. She never had to think for herself; everything was done for her. Then the harsh realities of being married, having to budget—she was totally unequipped for these things. And I feel I made a terrible mistake in that respect. On the other hand, you want to do what you can, and, of course, that was the way I was brought up, in a social setting. Hope was brought up in that setting, and so she has rebelled against this, somewhere along the way—to the point where it's hard for me to understand."

Hope's rebellion, however, was not unremitting. Her friend Michael Abbott had noticed Hope's pride in her breeding. He considered her a dual personality. She had an earthy streak, but she also thought herself a patrician, and acted that way. And indeed, at times the similarities between Hope and Honey were far more apparent than their differences. Both women were petite, blond, beautiful. Both smoked a lot. Hope nursed sick cats, sheltered runaway children, and made certain attempts to reach out beyond the given perceptions of Beverly Hills; while Honey was anything but earthy, there were occasional signs that her inner yearnings were not totally unlike her daughter's. Honey kept a book of religious poems on the edge of her bathtub, and she had clipped a maxim and taped it on her refrigerator door:

I SEARCH, THEREFORE I AM.

Monday was one of Honey's usual busy, well-organized days. She and Van had come back, just two weeks before, from a trip to Guatemala, and Honey had notes to write, people to make luncheon dates with, the Chips meeting at her house to prepare for, maids to instruct: besides her regular day maid, a middle-aged black woman named Gertrude, Honey had a Japanese student, a young woman named Kazue Tomita, working at her house part time. Late Monday afternoon Honey drove to her stepson's house and picked up two of his children, whom she and Van later took to dinner. They drove them home and got back to their house around eight o'clock.

Honey phoned Hope then. She thought her daughter still sounded strange, and Honey said she was coming up to see her. Hope put a man on the phone, who spoke calmly and reassuringly. He said his name was Taylor, that he was a friend of Bill's and that Hope and the children were fine, but something had come up about her divorce that had upset Hope. "In these divorce situations, there are always legal unpleasantries," Taylor told Honey, assuring her that Hope would come by to see her Tuesday and explain everything.

Hope telephoned Honey around eleven o'clock Tuesday morning. "Lock all the doors and turn on the alarm and don't let anyone in the house," Hope told her mother. "I'm coming down with Keith and K.C. because our lives have been threatened."

Hope had awakened Tuesday morning to find Taylor already showered and dressed, cheerful as ever, again cooking breakfast for the children, getting Hope Elizabeth ready for school. Hope begged Taylor to let her daughter stay home. "I'm taking her to school, and that's that," Taylor said firmly. He and the child left together. When he returned, he told Hope that Hope Elizabeth was safely in school and that all day the child would be watched by his people.

"Taylor, this can't go on," Hope said shakily. "Somebody is going to discover Bill's body. My God, it's been three days!"

"You're right," Taylor said reluctantly. "What you have to do now is call the ranch foreman and tell him someone's in the ranch house writing a book and doesn't want to be disturbed." When Hope refused, Taylor smiled. "You have to," he said. "You have no choice." But when Hope telephoned Jim Webb, there was no answer.

Keith and K.C. were tearing around the house, fighting, making an awful racket. "Please, please let us go to my mother's," Hope pleaded with Taylor.

"You can go when I say it's okay," Taylor said. "Right now I'm going out to do some shopping." He reached across the sofa and took her hand. "I owe you one antique white dress."

"Oh, God, Taylor," Hope said. "I don't want a dress. Please let me go to my mother's." Taylor shook his head. "I'm going to buy you that dress," he said firmly. "Where do you buy your clothes?"

"Never mind, never mind," Hope said, trying to keep her voice under control. "Please, never mind the dress."

"I am going to make it up to you," Taylor insisted.

Hope gave in. "Usually at the House of Nine," she said.

"The House of Nine. Where is that?"

Hope told him, and Taylor stood up. "Off to the House of Nine," he said brightly. "Don't answer the phone and don't answer the doorbell while I am gone." He reminded Hope that the house was being watched, the phone was being monitored, that the man across the street who looked like a gardener wasn't a gardener at all.

Hope sat on the sofa, smoking cigarettes, oblivious to the boys' racket. When the doorbell rang, she jumped, and her heart pounded. It rang and rang, so she finally went to the kitchen window and called out. "Who is it?"

It was the nurse of a little boy K.C.'s age, from a house down the street. The woman was very upset. She told Hope her little boy was lost and she thought he might have wandered over to Hope's. Hope said she hadn't seen the child, and when the nurse left, Hope was terrified that the woman would call the police and then, when Taylor returned and saw police cars on the street, he would think she had called them. She felt she had to reach him, to explain, so she called the House of Nine, where she was known. "Has anyone been in to buy a dress for me?" she asked frantically. They said no. "Well, if a man comes in to buy a dress for me, please have him call me," Hope said. She left her phone number, and sank down on the sofa again, trying to think. *If that little boy has been kidnaped,* she thought, *then there really are people out to get us; they must have thought he was K.C. But if Taylor can reach them and tell them they have the wrong child, everything will be all right.* She had to talk to Taylor; she was depending on him.

Meantime, though, the lost child had been found wandering in another neighbor's yard, and when Taylor returned, the neighborhood was quiet. Hope poured out the story, stressing her terror, and he put his arm around her. "It's all right," he told her. "Everything is going to be all right. I have checked around, and now it is safe to go to your mother's." He apologized for not having found the white dress.

After Hope phoned Honey to say they were coming, Taylor gave her last-minute instructions. She was to tell her mother the agreed-upon story of an unknown intruder in the night and her rescue, the next morning, by Taylor. He told her that if she drove anywhere but to her mother's, or did anything to attract attention along the way, everyone would be killed. He warned her that if Honey became agitated and called the police, everyone would be killed. He told her that Honey's phone was tapped, too, and that if anyone called the police it would be instantly known by all the people who were watching and listening and hovering, and everyone would be killed. He told her that he would follow her in the Lincoln and would watch to make sure she and the boys arrived safely at Honey's. When she arrived there, he said, she was to immediately drive the car to the lower parking lot at the Beverly Hills Hotel, with her mother following, then return to Honey's and wait until she heard from him again.

Just before they left, Taylor picked up K.C. and hugged him, then he put his arm around Keith. "I have some presents for you," he told Keith, and led him to the dining table, where he had laid out several items, including a portable radio and a Schick hot comb.

When Hope saw the car she was to drive, her heart began pounding again. It was the yellow car with brown trim. She was sure the brakes had been broken and that she and the children were to die that way, hurtling down the mountain road. "No, no," Taylor soothed her, when she told him of her fear. "I've driven this car myself. It's perfectly okay."

Hope put K.C. in the back seat and Keith in front beside her. Taylor backed out of the driveway in the white Lincoln and Hope backed out next; when she turned and headed up the Drive, he stayed very close. She drove so slowly that Keith noticed. "What's the matter?" he asked. Keith had observed that his mother had been acting strangely since she'd come home from the ranch, kind of nervous and scared and tiredlike, her hair all messed up. He had been told not to answer the telephone, even though it rang a lot, and he had been told that he wasn't going to school that day, though nobody gave him a reason. Keith hadn't been really worried, because the man who had come back with his mother had been so nice.

Taylor seemed to like kids a lot, even though he had made Keith clean up his room and pick up, a little, in the bathroom.

"What's the matter?" Keith asked again as they drove.

"Nothing," Hope said.

But Keith kept at it: "What's the matter? What's the matter?"

"Somebody's trying to kill us all," Hope blurted to the boy.

"Golly, m-maybe Hopie shouldn't have gone to school today," he stammered.

"No, it's okay," Hope said, instantly sorry she'd told him. "It's okay. We're going to Honey's now and we are going to be okay. Taylor is helping us."

Honey was watching from the living room window. When she saw Hope pull into the little half-moon driveway, she turned off the alarm. She stood in the doorway as Hope hurried the children inside.

As Hope went in, she looked back quickly and saw Taylor parked across the street, watching. She fell into her mother's arms. Honey called to Kazue to take the boys into the den; then she took Hope into her bedroom and closed the door.

Hope tried to stay calm so her mother wouldn't start crying. "You're going to have to keep complete control of yourself," Hope told Honey. "You cannot cry, you cannot become hysterical, you cannot fall apart. Bill is dead, and someone has threatened us. We are all in danger." She tried to follow her own advice to stay calm as she poured out the story of Bill's being murdered at the ranch by a stranger in the night, the contract and professional killers, and Tom Masters's involvement, the blood and the screaming and the vomiting and the planned bloodbath, her rescue by a man named Taylor. She showed her mother her wrists, with gummy adhesive marks on them, her right hand swollen and colored a light purple, bits of dried blood under her fingernails. "Darling, let me clean that for you," Honey said, but Hope yanked her hands out of her mother's lap. "No, no," she insisted, "this is reality to me. Every time I think I'm losing my mind, I look at my hands and I know everything has really happened."

Honey was aghast at Hope's appearance—filthy and disheveled, her skin gray, with sunken eye sockets, the way her own parents looked just before they died. Honey wanted to take Hope to the hospital. "I can't leave until the contract is canceled, don't you understand?" Hope screamed. "If I'm still alive in the morning, then I'll go to the hospital." Honey suggested getting a doctor, then, to come to the house. "No, no," Hope said. "Taylor said your telephone is tapped and it would be danger-ous to call anybody." Honey wanted to call Van, and Hope Elizabeth's school, to warn them of the danger, but Hope insisted they follow Taylor's instructions. "He told me that either he or his people would look after Hopie, and I'm counting on him."

Suddenly Hope jumped up. "My God, the car. We have to take the car back."

"You can't drive," Honey said. "You're in no condition to drive."

"Don't argue with me," Hope shouted. "The only reason we are all still alive is because I have done exactly what I am told."

"But is it safe for us to leave the house?" Honey asked.

"Yes," Hope said, "as long as we go straight to the hotel and come straight back and don't attract attention."

Honey told Kazue to keep the children in the den while she and Hope went on an errand. At the front door, Honey forgot she had turned the alarm back on after Hope and the boys had entered; when she opened it, there was a piercing shriek. Hope began to sob. "If the police come now, we are all dead, dead, dead!"

The Beverly Hills Hotel was only a few blocks from Honey's, at the corner of North Canon Drive and Sunset Boulevard. Hope parked the yellow car in the lower lot, left the keys in the car, and ran back to Honey's car. They were gone only ten minutes, but when they returned, Kazue told them a man had called, asking for Hope. Kazue had said she wasn't home.

Hope was frantic. "Now he won't trust me, now he won't trust me!" Honey tried to calm her, reminding her that Taylor must have known they had been out returning the car, as he had instructed her. She gave Hope a glass of wine.

Hope and Honey sat on the edge of the long sofa in the living room, smoking, trying to keep each other calm. They decided that one of them, not Kazue, should answer the phone because Taylor had said he would let them know when the contract had been canceled and they could safely call the police. Very soon, the phone rang. When Honey answered, she recognized the voice of the man she had spoken to the night before, the man who had said he was a friend of Bill's and that Hope had a small problem.

"We've just been out returning the car," Honey said.

"Yes, I know," the man said. He asked to speak to Hope. Their conversation was very short.

"He said he has to change locations and he'll call again," Hope told her mother when she had hung up.

"When he calls back, ask him to come here," Honey said.

But when he called again, saying the same thing—that he had to change locations and would call back—Hope just hung up, and Honey became upset. "You have to ask him to come here," she insisted.

When the fourth call came, Honey answered and again gave Hope the phone. But when Hope didn't ask Taylor to come to the house, Honey grabbed the phone. "Please get right over here to our house and explain what is going on or I will call the police," Honey said.

"Don't call the police," Taylor warned. "I can't explain now because I can't stay on the phone or this call will be traced to me. Your phone is tapped." He hung up.

Standing near her mother, Hope wanted to cry but didn't dare, for fear she would never stop. "Why did you do that," she moaned. "Why did you do that?"

"Because he has to come here and talk to us," Honey said.

Hope took several deep breaths. "Okay," she said. "Just be very, very careful what you say to him if he comes. Just listen to what he has to say and please, please, please don't get hysterical. He hates hysterical women. Be nice to him. Be very charming, and don't ask him too many questions."

In between the calls from Taylor, Honey was getting personal calls. "I can't talk now," she would say, hanging up the phone quickly. Shortly after three o'clock, Hope Elizabeth rang the doorbell, stopping by her grandmother's on the way home from school, as usual, and shortly after that, Taylor called again to say he knew the child was there and he was coming over.

Hope went into the den and took Keith and Hope Elizabeth, one at a time, into Honey's bedroom. She spoke to Keith first. "Something very bad has happened, Keith, and I'm going to tell you about it now. I don't want you to cry and I don't want you to make a big fuss. I want you to listen to me and not ask me any questions and then I want you to go back in the other room and take care of your little brother, because that is what I need you to do right now.

"Someone has killed Bill, and now somebody wants to steal K.C. I want you to stay in the den and watch K.C. and keep him quiet while I try to work this out."

She told her daughter the same thing, feeling that if she told them K.C. was in danger, it would bring out their protective instincts. Both children went back into the den after she talked with them, stunned but not crying.

The doorbell rang as Hope was with Kazue and the children in the den. When she came hurriedly into the living room, she saw Honey looking out the window. Hope ran to the window.

"It's Taylor! It's Taylor! Let him in."

Honey released the chain bolt from the door and turned off the alarm. She opened the door to a handsome, smiling man.

"I'm Taylor," he said.

"I'm Hopie's mother," Honey said. "Please come in."

She closed the door behind him, bolted the chain, and turned the alarm on.

"Did Hope explain to you that I'm the news photographer whom Bill Ashlock invited up to the ranch to do an interview and to take pictures?" he asked.

"Yes," Honey said. "Bill telephoned me last Friday to be sure it was all right with me to invite you up there. Aren't you the person I talked with last night on the phone at Hopie's?"

"Yes, I am," he said. "I'm sorry about lying to you on the phone, but Hope's telephone is tapped and I had to be very careful what I said. I don't know what might have happened if you had come up there, or sent the police."

Honey had many questions, but she remembered that Hope had told her to be charming. "Come in and sit down," Honey told Taylor. "Would you like a drink?"

"No, thank you," he said. "I'm too upset." He sat down at the end of the long sofa, nearest the door. "Are the children here? I know Hope Elizabeth is here because I watched her to be sure she was safe."

"Yes, they're all here," Honey said. "They're all in the den with the maid." She sat on the smaller sofa.

Taylor smiled at Hope. "Did you return the car?"

"Yes," Hope said.

"Did you go directly there and come right back here?"

"Yes."

"Did you put it where I told you to put it?"

"Yes, I put it in the lower parking lot."

"That's a good girl," Taylor said approvingly. "Did you stop and speak to anyone?"

"Oh, no, no," Hope said. "No, we didn't."

"How did that car get to Hope's house?" Honey asked.

"Oh, my people brought it up there for me," Taylor said easily.

Hope made herself another drink and Honey watched Taylor closely as he talked. She was impressed by the look of this man, tall, well-built, with broad shoulders. His brown wavy hair was well-groomed, evenly cut about two inches below the ears, worn very thick and full. She thought he had brown eyes, but it was difficult to be sure because he was wearing wraparound glasses with a light mauve tint. He was beautifully dressed in a brown tweed jacket with a pale yellow shirt, a gold and brown striped tie, well-polished leather boots. *Obviously intelligent, well-educated, well-born,* Honey thought. He was calm and self-confident, with a pleasant smile.

Taylor related to Honey how he had seen Bill in the city on Friday and had made plans to go to the ranch. But he didn't go until Sunday, Taylor said. He had arrived in Springville at 9:30 Sunday morning, but when he'd telephoned from town to the ranch to get final directions, as he and Bill had arranged, there was no answer. He assumed that Bill and Hope must be outdoors, so he just drove around the area until he found the ranch road, with the ranch name on the gate. He drove up the winding road and saw two houses; he assumed that Bill would be at the larger house. He went to the back door, found it unlocked, walked in, heard a woman screaming, walked through the kitchen into the living room and found Bill Ashlock shot dead on the sofa. Following the screams, he went into the front bedroom and found Hope naked and tied. "She was a real basket case, and she has been a basket case ever since," he said. "It was obvious from the way she was tied that she couldn't have had anything to do with Bill's death, and I untied her. She was terrified and just wanted to get out of the house, but she said she couldn't stand the thought of going through the living room where Bill was, so I moved Bill's body to the back bedroom, threw a sheet over the bloody sofa, and told Hope it was okay for her to go through the room. She ran out the front door to my car and I ran after her."

"How was she tied?" Honey asked.

"Very, very professionally," Taylor said. "Her feet had been taped together at the ankles, then her legs had been pulled up behind her and her hands taped to her feet. I removed the tape as gently as I could, but I know it must have hurt when I pulled it away from her skin."

"How did you know who she was?"

"Well, Bill had told me all about her, and I knew she was going to be there with Bill, and at our lunch he had showed me her picture." Taylor shook his head gravely. "You know, when I saw her, she was just barely recognizable as the beautiful girl in the picture. The man who did this to your daughter has to be insane."

Hope was pacing the room, smoking. "Why are you so nervous?" Taylor asked. "Sit down and relax." When he said this, Hope sat down immediately.

"After you untied Hopie and left the ranch, why didn't you drive straight to the nearest police station?" Honey asked.

"Because your daughter told me what had happened up there and she was terrified for the safety of her children. She said they were at home with her Mexican maid, and she said the killer had told her that if she notified the police before he said she could, he would kill her and her children and"—he gestured toward Honey—"you and your husband, too.

"She was worried that her husband, whom the killer said had hired him, had taken K.C. out and might not have brought him home. She only wanted to go home. So I took her home, and shortly after we arrived the killer telephoned, wanting to know who the man was who had brought her home." He bowed his head slightly, in acknowledgment. "And he told her again that if she notified the police, she and her children would never be safe. Never." He looked at Hope. "Not for the rest of their lives."

Hope stood up quickly and sat back down. "And if the police were notified, she must not identify him or she would be killed."

"Is there really such an organization of professional killers?" Honey asked. "Is it the Mafia?"

"Don't interrupt him," Hope said. "Just listen. Let him talk."

Taylor looked very serious. He leaned forward and clasped his hands together.

"In Los Angeles it isn't called the Mafia; it's called the organization. But I assure you they are very, very real. I know it is difficult for you to understand because they have never touched your lives or your way of life, but there are organizations, there are professional killers. They kill because it is a business with them. They are just doing a job, like any other job, that they are paid to do."

Honey stared at him.

"How do I know you aren't one of them?"

"You don't," Taylor said calmly. "But if I were, would I have brought your daughter home and guarded her day and night? Would I have sat up by the window all night with a gun so she and her children could sleep?

"In fact," he went on rather grumpily, "I am very tired because I have gone without sleep so I could sit by her living room window with my rifle. That sliding glass door in Hope's living room has been deliberately jammed so it can't be locked. They probably did that when they got the floor plan of the house."

"I looked through Taylor's rifle," Hope chimed in. "You wouldn't believe how far away you can see with that telescope on it."

"She has been in terrible danger," Taylor continued. "You are all in terrible danger. I am sure there is someone on the roof of the house across the street right now with a telescopic rifle aimed right at your front door."

"But aren't your people out there?" Honey wondered.

"Not anymore. I waved them off when I arrived here. But there may even be a bomb under your house right now, a bomb set to go off if you call the police. Haven't you noticed some suspicious-looking people around here lately?"

Honey had. She told Taylor that when she followed Hope to the Beverly Hills Hotel, she had noticed two men in overalls standing by a truck in front of the house across the street. They were still there when she and Hope returned. A black woman had been sitting on the doorstep of the house next door to Honey's. And she remembered the incident the day before, on Monday, when a man she'd never seen before had walked right across her patio, right up to the sliding glass door into the living room. Shielding his eyes with his hand, he had peered into the room. When he saw Honey, he turned, walked across the patio onto the lawn and over to the garage; he went in, came out with a hoe, and began to work. Honey had assumed he was a new man hired by their regular gardener.

Taylor nodded knowingly. "With all the glass windows and doors you have around here, there isn't a room in the house where you couldn't be shot by someone with a telescopic rifle.

"This killer has been very clever. He has always arranged to have one child away from Hope at all times. That way Hope could never contact the police, because one child was always in danger. But I have never left her unprotected. Any time I have had to leave her, I have had my people protecting her. One of my people was up there posing as a gardener."

"But when can we call the police?" Honey asked.

"Not until the contract has been canceled. I have talked with my people in Chicago, and from all they can ascertain, the contract is still out on Hope and her children and"—he paused again—"probably on you and your husband too, now that Hope has come here."

"You keep bringing up your people," Honey said. "Who are your people? Are you CIA or FBI or what?"

Taylor laughed. "I think the less you know about me and my people, the better," he said gently.

Two or three times during the afternoon, Honey went to the phone and picked it up to call her husband, in spite of Taylor's warning. But each time, Hope stopped her. "Mother, Mother, please listen to Taylor and do what he says." She stressed the word Mother, though Hope had not called Honey "Mother" for twenty-five years. So each time, feeling she was being warned of something even more sinister than the situation they were now in, Honey replaced the phone.

Taylor was explaining, too, why she mustn't call. "You know, they have people in the police department, too. How do you know one of them won't take your call? They have people all over. All over! Lawyers. Doctors. Police. Even in high places in government."

Honey was trying to straighten things out in her mind. "When you got back to Los Angeles and got the children, why didn't you drive to the police station then?"

"Because I am not an American national."

Honey said she did not understand.

"I am not an American citizen," he said patiently, "and this kind of thing could cause me all kinds of trouble with my passport."

Honey was annoyed. "I can't understand, under these circumstances, what possible difference that would make."

Taylor still spoke patiently. "I have moved a dead body and removed a material witness from the scene of a crime and disturbed the evidence of a crime. I could be in all kinds of trouble."

"Surely you could explain why you did all that," Honey said crossly. "You should have taken her right to the police. I can understand why Hopie wanted to get home to make sure her children were safe, and obviously she was too hysterical to use good judgment, but you seem like a mature, intelligent person, and you should have known to go straight to the police."

"It was too dangerous," Taylor repeated. "And I could have been in all kinds of trouble. What I need to do is see a lawyer, give a deposition, and take the next plane out of the country. In fact"—he stood up—"I think I will leave now."

"Oh, Taylor," Honey pleaded, no longer cross, "you rescued Hopie from the ranch. You saved her. The killer might have come back if you hadn't taken her away. And you have protected her ever since. Surely you aren't going to leave now, when you are her only witness? The police will need every detail of what you have done so they can find and identify the killer. Please, please stay."

Taylor looked at Hope and smiled.

"I'll stay." He sat down and lighted his pipe.

"Let's change the subject," he said smoothly. "Did you know that your daughter picks up filthy little babies and wipes their runny noses?"

He didn't explain, and Honey didn't ask him to explain.

"That doesn't surprise me," Honey replied. "She is the little mother of the world. Every person with a problem seems to come to her for help. Our dentist thinks it's extraordinary that she keeps bringing her Mexican maids to him to have their teeth fixed but she never comes to have him take care of hers. She has always helped people, and Bill Ashlock helped *her*. Bill was wonderfully helpful, and he enjoyed the children so."

Taylor abruptly set his pipe down on the table and stood up. Hope remembered he did not like to talk about Bill. "Would you believe Taylor is fifty-one years old?" she asked, her voice shrill.

"My goodness, fifty-one," Honey marveled. "Well, you certainly don't look it."

"And I have grandchildren," Taylor said. He no longer seemed upset; he sat down and picked up his pipe.

"I wonder what the killer's next move will be," he mused. "I wonder if he will ask for money. Perhaps that is why he let Hope come here, because he knows that you are the source of her money. Oh, he knows that; he knows all about you. He knows that your husband has had two heart attacks, and he has even been down to your husband's new office in the Arco Towers."

"My husband has often told me he would never pay a penny on a kidnap threat," Honey said, "and I'm sure he would feel the same way about this."

"Who would benefit if you were all killed except K.C.?" Taylor asked.

"If we were all killed, then all of my separate property would go to K.C. and then, of course, Tom Masters would have control of it."

Taylor looked thoughtful.

"Is it possible," Honey asked, "for someone to take out a policy on Hopie's life without her knowing it?"

"It's entirely possible," Taylor said, "but the premiums would be very high."

He puffed meditatively on his pipe, and Honey brought up some things she'd been thinking about.

"How was Bill shot?"

"He was shot through the back of the head," Taylor said. "He probably never even knew what was happening."

"I wonder why Hopie didn't hear the shot," Honey said.

"Oh, he probably used a silencer." Taylor demonstrated with his hands how Bill must have been shot. "Like in *The Day of the Jackal*. Have you read it?" Honey was so startled she did not reply. She had just read the book on vacation, and its deadly details were vivid in her mind. The Jackal. A man who slipped in and out of other people's identities and other people's lives. A cultivated man who dressed in custom clothes and burnished leather shoes, a man who relished fine food and who was at ease in fine hotels. A man adept at disguise: sometimes he put a Band-Aid on his cheek. Sometimes he wore dark wraparound glasses.

Once, when the phone rang, it was the ranch foreman, Jim Webb. He told Honey that Hope's car was still at the ranch but he hadn't seen her around and he wondered if anything was wrong.

Honey covered the phone with her hand and told Taylor it was Jim Webb. "Can I tell him?" she asked.

"No," Taylor said.

"Hope is here with me, Jim," Honey said. "But there has been a terrible tragedy at the ranch. I'll call you back as soon as I can. Please don't go into the house."

Honey hung up and turned to Taylor. "Terry Webb goes into the ranch house on Mondays to clean up after the weekend, and change the linens. She probably hasn't gone in because Hopie's car is still there. Isn't it too bad she didn't go in as usual, because then she would have called the police and they would have gone right to Hopie's house, looking for her."

"You are all just very lucky that they didn't go to Hope's house," Taylor said in a severe tone. "I told you that if the police had gone up there, everyone would have been killed."

"But if our phone is tapped and if they heard that conversation," Honey said anxiously, "then they must know that the word will soon be out. Can't I call the police now?"

"No, no," Taylor repeated. "You have to wait until Hope gets word that it is all right to call the police." He paused, then nodded slightly. "You're right, though. He certainly knows that time is running out."

Van came home a little before seven o'clock. "Darling, we have something very upsetting to tell you," Honey said, "but you should sit down and have a drink first and be prepared for terrible news. And perhaps you should get your pills, in case you need them."

She introduced Van to Taylor. "Would you like a drink?" Van asked the visitor. Taylor asked for sherry.

Van went to the alcove bar, which was fitted with a refrigerator, a sink, and folding doors. He brought drinks around to the sofa and the four of them sat quietly for a few minutes, sipping. Taylor was puffing calmly on his pipe.

Hope could hardly sit still. Her hands were clammy and she felt light-headed. After Kazue had gone to her Berlitz class at six o'clock, Hope had put the children to bed, all three of them in the one big bed in the second bedroom, the room that had been Hope's when she was a teen-ager. Hope knew the room well; she kept thinking of the long window across one entire wall of the room, overlooking the back garden. The draperies were closed, but Hope remembered what Taylor had said about the people who were outside, and how nobody was safe in a house with so much glass. She felt sick to her stomach, and so agitated that she suddenly burst into her story, trying to tell Van. Honey began to talk, too, with Hope interrupting her. When Taylor cut in, both women stopped talking.

Van listened as Taylor told the story, the same story that he and Hope had, separately, told Honey—that Bill was murdered, that an intruder at the ranch had hurt Hope and tied her up and warned her about a contract on her life, that she and everyone in her family were in danger. Taylor described his rescue of Hope and his efforts at guarding her, back at her house. He added some details that Honey hadn't heard, about threatening phone calls that had come on Hope's phone during the two days he'd spent there. "Isn't that right, Hope?" he asked, watching her closely.

"Uh-huh," Hope said, afraid that if she didn't agree about the threatening calls, he would pull out his gun and simply shoot them all. Honey had not seen Taylor's gun, but periodically, during the afternoon, Hope had seen him flick open his jacket several times, just long enough for her to see a part of the gun tucked into his waistband, and she felt he was warning her.

Van set his drink on the coffee table and stood up. "I'm going to call the police," he said decisively.

"You can't call the police," Taylor explained. "Your phone is tapped, and if the police are called, everyone in this house will be killed."

"I don't care," Van said. "I'm sixty-three years old and I've never broken the law in my life. I'm calling the police."

He walked toward the telephone on the game table across the living room. Hope screamed and ran to the phone, just ahead of him. She turned and faced Van, standing between him and the phone.

"What about my children?" Hope cried. "You're not just risking your own life. You're condemning my children, and they haven't even had a chance to live!"

Van stared at Hope. He looked back at Taylor, then he began to pace up and down the room.

"My foreman and his wife are in danger up there," Van said.

"What about the safety of your own family right here?" Taylor demanded. "Your foreman isn't in any danger from a dead body."

The antagonism between the men mounted as Van paced. Taylor talked again of a possible bomb beneath the house, set to go off if the police were called, and about a possible sniper in a tree. Van kept shaking his head, insisting that the police had to be notified at once. Hope seemed near collapse.

Taylor spoke calmly. "Do you know a lawyer, or do you have a friend in the D.A.'s office, whom you could call and ask to come here?" he asked Van.

Van whirled and glared at Taylor. "That's a hell of a thing to do to a friend," he snapped. "Ask them to come here and maybe get shot on our doorstep."

Then Taylor began to agree with Van about calling the authorities; he seemed to be trying to calm Van down. Eventually the debate simmered down to the question of whom to call.

"You can't just call anyone at the police station," Taylor said. "I suggest you call a criminal attorney first and get his advice." Again Van refused, saying that anyone who came to the house might be in danger.

As the conversation went on, Hope could see that Van intended to call the local police at the Beverly Hills station, two blocks from the house. "Call the FBI or somebody important," she begged Van. "If I'm going to talk to somebody, I want to talk to somebody with some experience and intelligence and the capability to deal with this whole awful situation. I don't want to talk to some four hundred dollar-a-month desk clerk."

She felt Van was ignoring her. "I'll call the police here," he repeated. "They'll know what to do. I'll go outside and call from somewhere else and ask them to send plainclothesmen in an unmarked car."

Taylor stood up. "It's better if I go out and call," he said. "I've been seen coming and going from this house, so it won't look strange if I leave." He sketched his plan: he would go to the Polo Lounge at the Beverly Hills Hotel, order a drink so as not to create suspicion, then after a few minutes he would get up casually and go to the men's room, where he would call the police from the pay phone there.

"You'll come back then, won't you?" Honey asked in a pleading voice. Taylor said he would return. He stood up, gave a little wave toward Hope, then he was gone.

Van strode down the hall to the bedroom and came back with two guns, a rifle and an automatic revolver. He laid them carefully on the game table in the living room.

Hope stared at the guns. "I've never made a will," she said shakily. "I want to write out a will." She made a pleading gesture toward Van. "Will you show me how to do it?"

"Just write it on a piece of paper and sign it," Van said, "and be sure to date it."

Honey got a piece of Van's business stationery from the telephone shelf in the kitchen and handed it to Hope.

She wrote:

2-27-73

In the event of my death, please allow my friends, Mr. and Mrs. Bill Pierce, to have custody of my three children. Tom Masters has arranged to have us all killed and my first husband shows no interest and is not able to care for them properly. Please keep the children together, as they are a little family within themselves and need each other. Please let whoever has the children have whatever money or property that I own.

                    Hope Masters

Sgt. Billy Ray Smith at the Beverly Hills station took Taylor's call at nine o'clock. It was a quiet night at the station, like any other quiet Tuesday night, when the few calls that came in seemed to involve dogs without leashes, maybe a burglar alarm going off in the neighborhood, probably by mistake. The caller told Sergeant Smith that he was calling from a phone booth on behalf of someone else, about a young woman who had been "involved in a killing" in northern California. Sergeant Smith didn't notice anything special about the voice—no drawl, no foreign accent—only that he seemed excited. The caller said that this young woman had witnessed a killing, and that the person who was dead had been killed by a member of the Mafia. He gave Honey and Van's address and asked that a plainclothes unit be sent there right away.

"What's your name?" Sergeant Smith asked.

"Taylor," the caller said.

"Well, do you live at that address?"

"No, I live at another address."

"Well, give me the other address," Sergeant Smith said. He was a little leery of the whole thing, besides—who knows?—maybe this guy was trying to sucker a policeman into an ambush or something.

Taylor said he lived on the Drive.

"Give me the phone number there," Sergeant Smith said.

Taylor refused. "Are you going to send a plain unit or not?" he demanded.

"I don't have a plain unit," Sergeant Smith said.

Taylor got mad. "Well, if I have to go through all this, forget it," he said. "I'll call the FBI." He slammed down the phone.

Sergeant Smith felt sure it was a crank call. Still, he radioed the patrol car in the neighborhood and asked the officer driving, William Clyde Stien, to check around those premises for anything out of order, any vehicles that possibly looked suspicious.

Taylor called the house. He said the Beverly Hills police didn't believe him and wouldn't come because he wasn't a property owner. "I'm going to call the police in Porterville now," he told Hope. "I'll call you back."

"We can't just sit around here and wait," Van declared. He picked up the telephone and called Information. "I want the number for the Beverly Hills police," he said. Hope watched him silently, her head splitting open. *This is it,* she thought. *This is it.*

Then Van was almost shouting into the telephone. "A murder, a murder—that's what I said, a murder!"

By the time Van called, Sergeant Smith had checked the family name in his cross-directory, and he decided to pay attention. The sergeant had told Taylor the truth—he really didn't have a plain unit—but when Officer Stien came back to the station to report nothing suspicious, Sergeant Smith told him to change clothes and go back, taking another officer with him, Phil DeMond.

Officers Stien and DeMond changed out of uniform and drove the short distance to Honey and Van's. Stien placed both men's I.D. cards on the clipboard he was carrying, walked up to the door, and rang the bell. DeMond waited a little way down the driveway, looking around. The front light over the door was on, and he could see all around the front of the house, the driveway, and sidewalk. Nothing seemed suspicious; nothing seemed odd. DeMond saw a man at the window, looking at them from behind the drapery. Then a woman opened the door a few inches, leaving the chain on. Stien showed her his I.D., but Honey refused to let him in; he looked suspicious to her. Van came to the door then, looked closely at the I.D. on the clipboard, and unfastened the chain.

As Officer Stien walked into the foyer, his partner right behind him, Hope rushed forward.

"If you are not the police, if you are *them,* please shoot me!" she cried. "I'm the one the contract is on, not my parents!"

She had a gun. Hope later said she was pointing it at the floor. In his report DeMond said she was "waving it above her head." Stien said "she was kind of pointing it away, not really right at us, but she had a good grip on the gun and she looked like she could use it very easily if she wanted to."

"I want to see sufficient identification," Hope demanded, so Stien showed her the cards again. Van took the gun from her, unloaded five rounds of ammunition, and set it on the table. He remained standing near the table. Hope and Honey and Officer Stien sat down. Officer DeMond stayed near the door.

"I think you ought to interview my daughter about this crime or whatever it might be, or murder or whatever it might be, that has taken place up at our ranch," Van said.

Officer Stien adjusted the clipboard on his lap and took out a ballpoint pen.

"Okay, what happened there? Start with a few facts about the ranch. What's the name of the ranch?"

Honey frowned. "We don't want any publicity," she said. "We don't want the name of the ranch or our names in the newspapers or anything."

"Well, you called us up here," Stien reminded her.

Van explained the partnership arrangement with the three other families. He was describing the ranch location when Hope broke in.

"Let me talk, let me tell them the story."

Once Hope started talking, she couldn't stop. She had been wanting to talk to the police for three days, and her story came pouring out: an intruder in the night; the screaming for Bill and the running through the dark house; the talk of a contract on her and Bill and the children; the blood, the vomit, the terror in the bedroom; the question of brushing her teeth. Mostly the officers just listened, because DeMond noticed that when they interrupted to ask her a question, she tended to start all over again, from the beginning, and later DeMond reported that he never learned whether or not she had actually brushed her teeth.

Honey thought Hope sounded hysterical and erratic, and even Hope knew she was repeating herself, but she felt she had to: they didn't seem to believe her. They seemed to be humoring her, just sitting there, so she talked more and more. DeMond remembered her talking about her divorce, about Tom Masters, about being taped and tied, about rubber gloves, and the killer being paid thirty-six hundred dollars for the job—although DeMond said he never did find out whether that meant thirty-six hundred dollars for all of them, or thirty-six hundred dollars apiece. She talked about a photographer named Taylor who appeared at the ranch in a white Lincoln on Sunday and rescued her and brought her home, and how terrified she was at home, and how she was afraid to call the police and how she wanted to give Bill a good burial and she wanted him cremated because that's what he always wanted.

The officers could tell she had been drinking, and she was extremely nervous, and as time went on, and her story went on—"rambled on," DeMond reported—they became more and more doubtful. When she was telling them about her wrists being taped, she was gesturing and pointing and waving her arms around. "She went into this whole thing about tape," DeMond said, so when Hope was saying to him, "See? See?" and holding up her wrists, DeMond didn't argue. He was standing by the door, five or six feet away, and although he didn't see any tape marks, "I just agreed with her that there was tape," he said. "I didn't even know there was any crime. She was telling us a story that was getting lengthy and she was going back and forth. She'd go into real exact details on certain aspects of the conversation, and then she wouldn't answer simple questions we'd ask her, to put in our report if we were going to write one."

When the officers asked her to describe the intruder, DeMond reported, "She waved toward me and said, 'He's about your height and he's about your weight, maybe a little heavier, maybe a little thinner.'" Stien reported that Hope had described the intruder as "possibly white or maybe Mexican, probably about six feet, one hundred eighty pounds, a pretty big, good-sized guy, long stringy hair about shoulder length, and he possibly had a mustache or a small goatee or something." DeMond thought she said "a beard, or whiskers."

The phone rang, and Van answered. "It's for you," he told Officer Stien. It was Sgt. Billy Ray Smith, calling Stien at the house because he had just had a call from a policeman up north in Porterville, in Tulare County, Sergeant Coley. Sergeant Coley called the Beverly Hills police because, at 9:40, the Porterville police had a call from a man who said he was calling from Beverly Hills, from a pay phone near his home. He gave his address and his phone number. He said that his stepdaughter, whose name was Hope Masters, had just told him of a terrible thing that had happened at their ranch in Springville, that there was a dead body there. When Sergeant Coley and another Porterville officer on the line had asked for more details and for directions, the man had given them directions and told them the combination to the lock on the gate and then had begun to shout at them. "Let's stop all the bullshit and quit asking me questions and get somebody up there and uncover the body and get something done!" Then the man hung up.

So Sergeant Coley in Porterville had called down to Sergeant Smith in Beverly Hills, and Sergeant Smith called Officer Stien.

"What's going on there?" Smith asked Stien.

"I'm not sure," Stien said. "There is possibly a dead body at a house on a ranch in Tulare County."

Sergeant Smith told Stien to stay there, that he would call him back. Stien sat down and picked up his clipboard. Hope kept talking. She had been talking about whiskers, and when the officers pressed that point— how long were the whiskers? A couple days old, or like hippie-type?— DeMond said she went into great detail: it was a mustache just like her husband's, or possibly it could have been a goatee. "She just went on and on about the whiskers," DeMond said wearily, and even after two hours, Stien said, "I just felt it was a big story."

Then the phone rang again.

Jim Webb was so scared he was not even shaking. He was just sitting like a stone on the edge of the bathtub, staring at the floor. The children were all in the living room, and Jim Webb wanted to be by himself. It was so unbelievable he could hardly think, hardly speak. When his wife saw him come in from outdoors with a very strange, chalky-white look on his face and go straight into the bathroom, she had followed him in. "You saw something," Teresa said. Jim didn't answer.

Around nine o'clock, just about the time Taylor was calling the Beverly Hills police from the men's room at the hotel, Jim Webb had taken a flashlight and gone outside, down the stretch of dirt road between the two houses, past the orange grove, making his way through the deep blackness, around to the back door of the main house. He had put on a pair of gloves, slipped a pair of socks over his shoes, unlocked the door, and gone in.

Jim Webb never could explain to the police exactly why he had entered. "I don't know why I went in. I don't know why I went in. I just felt something was wrong and I had to check it out. I just, you know, I don't —sometimes you feel like you got to do things, and I just felt like I had to go. I just did. Everything inside told me no, but something told me yeah, so I went over. If there was something wrong, I didn't want to get involved in it. I didn't want to leave any fingerprints, I know that."

That was why he'd gone over to the main house twice before, earlier in the day, because he thought something might be wrong. All day Sunday, all day Monday, and all day Tuesday the Vega had been parked over there, though he hadn't seen any people. The first time he went over, on Tuesday afternoon, he just knocked on the door, then left. The second time he'd looked in the windows; it wasn't very late, but the winter dusk came early in the mountains, and he'd used his flashlight, shining it into some of the windows. Through the window of the corner bedroom, the one nearest his house, he'd seen beds messed up, blankets all jumbled, but nothing wrong. Then, standing at the back door, looking through the storage room into the kitchen beyond, he'd shone his flashlight across the kitchen floor and seen a long white strip, a white powdery trail of something like Ajax, leading all the way across the kitchen floor into the hallway beyond, the hall that led to the back bedroom. Jim was surprised at the white stuff on the floor, because Teresa was such a good housekeeper. The very last thing she did, when she went over to clean the place after the city people had been up for the weekend, was to wash the kitchen floor, and she always put down a nice new coat of wax. Jim knew she did because he often helped her clean; he knew some of the owners could be pretty fussy, especially Hope Masters's mother. All the owners expected a lot for the $150 a month they paid the Webbs; although the Webbs also got a rent-free house with utilities paid, Jim had to take care of the grounds around the house, irrigate the orange trees, mow the lawn and cut wood, look after half a dozen horses, and do repair work around the place—all sorts of odd jobs, all sorts of things the owners wanted done.

After his second trip over, Jim Webb had called down to Los Angeles and had heard from Hope's mother about "a terrible tragedy at the ranch." He talked with other people on the phone, including Hope's stepfather, who told him that the police had been notified and that Jim must not go into the house. He had also talked with another of the owners, Nick Doughty.

Then he made his third trip, wearing gloves, and socks over his shoes. "I expected maybe to find somebody hurt," he told the police, "or maybe somebody just completely freaked out or something like that, but as far as what I found, no, I didn't expect that, because if I would have expected that, I *never* would have went in there."

Except for a light in the storage room, the house had been dark. Jim had turned on the kitchen light and walked through the kitchen, through the living room, shining his flashlight all around, into the two bedrooms on the east side of the house. One bedroom was neat, the beds made; in the other bedroom, the room he'd seen through the window, the beds were messed up, covers pulled back, but he saw nothing else. He walked back through the living room, shining his light onto the sofa. He saw that the sofa had a cover thrown over it, white, maybe a sheet or a bedspread. He walked past the dinette into the front bedroom on the west side, where everything was in good shape, nothing wrong in that closet or in the bathroom next door. Then he was standing in the small hallway between the dinette and the back bedroom, the last bedroom, the only bedroom he hadn't yet checked. The door was closed. As he walked toward that door, he stepped on a loose floorboard, and he heard a loud creak.

He pushed the door open and shone his light around on the beds, which were neatly made. He swung the beam around the room and brought it down along the floor. He saw the long bundle there, on the floor near his feet, something all wrapped up. It looked like a mummy.

He may or may not have closed the door. He may or may not have turned off the kitchen light. He may or may not have locked the back door to the house as he got out fast, around the orange grove, across the forty yards or so to his own house where he went right into the bathroom and sat for a good half hour or more, before he went out and called the Porterville police and then went into the bedroom, got down his own gun, loaded it, and lay it right out where he could get to it if he had to.

The Porterville station logged his call at 9:44 P.M., four minutes after the call from the man who said he was talking from a pay phone in Beverly Hills. In minutes the resident deputy in Springville, Doyle Hoppert, was on his way. Lieutenant Joe Teller was the second man to reach the ranch entrance road, followed by Sergeant Coley and Detective Jack Flores. Lieutenant Teller decided they would leave their cars parked down below and walk up the ranch road to the house, looking for possible tracks.

The four men climbed the muddy driveway in the blackness, their flashlights making sweeping arcs in their path. There was no moon. In the cold rain, the house seemed to lurk ominously beyond the drenched lawn, shrouded and mostly dark, although Teller thought he saw a dim light from a side window. They followed the light around the side of the house, to the back door. The door was locked. Deputy Hoppert hurried back to the driveway, around the orange grove, to get a key from Jim Webb.

Inside the storage room, they stood for just a moment, then separated. Detective Flores crossed the kitchen, heading for the rear wing. Lieutenant Teller walked into the living room; as he beamed his light around, he saw a plate of dried-up cheese and crackers on a table. As he headed for the front bedroom, he passed the bathroom and noticed four or five used towels on the floor. Then he heard someone calling him. He turned quickly and walked through the living room, through the kitchen into the back hall. Jack Flores was standing at the doorway of the back bedroom. He was shining his flashlight at the long, wrapped bundle on the floor.

The body was lying face down on a white mattress pad, wrapped completely in a yellow bedspread, approximately three feet inside the northeast bedroom, with the head pointed south.

Officer Doyle Hoppert made out the official report, doing his best to fill in all the spaces. Under PREMISES he wrote: "Large single frame residence in rural area." Under OFFENSE: "(V) was shot in the top of the head (middle and slightly toward the back of head) with unknown caliber and make of gun." Under EXTENT OF INJURIES: "Death." He had to leave blank the spaces for VICTIM'S NAME: LAST, FIRST, MIDDLE, OCCUPATION, and ADDRESSES, RESIDENCE AND BUSINESS, though he made a stab at DATE OF BIRTH and wrote "Approximately 25." Under MOTIVE: "Unknown."

The officers at the scene called back to their station. Captain Farris and Lieutenant Barnes, reached at their homes, headed over to the ranch, along with men from the crime lab. Then Sergeant Coley called back down to Beverly Hills, which is why Sgt. Billy Ray Smith called Officer Stien again.

Officers Stien and DeMond asked Hope where her car was. She said it was still at the ranch. They said they were taking her down to the station.

"What about Taylor?" Honey asked. "Please get a prowl car and start looking for Taylor. He must still be in the area. Maybe he's still at the Beverly Hills Hotel."

"Will I need anything?" Hope asked the policemen. "Should I take my bag?" They said she wouldn't need anything, then one of them added that she should bring a sweater. She put a pack of cigarettes into the pocket of her jeans.

"Please, please start looking for Taylor," Honey was saying. "You should have policemen looking for him at the airport. He said he would like to leave the country. Please, please put up police blockades at all the roads out of town."

A chilly rain was falling as Hope got into the police car, in the back seat. As they drove the short distance to the station, Hope thrust her hands over the back of the seat, dangling them between the two men in front. "Did you ever see hands swollen like this?" she asked. They said yes. "Do you think the swelling will go away?" They said yes.

At the station, she was given a sheet of paper headed ARREST AND BOOKING FORM. "I thought I was going to talk to a detective," Hope protested. They said the detectives weren't there just now. "What about my family?" Hope asked. "Is anybody watching them?" The officers said her family was fine, and Hope signed the form. It listed her name and address and vital statistics, her occupation as "homemaker," and the charge as "Suspicion PC 187." That was the number, in the California Penal Code, for homicide.

And that was the number on the license plate—CBX187—on a white, two-door, brand-new Chevrolet Impala that was rented at the Avis desk at the Los Angeles Airport at 10:30 P.M., the exact time that, at the ranch, the victim was being pronounced DOS—Dead on the Scene. The man who rented the car gave his name as William T. Ashlock and initialed the rental form W.T.A.

CHAPTER
SIX

THE DISCOVERY OF Robert Pietrusiak's beige Buick in a supermarket parking lot at the corner of Higgins and Cumberland in Park Ridge, Illinois, was good news only to Mr. Pietrusiak. It now bore a new Missouri license plate—YG9-902. The manager at Dominic's Market said that by the time the car was found, just before two o'clock in the morning on February 22, it had been there at least a week, maybe ten days. It was empty, except for a *Daily News* dated January 31, and there were no latent fingerprints. "The vehicle was searched with negative results," Bob Swalwell reported tersely.

By that weekend—the weekend Hope Masters and Bill Ashlock had driven to the ranch—Swalwell and the many other men involved in the search for G. Daniel Walker had other information, other leads, other cars. Lots of other cars, especially three Mercury Montegos.

Ronald Tonsel, the tall, slim Corrections officer whom Swalwell considered arrogant, had spotted a blue Mercury Montego, 1973 Illinois license BC 7806, following him one day when he was following Marcy Purmal. Tonsel thought the driver might have been Walker: white male, dark beard, wire-rimmed glasses. The license plate check led to Budget Rent-a-Car on Higgins Road, not far from Dominic's Market, where the clerks traced the rental back to February 2, by a Robert Zierk of Wheaton, Illinois, who had used an American Express card.

Mrs. Zierk sounded surprised when the police called. "The car is right here in our driveway," she said. "We had an accident with our own car and we rented this one while ours is in the shop." Swalwell asked her to please go outside, anyway, and check to make sure both license plates were on the car. When she came back she said yes, both plates were on the car, and she assured him the car had never been out of Wheaton. Anyway, the car was brown, not blue.

Back at Budget, Swalwell asked about a blue—repeat, blue—Mercury Montego that might be missing. One was: a four-door, 1973, light blue, Illinois license BC 7803, missing for nearly a month. Swalwell notified Chicago P.D. Communications Center, which put out a 1028, advising all units on the South Side to be on the lookout for said vehicle, possibly being driven by G. Daniel Walker, fugitive. That very night, an armed man robbed the Standard station on South Lake Park Avenue and drove off in a light blue 1973 Mercury Montego, Illinois license beginning BC, the rest of the number missing. Swalwell hurried over, but that wasn't Walker, either.

Swalwell wasn't deeply discouraged, but he had to admit he was keeping one eye on the calendar. The last time he had tracked this man, after Gus had been shot, it had taken eighteen days before Walker was run to earth, literally, in LaBagh Woods. He had been loose more than three weeks already, with no solid leads.

No, Swalwell corrected himself, that wasn't true. There were leads all over the place, infinite possibilities. Some of them led nowhere—staking out the volleyball court, or hanging around the Pizza Factory on North Clark Street for hours the night Marcy Purmal and a bunch of Legal Aid people had a party there after work. And some of them might have seemed pointless to anyone but Swalwell. He had always felt that the ex-convicts that Walker had hung around with in prison could be useful, and when he and Trooper Rowe had a few hours on their hands, they would often drive around to see one, just checking.

Swalwell was right in thinking that Walker kept in touch with some of his ex-con friends. Walker himself said so. In one letter to Marcy, he furnished a list of eleven people who were helping him in hiding, a list headed by three men—Leo, Tony, and Sam—whom Swalwell knew very well indeed, though he never was able to prove anything against them. "Knowing and not being able to prove it is a hell of a lot more frustrating than not knowing," Swalwell said ruefully.

Walker's letters did not surface immediately, as they were written; as Walker had pointed out, in Walker's midnight letter to Marcy on the day he walked out of Illinois Research, his letters wouldn't reach her "for awhile." Walker managed, maddeningly, to stay at least a day or two, a step or two, ahead of Swalwell and the assorted searchers. Not that they weren't very good cops, but Walker was a very good player at this game of cat-and-mouse. Walker, however, did not consider himself the quarry. In one of the first letters he wrote, dated February 6, six days after his escape, he called himself "Top Cat" and boasted gleefully that he had indeed been hiding in a building that the police had searched the day before:

> I was in a bind, thanks to approximately 16 Feds and 21 FBI and State Police who got me cornered in a building—but alas! This Old Fox is not an Under Cat because he has single moments of being Top Cat—I actually played with 'em. Yep! Played with 'em until it hurt. I knew an instant escape route, having cased the building over, and yet, when I realized and saw the spreading trap—I played with 'em. Just like old times, and twice the fun.

Some of Walker's letters were hand-delivered, such as the three notes in the black purse. Others arrived in the mail, sometimes with the name "Charlie Brown" in the upper left corner of the envelope, always with "Attorney/Client" typed on the envelope. In them, Walker freely mixed fact with fiction. "He'll give you a little tidbit of truth and mix it in with the garbage, to confuse you," Swalwell noted. Even the garbage, though, sounded good, such as the information Walker gave, in his February 6 letter, about his hideout with some "old and very dear friends of the family":

> With open arms they met me, sending a car and two back-up cars in the event of trouble or a tail. Like always, you first must eat—out to a little old lady's home in an old neighborhood. She did not know me nor did I know her. We were never introduced. Nine men came into her home, she served wine, lots of wine, and then set about preparing a dinner the likes of which you would not believe. Everything was homemade and beautiful. We sat around a huge kitchen table, were loud, and drank wine, and drank wine, and then coffee so strong it could serve as battery acid. Finally, The Man and I had our private little talk. He rejected much of what I told him was my plan, and I rejected much of what he wanted me to do. We settled on a compromise of sorts—he forced me to go-to-mattress. While I cannot tell you where, there are many spots around the city and out in the sticks where large homes and/or apartments are kept with stacks of

mattresses, kept in the event that large groups of men must go into hiding (an old holdover from the gang war days). My mattress was and is on the floor. There is TV and food and booze. (Excuse me, a phone call: would I like to be part of a three-man team being sent to a city in the East to take off a jewelry salesman? My end would be four big ones. Nope. Oh, yes, I have had several offers—the feeling-out process to determine whether I am back with all my heart or just willy-nilly.)

Anyway, after we finished at the old lady's house and it was time to be taken for my ride into the night, in pranced three young girls, 17 to 20. Which would be my choice? I explained a few more days would be allotted for you to come to your sense before I would undertake another—better hurry and come to your sense, my darling, for one looked like she would be a great lay.

As you can see, I am in great shape and being well provided for— you should have it so good. This morning two buttons drove by to see if I wanted any different types of food, needed pipe tobacco, and to bring a relief baby sitter—ah yes, even this side keeps me under constant guard. You see, someone must answer the door, phone, and be prepared to spirit me away in the event of trouble. I am being measured for I.D. shortly, and then a tailor will measure me for tropical suits, and then comes the barber. When the time is right— out of the city and into the blue I will go, and there is no doubt that I will make it now, unless a pigeon along the way spots who I am.

One might suspect I am happy—I am not. This carries a price tag, one you never get to see until it is too late.

From his own knowledge of Walker, and from his knowledge of the Chicago underworld, Swalwell discounted Walker's Mafia jargon, "going-to-mattress" and "The Man," as simply Walker's braggadocio, his attempt to sound very big time. And he was also dubious about the "price tag" ending, Walker's unhappiness, although with a guy like Walker, who could say? Fortunately, Swalwell was not assigned to deal with Walker's soul. But he didn't doubt for a minute that some of Walker's friends, both ex-cons and civilians, were helping him and, Swalwell admitted, doing a pretty good job of it so far. Even when a letter was postmarked Chicago, Swalwell knew that didn't necessarily mean Walker was still in town. Sometimes Walker specifically said he was not.

It is seven-ish, I am back in Denver with a Dr. Pepper at hand and the bath is slowly filling with extra hot water. I need it, yes indeed, do I ever need it.

Skiied Loveland Basin early this A.M. and then on over to Vail and the big monster Lion's Head this afternoon. Busted my ass but good, too. Not only that but ruined a new pair of $59.95 ski pants. The only saving feature of having blood run down my left leg was there happened to be a cute little blond ski with me who insisted I come right off the slopes and into her suite at the lodge, where she bathed and dressed my leg, and then fixed us a drink. Ah yes, escape can be pure hell. Actually, she was quite safe, for the other two gentlemen skiing with us also joined the first aid session—Jimmy was 5 and Brad was 7, both her sons. Actually, I met them first and they introduced mommy. (Daddy was off earning enough bread to keep them in the $100-a-day suite.)

Tell the boys at Illinois State Police to look for a fugitive with a limp for the next week or so, huh. . . .

Since it is eight where you are, I suspect you are playing volleyball or choosing up sides for who gets who after the game—I hate you! Not really. I love you and miss you and want you (and not necessarily in that pecking order, I'll have you know, Ma'am. Damn, it has been so long I am certain I must be a virgin, again).

Got to turn the water off and make a scotch (still your bottle of stuff, I'll have you know, sweetie-pants).

The letter continued on a second page:

Hi there, that didn't take long, huh. Sonny and Cher are on the tube (like her and can't stand him).

Now then, I have a problem. Due to good eating and five meals a day, I suddenly find myself getting pudgy again. What do you suggest? Actually, a steady diet of fucking probably would help considerably. Know anyone I could sign up to join me who is not Laura Lawyer and afraid of losing her ticket, and is guaranteed not to be a virgin or a nice girl? (What did I ever see in you, I keep asking myself. Ohhhhh, I kinda have an idea, lover.) . . .

Love and Stuff . . .

That letter was dated Friday, February 16. The next evening, Swalwell was notified that Ronald Tonsel from Corrections and Willis Stephans, the Parole Board agent who had intercepted the black purse, were on a flight to Vail, Colorado, due to arrive at 8:00 P.M., where FBI agents working out of Denver would meet them. Marcy Purmal was on board, too.

By Tuesday everybody was back. Swalwell met with FBI agent Baucom, who reported that his men couldn't find Walker in Vail, then with Tonsel, who told Swalwell all about the trip. Again, Swalwell made a terse entry in his report: "The results of the trip were negative, and it was never established that Walker was ever in Vail, Colorado."

Swalwell was not surprised; Walker himself had said he was moving on. But it bothered the hell out of the detective that some of the men involved in the hunt didn't share information as it trickled in; presumably they aimed to be the men who finally cornered Walker and got the glory. Swalwell had no particular aversion to glory, and it had certainly occurred to him that success on this case might get him out of uniform and into the three-piece blue suit permanently. He figured there would be glory to spare when this man, on whom the FBI had a fat file, was caught. Not if; when.

One of the most intriguing things about Walker's letters were the details he scattered about, apparently in an attempt to liven up the chase. Swalwell knew all about Walker's low threshold of boredom, so he was prepared when Walker taunted the police; as in a February 15 letter in which he not only named the dining room at his hotel—The Oak Room—but went on to itemize his dinner:

> First, a series of martinis (four or five in number), oysters on the half shell (six), followed by turtle soup and sherry, a lovely salad with house dressing, bacon bits, grated cheese, etc., etc., hot shrimp, and then a 10 oz. steak beaten with pepper on both sides and cooked to medium rare with mushrooms, green peppers, onions, and topped with a brandy and served flaming, accompanied by the normal, and trailed by four Irish Coffees and a strong desire to take the blond away from the guy at the next table who did not appreciate what he had.

While FBI men, directed by Baucom in Chicago, were combing Denver—it was amazing how many restaurants and hotel dining rooms had names like The Oak Room—Swalwell worked his territory. When he went back out to Park Ridge, where Bob Pietrusiak's car had been found, he talked with Detective McDonald of the Park Ridge police about a third Mercury Montego.

This one was white, 1973 Illinois license BC 7962, rented on February 8 at 1:30 in the afternoon by a man using an American Express card that later checked out as stolen. The man had given his local address as the Marriott, Room 102, his company name and address as "Zipco," on

Peachtree Street in Atlanta, Georgia. The car had been rented at the Budget rental place on Higgins Road that Swalwell knew so well by now, but when he and Trooper Rowe talked with the young clerk who had handled the rental, John Bianchi, and showed him Walker's picture, Bianchi was uncertain whether that had been the man.

Nevertheless, Swalwell and Rowe headed over to the suburb of Rosemont, because the American Express card belonged to a traveling salesman from Georgia who had been robbed in his room at the Regency Hyatt House, also on Higgins Road, but over the line, in Rosemont. Detective Wilezynski of the Rosemont police related that robbery to them.

Larry Burbage, a salesman who had flown in from Atlanta, said he had been sitting on the edge of the bed in his room, 877, at 10:30 on the morning of February 7. The door to his room was closed but not locked, because his boss at Agronomics, Anthony Kupris, had gone downstairs and Burbage expected him back any minute. Kupris had the adjoining room. The inner door between the two rooms was unlocked, too.

Burbage was about to make a phone call when suddenly a man was in the room with him, pointing a small blue steel revolver at him. "Up!" the man ordered.

Burbage stood up and looked closely at the man, who seemed about five feet eleven and thirty to thirty-five years old, wearing wire-rimmed glasses, very neatly dressed in a dark blue suit with a yellow shirt and yellow tie.

"In here," the gunman said, motioning toward the door connecting the rooms. "Lay on the bed face down and give me your wallet," he ordered, closing the door behind him. Burbage handed over his wallet, with eighty-five dollars in it. "Do you have any more money?" the gunman asked. Burbage said no. "Take everything out of your pants." Burbage did that, too. "Take anything you want," he told the gunman, "but leave me my keys."

"You're not the one I want," the man said abruptly. "I'm waiting for Kupris."

"He's in the lounge."

"Well, looks like we're in for a long wait," the man said casually. But then he ordered Burbage to go into the bathroom and strip. "What kind of watch you got?" he asked, still casually.

"It's an old one," Burbage replied.

"Forget it," the man said.

When Burbage was naked, he was told to put his hands behind his back. He felt them being tied with what he thought must be the cord from an electric razor. Then he was ordered to crawl under the sink and not to move. His feet were then tied with neckties, which were tied to drain pipes under the sink. Once again the man left, but when he came back, he had two pillows, which he placed under Burbage's head. He left again.

When, after a while, the man hadn't returned, Burbage wriggled loose, wrapped himself in a towel, and ventured out into the room. He heard noise in his own room, 877, so he went out into the hall and found a maid, who called the desk, who called the police.

Besides the cash, Larry Burbage had been robbed of his brown attaché case and a handful of credit cards, including a Mobil Oil card, a Bankamericard, a Master Charge card, and the American Express card that was used to rent the white Mercury Montego at Budget the next day.

Detective Wilezynski explained to Swalwell how he and his partner, Detective Magrowski, had been tracking the Burbage credit cards ever since, for more than two weeks. Swalwell was amused at the name of the team—Wilezynski and Magrowski, a mouthful for sure. Wilezynski said that the next use of the American Express card seemed to have been Friday, February 9, at the Marriott Inn in Ann Arbor. The person using the card had rented Room 109, the room in which, sometime that night and the early morning, a jewelry salesman named Taylor Wright of Benton Harbor, Michigan, had been beaten and robbed.

Swalwell asked Wilezynski for the addresses of Taylor Wright in Benton Harbor and Larry Burbage in Lilburn, Georgia. Then he called Agent Baucom, told him the story, and asked him to have his agents in those areas talk to the two salesmen and show them Walker's picture.

In a phone call to Marcy on February 17, Walker's tone suddenly changed.

P: Good morning.
W: How are you?
P: Oh, fine. How are you?
W: Good. Thought it was about time I said hello.
P: Well, that's awfully nice of you, considering what's been happening lately.
W: Well, what has happened?
P: Oh, shit, man, they're talking about—they're seriously talking about indicting me.
W: Well, did you go before the grand jury?
P: Yes, twice.
W: Twice?

P: Yes. And they had Friedman the first session and the second session they had Haddad, second-chairing him.

W: Uh-hm. You can't tell them what you can't tell them, can you?

P: No, but they've got this mis-identification thing.

W: You mean—

P: There is somebody who says that I was with you at two o'clock in the morning at a gas station up on the North Side, damn it.

W: (*Laughing*) At two o'clock in the morning up on North Side.

P: Um hm, um hm.

W: Uh—what day?

P: I'm not really sure. They—they haven't, you know, told me which day it—or which morning it is.

W: Umm—I almost [rang] you at the office. I figured you'd be over there.

P: That's—that's exactly where I was heading.

W: Oh, you were? Well, you haven't lost your employment.

P: No, not yet. But if there's an indictment, there's gonna be trouble. They haven't decided whether I'd be suspended or what, you know.

W: Uh huh.

P: What would happen.

W: Well, you okay otherwise?

P: Yeah—

W: What does that mean?

P: Well, it's just very difficult.

W: What day did you go before the grand jury?

P: Tuesday and Wednesday.

W: Tuesday and Wednesday. Well, I assumed if I broke all contact with you, or basically all contact with you, and that they knew you weren't in contact with me, they'd drop the whole thing.

P: Well, unfortunately, they haven't.

W: Well, we'll have to see what happens. I'll—I'll still, you know, stick by the agreement, though. If they indict you I'll come in.

P: Oh—

W: Well, I think it sounds silly, too. (*Laughs*)

P: Well, unfortunately, being an attorney, one realizes, you know, the seriousness of it.

W: Yeah, well—

P: Even, you know, one credible witness—

W: Well, I can only tell you that other than one night, I have not been out at two o'clock in the morning. And the night that I was out at two o'clock in the morning, I was with—I think there were five guys and three girls.

P: Well, is it possible—is it possible that one of those girls—

W: They're all shorties.

P: Well, what if they were sitting in a car?

W: They don't look that way. They're not pretty.

P: Thanks.

W: They're not pretty; they're ugly girls. And besides, I wouldn't be at a filling station at two o'clock in the morning.

P: Hmm.

W: Well dear, anything I can do?

P: No, I guess not. Not unless you want to turn yourself in.

W: Well, I definitely do, but I can't meet you on the steps at 26th and California today. I'm a little out of—

P: Hmm?

W: I'm a little out of the area. *(Beep)* So dear, that was the end of my change.

OPERATOR: It's now three minutes. Signal when through.

W: Thank you, dear. All right, love?

P: Okay.

W: Talk to you. Anything else?

P: Yeah, if you want, well, you can always call me at the office.

W: Okay. Will do.

P: Okay.

W: Bye, love.

P: Bye.

That evening Walker wrote in the same tone, mixing endearments with faint menace.

This is to advise you, Marcy—
that you will not like this letter any better than I enjoy writing it.

There was a note of fear in your voice today, something I never like to hear from someone I love. It makes me uneasy. Oh, I know what you must be going through, and yet, it all did not come as a complete surprise. Either ride it out or get off the trolley, ma'am.

Next, the missing purse really pissed me off, for I want you to have that, not to mention some of the notes therein could be dangerous—more to you than to myself. (I already know what I am in for and accept it.) Something about two secretaries calling the police and turning it over leaves me flat, nevertheless, I will accept that they did, and now they must accept what I do to people who piss me off. Therefore, if you like or have any love for either of the young ladies involved you might suggest they are in trouble with me. No, I shall not come back to harm them, however, I have made two phone calls (one to a Stone connection) and I am sure the matter will be resolved.

I can only say this, had you not hesitated when I told you to go pick it up this would not have happened. Each time you pause to play your role of equal time, we never get together or something goes astray. In the future, until our future is solved—jump when I say jump or get off the trolley, ma'am.

Next, I wonder why you were so late in going over to the office, which naturally makes me think you must have had a date or been out late the night before, which troubles me. Yes, I am jealous of you.

Ohhhhhhhhh, I could go on and on with what is bothering me, and yet, it ain't fair to you. No need of you catching it from both ends.

Yes, I will keep my end of the deal tonight. I am at the Kiandra Lodge, I will have cocktails in the Old English Pub and dinner in the Bully III—and no one will capture me for, darling, no one will recognize me. The room is not in a man's name and will therefore be passed over (eat your heart out, I am true blue and will stay that way if I don't have any more phone conversations like today). While I do not know whether you have been skiing or not, I can assure you it is next to impossible to recognize anyone who is not hiding their identity let alone someone who is doing so. I am going to love this eve.

Of course, I have packed my clothing in a car which was just picked up today and sometime after dinner I shall depart the area. Nevertheless, I gave you the first hot information of where I am and have been, therefore, this should take you off the hook and make a record of your being cooperative. Under other cover I am sending you information of who helped me in the Chicagoland area, and it will be interesting to see what you do with it, Marcy.

As for the other letter herein, I was mailing it and a bunch of others to a mutual secretary acquaintance, however, since those types are not dependable, plus it makes no difference whether I conceal where I am or not—what the hell, I ripped the package open and dropped 'em in the first box.

Interestingly enough, there was no 'I love you' in our telephone conversation, and when I told you it was impossible for me to talk on my end, all that comes forth from your end was long pauses and silence. It was either I force the talk or there was none.

All right—that is all the small stuff I have to get off my chest. Shall we move on in the field of big things?

If we continue like this, I am going to be captured and you under trial and all it brings. Interestingly enough, the first outing with the Illinois State Police found me making a deal for a small son who they were holding, and this time it appears they have selected you for the hostage. With a threat of an indictment over your head I am expected to come forth and surrender myself to save you, huh? I do not like it one bit. Went for that once. You are already in trouble, and you and I both know we never met in any filling station at 2 A.M. or any other place, for that matter, therefore I can only wonder what you hope to salvage by staying close and doing your thing in good ol' Chicago. Either come with me or get off the trolley, ma'am. The sound of fear in your voice did not excite me.

For the moment, I am going off—provided I make it tonight—to get things moving, and I will call you in a few days for a positive answer that encompasses statements and not long pauses and a lot of silence along the line. I will not tell you when, where, how or the time—but I will pull it off, that I assure you, my darling.

The time has come for you to stop promising me one thing and still leaving a bridge open for yourself back to the nice world. In for all, or out to face a world that has you guilty already.

I love you, Marcy, and we can make it together or we would not be in this position we now find ourselves. Just remember that they are using you to try and catch me. They may call it the Grand Jury or whatever. But here I sit in a suite at the Kiandra Lodge with plans to have some drinks I do not need, and a dinner I will not enjoy, and then drive all night to get to an airport and fly halfway across the nation to find myself another safe spot.

I love you and miss you—I'll call in a few days.

What Marcy called "this mis-identification thing" had occurred at a Standard station on North LaSalle Street. An attendant, James Mager, said he had been pumping gas at the all-night station on February 5 when, around 2:00 A.M., a man and a woman drove up in a yellow Karmann Ghia. While the woman, who stayed in the car, paid for the gas—less than five dollars worth—the man ran into the station and emptied the cash register. He waved Mager inside with a gun, jumped back into the car, and the pair sped off.

When Swalwell showed Mager pictures of five men, including Walker, Mager identified Walker as the robber. When Swalwell showed pictures of five women, Mager picked out Marcy. And, as Marcy had pointed out to Walker on the phone, her voice tinged with the fear he hated hearing, it only took one credible witness.

But the gas station incident became little more than an entry in Swalwell's long narrative report because, very soon, Marcy had begun to cooperate with the police, turning over Walker's communiqués and passing on assorted details, such as the information that the Valentine's Day gifts she'd received—the watch and the books, in the black purse—had been bought at the Dunhill of London shop on North Michigan. The gas station question also became submerged in the broader question of Marcy's relationship with Walker and the specific question: Had she helped him escape?

Swalwell never swerved from his belief that she had. "No ifs, ands, or buts." He believed, furthermore, that at least at one point she had intended to run away with Walker. In the letter in which Walker furnished his list of eleven helpful friends, he had discussed his plan for sending Marcy money, in amounts of five hundred dollars at a time, half of which she was to use to make car payments and pay other bills, the rest to be saved "for when we jump off." More than once, he reminded her to be sure her passport was in order.

Marcy always discounted those letters. "I don't think one could ever believe one single word Walker said," she declared. "Absolutely nothing. He was a very imaginative person."

"Some of the stuff I did might not have been too bright," Marcy conceded, "but there's a line one has to draw. Walker had made vague, amorphous threats about escaping, when he knew his appeal was being denied, and my answer to him was always 'That's not the way to go about it.' To say I helped him escape is not only ridiculous, it's pure crap. Bullshit!"

And even that question became secondary to the matter of catching Walker, as the trail led westward and tensions in Chicago eased. The Corrections men were not sitting around Marcy's apartment with shotguns anymore; Marcy was not indicated by the grand jury.

On the day the Pietrusiak car was recovered behind Dominic's Market in Park Ridge, the State Bureau of Identification notified Sergeant Lamb of the Illinois State Police in Aurora that the fingerprints found on the drinking glass on the Pietrusiak's kitchen sink were the left index finger and left thumb prints of Gerald Daniel Walker, ISB1049194. Sergeant Lamb said that although he had heard Walker was in Vail, Colorado, they definitely felt he would return to Illinois. The State's Attorney's office issued a warrant charging said person with burglary, auto theft, and theft.

Bob Swalwell, feeling a little more desperate than he cared to admit even to himself, went back to research his four-year-old Walker file. Although, by this second time around, he felt he had come to know Walker "better than I knew myself," he dug through all the old reports and documents again, till he virtually had them memorized. DATE OF BIRTH: August 10, 1931. DRINKS OF CHOICE: martinis, or gin and Fresca. HOBBIES: sailboating, ice-boating, collecting antiques. RELIGION: "bad-weather Catholic," which Walker had explained to a prison sociologist meant that when the weather was too bad for sailing, he went to church. Describing his family, Walker had called his wife Edna "as much of a wife as anyone could want"; his son Drew "the most beautiful boy in the world"; and his own parents, Virgil and Irene, as "cold, rigid people" who had given him many material things but not the personal attention he'd craved.

Both the sociologist's report and a pre-sentence investigation report by a probation officer agreed that Walker could be personable indeed. Probation officer Fred Connally, Jr., cited Walker's "friendliness" and his ability "to relate easily to strangers," describing him as "intelligent, very articulate, and, under the circumstances, extremely cooperative." Reading that old report, Swalwell couldn't help feeling that not the least persuasive proof of Walker's ability to relate to people was its closing section, in which the probation officer quoted Walker's goal in life, as stated by the subject: ". . . to convince people that material things are not the most important in life, but acceptance."

Six months later, though, when the prison sociologist, Wayne Michels, had interviewed Walker, the charm had apparently worn thin. Describing Walker as "articulate, clever, manipulative," the report pointed out that while "superficially, he appears cheerful and optimistic and he is probably quite gregarious socially . . . , this is an egocentric individual who describes himself in an almost grandiose manner, and it is apparent that status is particularly important to him. It is likely that beneath his facade of grandiosity lies a very poor self-concept.

"A significant aspect of this man's personality is the ease with which his emotions are stimulated and the extent to which he acts out his feelings in an impulsive manner. Diagnostically, the impression is that this is an anti-social personality. . . .

"Although this individual appears to be open and gregarious in his social relationships, it is felt that this is a facade . . . his underlying personality structure is basically sociopathic and he has little or no regard for the feelings of others, including his wife and child. Because of his drive, in addition to a manipulative ability, he has experienced occasional brilliant success in the business world; however, this performance has not been consistent over the years and it is doubtful whether this performance can be consistent unless there is a basic change in personality structure within this individual. There is an underlying element of rage and anger within the inmate which occasionally surfaces and results in impulsive and aggressive overt behavior. This rage undoubtedly has its roots in his relationships with his parents during his early formative years. . . .

"This individual is considered to be potentially very aggressive and perhaps homicidal."

One sentence in the report, from an evaluation of Walker by the Psychological Screening Board, particularly interested Swalwell, since it confirmed what he'd felt and thought about Walker as soon as he'd begun tracking him, long before he'd read anybody's reports. "Although he gives lip service to societal values, little internalization of these has occurred."

The psychologists had taken the words right out of Swalwell's mouth, though Swalwell's words were plainer: "A man who could shoot you, then sit down and eat his lunch right beside your body. A bad seed."

"We pick up the pieces, then we deal with the pieces."
Some of the pieces.

On Valentine's Day, a man using Taylor Wright's American Express card rented a bright blue Chevrolet Impala at Capitol Rent-a-Car, part of the Hertz system, on North Nineteenth Street in Omaha, Nebraska. He gave his home address as Benton Harbor, Michigan; his local address as the Blackstone Hotel; his firm as Zipco. When the week was up and the car wasn't back, the car rental people called Benton Harbor. Mrs. Taylor Wright said her husband had been beaten and robbed, and his billfold with his American Express card was still missing, and he had certainly not rented any car in Omaha. The Hertz manager called the Douglas County Attorney's office, which issued an arrest warrant for John Doe.

Half a dozen rooms at the Hilton Inn in Omaha were burglarized in mid-February. Richard S. Powell, an insurance salesman from San

Bernadino, California, who was in town for meetings at his home office, Mutual of Omaha, lost his green attaché case. His partner, Scott Johnson, lost a calculator.

The blue Chevy Impala was eventually found in the parking lot of the Sheraton Inn on Quebec Street in Denver, near the airport. It contained an empty soft drink can, one glove, a partially empty bag of doughnuts, and a pair of men's slacks covered with a reddish-brown substance, either mud or blood. The car keys were missing. Between February 14 and 17, it had been driven 1,040 miles.

On February 17, a man checked into Room 310 at the Sheraton on Quebec Street. He used Larry Burbage's American Express card, giving a home address in Evanston, Illinois. Under MAKE OF CAR he wrote "Mercury" and he listed a Colorado plate. Under COMPANY he wrote "Self-employed."

On February 18, that man checked out. Two Sheraton clerks, Mary Bittle and Sharon Reffel, remembered him. Mary Bittle thought he had acted very arrogant. Sharon Reffel said he had left the hotel with a tall blond woman, five foot eight or five foot nine, maybe thirty years old.

That weekend, a man used the same Burbage American Express card at a Hertz rental office in Denver. He showed a valid Georgia driver's license and said he would be keeping the car one week. The car he rented was brand-new, only 248 miles on the odometer, a four-door Ambassador. The car was yellow, with brown trim.

On February 21, a man presented the Larry Burbage credit card at a Sears Roebuck store in Albuquerque, New Mexico.

> Sunday/18th . . . 11:30 P.M.
>
> Yes, I did say Albuquerque, for the International Hot Air Balloon Races. Which really were not much, so to speak. You put out much more hot air across a hospital bed than they did across forty miles of countryside. But then, they do go, and thus far you have been no-go, therefore, one must assume you are equally exciting. . . .
>
> I am about ready to dash out to an all-night gas station and see if someone is awaiting me. At least that seems to be the game plan in the Chicagoland area—who knows about Albuquerque?
>
> I don't expect too much from this town. It looks dull and not to my liking. However, the hotel is very nice and dinner was not all that bad.
>
> For some reason I have been having nagging thoughts about you all this day. I was really turned off over the telephone with you

yesterday—perhaps it was me and not you. I wait and wait and wait to call you, and then when I get you on the line I have all these dreams of what we are going to talk about, only to discover they are never mentioned. Perhaps I am guilty of not taking the situation as seriously as you do, therefore, I am more on a lark and you are struggling to keep your head above the level of what is respectable. I could give a shit less what happens or does not happen, I suspect.

Already I have had enough kicks to keep me going for five more years, if they snag me tonight. . . .

But they did not.

CHAPTER
SEVEN

"IF SOMEONE WANTS to hurt you," Officer Stien told Hope when she was booked at the Beverly Hills station, "this is the safest place you could be." But she didn't feel safe, lying on the narrow bed in her cell, listening to the night rain. She was afraid for the children; they had lost Bill, and when they woke up in the morning, they would find her gone, too. Or maybe they wouldn't wake up; she felt sure Taylor wouldn't kill them, but a bomb under the house . . . Or maybe her parents would be shot, and the children would wake up to find a living room scattered with dead bodies.

And she was afraid for herself. She was the only prisoner on the women's floor, and she clearly remembered Taylor's warning that "they" are all over, even in police departments and doctors' offices, even in prisons. So at one o'clock in the morning, when her door was suddenly unlocked and someone said, "Your attorney is here," she was instantly tense. She had never seen the man before in her life.

But when the tall, distinguished-looking, gray-haired man began to talk, she felt more confident. He didn't say much, because in his experience, he'd found that jailhouse conversations were not as private as a compact, six-by-eight-foot room would lead one to believe. He told her briefly who he was; he listened briefly to what she had to say. He told her to make no more statements to the police; he told her to get some sleep and that everything would be taken care of in the morning. *Thank God, somebody's been brought in who knows what the hell's he's doing,* Hope thought as she crawled back under the blanket.

Ned Nelsen had a solid reputation for knowing what he was doing. He had practiced criminal law in Los Angeles for more than twenty years, starting with a murder case when he was fresh out of the University of Southern California law school and working as a protégé of the famous trial lawyer, Grant Cooper. He'd won that case and, in the two decades since, no one Ned Nelsen defended had ever been convicted of murder, not even the man he'd defended shortly before he met Hope, a man who'd killed his brother-in-law by shooting him right between the eyes with a .38 at a distance of three feet. Even though the dead man had been unarmed, and the man with the gun knew he was unarmed, Ned's client pleaded self-defense and the jury had acquitted him.

Not long after Hope went away with the police, Van had reached Ned Nelsen at home. The attorney listened to Van and Honey and agreed to talk with Hope. Ned Nelsen seldom declined to defend anyone, although sometimes, as he pointed out, "when I explain the fee structure, they decide to seek representation elsewhere." His fee structure was not difficult to explain: a twenty-five thousand dollar retainer and one thousand dollars a day for the services of Nelsen and his young associate, Tom Breslin; or six hundred dollars a day for Breslin alone.

Van didn't know Ned Nelsen personally, but he knew his professional and social credentials. Ned lived in a gracious old house in the Hancock Park section of Los Angeles, with his beautiful wife and their beautiful teen-age daughters, where he presided with urbane charm at gourmet dinners he cooked himself. He was a dedicated hunter—as mementos of a recent safari in Kenya, he carried an elephantskin briefcase, and the seven-foot tusks were mounted above the double doors of his dining room. As a chef, his specialty was venison chili. He'd once cooked a dinner of wild Canadian goose for seventy people. At the time he met Hope, he was making final preparations for an annual charity dinner at the Beverly Wilshire Hotel, an invitational, black-tie affair which, as chairman, he orchestrated through nine courses and half a dozen wines. There would be champagne with pâté of pheasant and smoked wild mallard duck; consommé with sherry; Montana trout poached with bay shrimps and served with Chardonnay; grouse with wild rice and Pinot Noir; sherbet; saddle of venison; artichokes stuffed with chestnut purée, Cabernet Sauvignon; fruit, Brie, and port. In his quiet, paneled office, Ned Nelsen had a big glass jar containing a million dollars, shredded.

Ned Nelsen was not as sanguine, though, as he'd sounded when he visited Hope. Although he didn't think she had killed Bill Ashlock—she had no motive, he pointed out, and while prosecutors didn't need to show motive, things usually didn't hang together without one—he was concerned about the two days she had spent at her house with the man named Taylor, giving him backrubs, making no overt attempt to escape or to call the police or her parents or to call for any assistance at all. He had to tell Honey and Van there was evidence implicating Hope and that if Taylor didn't turn up, she would be in enormous trouble. Most of all, Ned Nelsen wished he had been summoned earlier, before Hope had rambled on to the police for two-and-a-half hours about an intruder. "I would have had a heart-to-heart talk with her about just exactly who this stranger was," Ned said with wry understatement.

Even with the unusual activity surrounding the arrest of a female murder suspect in the middle of the night, the Beverly Hills police station was hushed, compared with the scene up north. All over Tulare County, it seemed, detectives and deputies were being roused from their beds by shrieking telephones.

Sgt. Henry Babcock and Detective Ralph Tucker left Porterville shortly after midnight, heading down the freeway to Los Angeles. At the ranch house, ablaze with light, Deputy Michael Scott was making two continuous chalk lines outlining the trail from the living room, through the kitchen, to the victim's body in the bedroom. He dusted for prints and was able to produce and lift latent fingerprints in different areas of the house, from different items. He collected a number of things and tagged them as evidence, including a balled-up piece of white adhesive tape found in a yellow trash can in the kitchen, about halfway down in the can. He saw a Band-Aid stuck inside the ball, with what appeared to be hairs.

At 3:20 A.M., Detective Jack Flores, who had been standing by the door of the bedroom where the body lay, for more than three hours, was relieved of that duty. He left the house and walked across the orange grove to talk with Jim Webb. The Webbs were still up, and Flores asked Jim to relate, in his own words, what he knew about all this.

Jim Webb started with Friday night when, he said, he and Teresa and the kids had come home late, around 11:30. They'd seen a car parked at the big house and some dim lights on inside, but nobody moving around.

Early Saturday morning, Jim said, when he left for work around six o'clock, he saw another car parked at the house, a late model Lincoln, white, with either a dark blue or a black top.

After work on Saturday, Jim went by his mother's house on Cottage

Street in Porterville to visit with his brother, Junior Edward, who was up from Ventura with his wife Betty and her sister Sharon, and Junior Edward's oldest boy and Sharon's girl, and his other brother Gerald from Fresno. Gerald and Ed told Jim they'd been up at the ranch looking at the cattle and some people there had asked the Webbs to saddle a horse for them. When he heard that, Jim drove on up to the ranch with one of his brothers and talked with a young woman he knew as Hope—he didn't know her married name. He said she told him that a man there from the *Los Angeles Times* wanted to take pictures and they needed a saddle for the horse. When Jim couldn't find the key to the tack room, he called Teresa, down at his mother's, to ask if she knew where the key was.

Teresa said she didn't know, so Jim called Hope to tell her he couldn't find the key and could it wait till the next day. She said no, that the fellow from the *Times* had to go back that afternoon and he wouldn't be there the next day. Hope told Jim her mother had given her a key to the tack room, and she asked him to come over and take a look to see if it was among the keys she had. Jim said he'd gone over and knocked on the door and was introduced to two men. One fellow was introduced as a photographer from the *Los Angeles Times*. Jim didn't remember his name; tall, six feet, maybe six one or six two, kind of dark brown hair, maybe sandy brown, well-dressed, wearing a dark leather coat. The other fellow was shorter, with curly dark brown hair, about twenty-five to thirty years old. His name was Bill.

Jim said those two men, and Hope, were the only three people he saw at the ranch all weekend.

Jim and his brother went around to look at the cattle and when they came back, about forty-five minutes later, the horse was tied up in front of the house and the people weren't around. Jim put the horse back to pasture, then the Webbs left to go down to his mother's house in Porterville to look at slides of Jim's vacation, and as they were driving out, they met the Lincoln that Jim said he'd seen early that morning, coming up the drive toward them. Jim backed up and let it pass. He saw three people in the car, but he couldn't say for sure who they were.

When Jim and Teresa and the kids got home about nine Saturday night, they saw both cars parked by the house, the Vega and the white Lincoln, and lights on in the big house.

When Jim left for work early Sunday morning, around 6:00, both cars were still there, and when he got home around 7:30 that evening, the Lincoln was gone. Same thing all day Monday: the Vega parked by the side of the house, one light on, no sign of anybody. Same thing Tuesday morning. Same thing Tuesday evening, when he came home from work, and by then, Jim said he was getting concerned, because it was pretty unusual not to see anybody around once in a while. He asked his wife if she'd seen anybody around. She said no. He asked the kids. They said no. He tried the buzzer between his house and the main house, but no one answered. He dialed the ranch number on the regular phone, let it ring six or seven times, but no one answered.

He walked over to the house and knocked, but no one answered. He said he'd peered into the house, whether it was right or not he didn't know, but anyway, he peered through the window and noticed a blanket laying on the couch, kind of a spread or something. There was some sort of a dim light on; he thought it was a bathroom light.

He went home, got his flashlight, came back, and shone it in a couple of windows—the living room window, the corner front bedroom, and the side door into the kitchen—but he didn't see anything.

He said he didn't really want to call Hope's father because he'd heard he'd had a heart attack, but he felt that by this time he should. So he called Information and got his number and gave him a call. Hope's mother answered. He asked if she'd heard from her daughter. He said Hope's mother replied, "She just walked in." Jim told her he was concerned about the car sitting in one spot all the while, and nobody around. He said Hope's mother told him there'd been a terrible tragedy and she would call him back.

Almost as soon as he hung up the phone, Jim said, his other phone rang. It was Mr. Nick Doughty, one of the other owners, who kind of ran the ranch, and who Jim guessed was his boss. Jim said Mr. Doughty was calling to see how things were with Jim.

Jim told him about his conversation with Hope's mother. Mr. Doughty told him to hang on, that he would call him back. When he called back, he said he had talked to Honey and Van and they had a problem. Jim said Mr. Doughty told him it was not the ranch's problem and it was not Jim's problem and he advised Jim to take the wife and kids and go someplace for the night. Jim said that sounded good to him, he was sure ready to leave, but Hope's mother had said she would call him back. Jim told Mr. Doughty he would lock all the doors and stay inside his own house.

Jim said at 9:30 Van called to say his daughter had told him there had been an intruder in the house and someone had been shot and it was a Mafia sort of thing, and the whole family had been threatened. Van said he was going to call the Beverly Hills police. Jim and Van talked about whether to call the Porterville police or the Porterville sheriff's office, and finally Jim called the sheriff's office himself.

"That's about all I can say up to now," Jim Webb told Detective Flores. Later he said more.

Hope woke early, hearing someone walking in the hall outside her cell. "Hello," she called.

A man came to the door. "Are you starting up so early?" he yelled.

"Well, the officer last night said if I needed anything to just call out," Hope explained.

"What do you need?"

"I'd like a match," Hope said.

The man brought a pack of matches. "Don't throw cigarettes on the floor," he warned.

"I am not accustomed to throwing cigarettes on the floor," Hope replied, in a tone her mother would have recognized. "Furthermore, you don't know who I am or why I am here."

After the matches, he brought her a breakfast tray of dry corn flakes with no milk, and black coffee in a metal cup so hot she couldn't pick it up.

Downstairs, Sergeant Babcock and Detective Tucker, who had arrived from Tulare County around 4:00 A.M., were talking with Officers Stien and DeMond and their boss, Lieutenant Mann. The young officers had listed three subjects in the case:

Subj. #1: MASTERS, Hope, WF, 31 years
Subj. #2: TAYLOR, Tyler
Subj. #3: WM, 6'0, 185, brn hair shoulder length and straight, mustache or goatee

Stien and DeMond told the story that Subject #1 had told them about a Mafia killer who had killed the victim and was supposed to have killed her and her children. All the officers discussed why a hired killer who had been hired to kill her, her children, and the victim would have let her live after killing the victim. They also discussed, at length, the fact that Subject #1, who was a witness to the alleged crime, had left the scene and had not reported the crime for approximately two days. Stien and DeMond said Subject was vague on the male who had been driving a Lincoln Continental and had driven her back to L.A., and could say only that his name was Taylor or Tyler and that he was a reporter or photographer for the *Los Angeles Times*. They said her parents "cannot or will not" identify the subject driving the Lincoln. The Beverly Hills men also told the Tulare men that Masters's attorney had been there to talk to her.

Sergeant Babcock telephoned Van and asked if he would come down to the station to make a formal statement. Van agreed, and he arrived quickly, just before 6:00 A.M., still crisply dressed in the suit he'd worn when he arrived home from the office the evening before, so businesslike and imposing that Babcock called him "sir," which Babcock did not always do when discussing a homicide.

"Are you agreeable to tell us what you know about the incident, sir?"

"I'm agreeable to telling you what I know about the incident," Van said carefully, "but you should know that the only things I know about the actual incident involving the death of a man, I got from my daughter."

Babcock nodded. "All right," he said. "Let's start from the beginning."

Van told how he had arrived home from work the evening before, to find his wife, and Hope, and a man whose name was Taylor, gathered in the living room. He described Taylor as a white man, around forty-five years old, about six feet tall, 185 pounds, with reddish-blond hair.

"Is he a friend of your daughter?" Babcock asked.

"No, he is not a friend of my daughter," Van replied. "In fact, I do not believe my daughter had ever met the man until he arrived at the ranch after the incident."

"Do you know what this man does for a living?"

"I can give you that only by what he said. It's my understanding that he writes articles, I suppose for either newspapers or magazines."

"Do you know why he arrived at the ranch if your daughter didn't know him?"

Van said the writer had gone up to the ranch to do a story about Bill.

Babcock frowned slightly. "This gentleman, Bill—I presume he's the deceased—was he a noteworthy person, famous, did he do something that would be newsworthy?"

"No, Bill himself was not noteworthy, as I recollect, but he was engaged in a line of business that involved motion pictures or theatrical business."

"That would be easy to find out," Babcock said. "All right, sir, going back now to what you were told about this incident by your daughter?"

Van drew a deep breath. "Well, the story that my daughter told, since she was in a considerable state of agitation still, was an extraordinarily lengthy story, but let me just give you the extreme highlights, and then you can ask me to fill in if you want.

"As I understand it, my daughter and Bill got to the ranch on Friday. She said nothing to me of what they did on Saturday during the day, but she did say that she lay down in one of the bedrooms to take a nap on Saturday afternoon. And she requested him to wake her up in time to play a card game."

Babcock interrupted. "This was told to you by your daughter?"

"Yes."

"Personally?"

"Yes."

Babcock nodded. "All right. Go ahead, sir."

"To play a card game, or something of that nature," Van continued. "She did go to sleep, but she was awakened, not by Bill, but by the—this individual—the intruder—let me call him the intruder—who was pawing at her and grabbing at her. And she was able to squirm out of his grasp, and she called for Bill. She ran into the living room, which adjoins the bedroom. This is a very small house we're talking about. She ran into the living room and saw Bill lying on the couch, ran over to him, and, calling his name, took him by the shoulders and shook him. And she said she noticed his head wobbling as she shook him, and while she was shaking him, the intruder was either coming up behind her, or started to, and he said to her, 'No, he can't help you. He's dead.'

"He said that several times, perfectly commonly. And finally, when my daughter stopped shaking Bill, the intruder then said, 'Look at your arms.' And she looked at her arms and noticed that they were covered with blood. I didn't mention that this took place during the nighttime hours, Saturday night or Sunday morning, depending on what the clock said. My daughter was completely unable to tell us about the time. She did say that the individual was with her for a matter of four to six hours and that the individual left while it was still dark."

Babcock cut in again. "How did he leave? Did she say?"

Van frowned. "No, I don't believe she said. You mean by vehicle or walking out? She didn't, and if she said, I've forgotten. Shall I continue?"

"Sure, please."

"The man grabbed her. He tore off her clothes and he either attempted to rape her or he did rape her. I'm fuzzy; I'm unclear on which of those two events actually took place. At one point, whether it was a subsequent assault or whether it was the first assault I don't know, but she said that the man started to rape her but stopped when she showed no interest. She —the man tied her up, I presume earlier, with adhesive tape, with her hands behind her back and also, I believe, put adhesive tape on her feet.

I do not recall whether my daughter said she was tied to the bed. I'm sorry, I've forgotten about that.

"Apparently she and the intruder had lengthy conversations in which this intruder told her, among other things, that he was doing the job on a contract, that he was being paid thirty-six hundred dollars for doing the job." Van explained that the intruder told Hope that her two older children were to be killed, too, but not the baby, in case he showed up. He told Babcock the names of Hope's two husbands, though he didn't know where either of them lived in Los Angeles.

"My daughter said that somehow or other she was able to persuade the man not to kill her."

"What kind of weapon did this man have?" Babcock asked.

"My daughter said that he had a handgun with a great big barrel, that the man tried to push the barrel of the gun into her mouth and the barrel was too big to go in."

"Then what happened?" Babcock asked.

"Well, the man left, somewhere at a time that my daughter could not identify. She could only say that it was four to six hours after she was awakened."

"Then what happened?"

"Well, I don't want to tell you anything that I'm surmising," Van said carefully. "The next incident that my daughter mentioned to me was when Taylor or Tyler, the photographer-writer, arrived at the house."

"What time did he arrive, according to her?"

"She has no idea at all, but at this stage of the game, Taylor, who was present in my house last night, as I told you, picked up the story. He says that he arrived at the house around eleven or twelve o'clock Sunday morning, and the first thing I can remember him saying was that all he could hear were screams coming out of the house. Yells. He went into the house and then saw Bill, the deceased, lying on the couch, but didn't pay any attention to that and followed down the screaming to where my daughter was lying on the bed, bound with the adhesive tape.

"My daughter wanted to get up and go to the telephone—I've forgotten who she was going to call—but in order to do so she would have had to go through the living room. And she was in a state, according to Taylor, of extreme agitation—I suppose that means hysterics—and she would not go into the living room where the body was. Taylor tried to persuade her to go, and asked what he was supposed to do about it."

"He was telling you this, right?" Babcock said. "He told you this, right?"

"With her present," Van said. Babcock nodded again.

"He asked her what he was supposed to do," Van continued. "And she said, 'Move the body.' She said, 'Get Bill out of there.' So Taylor did move the body. He put the body on a bed in one of the other bedrooms. I don't know which one." After that, Van said, Taylor and Hope left the ranch in Taylor's car.

"Do you know where this gentleman is now?" Babcock asked.

"No, I don't."

"Well, eventually we'll contact him," Babcock said. "Of course, it's a little bit unusual for the man originally to be involved in contacting the police and then make himself scarce. Something's wrong there." He paused. "Does your daughter own any weapons, any firearms?"

"She not only doesn't own them, they frighten the hell out of her," Van said emphatically.

"How about your wife?"

"She has the same attitude toward guns that my daughter does. She's scared to death of them."

"Do *you* own any firearms?"

"Yes, I do," Van said firmly. "I own a .12-gauge shotgun, a .45 automatic, and a .38 automatic and, incidentally, none of these guns has been fired, as I recollect, for ten to fifteen years. I also won, however, a .22 rifle that I take up to the ranch for the purpose of trying to shoot ground squirrels, and I also own a .22 Colt Woodsman handgun." Van explained that he had bought the two automatics more than thirty years before, when he had been in the navy, and that the shotgun, the Colt, and the rifle had been gifts.

"All right," Babcock said. "I just got about two or three more questions to ask." Actually, he had four.

"One, has your daughter ever been arrested, and if so, for what?"

"My daughter has never been arrested, to my knowledge, other than for traffic violations."

"Number two. Why do you think the man let her live?"

When Van did not reply promptly, Babcock leaned forward in his chair.

"Mind you, now," the detective reminded him, "you have a man who, at least coming from your daughter's lips to you, has been told that the man was paid to kill. The man sees a lady—a woman—a witness—who can identify him. Why—why didn't he kill her?"

"I cannot answer that question," Van said slowly. "If indeed he was a paid killer, as he said he was, then I have no answer for your question, and I'm every single bit as puzzled as you are."

"And another thing," Babcock pressed. "Why wait so long to report this crime?"

"The reason that my daughter gave me, and this was verified by Taylor, is because she had been told by the intruder, the killer, that she was not to report anything to the authorities, that he would be in touch with her and that he would let her know when, if ever, she could report to the authorities and that he was going to watch her and her family—namely me, her mother, and her children—and that if she did not obey his instructions, everybody would be killed.

"She was frightened into doing this and, uh"—uncharacteristically, Van stammered a little—"uh, let me just say editorially that I think it was a mistake, but on the other hand, you had a forty-five-year-old man going right along with it."

"Let me ask you this," Babcock said slowly. "Your own opinion, naturally. Do you think that possibly your daughter and this gentleman might be involved in the killing?"

"I—I—I—I think—"

"Think it's a possibility?" Babcock prodded.

"I think—I think it's absolutely inconceivable from any standpoint," Van said.

"You don't think it's conceivable that your daughter and this other gentleman would be involved in this killing as perpetrators?"

Van stopped stammering. He spoke very firmly.

"I think it would be absolutely inconceivable either one of them could possibly have been involved."

Hope's coffee cup had just cooled enough for her to handle it when the jailer came to pick up the tray. "Your attorney's here," he announced. Again, the man was a stranger; again, trembling slightly, she asked to see his identification.

Tom Breslin was feeling moderately cranky when he was led into the cell and the door locked behind him. He'd been awakened at home by Ned Nelsen, telling him to get on down to the Beverly Hills jail to talk to a woman named Hope Masters, that it was a homicide. Tom had spent an hour driving around, trying to find a shop open so early, so he could buy a notebook. He sat down on the edge of Hope's cot and regarded her sternly.

"Don't lie to me," Tom Breslin warned her. "The last person who lied to me got the death penalty!"

When he looked closely at his new client, though, he softened. In the harsh white light of the cell, he thought she looked awful—skinny, even gaunt, with huge purple circles under her eyes, very shaky, very scared. So he smiled his open, Irish smile and tried to put her at ease by joking about the decor of the cell, especially the open toilet, no lid, on the opposite side. "That's very picturesque, don't you think?"

Hope smiled a little, and Tom took out his new notebook. Before she began talking, he told her she should be very courteous to the police but she must not say anything more to them, anything at all. He did not have the heart to tell her she'd already said too much.

Van came home to pick up his guns. He took them down to the police station while Honey dressed, and when he returned, she went down to give her statement.

"May I see Hopie?" Honey asked. They said she could not.

"Does she need anything?" Honey asked. "How is she?"

They said she didn't need anything, that she was fine, and they reminded Honey she was there to give a statement.

Honey told the Tulare detectives about Hope arriving at her house the day before in a yellow car that Honey didn't recognize, and how terribly upset and distraught Hope had been as she told a story of a contract on their lives and tapped telephones, of a killer in the night who had told Hope her husband wanted her dead.

"She'd hesitated for a moment," Honey said, "because she's been married twice."

"Which husband?" Babcock asked.

"That's just what she said to him!" Honey exclaimed. "Which husband? Which husband?" She recounted to Babcock some of the conversation between Hope and the killer, conversation about the house keys. "You understand now, everything I'm telling you is just what my daughter has told me," Honey pointed out.

"Right," Babcock said.

"And I have every reason to believe her explicitly," Honey said firmly. "She's a very honest person. *Totally* honest."

Honey explained that the killer had told Hope that the baby was not supposed to be hurt, and in fact was not supposed to be there at all, because her husband was going to pick up the baby, and when Hope heard that, she had known which husband the killer was talking about.

"Which husband was he talking about?" Babcock asked.

"Tom Masters," Honey said.

Babcock merely said, "All right," and Honey continued with Taylor's account of his arrival at the ranch, moving Bill's body to the back bedroom and bringing Hope back to the city. She told how frightened they all had been, including Taylor. "He was obviously frightened for his life," Honey said. "He said he had been switching cars and doing all kinds of things to avoid being seen or being followed by these people. Taylor was obviously terrified." She told how Taylor had left to call the police, and how Van himself had then called. "He had a terrible time persuading anyone from the Beverly Hills police to come," Honey said tartly. She began to describe Taylor in detail—his boots, his glasses, and his unusual pipe— but she was cut short.

"Do you believe your daughter's story?" Babcock asked sharply.

"Completely. *Completely,*" Honey said. "Taylor, who seemed to be a very rational man, believed it completely, and even Van, when he came in—he believed it too."

"Why hasn't Taylor made himself available?" Babcock wondered.

"I don't know," Honey said. "Whether he was afraid to come back to the house for fear of these people killing him, or whether he was afraid for himself. He—he realized he had done a very stupid thing in moving the body and then not telling the police right away."

"Let me run through this now," Babcock said. "It sounds—well, let me run through it. First of all, the gentleman Tyler or Taylor, if that's his correct name, we know of no address on him, right? And he has not made himself known to the police of his presence, right?"

"He promised he would come back," Honey said plaintively.

Babcock could not contain his skepticism. "Let me ask you this," he said bluntly. "Do you think it would be likely for a Mafia-type professional killer to let the only witness to a murder live? It doesn't seem logical, does it?"

"No, it doesn't," Honey admitted, "except I think she convinced him that—" Babcock cut her off again.

"We're talking about a professional killer, right?"

"Right," Honey agreed.

"It doesn't seem logical, does it?"

"No, it doesn't," Honey said again. She looked at Babcock and clasped her hands fervently. "I think it's an absolute miracle."

Babcock looked at her, perhaps seeing her for the first time not just as a subject being interviewed, but as a mother. "We're not out here to persecute your daughter," he said, less sharply. "But we have a dead man on our hands."

All Dr. Hayes knew, when he got to Myers Chapel in Porterville, was that the body had a lot of blood on it. When he saw the small hole in the back of the head, apparently a gunshot wound, he sent the body over to the Sierra View District Hospital for X rays.

When the body was returned, Dr. Hayes began his autopsy at 4:10 A.M. He asked Sgt. Vern Hensley to photograph the body clothed, because of the pattern of the bloodstains; there was a great deal of blood, clotted and dried, on the shirt, both in front and in back; on the pants; on the hands; and in the victim's mouth. In fact, the chief source of blood seemed to be from the mouth.

Ted Goode of the funeral home staff helped Dr. Hayes undress the victim, then, and Sergeant Hensley took more pictures. Then Dr. Hayes put on surgical gloves and continued his work. He found no defense wounds, indicating no struggle—no markings on the knuckles, no hairs under the fingernails. From the discoloration of the body, he determined that the body had been in two positions: first, lying up against some solid object, then lying face down.

Because of the areas of the brain that were injured, and the massive bleeding, Dr. Hayes thought that death had been instantaneous. He concluded that the bullet had fractured the bones at the base of the skull and emerged through the palate. The bullet was fragmented. The head wound measured three millimeters in diameter and since it had seared edges, with no powder burns, he decided the gun had been fired at a minimum distance of two to three feet. He estimated the man had been dead from one to three days.

Lieutenant Becker of the Coroner's Division, whom Dr. Hayes knew from other autopsies, other cases, was standing by, but the doctor didn't know the other officers; unless someone was specifically helping him at an autopsy, he didn't pay any attention to the people wandering about.

Sergeant Hensley took the clothing as evidence, as well as seven small metal fragments and a hair sample. Dr. Hayes drew blood and sent it to the crime lab, where the analysis showed blood alcohol concentration of .23 percent, eleven or twelve drinks. He drew as much urine as he could, but there wasn't much, only 144 cc's, about a tablespoonful; that analysis showed a spot characteristic of morphine, which could have been present if the victim had taken codeine, heroin, or morphine within three days before the examination. The victim's stomach contained rice and some dark brown material, possibly beans, which had been in the digestive system one to five hours.

Dr. Hayes did not sign a death certificate. On the documents sent to the lab with the samples he wrote "John Doe."

The autopsy took two hours, about the usual amount of time, just as it was usual, Dr. Hayes reflected, for a homicide autopsy to be done at 4:00 in the morning. The only thing unusual in this case, to him, was the fine physical condition of the body. He had been told the victim was forty-three years old. "This man doesn't look like a man who is forty-three years old," Dr. Hayes told one of the detectives. He thought the man appeared much younger.

Hope and Tom Breslin were still talking when someone came to her cell door and announced that the Tulare police were ready to transport her up north.

Tom helped her as she got up, shakily, to her feet. He squeezed her hand. "Don't worry," he said. "And don't talk to anybody till you see me again." He walked downstairs with her, the guard leading the way, around to the parking lot behind the jail, where he introduced himself to the two detectives. "Mrs. Masters might want to talk to you while on the trip," Tom said, already aware of Hope's flair for talking nonstop. "But I've advised her not to talk, and I'd appreciate it if you don't discuss this case with her."

Sergeant Babcock brought out a pair of handcuffs. "Not too tight," Hope said. "My hands are really hurting." He snapped on the cuffs and led her to the back seat, where there were no door handles on the inside. He and Detective Tucker got in front, and they left Beverly Hills at 10:26 A.M.

Cliff Einstein kept thinking Bill would walk in any minute. They had an important layout to show this morning, and Bill couldn't possibly have forgotten. It was an important presentation, one Bill had been working on for weeks.

This morning, Wednesday morning, was the first time Cliff felt really concerned about Bill, even though he hadn't seen him since Friday afternoon. "Where's Bill?" someone had asked Cliff on Monday, when Bill hadn't come in, and although Cliff didn't know, he didn't think too much about it then. Bill had some vacation time coming and he'd talked about taking a three-day cruise some weekend, running into Monday. Bill had never before failed to tell Cliff when he'd be out, so Cliff thought maybe Bill had told him and Cliff had just forgotten.

Cliff had flown up to San Francisco Monday afternoon. When he got home early Tuesday evening, around 5:30, his wife said that Fran Ashlock had called, because Bill's friend Sandi had called Fran to ask if she knew where Bill was. Sandi had called Bill at his office, and when they told her he hadn't been in since Friday, Sandi got worried. She told Fran she was afraid maybe Bill had had an accident. Then Fran got worried.

When he got that message from his wife, Cliff was a little concerned too, but he didn't call anyone—for one thing, he didn't know whom to call, Fran, Sandi, or Hope Masters. "Well, when I go in tomorrow, I'm sure he'll be there," Cliff told his wife.

But Bill wasn't in Wednesday morning. Helen Linley said she'd tried to reach him on Tuesday, and Barry Carter from the art department told Cliff he'd called Hope's house a couple of times on Tuesday, but the maid told him Mrs. Masters couldn't come to the phone. When Barry asked the maid about Bill, the maid once said she didn't know where he was, but the other time, she said Bill was at the ranch. Then the production manager, Gene Wollenslegal, who lived near Bill's apartment, thought maybe Bill was sick, and he'd driven over to see whether Bill's car was in the garage. It wasn't, so they thought maybe Bill was still up at the ranch. Cliff thought the missing car didn't mean much, since he knew Bill was living mostly at Hope's, but he didn't have time to talk about it just then, because the client had arrived for the presentation.

Cliff thought Bill's layout looked magnificent: a large white board with a picture of a beautiful woman in the center, the woman wearing a sweetly serious look, holding a long-stemmed red rose. The white paper was bordered in black, with a bold black caption: WHAT IF SHE DIES FIRST?

Cliff was just describing the picture when the door to the layout room opened and one of the girls beckoned to him, urgently. Cliff excused himself and went out into the hall. "Bill's dead," someone said. "Helen's on the phone about it."

Cliff hurried down the hall into his own office, past Helen Linley who was talking on the phone, her face drawn with shock, trying to write down what the caller was saying. He picked up on the call from Hope Masters's father.

"Can you please tell me again what you just told my secretary?" Cliff asked.

"Bill Ashlock has been shot," Van said.

"Where? How? How did it happen?"

"At my ranch in Springville, which is near Porterville," Van said.

"When?"

"Sometime late Saturday night or early Sunday morning," Van said. "An intruder broke in, somehow got in." Cliff listened as Van told how the intruder had then grappled with his daughter. She fought off the intruder, Van said, ran to Bill for help, and found him dead, shot in the head.

"Who was this?" Cliff asked. "Who is he?"

"My daughter says he was a hired contract killer, and he gave her a rough time, but she finally convinced him to go away."

"How?"

"By telling him either that he already killed one person and that was enough killing, there was nobody there he should kill, or that he had the wrong family, it was a mistake."

"How is your daughter?" Cliff asked.

"She's in difficult shape now," Van said. "She's being held, having been the only one on the scene, the only one there." Van's voice was strained, but he spoke clearly.

"Do you have any idea who this could have been?" Cliff asked. "Somebody who was mad at Bill or something?"

"No," Van said, "but I want to make it clear it was our family he was after, not Bill. He was the innocent victim of something he wasn't involved in. Do you know anything about a photographer who might have been involved, or something?"

Cliff thought quickly back to Friday, and told Van what little he knew of the man who had come by to take Bill to lunch, the man who had interviewed Bill for three hours without taking notes. He wanted to talk further with Van, but Van said he had to hang up. He gave Cliff his office phone number.

Cliff looked in the personnel folder and found the name of Bill's brother in Columbus, Ohio. He called Robert Ashlock, then he left the office and got his car to drive over and tell Fran. He did not call Sandi.

When he finished talking with Cliff, Van called a man he knew at the *Los Angeles Times* and asked him to try to find out if a reporter named Taylor was doing a story on the ten most eligible bachelors around town.

Honey called a few close friends. She asked one of them to call around and tell everybody that the Chips luncheon had been canceled.

She had just hung up the phone when it rang.

"May I speak to Hope?" a man asked.

"She's not here," Honey said. "Who's calling?"

"This is Taylor."

"Oh, Taylor!" Honey cried. "Thank God you've called! Oh, Taylor, Hopie is in desperate trouble. She has been charged with murder."

"Well, I have been to see my lawyer," Taylor said calmly, "and he has taken my deposition. Where is Hope now?"

"They took her to Visalia."

"I'll see to it that they get my deposition right away," Taylor said.

"Oh, Taylor, please call the Beverly Hills police and let them know you exist," Honey begged.

"After the way they treated me last night, I'm not interested in wasting my time with them," he announced.

"But Taylor, they must talk to you. They are looking for you now. You are Hopie's only witness. You are the only one who can help her. What are you afraid of? Nothing can happen to you."

"Oh, yes it can, in the business I'm in," Taylor told her. "I'm not a national, and they can keep me from leaving the country."

"Will you please tell me where you can be reached?" Honey asked.

"No," Taylor said.

"Will you tell me your last name?"

"No."

"Then will you tell me the name of your lawyer?"

"No."

Honey began to cry. "Oh, Taylor, you can't do this. Taylor, Hopie is in such serious trouble, and the police need your testimony to clear her."

"I'm sorry," Taylor said. "How are the children?"

"They're all right," Honey said, "but they need their mother."

Taylor was silent for a moment. "How much is her bail?" he asked.

"It hasn't been set yet," Honey told him. "They will probably arraign her tomorrow."

"Oh, well, then," Taylor said lightly, "good-bye."

Honey screamed into the phone. "Don't hang up! Please don't hang up! You can't do this, Taylor. You have to help Hopie! Please help Hopie!"

"Will Van be in his office this afternoon?" Taylor asked calmly.

"Yes, I think so," Honey managed to say.

"I'll call him later," Taylor said. Then he hung up.

Honey found a tissue and stood for a moment in the kitchen, collecting herself, before she went into the den, where the children were watching television. She tried to keep her voice natural and easy. "Keith, do you know Taylor's last name?"

"Yes," Keith said. "Taylor Wright."

Hope was not in Visalia. She was taken first to the Porterville holding tank, after a drive she had thought she might not survive.

In the back seat of the police car, she was hunched over with pelvic cramps; her wrists were throbbing from the tight cuffs. Beyond the grill that separated the front seat from the back, she could hear the policemen talking; she was sure they were threatening her, indirectly. At first they had seemed pleasant and understanding. "I can understand what you did, it must have been self-defense," one of them said.

"No, no, it wasn't that way," Hope said. "Bill would never, never hurt me."

They talked some more, but when she wouldn't say anything about Bill, they seemed to get angry. "We'll just have to throw her in the hole and let the black dykes take care of her," one officer said loudly.

The car stopped then; she raised her head and saw that they were in the parking lot of the Ranch House, a restaurant along the freeway. "Oh, I have to go to the bathroom," Hope said.

"You have to stay in the car," one of the men told her. "What do you want to eat?"

"I'd just like a plain vanilla milkshake," Hope said. They locked the car, and she saw one of them enter the phone booth near the restaurant door.

In the hot stuffiness of the car, the midday sun beating on the roof, she felt dizzy and sick; she fell over sideways on the coats they'd put in the back seat with her. One of the men was very angry when he came back to the car. "Get off those coats. What do you think you're doing on those coats?" he yelled.

Hope pulled herself up and took the milkshake between her cuffed hands, but after one sip she thought she would vomit, so she just held it the rest of the way. The men got into the car and, before they drove off, one of them read her her constitutional rights. Then they said nothing more to her.

When they stopped the car and told her to get out, she didn't know where she was. They led her into a small cinderblock building, with barbed wire around the back.

"I have to go to the bathroom," she said again, and someone took her into a closetlike room with cement walls, a window covered with cardboard—no light—a toilet, and a combination drinking fountain-sink. Hope thought the room smelled like a year's worth of vomit and urine that hadn't been cleaned up. There was a bunk along the wall with a mattress on it, but because it was so dirty, Hope was afraid to lie down; she thought she might catch some disease, so she didn't use the toilet, either.

Outside the room, she could hear people talking. Twice she heard a phone ring and a man say, "Hope Masters is not here." She knocked on the door when she heard that, but no one came. *Don't be scared,* she kept telling herself. *You have an attorney and eventually someone will find you. Don't be scared.* She bunched her sweater into a ball and leaned her head against it and closed her eyes. After a while—she had no idea when— someone opened the door and told her to come out. She was fingerprinted and photographed, examined for needle marks, then handcuffed again and put back in the police car for the ride to the county jail.

Sergeant Hensley was tired by the time he took Hope Masters's fingerprints, and he wasn't finished for the day yet; he had to go over to the crime lab and start processing the evidence. When he'd finished helping with the autopsy, at dawn, he'd gone to the crime scene, help-ing Mike Scott and the other deputies. Scott had taken the photo-graphs, using a 35-mm Pentax until he dropped it and then had to use Jack Flores's Kodak. He took two rolls of color film from the Pentax and put it in the crime lab truck to be taken to the Main Drugstore for processing. Then he took black-and-white photos of everything he'd taken in color.

Besides the dusting for prints and the photographs, the officers were collecting evidence throughout the house, including bedding, suspected bloodstains from various locations, pieces of clothing, towels and wash-cloths, a first-aid kit, wadded tissues, and a yellow waste basket that had a white pillowcase with red stains on top of it and the ball of adhesive tape, wadded up, halfway down in the basket. When they were finished, Ser-geant Hensley had recorded forty-nine items taken into evidence and sent to the crime lab. Some items were marked directly, others put into containers, tagged and marked with a felt marking pen. Number 49 was listed as "one sheet and one mattress pad." Later Sergeant Hensley had to correct that. The mattress pad was an item of evidence, having been found beneath the body, but the sheet belonged to the people at Myers Chapel.

A tall, handsome woman smiled at Hope through the bars at the Tulare County Jail.

"Oh, I have to go to the bathroom, please," Hope said.

"You can use mine," the woman said. She led Hope to a small, im-maculate white bathroom and opened the door. *Oh, thank God,* Hope thought. *I can use a clean toilet. I can relax for a minute. I can wash my hands.*

Once again then, Hope was photographed and her fingerprints taken. She was given a set of clothing: a flowered flannel nightgown with a number on it, a pair of underpants, a pair of jeans, a light blue shirt and a sweatshirt, a pair of white socks, and rubber thong sandals.

The matron, Elisa Arenas, watched Hope as she took off her own clothes and slipped into the gown. She thought Hope seemed very upset, very tense and nervous.

"I'm going to ask to take you over to the hospital," the matron said. "I'm going to ask them to remove the handcuffs on the trip, and I'll take the responsibility."

"Aren't you afraid of me?" Hope asked. "If I did what they say I've done, wouldn't you be afraid of me?"

"No," the matron said. "I'm not afraid of you. I'm a good judge of people."

Still, Hope was loosely handcuffed for the ride to the hospital in the police car, with a man driving and Matron Arenas in the front seat, and Hope in the back. During the thirty-minute ride, Hope talked.

At the hospital, Hope and Elisa Arenas sat on a long bench in a waiting room jammed with people. Once again, the scene seemed unreal to Hope —sitting in a flannel gown, handcuffed, in a strange room filled with strangers. She had no idea of the time or precisely where she was; she only knew it was dark outside. Still, she felt safer in the hospital, a lot safer, than she had felt in the little Porterville jail. She felt here she was in a place with rules, with some kind of order. Only once, as she sat on the bench next to the matron, did she feel threatened, when a young man suddenly stood over her, holding out a Life Saver. He knew she couldn't take it because of the handcuffs, and he wanted to put it directly into her mouth. Hope bent her head toward the floor; she thought the mint might be poisoned.

"I hope the doctor will keep you here," the matron said. Hope wished that, too, but he did not. When Dr. John Wing Hing Wong examined her, with the matron present, he saw two small areas of what appeared to be adhesive tape marks on her left forearm, but he reported no bruises, no evidence of trauma connected with rape. After the pelvic examination, he said she could return to jail. "How long will it be before I know if I'm pregnant, or have a veneral disease?" Hope asked.

"About three months," the doctor said. Hope was aghast. "The doctors I've dealt with could tell you in about three days, or a week," she informed him. The doctor did not reply; he thought she seemed emotionally disturbed, and very talkative.

"I'm sorry the doctor didn't keep you, but I have no control over it," Elisa Arenas said. "Have you had a phone call?"

"No," Hope said.

At the jail, after midnight, she used the phone under a sign: WHEN YOU'RE BOOKED, ASK FOR YOUR PHONE CALL. When Honey heard Hope's voice, she began to cry.

"I don't have much time," Hope said. "Put Keith on the phone.

"Keith, listen to me," Hope said. "I just want you to know I'm in a regular jail, and I've seen a doctor, and I'm okay. Keith, listen to me. You have always been my sunshine boy, and I expect you to keep your brother and sister happy until I can get back to you. Will you do that for me, Keith?"

"Yes," Keith said.

"I love you," Hope said.

In the den at his grandmother's house, Keith hung up the phone and turned to his ten-year-old sister. "We're never going to see Mom again," Keith told her.

In the hallway at the jail, Hope hung up the phone. Then she leaned her face against the phone and began to cry.

Elisa Arenas put a hand on her shoulder. "Don't do this to yourself," she said gently. "I know how you feel, but don't let go. It isn't going to help you or them." Hope straightened up. "You have to come with me now," the matron said. They rode up in an elevator with no numbers on the buttons. "I'm going to put you in with a black girl, but she's okay," Arenas said.

"Could I please have a cell by myself?" Hope asked.

"No, single cells are for special cases," the matron said. She paused. "Now, I have to tell you that the other matrons might not be nice to you. But just remember that some of them are young and frightened. If it gets bad, just hold on and wait for me to come back."

"When will you be back?" Hope asked.

"I only work part time," the matron said. "I won't be back for three days."

The elevator stopped and the door slid open. They walked down a long corridor lined with cells, each cell with bars looking onto the corridor. Suddenly, as they walked along, there was screaming and yelling; Hope saw hands thrusting out of the tiny windows, waving, grabbing at her. One of the hands almost got her by the hair. She shrank closer to the matron.

About two-thirds of the way down the corridor, the matron stopped and took a key from her belt. She opened the door and Hope went in. Most of the yelling died down, as Hope passed each cell, except for the noise coming from a cell down at the end of the hall. Hope found out the woman in that cell was withdrawing from heroin; she heard her thrashing about, screaming and vomiting all through the night.

CHAPTER EIGHT

BEVERLY HILLS SOCIALITE HELD AT VISALIA IN RANCH SLAYING
(Los Angeles Times)
MYSTERY VEILS SOCIALITE ARREST *(Los Angeles Herald-Examiner)*
SOCIALITE BOOKED FOR MURDER *(Oroville Mercury-Register)*
SOCIALITE HELD IN SLAYING OF EXECUTIVE
(Santa Monica Evening Outlook)
SOCIALITE FACES MURDER CHARGE; VICTIM IDENTIFIED
(Visalia Times-Delta)
SOCIALITE DENIES GUILT IN SLAYING *(Fresno Bee)*
PROMINENTE DAMA DE SOCIEDAD PRESA EN TORNO A UN HOMICIDIO
(Los Angeles La Opinion)

BY MUTUAL AGREEMENT, the socialite was scrubbing the toilet and the sink with a bucket of disinfectant while her cellmate scrubbed the floor. When Hope was told the scrubbing had to be done twice a day, she winced, feeling a stab in her back. "Would it be okay with you if I do the toilet and sink and you do the floor?" Hope asked her roommate. "Sure," Vanessa said.

Hope liked Vanessa. When Hope was escorted into the cell Wednesday night, there were just the two of them in a cell with eight bunks and a toilet. But Vanessa explained that the cell would fill up over the weekend, when the hookers and junkies were rounded up, and she suggested that Hope take a lot of blankets before then, because later there wouldn't be enough to go around. In fact, Vanessa helped Hope pick out some of the best blankets, though they all had holes in them, Hope noticed.

"What's she in for, Vanessa?" a woman yelled from down the corridor. Nobody could see into anybody else's cell, but everybody seemed to know what was going on.

"Oh, leave her alone," Vanessa yelled back. "She's sick."

Some of the women on the floor were waiting to go to court; others were serving sentences. Vanessa told Hope she'd been in jail for two months, on a charge of stealing a car, and was waiting to talk to a public defender. She said she'd been working for a woman who was an alcoholic, taking care of the woman's children, without salary but with room and board and sometimes the use of the woman's car. Vanessa said she'd asked the woman if she could take the car and drive down to L.A. to visit her sister, that the woman had said okay and then had put out a stolen car warrant on her.

Vanessa was so friendly that Hope talked to her a lot.

Even with the extra blankets, Hope was freezing, even wearing the socks and the sweatshirt over her gown. She'd hardly slept. The woman down the end of the hall had screamed and vomited all night, the overhead lights glared all night, and, three times during the night, a guard strode down the corridor, running a gun over the bars on the cells, calling each inmate's name, over and over: "Vanessa! Answer me! Vanessa! Hope! Hope! Hope!"

The first time this happened, Hope sat up on her bunk, terrified, her heart pounding, but Vanessa told her not to worry about it, that the guards were just checking to make sure everybody was still alive. Once in a while, somebody managed to commit suicide; and not long before, she was told, a woman who had been brought in with broken ribs had screamed all night and been found dead in her cell in the morning; a rib had punctured her lung.

Only one good thing had happened Wednesday night, though at first it didn't seem good at all. Hope was sitting on the edge of her bunk, talking to Vanessa, when someone came and said, "Come on, your lawyer's here." Hope followed the guard into the corridor, down to the end, where she saw Tom Breslin standing with another man. She glanced at Tom, then stared at the man with him. He was huge. Not fat, but very big and muscular. He wore two or three diamond rings and a diamond bracelet. He looked very smooth and very menacing; to Hope, he looked exactly the way a Mafia hit man would look, so she turned, without saying a word, and ran back to her cell, where she huddled on the far end of the bunk.

She was brought out again and taken to a small, windowless room, where Tom and the big man were sitting, smoking. Again Hope shrank back. "It's okay," Tom told her, as he introduced Gene Tinch, a private detective whom Ned Nelsen had called in on the case.

"I'm dying for a cigarette," Hope said. Tom handed her a pack of Luckies, and soon the three of them were enveloped in smoke, talking.

Tom looked a wreck. After driving up from Los Angeles, he'd been driving all over Tulare County, getting what he called "the runaround" from the local authorities. At the District Attorney's office in Visalia, where he'd asked to see the arrest reports, he'd been told they were in Porterville. Nobody could tell him how to get to Porterville. When he found out—it was nearly an hour's drive—and got there, he was told the reports were at Visalia. Or, if not there, maybe at the printer's, being photocopied. When he and Gene tried to scout around at the ranch, they were turned away. But Tom told Hope not to worry, that they were checked into a nearby motel and he'd see her in the morning.

"Did you call Porterville this afternoon, looking for me?" Hope asked, remembering the calls she'd heard when she was in the dirty toilet, hearing someone say, "Hope Masters isn't here." When Tom said he hadn't called, Hope knew who the caller must have been.

Tom had heard only part of the long story from Hope at the Beverly Hills jail. Now she developed it further, but basically it was the same story of an intruder in the night, a man with a goatee, possibly Mexican, and the man who had rescued her, the man named Taylor.

"Try to get some rest," Tom told Hope. "I'll see you in the morning."

"Would you bring me some cigarettes?" Hope asked.

"Sure," Tom said. "And by the way, don't talk to your roommate. They could use her against you in court."

Very early on Thursday—Hope wasn't sure when, without clocks or windows—there was a tremendous, deafening noise, the slammer: forty cell doors being yanked open simultaneously and, when the women had stepped out into the corridor, being simultaneously slammed shut. At breakfast, she was given a spoon—no knife or fork—and an enormous amount of food: oatmeal, eggs, bacon, toast, pancakes, and coffee. Hope still had bad cramps; she was nauseated. "Oh, God, I can't eat any of this," she said to the trustee. "Could I just have a glass of milk?" The trustee said no milk in jail, and Hope didn't argue. She was afraid of the trustee, a short, squat woman who looked part Indian. Vanessa told Hope that trustees didn't get that job depending on how much they could be trusted, but depending on the length of their sentences. The short, squat woman was serving six months for permitting child abuse; her boyfriend had mutilated the sex organs of the woman's three-year-old son.

By 5:30 A.M., everybody was dressed and fed and the scrubbing was finished. There was nothing more to do. The trustees had TV sets and radios and sewing machines in their cells, but in the day cell used by the rest of the women, with eight benches bolted to the floor, and one table, there were no books or magazines, no TV, only one jigsaw puzzle on the table. Vanessa was doing the puzzle, and Hope started to work on it, until it occurred to her that Vanessa might not get another puzzle for a while and she probably wouldn't want to finish it real fast. So Hope went back to one of the other benches and just sat there. Down the hall, someone had set a fire in a cell; a few women were scooping water out of the toilets in their cells and talking through the pipes to the men on the floor below. Hope just sat there, waiting, listening, reading the graffiti over the toilet in the day room. She thought it interesting that although a lot of the women had started the morning by yelling "Fuck!" back and forth, the graffiti was quite different. One scrawl said, "I got out and you will too." Another was, "God is everywhere—even here."

Like most of the sheriff's men, Sgt. Vern Hensley did whatever job needed doing; Tulare County had only twenty-two adult felony investigators, and a situation like this one put a strain on the manpower. He had helped with the autopsy; he arranged for Pat Tomlinson of the M & W Flying Service in Porterville to take aerial photographs of the ranch from a helicopter. Mostly, though, Vern Hensley worked with evidence, specializing in fingerprints. He had been with the Tulare County Sheriff's Office for fourteen years, in charge of the crime lab for thirteen. Just after noon, Sergeant Hensley got a copy of a driver's license bearing the name and the right thumbprint of a William Thomas Ashlock, from Lt. Forrest Barnes. He compared the thumbprint on the license with the thumbprint of the decedent and concluded they were identical.

Other deputies and detectives had been at the ranch continuously since Tuesday night, searching it or guarding it or both. Sheriff's men had sealed off the property; Jim Webb, Teresa, and the kids had moved down to Porterville, to Jim's mother's.

At the Porterville substation, Detective Jack Flores interviewed Jim's thirty-two-year-old brother, Gerald Ray. He asked Mr. Webb to tell him what he knew of the incident at the ranch, in his own words. Gerald said he worked swing shift at Sperry Rand and was a minister of the Free Will Baptist Church in Orange Cove. He told how, on Saturday, he and his other brother and their families had gone from their mother's house to the ranch where Jim lived, to see the cattle and take some color slides and let the kids see the newborn calves. As the whole group, four adults and three children, was leaving the ranch to drive back into town, Gerald saw a gentleman in his late twenties, with dark curly hair, medium build, olive complexion, in a green Chevy Vega. The man asked the Webbs who they were. When Gerald told him, the man asked if any of them could saddle a horse. They told him no, but that Jim would be off work after three and would probably be up at the ranch then.

Gerald said he saw a two-tone Lincoln Continental behind the Vega, but he didn't get a good look at the man in it.

Back in Porterville, when Jim got home from his job at the state hospital, Gerald told him there was somebody at the ranch waiting to get a horse saddled. Jim asked Gerald if he'd like to drive up with him, so Gerald went along in Jim's car, which he thought was a late-model Mercedes-Benz.

When Gerald and Jim arrived at the ranch, Gerald saw both cars again but he didn't see any people. Jim looked for the key to the tack shed to get a saddle, and couldn't find it. Gerald said Jim told him somebody had just broke into the shed a week or so ago and stole some saddles. Gerald asked Jim if they couldn't just pull the hinge off the door, but Jim said no, he had fixed it back to where it wouldn't pull off very easily. They tried to get in the back window, but couldn't. So he called over to the main house to tell them.

While Jim was in the house calling, Gerald stayed out in the yard, where he saw two men and a girl looking through the orange grove. Gerald saw the one gentleman he had seen previously—dark curly hair, in his late twenties, medium build—and he saw another man, bigger, about six feet, maybe 185 pounds, very well-dressed, with the new type of sunglasses that look like they change colors with the light of the sun. He had a very fancy pipe, kind of a Sherlock Holmes pipe, and seemed well-mannered. He had long brown hair—not extremely long, not like a hippie—wavy but not curly, the way you fix hair with a hot comb.

The other man, the smaller man, was about five foot eight or five foot nine; his dark hair was curly but not really kinky, more like the hair of an Italian fellow Gerald knew. Gerald said that man did not have a mustache and he thought the girl called him "Bob," but he wasn't positive. He did notice her attitude toward that man, though; it seemed to Gerald like she treated him like a valet or something, but the other fellow she treated more or less as a dignitary, because later on, when the horse wanted to eat grass and wouldn't move, Gerald said the girl said to the curly-haired fellow, kind of snotty like, "Here, you take her, that's what you're here for, anyhow." Then the bigger fellow just went over and got the horse and led the horse off. And just as they were all getting to the edge of the trees, Terry Webb and Gerald's wife came driving up in the Dodge, and the girl yelled something at Terry. Gerald thought the girl was just acting like, well, I'm the boss here, you'll do what I want you to do.

Jim went over to the main house, and when he came back, he told Gerald they were all drinking over there, and a little later he said something else, something about the affluent society. Gerald himself thought the girl was acting like she had been drinking or taking some kind of a drug. She wasn't acting normal, because Gerald remembered one statement she made when she and the two men were coming down from the pasture toward where he and Jim were standing; she was saying something about getting stoned and then sitting down in the middle of a river and listening to the kids laugh. Gerald thought it was weird.

Gerald said that while Jim was getting a knife to cut off a rope for the horse, the girl was talking, more or less bragging, about the movie actors she had been around. Gerald thought the curly-haired fellow looked like he had been drinking, or was on drugs or something; not completely incoherent, but not really with it. In other words, he wasn't alert and bright and he said very little. Gerald said the girl was definitely more attracted to the brown-haired fellow, the fellow that was supposed to be from the newspaper, than to the other one.

Gerald said the fellow with the pipe seemed like an educated man, a very likable individual. It sure seemed to Gerald like the girl was trying to impress him, and he didn't seem like he was too impressed. Gerald said she asked the fellow, "Will this be all right, without a saddle?" and he had said, "That will be fine." It did seem to Gerald that the fellow had come up to get a picture. It seemed sincere to Gerald, not like there was anything wrong in that regard at all.

Gerald said he had said to Jim, on the way up, "This must be some kind of a dude that you have to come up and saddle their horses for them." And he made some comment like, "Do you have to help them up on their horses, too?" When they'd passed the cars, Gerald had looked, because he just liked to see what kind of cars people had, and he thought the big car was a Cadillac but Jim said, "No, it's a Continental."

Sometime during the afternoon, Jim and Gerald drove on up behind the ranch, because Jim wanted to show Gerald a place where cattle could have gotten through the fence. Two people were fishing out in the pond. Jim told Gerald to go ahead of him, while he went up to the lake to see who they were.

When the Webbs all left the ranch, on the way out, around the second bend in the road, they met the Lincoln coming back up the road with its lights on. There were three people in it, and Gerald just presumed they were the same three he had seen before. Jim backed up his car, and the Lincoln came on ahead and stopped for a minute, and someone said, "Thank you, Jim." And that's the last Gerald knew about anything.

"There's one little thing I'm concerned with, and this is in regard to the deceased," Detective Flores told Gerald. "As near as I can remember in your conversation here, this fellow in his late twenties—five foot eight, about one hundred seventy or one hundred seventy-five pounds, olive complexion, dark curly hair and no mustache, now, could you have been mistaken at all that he had dark curly hair and no mustache?"

"I know I'm not mistaken about the curly hair and I usually—well, as many people that have mustaches today, I usually notice it," Gerald replied. "And I definitely don't remember a mustache. I really don't."

"In other words, you were that close to him that if he would have had a trace of one, you would have noticed it?"

"Yes, I believe I would have noticed it," Gerald said. "I know he didn't have a full mustache. He may have—now, when my brother first mentioned that he had a mustache, I thought, well, maybe he could have had one starting, but when he said a full mustache, no, no way."

"Would you have any objections if I took you to the chapel and let you see this body?" Flores asked.

"No, wouldn't have any objections at all," Gerald said.

"In other words, you have no reason to hesitate or say, well, I don't care to see him or to identify him? In other words, you would be going out there to view him of your own free will?"

"Yes sir," Gerald said.

Twenty minutes later, Gerald Webb and Detective Flores were at the funeral home, with Carson Dykes of the funeral home staff standing by. Detective Flores talked into his tape recorder.

"The time is four-thirty P.M. At this time we're at the Myers Funeral Chapel where we're about to uncover the deceased's face and head so Mr.

Webb can look at it and tell if it's the same subject that he seen at the ranch.

"Mr. Webb, would you kind of take a look at this fellow here and tell me if this is the same fellow you seen at the ranch?"

"Let me go around on the other side to make sure," Gerald said. "Would you move that down just a little bit from right there." Carson Dykes moved the sheet a little. "No, it does not look to be the same individual that I saw at the ranch at all," Gerald said.

"Would you speak up a little bit, please?" Flores asked.

"No, this does not look like the same—either of the individuals I saw at the ranch on Saturday, February 24, 1973."

Jack Flores paused. "Well, tell me, Mr. Webb, what makes you think this—any of the characteristics you could point out?"

"The hair doesn't—the gentleman, the one gentleman that I—was of this build and had darker hair and it was more curly and I can't remember him having a mustache at all, and this fellow here has a mustache."

"All right," Flores said. "How about his facial features—that is, maybe the forehead and the mouth and cheeks and nose?"

"I didn't remember him having full lips like that. I don't know if his lips now are the way they would have been then, or if they swell up more after death or something. Is that a normal characteristic? Now the face —the size of the fellow—it doesn't—I don't know, maybe he's the same size, but it just doesn't look like the same fellow at all to me."

"I think this will be enough for now," Flores said. Then he paused again. "Will you take another good look at him, though, please?"

Gerald took another good look.

"No, it doesn't look like the same individual at all."

"Okay," Detective Flores said. "Thanks a lot."

Gene Tinch was a private eye in the best fictional tradition. Besides the diamond rings and the gold-and-diamond bracelet, he carried his cash in a gold clip and a gun in his car at all times. He called a woman's legs "gams." He was big and handsome, funny and sociable and tough. He had been a cop, Los Angeles Police Department, for nearly twenty years, during which time he'd been shot at thirteen times and he had shot and killed two people. Now, after early retirement, he'd set up a private detective agency with a partner. The name of the agency was The Tin Goose.

As soon as Ned Nelsen took Hope's case, he suggested to Honey and Van that a private detective—specifically, Gene Tinch, whom Ned had worked with before—could help a lot. "If the client has the funds, I always hire a private investigator," Ned explained. "For two reasons. One, a private investigator can get a lot of legwork done that would be time-consuming for a lawyer, and two, most good private investigators have access to police information that a lawyer doesn't have." Although Ned's client did not exactly have the funds, Honey and Van agreed to hire Gene at a rate of one hundred fifty dollars for an eight-hour day, to a maximum of five thousand dollars, with twenty-five hundred dollars to be paid right away and with all expenses—mileage, meals, motels—to be itemized, with receipts. Ned had called Gene at home and, first thing Wednesday morning, before he drove up to Tulare County with Tom Breslin, Gene paid three hundred to a pair of electronic technicians to go by Honey's house, and Hope's house on the Drive, to debug, if necessary.

After he'd talked with Hope, though, Gene wasn't sure he wanted the job. "Extremely bizarre and highly unlikely," Gene pronounced her story, at the outset. "Being a policeman as long as I have, and having worked as many murders as I have, having heard as many bizarre stories as I've heard—stories that later turned out to be nowhere close to the truth— I'm now supposed to just sit there and believe her?" he demanded of Tom. "No *way.*

"I ask her a simple question and it takes her thirty minutes to tell me absolutely nothing," Gene complained. "She rambles on, I can't shut her up, and by the time I get an answer, if in fact I ever get an answer, I've forgotten what I asked her.

"Attorneys have a different outlook," Gene reminded Tom. "You take that damned Hippocratic oath or whatever, so you're bound by ethics to defend a client to the fullest. If somebody says to you, 'I didn't do it,' and never tells you different, then you have to believe her and defend her. But me, I don't have to do that, and personally, I don't want to work for a client who's lying to me, because somewhere down the line, it's going to make me look foolish, and I don't need that. I don't need the money that bad, and I don't need the headaches."

Gene Tinch didn't really believe Hope Masters had pulled the trigger on the gun that killed Bill Ashlock, but neither did he really believe her rambling story of the intruder in the night, the man with the goatee, possibly Mexican, sent by the Mafia. "Mafia are out for connections, or for money, or for dope or something," Gene said. "They're not just out to cause trouble for some little girl." Gene had a gut feeling that something was wrong here. But whatever it was, he admitted to himself, it was interesting, so he decided to stick with the case for a while and maybe find out what it was.

Sergeant Babcock and Detective Tucker checked into the Mayfair, downtown, where police officers got a good rate; then they reported in to the Los Angeles Sheriff's Office on West Olympic Boulevard. A little after midnight on Thursday, they drove over to Tom Masters's apartment.

Sergeant Babcock spoke first. "Now, Tom, I'm going to read you your rights. I want you to listen to them. You have the right to remain silent. Anything you say can and will be used against you, in a court of law. You have the right to talk to a lawyer before you are questioned and to have him present with you while you are being questioned. If you cannot afford a lawyer and if you want one, you have the right to have a lawyer appointed to represent you before any questioning. Now, Tom, did you understand what I read to you?"

"Yes, I did," Tom Masters said.

"All right. Now, do you wish to continue this interview? Do you wish to talk to us?"

"Yes, I do."

Sergeant Babcock had Tom sign a waiver, then he came right to the point. "I earlier told you that your wife, who is in custody, had advised us that you were responsible for this homicide. Is that so?"

"No, it is not," Tom said.

"I told you that, though?"

"You did tell me."

"Do you know of any reasons why she would say this?"

"No, it's incomprehensible to me," Tom said. "I do not know the reason why she would say that. I do not know."

Tom told the police that he had been to the ranch about five times altogether, most recently about nine or ten months earlier, with Hope and another couple. He said he and Hope usually spoke to each other about twice a week, but that he hadn't spoken with her in person since the previous Thursday, when he brought K.C. back to the Drive about 7:30 in the evening, the night Tom and his girlfriend Nadine later went to the premiere of *Walking Tall.* He said he had met Bill at Hope's house five or six times, and he knew Bill drove a little green Triumph or Spitfire. Hope had told him Bill was forty years old.

"What type of relationship did she have with this Bill?" Babcock asked. "Was it platonic? Was it a boyfriend type thing, or what?"

"Yeah, I mean, it's—uh, as best I can recollect—I've kind of divorced myself from her personal life only because I've found that I was even happier when she was involved with somebody, because it did mean she didn't hassle me—uh, she was involved with a man named Lionel, I don't remember his last name, who's now in London, before that. It seems that every man she meets, she does have kind of a—they both get all involved. I know I did when I met her four years ago, and this guy, uh, as best I could recollect, I believe if he wasn't living there full time for the past month or so, he was at least there most of the time."

"How old of a man was Lionel?"

"Lionel? He was probably about the same age, maybe a little bit older."

"Remember his description?"

"Yes, he was probably about five foot ten, weighed one hundred fifty, one hundred fifty-five, and he's a television producer. At least that's what he said he was."

"Hair color?"

"Brown. Dark brown. British guy."

"British accent?"

"No, not an accent, but, uh, kind of a world traveler, European type of guy."

"Sophisticated type?"

"Yeah, yeah, quite sophisticated. He was working in connection with Winters-Rose Productions, which is a big television production firm here in town."

"What kind of a car did he drive?"

"He rented a car all the time, a Pinto or something like that, because he really lived in Europe and he'd come over here for three or four months at a clip."

"How long has he been gone?"

"He's been gone—I think he left just before Christmas, as a matter of fact."

"What broke up their relationship?" Babcock asked bluntly.

"Uh, I don't know," Tom said. "I don't really know, but I know that he went—she told me—this is all through Hope—she told me that he went over to Europe, to London, to do a special *Dr. Jekyll and Mr. Hyde* or something. I know the production company he said he was with did produce, you know, a television picture over there called that."

"Does Lincoln Continental mean anything to you?"

"Very interesting you should say that," Tom mused. "Uh, probably a white Lincoln Continental."

Babcock seemed to hedge. "Well, we could say a light color, in a way."

"Okay, well, uh, the only Lincoln Continental that means anything to me would be Hope's mother's car," Tom said. "She's got a Lincoln Continental, dark blue one, I think a black vinyl top maybe. She had a dark blue one."

"How new is it?"

"Brand new. I think last year's, '72. A four-door Continental, not a Mark IV type like you see, but the more sophisticated Establishment-type car."

Tom said when he'd brought K.C. home on Sunday, he saw a white Continental in Hope's driveway, it looked just like Honey's except it was white.

He gestured slightly toward the young woman with him now. "The reason why Nadine is really here is that she was with me all weekend, so she can substantiate a lot of this, and I thought it probably would be good that she was here." Babcock agreed that it was a good thing. "Plus, I wanted somebody to talk to," Tom said.

He said Nadine hadn't been with him when he took K.C. on Saturday, because Nadine worked Saturdays, but she was with him on Sunday when they picked K.C. up around one o'clock and took him down to the beach, near Nadine's apartment in Playa del Rey. She was with him when they brought K.C. back, around six o'clock.

"Was the lady with you then also?" Babcock asked.

"Yes," Tom said.

The detective turned to Nadine. "Can you confirm that, ma'am?"

"Yes," Nadine said.

Tom said he knew that Hope and Bill had gone to the ranch because he saw Bill's car in the driveway on Saturday, and again on Sunday, when he'd also seen the white Lincoln.

"I made a remark of it," Tom explained, "only because I thought, gee, you know, we've gone to the ranch before and you never get back at six o'clock. It's about a three-hour drive, I guess, from Porterville to here, and we always got back around eight or nine. And I thought to myself, gee, I knew they had taken her car to the ranch—only assumed that because it was gone on Saturday, and it's a station wagon so they could carry supplies in it."

"Any other men friends of your wife's that might drive a Lincoln Continental?"

"I don't know for sure," Tom said. "I know she's got a friend who she kind of goes out with in between relationships or something. His name is Michael Abbott, he's an attorney, he's just out of law school, and he's just—"

"Young," Babcock supplied the word.

"Young," Tom agreed. He said he didn't know whether Michael drove a Continental, he just knew that Hope saw Michael quite often, and that she also saw an attorney and stockbroker named Gary. "These are wealthy people," Tom pointed out.

"Does the name Taylor mean anything?" Babcock asked.

"You have a first name?"

"No," Babcock said.

"No, Taylor doesn't mean a thing."

"Tyler?"

"Tyler, Tyler," Tom repeated. "No."

"Sumner?"

"No."

"How about newspaper reporters, photographers?"

"Newspaper reporters, photographers," Tom repeated.

"Authors, free-lance type?"

"It's funny that you say this now," Tom said again. "This is when her husband—her boyfriend, Bill—he worked for an advertising agency. I don't know which one, but one in town here. Now on Thursday I believe it was, or could it have been Friday now, damn it, she had called me— I can't remember. I know the last time I spoke to her in person was Thursday night, now she might have called me Friday morning. I can check with my answering service to find out if they took the call, exact date and time, but she— Very interesting, you know, in my business I handle most of the entertainers. I do their public relations, promotions, publicity, but I also handle some restaurants on occasion, and she called me and she said to me, 'You know,' she said, 'there's the *L.A. Times* or some writer going to interview Bill as one of the town's clean young bachelors, and they're going to do some posing—"

Again Babcock cut in. "What day was this?"

"I can't say exactly. I can find out. Thursday or Friday."

"Thursday or Friday for sure?"

"Right, right."

"About what time?"

"Uh—let me say, Wednesday, Thursday, or Friday. I—I, you know, I get confused on the dates now that she's— It was in the afternoon, probably, around three, but I can't say for sure." Tom said Hope hadn't told him the reporter's name, only that he was from the *Los Angeles Times*, and she'd asked Tom if he wanted any restaurants mentioned that he handled, for the publicity value, or so they might get a free dinner out of it. "I don't like to get involved with her in business at all, naturally, for obvious reasons," Tom said. "So I said, 'No, I don't know of any. I don't think anybody would go for it.' And that was all. I dropped it."

"Do you know of any middle-aged men, fifty-ish, she might have gone out with, to your knowledge?"

"No, I know that on occasion she tells me, you know, 'I met a guy who is too old for me, or wants to take me to dinner,' but I don't know any names. I just try not to get into that with her."

"Do you own a weapon?" Babcock asked suddenly.

"No," Tom said. "I do in Massachusetts, where I come from—mainly hunting, you know, but I own nothing out here at all whatsoever."

"To your knowledge, does your wife have a firearm?"

"No, I don't know her to have one, and never have," Tom replied.

"She's not familiar with firearms?"

"Not to my knowledge, not at all, not at all."

"Has your wife ever used narcotics?"

"She's smoked marijuana that I know of."

"Any hard narcotics?"

"Not that I know of."

"Barbiturates? Amphetamines?"

"Well, she takes quite a few sleeping pills, and I know she's got a bad back problem and she takes drugs, but these were all prescribed by a couple of doctors that she has."

Babcock turned to his partner. "Detective Tucker, you got anything I'm missing here?"

Ralph Tucker had something. "Your financial status?" he said inquiringly to Tom.

"What do you want to know about it?"

"What do you make?"

"What do I make?" Tom repeated. "I—I—uh, it's hard for me to say, exactly. Last year I grossed twenty-five thousand dollars."

"How hard would it be for you to come up with thirty-five hundred dollars?"

"Pretty difficult," Tom said.

"At this time?"

"Extremely difficult, right. I have a business manager who could show you my books for the past year, the past three years, so you could substantiate that."

Tucker was not deflected. "Where do you bank at?"

"Well, *he* banks," Tom said. "I have a business manager. The man's name is Mr. Lou Grant, and they have a business managing firm named Zulk, Grant, and Zulk, and all their clients' money is in one trust account, which mine is involved in. And I believe it's the Security-Pacific Bank at Fulton and Riverside in, uh—"

"Can you write checks on this?"

"No I cannot."

"Do you have a savings account?"

"Yes, we do, but it's involved again with this same trust situation. I mean, I cannot write a check. They have total power of attorney."

"And you have no way that you could get hold of any money?"

"Not unless, I suppose, I went to a friend and asked for thirty-five hundred dollars," Tom said. "That's the only way I know of how I could get hold of it."

There was only a slight pause.

"Getting back to this gentleman from England. What—"

"Lionel," Tom said. "I know him as Lionel."

"Was he clean-shaven?"

"Yeah."

"Did he smoke a pipe?"

"Seems like he did," Tom said.

"A great big pipe? Have you ever seen him with a—"

"No, no," Tom corrected himself. "He seems like the type who— would smoke a pipe, though, from the sophisticated air about him."

"Clean-cut, neat?"

"Clean-cut, very neat, yeah. Meticulous."

"Do you know if Bill has guns?"

"No, I don't know."

"Is there a gun stored at the ranch?"

"No, uh, no," Tom said. "And this is what I can't understand. I just don't think Van, her father, would allow that, because there are different families that go up there for weekends with kids."

Speaking of the ranch, the police brought up Jim Webb. "Do you know of any possible trouble between the foreman and your wife or Bill or anything like this?"

Not between those people, Tom said, but he told of a problem Van had once had, when he'd ordered ten or twenty dead orange trees cut down, and the foreman, by mistake, had the tree removers wipe out the entire grove, one hundred fifty trees or so. Tom said Van had been very, very upset.

"When your wife went up there, or any members of the family, did they go to any bars, any restaurants, any places they hung out at?"

Tom recalled a restaurant near Lake Success where he and Hope had once had dinner, and he remembered a little grocery store in Springville,

where they still sold ice by the chunk. At a little beer bar in the center
of town, with a pool table, an Indian had once made a remark about Tom's
long hair. The Indian was carrying a snake, and he was in a group of about
six Indians, while Tom only had one friend with him, so Tom just said
"Peace," and left.

"Does your wife use credit cards?"

"No, except for a Union Oil card," Tom said. "For gas. Cash only, or
writes a check."

"How about Bill?"

"I don't know anything about him," Tom said, more emphatically. "I
know that she always told me—that, uh, he bought her things and took
her to dinner but—but—was never going to make much money, something like that, referring to the fact that in my business I can make
twenty-five thousand dollars one year and one hundred thousand dollars
the next, if I get lucky with a couple clients. In his business he was more
or less in a salary position."

"What type of nature does your wife have? Is she a violent person?
Like, say, say if she's intoxicated or she's feeling good, would she be
violent?"

"I have never known her to be," Tom said. "I have never known her
to be absolutely violent. I know that when she does get a little drunk, I've
always had a problem with her."

The detectives were very interested. "What kind of a problem?"

"Well, just that she would be very silly and incoherent and, uh, would
drink, even though she knew she shouldn't drink any more and would—
uh, uh, uh—would swear, and cause a lot of problems. For instance, many
times we double-dated with my business manager and his wife, when
Hope and I were married and living together, and one night with them
she had three or four drinks. Evidently the combination of this medication
she was taking, and the drinks—she never realized it affected her. I would
have to physically put her in the car and take her home, or carry her into
the bedroom and then she'd pass out. Never really a streak of violence,
just incoherent and, like, a who-gives-a-hell type of attitude. This I've
noticed."

"This Webb," Babcock asked then, abruptly. "Did she know this
Webb? Any type of relationship there?"

"I don't know," Tom said.

Jim Webb told the police he hardly knew the girl. "They know more
about who we are than we know about who they are," the foreman

explained, "because they only come up maybe every four or five months, something like that." He said he had never been invited to any of their social gatherings. "Definitely not, definitely not." Jim knew she had long blond hair and was sharply dressed when he saw her, Saturday afternoon, with the other two fellows, but he didn't know much about Hope Masters at all. One thing he did know was that when he saw the powdery trail on the kitchen floor, like a trail of cleanser, he knew his wife wouldn't have left that kind of trail because she was a meticulous housekeeper and besides, if she didn't clean up just right, the owners would let her know about it. And he knew Hope Masters couldn't have left it, because "from what I heard, she had never done any cleaning in her life."

In his subsequent statements to the police, after his first predawn statement on Wednesday, Jim Webb admitted that he'd gone into the house, with gloves on, and socks over his shoes, not just stood outside and shined in the windows with his flashlight, the way he'd told it the first time.

Sgt. Richard Morris, who was conducting the interview along with Detective Flores, was very polite when he spoke to Jim Webb. "Would you care to explain why, when you were giving the first statement, when you had the first opportunity to tell what you knew about this situation, that you didn't tell about going into the house?"

Jim said in the first place, he was scared to death, and in the second place, when he called the police Tuesday night, after he'd talked with Van, the police had told him not to go into the house, and Jim didn't want to get into trouble by telling them he already had.

Before he talked with Jim Webb again, Detective Flores had talked with a man named Ed Pillstrom, who knew Jim. Ed Pillstrom told Flores that when he'd talked with Jim—"I was kind of kidding him about that crime wave they were having up at the ranch, and I asked him why he didn't find the body, because I know he works up there"—Jim had told Ed Pillstrom he was going down to the substation to change his statement about a gun.

But when Detective Flores asked Jim about a gun, Jim said he had not mentioned the word "gun."

"Definitely not," he said, adding that maybe Ed Pillstrom had mistaken the word "gun" for "gone." "Maybe I told him I had *gone* into the house," Jim said.

Before he talked with the police on Thursday, Jim Webb had the Miranda warning read to him by Detective Flores, and after he talked, late Thursday night, the deputy district attorney had asked him to take a lie detector test. Jim said he would take one after he'd had some sleep and had talked with his lawyer. But the D.A. had wanted it done right then. "I can get you the best guy from Bakersfield; I can have him here within the hour," the D.A. told Jim. But Jim still said he wanted to wait.

Honey kept going over and over in her mind the afternoon and evening when Taylor had sat talking, at the end of her velvet sofa. She remembered his anecdote about Hope picking up the runny-nosed baby at the market, but she also remembered him saying he hadn't arrived at the ranch until Sunday morning. "When could that have happened, if he didn't arrive till Sunday?" she asked Van.

She also remembered Hope pointing out to her that Taylor was fifty-one years old. She'd spoken in such a strange, shrill voice that Honey was startled, and now it occurred to her that Hope was perhaps trying to get Honey to take a really good look at Taylor. Honey had taken a very good look and had written a complete description of Taylor, which didn't seem to interest the police at all. "They just told me, 'Well, if you hear from him, have him turn himself in,'" she reported to Van. Honey kept going over the notes she'd made, trying to remember everything Taylor had said, everything Hope had said. As she thought about it, Honey began to wonder why Hope hadn't telephoned the minute she was safely away from the ranch; surely, Honey thought, the public phones along the highway would not have been tapped.

Honey was so upset and fearful about it all that when Tom Masters telephoned, the phone trembled in her hands. Tom said he was calling to ask about Hopie and the children.

"K.C. is well and happy and being well cared for," Honey told Tom. "Somebody will be in touch with you soon."

She hung up as quickly as she could and phoned the Beverly Hills police. She told the officer they were all very frightened, and she asked for a policeman to come around and guard the house. When they told her the case was out of their jurisdiction, and they couldn't send a man, Honey was furious. "The fact that I have been a resident of Beverly Hills for forty years, and a property owner, doesn't matter to you at all!" she exclaimed. Van called his son Michael, who was a reserve deputy in Los Angeles; Michael came over and sat all day in the living room with his loaded gun.

Tom Breslin was in and out of the jail three or four times, bringing Hope cigarettes, a toothbrush, a hairbrush. "Don't worry," he kept saying, so Hope tried not to as she lay on her bunk, gazing at the ceiling. She had been moved into a single cell, a cell for special cases, so she figured something would happen on Friday, but she tried not to think about anything, even after she'd heard a news bulletin about the murder, coming from a radio in one of the trustee's cells. She listened to the women singing—sometimes from several cells at once, sometimes from one, then another, one woman picking up where another had left off. She recognized Vanessa's voice—sweet and clear and mournful—but she didn't recognize any of the songs; they were made-up songs, Hope realized, more like laments, about their men and their children and their loneliness and troubles. *My God,* Hope thought, *this is the real thing. This is the Jailhouse Blues.*

Thursday/March 1, 1973

Ms. Marthe C. Purmal
Attorney at Law
422 East 47th Street
Chicago, Illinois 60653

Marcy,

This may be my last letter from freedom, for, I fear that tomorrow I must go into a district attorney's office and spill my guts to get a woman out of jail and charges of murder, all because she refuses to talk, thereby protecting me.

This seems to be the season for women coming into trouble and/or jail for me.

First off, I am enclosing a brief story from the front pages of the S.F. paper, which tells a bit of what is up in the fast-moving life of Run-Dan-Run! Next, I am enclosing a picture of Hopie (her name is Hope but is called Hopie) and I took the picture in Hopie's garden in L.A. (Yes, I'll just bet I have some explaining to do—later.) Actually, I have several hundred pictures and slides I have taken along the way to share with you, however, I have been waiting to send them or show them as things meant for you tend to end up with "them."

Of course, on to more important matters—while you sit in Chicago and feel sorry for yourself about becoming involved with me, tending to feel I am playing games with you and that you might be indicted, Hopie is spending her second night in the Tulare County Jail, has been already arraigned, and continues to be silent solely to protect me and give me time to run away, and is willing to stand trial.

All right, as you can see by the article, Hopie's father is part owner in a large ranch up in the hills of California at Springville, and I have been staying there along with Hopie, her children, and several other friends—the place has many bedrooms, but eat your heart out where I was sleeping.

Hopie's daughter, Hope (10) had a dental appointment, and the other two kids (Keith, 12 and Casey, 3) were ready to give up the wild life at the ranch, and two women (nameless L.A. socialites) had to go to L.A., which is approximately a 3 hour drive. Otherwise the body would not be that of William T. Ashlock, Creative Director for Dailey & Associates Advertising of Los Angeles, but would be that of G. Daniel Walker, for Bill Ashlock was the only man present at the ranch and assumed to be your true love.

Hopie was nude, bound with adhesive tape, and had been raped when I arrived, and yet, she gave me an accurate description of what had happened and who had accomplished the task. I tossed her into my car and drove to the private airport at Porterville where I rented a small plane and flew to L.A., dropped Hopie at her home and headed for where I knew my friends would go. Unfortunately, only one showed up and I left his body across a bed, which I am certain the police will discover shortly, and given enough time they would have a second one also.

Meanwhile, Hopie promised not to say anything until she had to, thereby giving me enough time to accomplish what I must and get away. Unfortunately the ranch foreman entered the ranch's main house and then called Hopie's father, who had no other choice but to call the authorities since a body was in the ranch house.

Since the ranch foreman was questioned he told that Hopie was there with friends of hers. The police arrived and Hopie and her children refused to answer any questions, and Hopie elected to go to jail to give me enough time to finish my manhunt in L.A. and get away.

My missing guy has flown to San Francisco, I am right on his tail, and assuming things go well and he gets his good tonight, I plan on driving to the Tulare County area and get Hopie out of jail. Ohhhhhhhhh, I shall not tell all, my dear, but fake it and hope to hell that my identity gets past the law folks, and yet, I tend to guess it won't.

In the event it all goes wrong, I am truly sorry that you were such a prissy bitch that you could not do what others have done—come along with me and enjoy a few days. It has been a ball, one you would have liked, but then anyone who would fly to Vail with an Illinois State Cop and State's Attorney has got to be a bum lay with a broken heart.

Love you, darling, and yet, it is amazing that while the authorities cannot find me, other folks with different strokes sure did—bang! Bill Ashlock was one great guy, he and Hopie were going to be married. (See, there is not that much to tell, after all).

Wish me luck.

love and stuff . . .

CHAPTER
NINE

MELVIN EUGENE PARKER was the only person in the Ashlock murder case who ever referred to the aristocratic Honey as "Hope's mom."

Gene Parker had never planned to be a cop. He was not from California, but from "back east," by which he meant Paragould, Arkansas, where he grew up on a one hundred sixty-acre farm and played baseball so well, at Oak Grove High School, that the Philadelphia Phillies picked him up for their farm club in Carthage, Missouri. A player then was paid either sixty dollars a month with room and board, or ninety dollars a month without, so Gene drove back and forth every day from Paragould to Carthage. He washed out after one year and, with nothing else to do except go back on the farm, decided to go west.

He worked on construction jobs up and down the coast, ending up, for no special reason, in Porterville, California, where he bought himself a little grocery store. It was a nice, slow, easygoing business, with lots of time to talk to the people who came in. "I got a vacancy coming up in Woodville," the sheriff told him one day, but Parker shook his head. "No thanks, I don't want to be a cop," he replied and, next thing he knew, he was driving around Woodville with the deputy who was leaving. The deputy introduced Parker to the barber and to the man who ran the gas station, then he parked the car and handed Gene the keys. "It's all yours, kid," he said.

Parker came to like his work a lot. "It kind of grows on you," he said simply. He liked it mostly because it involved helping people. "I am not a college degree person," Parker said. "But if your neighbor has a burglary, or gets hurt, or there is some trouble, you do not have to be a college degree person to get your neighbor's stuff back, or help him out, or stop the trouble. I always felt that if a guy had a gun on me, I wouldn't say nothing to him. I wouldn't stand still, either, 'cause I'd have to keep my feet going; I would walk up to him and take the gun away. That's just common sense, 'cause if I go for my gun, or start talking, he'll probably shoot." Parker paused, searching for words to define his philosophy. "Common sense," he repeated. "It does not take a college degree person to do your neighbor right."

Parker was assigned to the Ashlock investigation on his fortieth birthday, March 1. Some of his kids—he had five of them—had painted his toenails red while he slept, as a birthday surprise, and when Parker got the call to go down to L.A., he went so quickly he didn't stop to remove the nail polish.

Gene Parker and his partner, Detective Jim Brown, never knew why they were picked for the L.A. job, but they did know that this was the first time in the history of the Tulare County Sheriff's Office that men had been sent out of the county on an investigation, and they were looking forward to it. They checked in first at the Los Angeles Sheriff's Office to let them know they'd arrived; then Sgt. Ed Harter of the Los Angeles Sheriff's Office (LASO) took them over to the Mayfair, where the other two officers from Tulare County, Babcock and Tucker, were already staying, at the special police rate. Brown and Parker had a room with a view of a flashing neon sign across the street for a topless, bottomless bar. They slept very well, their first night on official business in L.A. and their first night on waterbeds.

Mary Bowyer, Van's secretary, took the call shortly after noon on Friday. She said Van was away. "Is there a message? May I ask who's calling?"

"This is Taylor."

The secretary caught her breath. "Mr. Taylor, what is your number, please? I'll have him call you."

"There is no number," Taylor said. "I'm Hope's friend. She is being arraigned at three o'clock today in Porterville. I want to get word to Van. I have some information."

"Why don't you go to Porterville?" Mary Bowyer suggested. "You have plenty of time to make it. You could help Hopie so much—they all need your help."

"I want to help," Taylor said, "but I am not going to make a personal appearance. The arraignment is to be in the Porterville Justice Court at three o'clock. I am going to call there around three o'clock."

"Please, please call before three o'clock, before the hearing begins," Mary Bowyer urged him.

"I will probably call around ten to three," Taylor said. "Is there an attorney on the case other than Van?"

"Yes, his name is Ned Nelsen," Mary replied. She spelled the name, emphasizing the second e, and gave his phone number. "Please go to Porterville," she said again. "Do you realize what you are putting the family through? You could clear Hopie, if only you would."

"I want to help, but I have to do it my way," Taylor declared. "I am not going to make a personal appearance. I am not an American national and I am not going to be picked up. I would be in deep trouble myself. I have a telephone number for the justice court in Porterville and will call there. Is there any way you can reach Van?"

"I don't know," Mary said. "He's on his way to Porterville now. But I'll try."

When she hung up, Mary Bowyer called Mildred Maguire, Ned Nelsen's secretary, but she was out to lunch. Mary called again at 1:15 and, just before 2:00, Mildred returned her call. Mary told Mildred about Taylor's call. "What do you think I should do?" Mary asked.

"Well, there's no point in your calling Porterville, because you really don't have anything tangible," Mildred said. "We have an investigator up there. I'll call him, and if Taylor does call Porterville, perhaps the call could be traced. Did you try to have Taylor's call traced?"

"No, I had no way of going off the line without putting him on hold, and I surely didn't want to put him on hold," Mary said.

As the secretaries were talking, at 1:54 P.M. on Friday, March 2, a man rented a new Thunderbird, brown over gold, California license 139GFK, at the San Francisco International Airport. Janet Bender, the Hertz clerk, took the Bankamericard and filled out the rental form: William T. Ashlock, Checkmate Productions, 211 South Lafayette Park Place, Los Angeles, California.

Hope knew she looked awful when she arrived at the Porterville Justice Court for her arraignment. Matron Arenas had given her a rubber band to hold back her hair, but a reporter was right when he described her as "wan and frail . . . very thin . . . wearing baggy red corduroy pants and a drooping knitted vest . . . she appeared exhausted." She was led into the courtroom through the back entrance, the prisoners' entry, from the parking area with the barbed wire atop the fence, around the little cement blockhouse where she had been held for a while on Wednesday, through a shadowy, cement-walled corridor into the courtroom.

Honey and Van were already seated on one of the narrow, straight-backed pine benches that made the little justice court look more like a plain country chapel—maybe even plainer, with no stained glass, its only color furnished by an American flag and the California state flag with a brown bear on a red background, gold-fringed. When she saw Hope being led in, looking so sick and scared and miserable, Honey began to cry.

Ned Nelsen and Tom Breslin stood with Hope at the counsel table, as Judge George Carter walked to the bench. He yawned, then smiled at the attorneys. "Gentlemen, you'll have to bear with me," he said. "I am very tired. I just got back from taking the bar exam."

Hope pleaded not guilty. She stood tensely between Tom and Ned, clutching a black sweater and a pack of cigarettes as Ned argued that if the man known to them as Taylor could be found, he was confident that the charges against Hope would be dismissed. "While Mrs. Masters did not use the best judgment," Nelsen argued, "she certainly did not kill Mr. Ashlock." But when Deputy District Attorney James Heusdens argued that she be held without bail until the preliminary hearing, Judge Carter nodded, and ordered her returned to custody.

There was a moment's hush, then a voice was heard from the middle of the courtroom. "I wish to address the court."

The courtroom stirred as Van moved forward and stood beside Hope. He put his arm around her and looked directly at Judge Carter, speaking in a firm, steady voice.

"My daughter is not well," Van said. "I don't know what even a few days in jail would do to her. I fear for her."

Now the courtroom was dramatically stilled as Van told, briefly, the story Hope had told him of the weekend at the ranch and the man who had come to his home on Tuesday.

"We are still trying to find out the identity of the man who came to the ranch, found the corpse, and discovered my daughter tied to a bed," Van said. "This man brought my daughter back to Los Angeles, but he refuses to give his name—or his proper name—because he apparently is not a citizen. He claims to be a free-lance foreign correspondent and has told my wife by telephone he will send a deposition to the district attorney in Visalia.

"He's still in town. He's still around. I'm hoping we can find him, but it's hard to find a person like this. I need my daughter to straighten out these unknowns." He gave the court his personal guarantee that Hope would return for the March 15 hearing, adding that she and her children were almost entirely supported by him and she had no money to flee.

Judge Carter looked closely at Van, then at the girl. He did not feel sorry for her at all. The way he saw it, somebody was lying dead, and this girl had been involved in some way, and maybe without all the drugs and things up at that ranch, maybe somebody wouldn't be dead. But he was very impressed with Van, with what Van had said and the way he'd said it, so Judge Carter called a recess to consider whether Hope Masters would be released on bail.

"This is Taylor again," the caller said. "Were you able to reach Van?"

"No," Mary Bowyer said. "Were you?"

It was 3:35 P.M.

"I called," Taylor said, "I got a court clerk or someone, but they would not bring anyone to the phone, court proceedings going on. Could not leave a message because I did not have a number to call back. You haven't heard anything from Van?"

"No," Mary said sharply. "I told you I had not heard from him."

"Put in another call and try to reach Van," Taylor ordered. "I will call you back later. How is Hope?"

"Hopie is ill, and being in jail has not helped," Mary retorted. "Mr. —what did you say your name was?"

The man laughed. "Just call me Taylor, honey. No one knows my name and I want to keep it that way."

Mary Bowyer tried pleading. "How can you do this to Hopie? She is so ill, so tiny—"

"Jail is not the most pleasant place to be," Taylor agreed. "But don't worry. She will be out today, and Van and Honey will see she gets the care she needs. How are the children? Are they with Honey and Van?"

"I am sure the children are being cared for," Mary said, "but they need their mother. Why don't you come forward and help Hopie?"

"She will get my help, but I have to do it my way," Taylor said firmly. "I am not an American national and I am involved in an internal triangle. I cannot make an appearance and chance being picked up. Hope is fragile, but things will work out for her.

"I do want to help, and I have made an affidavit that will throw much light on the matter. Too bad I could not get through to Nelsen or Van. You try again to reach Van. I will call later."

Van's secretary called Ned's secretary again, and again they decided there was no point in calling Porterville, with nothing to report. Each woman had checked on how to trace a call, each told the other, and each had been told it could not be done.

Virginia Anderson, the court clerk, was not a clock-watcher, so she was never certain of the precise time she'd noticed the well-dressed man in the last row of the courtroom, on the bench nearest the door. She saw him there just before Hope Masters's arraignment began, and during the first part of the proceeding, before the recess. She was struck by how well-dressed he was, in a white or ivory-colored turtleneck and a camel-colored jacket. He had dark brown hair. Although she only observed him seated, she took him to be tall, about six feet, 175 to 185 pounds. She thought he might be an attorney; she didn't see Hope Masters speak to him, or make any gesture, but she did see Mrs. Masters turn.

During the recess, which Mrs. Anderson thought was between 3:30 and 4:00, approximately, a court employee handed her a note for Mr. Nelsen, telling him that a Mr. Taylor was calling. Virginia Anderson didn't recall seeing the well-dressed stranger after the recess, though she never saw him leave, either. Neither did William Thompson, the bailiff, though he too had taken note of the immaculately dressed man on the bench nearest the door. Bailiff Thompson had worked in this courtroom for twelve years and knew most everybody who came in, but he didn't know this man. The bailiff was certain of the seat the man had taken, because it had always seemed a favorite seat and he'd seen many people try to take it, over the years, maybe because it was right at the door and a person could get out quickly.

Judge Carter had told the truth when he said he was tired. He had just driven back from San Francisco after a three-day bar exam that he had found a grueling, even a humiliating experience. Although as a justice of the peace, he was called judge, he was not an attorney, and he had heard that the system was due to change; with the district growing, the justice court would become a municipal court and the judicial requirements would be stiffened. George Carter felt comfortable in court, after fifteen years as a probation officer, so, in order to stay on the bench, he had been going to law school at night. This meant driving over to Fresno and back after a full day's work, tired before he even started out, sometimes fighting ground fogs so thick the roads were technically closed, one hundred and fifty miles roundtrip, three nights a week. He had talked Jim Heusdens into going to law school with him, and Jim had passed the bar—he was now a deputy D.A.—but George had taken it once, failed, and now had tried again. He was beginning to think it wasn't worth the trouble and, at age fifty-three, he thought maybe he ought to forget about the law, say "the heck with it," and concentrate on his family, his cattle, and his grove of tangerines.

Meantime, however, he had to decide on bail for the accused. If he hadn't been so tired, if he'd had a good night's sleep, he reflected later, he probably wouldn't have done it. But being so tired and worn down, he kind of gave in, and announced that upon consideration, he had decided to set bail for Hope Masters at fifty thousand dollars.

Hope slumped in relief. Tom Breslin smiled broadly. Hope had been horrified when Judge Carter announced he had just taken the bar, and she had complained to Tom about it during the recess. "I thought judges had to have some legal experience," she said in annoyance. "I didn't think they could be appointed right off the farm."

But Tom liked Carter; he had a kind of slow, steady air about him, a placid, creased face that seemed kindly. "He's a nice fellow," Tom told Hope. "And I don't mind anybody not passing the bar. There's some real good people don't pass it."

The district attorney's argument for no bail had come as an unpleasant surprise to Tom Breslin. He had expected a fifty thousand dollar bond to be asked. Van had already arranged for that amount, through his Los Angeles bank to a local bank, so he was able to present a certified check within minutes. Then Ned Nelsen was steering Hope out the door, through a clamor of reporters and photographers, some of them local, but others from San Francisco and L.A. and the wire services. Hope covered her head with the black sweater, but the cameras didn't stop clicking, and the UPI photograph that went out showed a skinny, headless person with the caption: "Camera Shy."

Hope's stepbrother Michael pulled a black Cadillac up in front of the courthouse. Ned opened the door quickly and almost pushed Hope into the back seat. Ned shook Van's hand, and Tom shook hands with Van with special warmth. Tom had met Van for the first time today, and he was impressed. "He didn't up-play his status, but you knew he had the status," Tom explained. "He was the one who swung it with Judge Carter." Ned told Van he'd call him in the morning; then Van got into the front seat with Michael, and Honey sat in back, next to Hope. Honey was smiling now, chic and beautiful in her mink coat.

Cameras kept clicking as the Cadillac moved down Morton Street to

Main, and out Main to the highway. Within minutes the car was out of town, passing groves of olive trees with their silvery-green leaves, bushy and sturdy, among the oldest kinds of trees on earth. The Cadillac turned onto the highway, heading south.

It was just one week since Hope had traveled this highway in the opposite direction, driving up to the ranch with Bill. One week. Friday to Friday; dream to elaborate nightmare; a week of blood and terror and heartbreak concluding in fine dramatic fashion when the stepfather she'd never gotten on with strode forward and clasped his arm around her trembling shoulders. "My daughter is not well. I fear for her." Now Hope was safely nestled in the deep softness of her stepfather's car, sleeping peacefully on her mother's shoulder, going home.

When they arrived, they began to argue immediately.

Gene Parker and Jim Brown had slept fine on their waterbeds and had had a busy day, starting at breakfast with the other Tulare team, Babcock and Tucker, who had been up late interviewing Tom Masters.

Parker and Brown got along well with Ralph Tucker, less well with Henry Babcock. As a sergeant, Babcock outranked them—the steps on the scale were deputy, detective, sergeant, and lieutenant—and he never seemed to let them forget it. In police language, Babcock was badge-heavy. Jim Brown had once heard Babcock refer to himself as the only educated person on the Tulare County Sheriff's staff. "I've always thought there was a big gap between education and intelligence," Jim Brown said dryly.

Jim wasn't a college degree person, either. He'd grown up on a farm in Ardmore, Oklahoma, until his family fled the Dust Bowl, when Jim was a little boy. They'd bought a farm in northern California, but Jim never cared much for farming, and when he finished high school in Tulare he'd worked as a salesman—used cars, potato chips—before he decided to try police work. When he joined the force in the spring of 1967, Jim said, he was "greener than a gourd," but the man he was assigned to work with, Gene Parker, broke him in quickly. They made a good team. Parker talked a lot, very fast, in a deep voice; Brown talked slowly, almost in a drawl, and said less, and they got along famously. They both had a quick, dry humor and would have tried to make a joke out of it if people told them they were good cops, which is what people said. Together they had the highest crime clearance rate of any detective team in the Tulare office; for all the fun they poked at themselves, they ranked high every month at the practice range—day shooting, night shooting, left-handed, right-handed. What they lacked in college credits they made up for in not-so-common sense. When a puzzling double homicide occurred in Exeter—a man shot five times, a woman shot twice, both bodies lying in the front yard, near a car, both weapons nearby—Brown and Parker figured out how the thing had happened and, though nobody at the barracks believed them at the time, it turned out later, from the dead woman's son's eyewitness account, that Brown and Parker were absolutely right.

In Los Angeles, however, they had to work with Babcock. "You stay outside," Babcock told them, when they all got over to the L.A. Sheriff's Office on Friday. "I'm going in to get the lay of the land." But Parker and Brown and Tucker had only been waiting in the hall a minute when the door opened and they were asked to come in.

"I'm Arthur Stoyanoff," said a tall, dapper man behind the desk, reaching out his hand. "I want everybody who's involved in this damned thing to be in here, so everybody can hear the same thing." Parker and Brown were delighted, and a little awed at the size of the place. "I counted fifty-four homicide investigators just sitting around there in the L.A. Sheriff's Office," Parker said, marveling.

They talked. Captain Stoyanoff assigned two of his men to help the Tulare men with anything they needed, so Parker and Brown talked more. Babcock and Tucker were working the Hope Masters angle; Parker and Brown were to check out the victim. They planned to start where Swalwell had started, with the pieces. "First we had to work up a background on Ashlock," Parker explained. "What does he do? Who does he associate with? Has he had family problems? We didn't know, one way or the other, about a third person at the ranch. We just went in with the idea of finding out what we could find out and put it all together and then try to determine what we've got here."

At Bill's apartment, the building manager, Mrs. Oezkan, was very friendly. She telephoned Ashkenazy Property for permission to enter, then she let the policemen into Apartment 104 and followed them inside.

The apartment was small, one room, with a piano and a sofa and a tiny kitchenette behind a bar. Mrs. Oezkan said that Mr. Ashlock had moved in on November 14, 1971, and had always seemed pleasant, a quiet person who kept pretty much to himself. She said he had a tall blond girlfriend and, just recently, she said, she had seen him with a short, dark-haired ladyfriend, about the same height as Bill.

Although Mrs. Oezkan said Mr. Ashlock was a nice dresser, with a good variety of suits and sport coats, the detectives found only a couple pairs of pants and one or two shirts. They also found a few scraps of paper with names and addresses on them, and photographs of two women. They gave Mrs. Oezkan a property receipt for the pictures, which turned out to be photos of Hope and Sandi. As they left the apartment, the detectives noted that the peephole in the door had been covered.

The detectives then went to Bill's office and talked with Helen Linley. She told them that Bill had left the office on Friday afternoon, early, and hadn't come in on Monday. When he still hadn't come in on Tuesday, she called Hope Masters's house; the maid told her Mrs. Masters was in bed and could not come to the phone. Later that day, Barry Carter, an artist with Dailey & Associates, had called, and the maid told Barry that Mrs. Masters had said Mr. Ashlock was still at the ranch.

Mrs. Linley said that a woman Mr. Ashlock knew, named Sandi, telephoned the office. She had said she wanted to change a dinner date she had with Mr. Ashlock from Tuesday to Wednesday. Then Mrs. Linley talked about Van's call, telling of the murder, and she told Parker and Brown what a nice man Bill Ashlock was, a gentle man, easy to get along with, possessing a quiet but keen sense of humor. Later, they heard the same kind of thing from Barry Carter, from Cliff Einstein, from Fran Ashlock, from Bill's brother Bob, and from Sandi. "Everyone liked him," Jim Brown wrote in his report.

"I liked Bill," Martha Padilla was saying, a little wistfully. "He was nice to me."

Martha and her twin sister Mary were at the Los Angeles Sheriff's Office, talking to Sergeant Babcock and Detective Tucker. Martha spoke in Spanish, through a translator, Dora Britton.

Martha told the detectives how Mr. Ashlock and Mrs. Masters had left for the ranch the Friday before, in Hope's station wagon, leaving Bill's little green car in the driveway. But when Martha returned Monday night around 11:00, neither of those cars was there, she said. "Two new cars were there, one white, one yellow." She had never seen either car before.

Inside, she said she met a man whom Mrs. Masters told her was Bill's friend. "He had long hair, and he wasn't bad looking," Martha recalled. Not fat, not skinny; "medium." She remembered he'd told her not to eat too much or she would get fat. Martha noticed his pipe because it was so large, so strange; it seemed to have been cut from the bark of a tree. He told Martha he was from London.

That was on Tuesday morning, Martha said. She didn't speak to him Monday night, because he and Mrs. Masters were in the living room, with the door from the kitchen closed; Martha had opened it, seen them, and closed the door again. "I saw them lying down there," she said. "She was rubbing his back, giving him a massage."

"Did you see them together in the bedroom?" Babcock asked.

"I saw them lying down on the living room floor," Martha repeated. "They had blankets, and there were a lot of suitcases. The children were in the bedroom. It is my thought that they were not in the bedroom because the children were occupying the bedroom."

"Did they sleep together that night?"

"They closed the door to the kitchen," Martha said. "They were lying down on the floor of the living room when I saw them—on the carpet, and I didn't see them again that night."

"Did you see them kiss each other, or hug each other?"

"No. What I did see was that they were both lying down and she was rubbing his back."

"Did they drink? Were they drinking?"

"Yes."

"Did Bill's friend have his shirt off?"

"Yes."

"Did Bill's friend stay all night?"

"Yes."

"Do you know where Bill's friend slept?"

"I believe they both slept on the carpet. On the floor."

"Did you see that they were lying down together when you came home?"

"Yes."

Martha said when she got up Tuesday morning, the man was in the kitchen, cooking breakfast, and that was when she chatted with him.

"Did Mrs. Masters receive any phone calls at the house while you were there?"

"Yes," Martha said. "One who called was Bill's boss. Mrs. Masters told me it was Bill's boss and to tell him that she was very ill and that Bill was at the ranch."

"Did Mrs. Masters give you any instructions about the telephone calls?"

"Yes, she told me that if anybody called, to write it down and not to tell anyone that she was there. That I was to say that I didn't know where she was and that I did not know where Bill was. And she told me she was going to the hospital because she was very, very ill."

"Did you see Mrs. Masters cry or act upset?"

"I saw her upset, and she was sad and very weak and with her eyes very sad, and she was very downhearted."

"Why was she like this?" Babcock asked.

"I don't know."

"How many telephone calls did she receive on Tuesday?"

"A man called about ten times, but I don't know who he was."

"Does the name Mr. Webb mean anything?"

"I don't recall."

"Does the name Troy mean anything?"

"No."

"Did you ever hear Mrs. Masters call Bill's friend by his name?"

"Yes, but I don't remember his name."

"Does the name Lionel sound like it?"

"No. I don't remember."

"How about the name Tyler, or Taylor?"

"I don't remember."

Detective Tucker asked Martha, then, whether Hope had told her she'd been raped.

"No, no, nothing like that," Martha answered. "The only thing I saw was that she was ill or weak, and her eyes were sad and she seemed upset and without any strength. She wanted to be resting and lying down."

"Did Mrs. Masters act as if she was afraid for her life?"

"She was nervous. I don't know why. She was looking for her pills for her nerves."

"Does Mrs. Masters smoke a lot? Take pills? Drink liquor? Or smoke marijuana?"

"She drank a lot with Bill. But when she came back from outings—going out with Bill—her eyes looked like she could have been smoking marijuana. She took medication and pills, but I don't know which kind."

"Was there anything that Bill's friend brought to the house?"

"He brought several suitcases. Many. There were three black ones, and they were still in the closet. I saw them there yesterday. I think they are the same ones. The rest he took with him."

Martha's sister had little to say, except that she'd stayed overnight with her sister at Hope's house, sharing the small bedroom off the kitchen. When she left the next morning, a little after 7:00 A.M., she saw two cars in the driveway, a yellow car and a white car.

Taylor called Mary Bowyer once more, at ten minutes to five.

"Did you get through to Van?"

"No," Mary said. "I called, but was told about the same thing you were told."

"They are probably on their way back now," Taylor said. "Will they go to Van's?"

"I think so," Mary told him. "Why don't you call there?"

"No, I will call Ned Nelsen," Taylor said. "That will probably help."

"You mentioned an affidavit," Mary reminded him. "What are you going to do with it? It won't help anyone as long as only you have it. Why don't you read it to me? Or send me a copy?"

"Yes, I have a four-page affidavit," Taylor said. "Perhaps I'll get it to Nelsen."

"Well, get it to someone so it can do some good," Mary said sharply. "It's doing no good in your hands. Please call the family at home tonight. They need your help so badly."

"Stop worrying," Taylor said. "Everything will work out all right. I am sure Hope is with her family now and will be okay."

Mary Bowyer was angered at his cheery tone. "Our talking has accomplished nothing," she said. "Call them at home tonight."

"Stop worrying, stop worrying," Taylor said. "I've made about twenty phone calls today on this and I'll be making more before it's over. But I'll do it my way."

At Coco's Coffee Shop in Long Beach, Fran Ashlock said Bill had never made trouble for anyone and was not a violent person. Fran described Bill as such a gentle person that sometimes she would lose her temper because he would never lose his temper. Fran said that although she and Bill had been separated for some time, she saw him nearly every week, and she was aware of his female friends, including Hope Masters. She said that Bill had discussed that relationship with her and had indicated he might not be able to handle "the fast living situation."

At Junior's Coffee Shop in Altadena, Sandi said Bill was a mild-mannered person, a man who avoided distasteful situations, and she could think of no one at all who would possibly harm him for any personal reason. Sandi was upset as she talked, but the detectives felt she was trying to cooperate. She said that just before Christmas, two months earlier, Bill had told her he'd moved in with Hope Masters, but Sandi told the detectives that nobody was jealous of anybody else, and she and Bill had continued to see each other from time to time.

Sandi told the detectives she didn't know any of Hope Masters's friends, only that Bill had talked about some of the expensive parties he and Mrs. Masters attended, and about the wealth and social position of Hope's family. Sandi said Bill had described Hope as a demanding type of person who would become highly outraged if any given situation was not up to her expectations.

As Parker and Brown probed into Bill's background, they learned he'd been married before he married Fran. When he was 24, starting out in the air force, he'd married a girl he met while stationed in Arizona. They'd been married four and a half years, and had one daughter.

Hope hadn't known that.

Taylor called that weekend. Gene Tinch had attached a recording device to the phone and, with the recorder and people listening in on the four extensions, and people giving instructions and advice in the background, it was sometimes difficult to hear Taylor clearly. But Gene was excited; this was a chance to pick up clues about this elusive, mysterious man.

Taylor asked for Hope, but she wasn't home. Honey told him Hope had been taken away for questioning.

"Who took her?" Taylor asked, sounding concerned. "Where can I reach her?"

"Her lawyer and another man," Honey said.

"Then she knew him, so that's all right," Taylor said, sounding relieved.

"Oh, Taylor," Honey said, "she has been charged with first-degree murder. They weren't even going to let her out on bail."

"I know that," Taylor said.

When he called back, Hope was home. "How are you?" he asked. Without waiting for an answer he said, "I know you're very bad. I will stick around and see you out of this whole mess."

"Oh, please do," Hope moaned. She was desperately grateful to hear his voice. "There are three private people who will meet you anywhere." She gave him Gene's home phone number.

Taylor talked about the contract. "It was bought through Chicago," he said.

"Oh, God, I can't believe who would do that to me," Hope said, feeling dazed. She paused. "I'm worried about you."

"Why are you worried about me?" Taylor asked.

"I don't want you to get hurt," she said. "You know that."

"That's neither here nor there," he said briskly. "I must enjoy what I'm doing. You take for so many years, and all of a sudden it's your turn to give."

Hope did not know what to say. "Can you call me later?" she asked.

"Sure," Taylor said brightly. "Take care of yourself. Good-bye."

Taylor called Gene Tinch very soon thereafter. "Hope asked me to call you," he said. "What has she told you so far?" Gene gave him a résumé of Hope's story about the Mafia contract and the intruder, the man with the goatee. "That is substantially correct," Taylor said. "However, there are a lot of loose ends."

"Can you tie them down for me?" Gene asked.

"The original contract was on Hope and her two older children," Taylor explained. "The original contractor was sent out from Cleveland, but he spent the money and did not do his job. So he was eliminated in a grubby motel, Room 7, on Sunset Boulevard, about two weeks ago. He was killed with the same gun that was used at the ranch, and the slugs should match."

A murder in a motel, thought Tinch. *That's something we can check.* "Can you tell me about what took place at the ranch?" he asked.

Taylor rambled on for a while, saying he'd moved Bill's body and had freed Hope, then brought her back to Los Angeles. "My people have found out that the tape was bought in a small drugstore across from Sears in Porterville," he told Gene. He paused. "I was in Porterville too, on the day of the arraignment, but I talked to two of the detectives there, and I know what's going on."

"I'd like to get together with you and discuss this," Gene said. "If you have talked to detectives and you know what's happening, you know you are important to Hope's defense."

"We will probably never meet in person," Taylor replied. "However, I will have a cassette tape delivered to you with my statement." He ended with a reassurance. "Please call Hope and assure her I will stay around and see her through this. I know her father has had to put up fifty thousand dollars bail, and if she needs money, my people will see that she gets it. Please assure her I will keep in touch."

Gene immediately called a man he knew at LAPD and, pretty soon, he got a call back. A homicide had been reported on Friday, February 23, at the Hollywood Hills Motel on West Sunset Boulevard. The victim had been identified as Richard Orin Crane, an unemployed engineer from the state of Washington, who had checked into Room 8 at the motel under his true name at 1:10 P.M. the day before. He had arrived alone, driving an eight-year-old Rambler station wagon. Richard Crane was a big man —six feet, two hundred pounds, thirty-two years old. When he did not check out on Friday, the manager used a passkey and found Mr. Crane slumped over the bed, with a gunshot wound in his head.

The men at LAPD had not been particularly stirred by the case, and neither had the newspapers. The murder had not been written up anywhere, and the LAPD investigators had filed it under "Miscellaneous Crime Report." But Gene Tinch was stirred. It was now clear that Taylor, whoever he was, was a formidable factor in this case. To say the least.

Taylor was right: Hope was "very bad." She ached all over, with heavy vaginal bleeding and cramps. Honey had tried to make her eat, but Hope said she would throw up if she did. Honey had called her gynecologist, explaining the situation at the house and the danger. So when Dr. Frances Holmes came to examine Hope, she came in golf clothes, carrying her medical gear in a brown paper grocery bag.

Dr. Holmes put Hope on Sustagen, a liquid food, a teaspoonful at a time. "Don't try to take a whole glassful, and don't worry," Dr. Holmes said. "You're going to be all right." Hope felt better, then; she trusted Dr. Holmes, whom she'd known half her life, and she felt she cared. Hope remembered how Dr. Holmes had insisted she stop nursing, when she had begun losing weight a lot. "I know your babies tend to have colic, but you have to stop," Dr. Holmes had said, and Hope had followed her orders.

When Dr. Holmes had gone and the house was dark, Hope lay wide awake in her mother's guest room. The bed was king-size, and all three children slept with her, partly because in this multimillion-dollar, two-bedroom house, there was no place else for them to sleep, and partly because since she'd arrived home, the children wouldn't let her out of their sight. They kept clutching at her, climbing over her, grasping at her, especially K.C. and Hope Elizabeth, with what seemed something like terror, desperation. Keith had the far side of the bed, with K.C. between him and Hope; her daughter was on the other side. Every night Hope Elizabeth fell asleep with her hand clenching her mother's so tightly that Hope could compare it only to a person dangling over the side of a cliff, clinging to a rope.

Hope was scared about so many things she could hardly sort them out in her head: a bomb under the house, someone waiting, watching, somewhere, with a telescopic rifle. She kept hearing footsteps up and down, up and down, pacing, beyond the wide window—maybe Gene Tinch, maybe a policeman, maybe not.

Several nights after she came home she couldn't stand it any longer. She crept out of bed, disentangling herself from the sleeping children, and slipped through the guest bathroom into Honey's room beyond.

"I have to talk to you," Hope whispered.

Honey awoke instantly, reached for her robe, and followed Hope through the bathroom, through the guest room, and into the den. Hope closed the den door and switched on a dim light. "I have to talk to you," she said again. She sat on the sofa; Honey sat next to her.

"Don't get upset," Hope said. "Don't say anything to Van or anybody. But I have to tell you, because if I am killed, there has to be somebody who knows. There has to be somebody who knows the truth."

Honey stared at Hope, her face pinched with tension.

Hope stared straight ahead for a moment, at the dark wall of the den, then she turned and grasped Honey's hands.

"It's Taylor," Hope said, her voice sounding urgent, like a hiss. "Taylor is the one who came into the bedroom. Taylor is the one who killed Bill."

Honey twisted her hands out of Hope's grasp and clenched them around her daughter's hands. Then she drew them back into her lap and held them tightly together, to keep them still.

"All right, Hopie," she said.

But still Hope lay awake at night, night after night. She was drained by her fear; she was so fearful that she had not yet let the children out of the house. The days were filled with commotion and chaos, the children squabbling, the phone ringing, Van and Hope quarreling, with Honey often stepping in, weeping. Disagreements lurched into discord, anxieties into anger. In this house throbbing with people—three children and three adults full time, other people in and out constantly—Hope felt emotionally stranded. Especially at night, lying in the darkness, she yearned, she ached, for someone she could talk to, someone who would truly understand.

She thought about Bill.
She thought about Lionel.
She thought about Taylor.

CHAPTER
TEN

"How ARE WE going to tell him we're not getting anywhere?" Gene Parker asked Jim Brown as they drove over to see Lieutenant Barnes.

Brown shook his head glumly. Throughout the long drive up from L.A., since they'd been summoned back up north to give a report, he'd been wondering that himself. Neither of them was afraid of the lieutenant; he was the kind of person you called "lieutenant" or "sir" on duty, but whom you could be casual with, call him by his nickname, other times. Because of his silver-streaked hair, Forrest Barnes's nickname was "Frosty."

Besides liking him, Jim Brown had had special respect for Lieutenant Barnes since Jim's beginnings on the force, when Barnes had said something Jim had never forgotten. Simple, but very meaningful to Jim. "As a law enforcement officer, don't ever take anything for granted," Barnes told Jim Brown. "Don't ever assume anything. When a police officer says, 'I assume,' this is what happens." Barnes took a piece of paper and printed the word ASSUME. Then he printed it again, splitting the word with hyphens: ASS-U-ME. "When you assume something, it makes an *ass* out of *you* and *me.*"

Still, it was not going to be easy to tell Barnes that they were getting nowhere fast. Getting nowhere partly, they felt, because they didn't have an overall picture of what was going on in the case; they'd noticed that

Sergeant Babcock almost never made a phone call in their presence, and they felt that in a way, Babcock was making their job harder. They'd heard that when Babcock had first interviewed the young officers at the Beverly Hills station, he'd read them their rights and made them sign a waiver. For a police officer to advise other police officers of their rights was, even for Babcock, really, really badge-heavy.

And partly they were frustrated because, for all their hours of driving around and talking, for all their pages of notes and reports, they had yet to come up with anything remotely resembling a motive for the murder of Bill Ashlock. They had not heard of one single person who didn't think Bill Ashlock was a really super guy. A nice man, very quiet, very well-liked —so unanimously well-liked that he'd ended up on a slab in the cold room at Myers Chapel with a bullet shattered throughout his brain.

"What are we going to tell Barnes?" Parker asked Brown.

"Well, shoot, we're just going to have to tell him the truth," Brown said. "He's going to catch on, anyway." So that is what they were telling Forrest Barnes in his office Monday morning, March 5, when he got the call, long distance from Chicago.

Hope used the phone in the bedroom, when she had a moment's privacy. She couldn't make the call she'd been wanting to make since the weekend at the ranch—to call Fran to tell her, personally, about Bill, so that Fran could pass on Hope's feelings to the little girls. With Bill dead over a week now, and the whole mess in the newspapers, and with the word she'd had of Fran's plan to file a civil suit against Hope—deprivation of income, wrongful death—obviously it was too late for that call. So she called Bill's office.

"I can't talk long," Hope told Helen Linley. "I'm not supposed to make phone calls, and I don't know if the phone is tapped." She paused, then continued quickly.

"I'd like you to give Fran Ashlock a message, please. I'm sorry I can't deliver it myself, but I can't.

"I want you to tell—to tell Fran how happy Bill was, all the way up to the ranch, and how lucky he was. He had no problems with his wife, she was a very understanding person, and he could see his children whenever he wished, and he loved his job and the people he worked with, and he loved me and my children."

Helen Linley took notes as she listened.

"He probably never could have known what happened," Hope said. She went on to say that Bill didn't believe in God, but she did, and she had been trying to convert him, and one day after he had gone with her to the Self-Realization Garden, or maybe it was a temple, on Sunset, he had been impressed and had said he wanted to go back again sometime.

Hope asked Helen Linley about the funeral service, because her family wanted to do what they could. Helen Linley said the services were private, and it was all over. Hope asked how they'd learned of Bill's death; Mrs. Linley told Hope her father had called.

"I never thought I would be blamed," Hope said.

There was a brief silence.

"I will pass the message along to Mrs. Ashlock," Helen said.

"And tell her I've been praying for Bill."

Helen Linley told Cliff Einstein about the call and, the next day, Cliff discussed it with Parker and Brown.

"It had the same emotional qualities of somebody who had done somebody harm and at least was causing the harm to be slightly less severe, by making it clear that there was not suffering accompanying the harm," Cliff Einstein told the police.

When the doorbell rang that evening, Van opened the door an inch or two, without taking off the chain. "Special Delivery," said the young black man on the doorstep, handing Van a large brown envelope through the opening.

Van laid it on the table and called Ned Nelsen at home.

"What should I do?" Van asked. "Open it, or what?"

"Call Gene Tinch," Ned said.

"What should I do?" Van asked Gene. "Open it, or what?"

"Open it," Gene said. "I'll hold on."

Van used a pair of ice tongs from the bar drawer to pick up the envelope while he cut off the top with a scissors.

"It's a cassette tape," Van told Gene.

"I'm coming over," Gene said. Van called Ned, who said he and Tom were coming, too. Thus a sizable audience assembled to hear Taylor's first tape, which was clearly not what Taylor had had in mind at all.

> I do not want any members of your family listening in. I do not want any of your lawyers to listen in. I just want you to follow the instructions I give you.
>
> I will stick by you to the bitter end and I will get you out of this mess. I will not leave the country. I will not leave the area until I know all the charges against you have been dropped. I will do everything I

can to solve your problems for you, problems that were brought on basically because of some of my actions, but I'm not going to get into that because I don't know yet whether this tape is going to fall into the wrong hands or not.

I do want you to know that your telephone has a tap on it. I am talking about your mother's telephone and I would presume also the telephone at your house; however, I have not used it. To assure anyone that may intercept this, I have not touched the paper nor the envelope this is being mailed in, nor the cassette. They may rest certain that there are no fingerprints or any other means of identification upon the cassette, the outer box, or anything else which could lead to my identity.

Now then, let's get to matters. . . .

I was at Porterville yesterday, although I didn't come into the court because that is a very small building and a very small court, and frankly, I wasn't too sure what you might do if you saw me, although my appearance, my basic appearance, had been changed to the point that I doubt if even you would recognize me. But there was that off-chance that you might recognize me and suddenly shout out, 'Oh, Taylor, help me!' or something, so I had to maintain a little bit of distance.

But I did see you. I saw you close enough through a pair of binoculars to realize that you really looked awful, that you'd been through hell and, you know, there's nothing going to change that, no magic words I can utter into this microphone and say, 'Oh, God, I'm sorry.' Of course I'm sorry—but it's happened. You've been through it. You know what the experience is like.

Now you're back home. I had tried to call you earlier today, and your mother told me you were off being questioned by the police. Now, I don't know what that's all about, but hopefully before this cassette reaches you I will have talked with you on the telephone and had a few brief words with you about what the situation is. I must forewarn you that I'm not going to hang on the phone and talk to you at great length because, knowing that your phone is tapped, I must also assume that they have a back tracer on it where they are attempting to determine where I'm calling you from, and once they determine where I'm calling you from, they will send authorities to attempt to apprehend me.

I presume I'm wanted very badly. In fact, if my information can be relied upon, one of the main reasons for letting you out was that they figured you would eventually lead them to me through design or by accident or something of that nature.

But we're not going to allow that to happen. They needn't worry about that, and I don't think you need worry about that. However, I will attempt to stay close enough that I can protect your best interests. I don't believe that—while your family means well, your mother and your stepfather and the various people around you, I just don't believe that they are equipped to handle this situation. The attorney that they've hired for you, Ned Nelsen, is not my idea of the best sort of attorney for this type situation. Oh, I know he has a great reputation, but there are other people in California, and if the events take such a turn to the point that the charges against you continue to linger, I am going to suggest that you hire a certain attorney. I know who this attorney is already. I have spoken with this attorney. This attorney knows, shall we say, everything, and would be better equipped to provide you with some sort of assistance.

Obviously I have more information from my sources and things like that than either your family or attorneys or the authorities persecuting —I'm not going to say prosecuting, because at this point it's more of a persecution-type thing. But I have more information than all those forces combined could ever hope to develop.

I'm somewhat tempted to blurt some of it out on this tape. However, I don't think that's wise, because I would prefer to use the information I have as bargaining and bartering material to have the charges and harassment against you dropped.

I have kept track of the kids. I know they're staying home from school. I talked to Keith the other day on the phone but, as I say, I'm not far away, dear. I'm going to stay close. I'll see you out of this one. Mr. Fix-it will get you through this one.

And I found a stunning white dress, size 3. Oh, it's great. Oh, I know this is not the time to talk about things like that, but nevertheless I found one.

I must say I'm anxious to find out how you found jail. Was it comfortable? Was it all the things you thought it would be? I'm sure it wasn't. Oh, come on, smile. You can smile a little bit.

Well, here we are. You're there. I'm here. And there's that whole big army of people between us. I don't know what to say. . . .

I know that you owe me nothing; I owe you nothing. What happened happened, and it would make better sense if I just disappeared into the night, but I think if my disappearance would happen now, and you were left to stand alone, I think that, knowing the forces of justice in the United States, that you would probably be persecuted and prosecuted into prison or a mental institution. It's hard to say.

Well, hang in, dear. Know that I care for you and know that I respect your position and remember this: that I didn't take you out of that ranch house all the way back to Los Angeles to be with those three kids only to have a bunch of police officers in their funny uniforms, with their guns on their hips, drag you away from them. I'm gonna see that you stay there in that house with your three children and that you have a better life than you've had thus far. So hang on. I'm going out to try and call you on the phone, and I'll get back to you a little later. Much love.

Back again. You were not available. I'm just beginning to think I can't get through to you. You know, you're being held up there in the county jail. I called several times and had talked to the fellow there at the jail desk and attempted to seduce him into putting you on the telephone and—let's see—I've also talked to the detective that's investigating the case, I've talked to the court bailiffs over in Porterville, I've talked to the District Attorney's office up there where you were originally being held. I've talked to any number of people and in the event that anything would happen to me, and knowing your position, I did have an affidavit drawn up, and I'm going to read it to you now —the normal affidavit form, Los Angeles County, state of California, and then it reads:

The undersigned is disposed to state under oath the following:

1. That I am not an American national and under the instructions and orders of my government, I am prohibited from having direct contact with local and/or domestic authorities and thereby allowing my identity and purpose within these borders to become known.

2. That by mere accident I have become involved in a situation whereby the laws of the state of California and perhaps the United States have been broken in that, on the twenty-fifth day of February 1973 I did become aware and of the knowledge that the murder of a Caucasian male believed to have been named William T. Ashlock at a ranch house in the Springville, California, area. Said body was on the sofa in the living room of said home, face down in a pool of dried blood, with its legs across the coffee table.

3. That in the front bedroom I did also discover the person of

Hope Masters, Caucasian, female, approximately thirty-one years of age, ninety-five pounds, long blond hair of a blondish hue. Hope Masters was nude and her hands were tied behind her back with a piece of adhesive tape and her feet at the ankles were also so bound that on untying this woman I determined that it would have been impossible for Hope Masters to have bound herself. Thereby I was inclined to believe her story of an intruder and the murder of the man on the sofa in the next room.

4. That I had no desire then, as I do now, to become involved in a domestic situation. Therefore, I was quite agreeable to the demands and pleadings of one Hope Masters to remove her from the scene of the murder and to a Los Angeles, California, area, and that I could further understand and appreciate the hysteria of Hope Masters, wanting the body of the man removed from her view prior to her leaving the bedroom. That of my own free will and at the request of Hope Masters, I did place a sheet, bedspread, and pad upon the floor, did roll the body up on same and did drag same out of the living room and through the kitchen into a rear bedroom whereupon I did help Hope Masters out to the automobile I was driving.

5. That I did then return to the inside of the home/house and did pick up and remove anything which I had touched and could possibly lead to my identity through fingerprint identification, i.e., adhesive tape that bound Hope Masters, etc., etc. However, I did not remove anything nor did I move and/or conceal anything that might have been a weapon or instrument of death of the man upon the sofa.

6. That I did drive Hope Masters to her home in Beverly Hills, California, or Los Angeles, California, and did stay in said home with and offer protection to Hope Masters and her three children until Tuesday, 27 February 1973, at which time Hope and her three children were transferred to the home of Hope's mother and stepfather.

7. That the entire time your affiant was in the presence of Hope Masters, she voiced and displayed signs of fear for her life and the lives of her children, and the mother and children did not wish to be in any room in her home other than where I might be present. That said fear apparently was based upon the belief

of Hope Masters and the facts of what occurred in the ranch house/home that a husband of Hope Masters had hired someone and/or several persons to murder Hope Masters and two of her children, namely, the older son, Keith, and the daughter, Hope.

8. That after accompanying Hope Masters and her children to the home of her mother and stepfather I did depart and leave Hope. However, later I did inquire via telephone as to Hope's safety and plans, whereupon she informed me that her mother insisted the police be notified and I did go to her parents' home in Beverly Hills, California, engaged in conversation with her parents.

9. When it was agreed that the authorities should be called, it was this affiant who left the home and first called the Beverly Hills Police Department. However, the two policemen that I spoke with were trying and difficult to convince that a crime had been committed and/or that an unmarked car should be sent to the home. Whereupon I called Hope Masters and told her to have her stepfather call the Beverly Hills police, while I called the sheriff's department in Porterville, which I did accomplish and did encounter much the same difficulty in convincing the sheriff to undertake an investigation without complete access to this affiant's identity.

10. That based upon a telephone conversation with Hope Masters's mother upon the twenty-eighth day of February 1973, midafternoon, I believe that Hope Masters has been arrested and removed from Los Angeles, California, to the county wherein the ranch house/home is situated. Therefore I am issuing and making this affidavit in support of this affiant's belief and knowledge that Hope Masters did not kill or cause to be killed one William T. Ashlock in the aforementioned ranch house/home; that Hope Masters did nothing to remove said body from the sofa to the rear bedroom, that I did so as Hope was too frightened to pass through the living room to leave the house and that I did move the body of my own free will; that I did actively encourage and insist that Hope Masters not call the authorities and report the death of William T. Ashlock for reasons of protecting my identity as well as protecting Hope Masters, who was frightened that her husband, one Tom Masters, was intent upon causing harm and/or death to

Hope Masters and two of her children, and that this advice was continuing throughout our travels together; that Hope Masters did not know or have ever made my acquaintance until the day at the ranch house/home nor did she know my person in any form; that Hope Masters does not know my true identity, does not know from where I come or what my intent and purposes might be within the United States; that Hope Masters was under your affiant's control and custody from the time I entered the ranch house/home and returned her to the Los Angeles area and until I accompanied Hope Masters to the home of her mother and stepfather.

11. That your affiant is willing to answer any and all questions concerning his personal knowledge of Hope Masters and her children and what occurred at the ranch house/home in Springville area and the body of one William T. Ashlock and the actions of the affiant in relation to this incident. However, this must be done outside the United States in jurisdiction of the authorities so desiring to put forth questions or seek drawings or diagrams and perhaps wish to view and test the various items which the affiant carried out of the ranch house/home in order to protect the identity of the affiant.

Further your affiant sayeth not.

And this has been signed.

Now, I'm not too sure that this is the type of affidavit you want. It's sketchy. It doesn't have much detail. I'm sure that in this situation I could easily run it into a thirty- or forty-page affidavit, which I think might be the most useful to your particular situation at this time. I think that the more facts that are known, the better it will be for you. For example, while— I'm gonna give you a few little bits of information which could be very helpful to you.

The bullet that was in William Ashlock can be matched up to a weapon that ballistically fits another death. There was an unemployed engineer from the Washington-Oregon area who was originally hired with the intentions that he was to kill you and either one or two of your children, and also Ashlock. That he set out and proceeded to follow you and accomplish his task for quite some time; however, he failed in doing so. He had spent a major portion of the money which had been paid to him for this task, and that he was found and eliminated. I know where his car is parked. I know all the basic facts to that situation, which I am sure would more than cover you in that you were elsewhere at the time this other crime occurred.

My people can also trace back how the weapon traveled to the West Coast. That it was part of a package agreement that someone would come out here and would kill you and your children. And there's other little things, except that I don't know where this tape's gonna go, and I don't know whether you're going to be completely trustworthy and not allow anybody else to listen to it; I'm going to hold back on what basic information I have until I know we have some sort of agreement on what we're going to do.

It's not a fact that I distrust you as a person. I know that you're a very trustworthy person and that your word is good, but I also know that you're in an impossible situation, that you're surrounded by family and strangers who are pushing and pulling and questioning and asking, and from the comments that have been passed around, they're somewhat of the suspicion that you are deeply involved in this, and they're not too sure that you're blameless, so you might bear in mind that there's a lot of little things going on around you that I'm more aware of perhaps than you're aware of.

For example, the other day your father's—your stepfather's—secretary thought she was being very cute by having somebody listen in to my conversation. They were using a means of—they had— First they thought they were going to do this and they were going to do that— but she obviously thought she was being cute and that I wouldn't realize what was going on. But I'm a pretty perceptive person—yes, yes—I'm not new to the situation, so I'm up on most things.

But we're not here to talk about me. We're here to talk about you. Keep your head. Be cool. Don't get rattled. And for God's sakes, don't tell the police any more stories. You should never have made an original statement without an attorney being present, and this is where the mistake is, because the minute they can start tripping you up on this little fact or that little fact, or things like that.

I think the first thing they grabbed hold of was they couldn't find the tape that you were bound with. Well, I carried that away because obviously I touched it with my bare hands, and adhesive tape has a way of making fingerprints that—you know, in the sticky portion— and I wasn't about to leave that around. I have attempted to sow some fingerprints that will lead to the identity of somebody else, but I don't know how successful that'll be. I'm involved in many different areas, and one way or the other, we'll solve this problem for you.

It's unfortunate that you know absolutely nothing about what happened. You weren't prepared for what happened, and you come out being the heavy guy. It is nice that the newspapers recognize that you're a socialite, and that's the kind of publicity you want least in life. At least that's what I would say.

You're an awful nice person. Nice girl. You have a lot of redeeming features and qualities. You have some I don't like. In fact—hang on a minute. I want to get a list of something that I made up when I was trying to call you up there at the jail. I was going to talk to you and tell you that I wasn't gonna go away, and that I was gonna stay around and help you, but you have to make five promises.

The first one was that you stop taking all kinds of pills. The second one is that you would gain ten pounds. The third one was that you become a good housekeeper by closing drawers and picking up your clothes, etc., etc. Four would be wait. Just wait, period. And five; save those backrubs. Oh, I thought maybe it might make you smile a bit there. Yes, well, I'm sure that it probably won't now, but I don't know. You can smile even in a bad situation like this. Sure. There's always room for a smile.

Well, let me look at my list of things that I wanted to cover with you. Oh, I do wish to impress upon you that your father's home phone is tapped and is being monitored by the police, and I would suggest you stop your cooperation with the authorities in giving them statement after statement after statement. They've elected to charge you now. The evidence they're going to bring forward, if it goes that far, would—could be blown apart by just one appearance of one witness. I have no desire to come into court and take the witness stand and give testimony for you. I have no desire for the authorities to know my identity. I have no desire for a number of things, but before I would see you separated from your children, I would do that for you. I don't know why I'd do it for you. I mean, I don't owe you a damn thing. Yeah—besides, you're so ugly. Mmmm . . . don't like you a bit. Right. No, can't stand anybody who won't kiss before they brush their teeth. Yeah.

See, aren't you glad you didn't let anybody listen to this tape? I wish I could be more frank, more candid with it, but until I know where the tape went, until I know that we're respecting each other mutually, that we're out for the same purpose, to extract you—extradite you—out of this trouble, and see you're restored to a reasonable position in society and, you know, back and join your children, I'm going to be a little hesitant about being—about just letting it all hang out on these tapes.

From time to time I'll contact you. Obviously I'm not going to send somebody by with these tapes because that person would be arrested. It's becoming more difficult to watch and provide you some protection. I've been a little bit happy while you've been in jail, as a matter of fact, because that was one of the safer places for you. While I couldn't get to you, nobody else could either. But there'll be somebody around close, never too far. There's going to be that buffer of the police in between, watching you, but who knows? One or two of those may be in my team. You never know what happens. It's a funny world.

I'll do what I told you I was going to do. I will do it at the appropriate time. I think we both know what we're talking about, and that party has been with someone ever since this whole thing has come up, but certainly he's not going to get to you. No, I'll make sure he doesn't get to you. Just have a little faith and a little trust in me. I haven't let you down completely yet, have I? Obviously the minute I knew you were arrested I could've left the area, left the country, and sat back and watched the newspapers and laughed, but I didn't do that, so I'm taking the risk of staying around. I'm taking the risk of trying to help you, and I will help you, but have faith in me and know that when the proper time presents itself to take care of that situation to see that you are never bothered or troubled by that individual again, it will be done.

Moneywise, it would be very unwise for me to give you any money or see that your life is made more comfortable at this particular time. You're going to have to suffer it out. It would be one of those things you would have to explain where it had come from; it would create more problems than it's worth. So be poor. Enjoy being poor. There's lots of people in the world who don't know how good it is to be poor, so enjoy being poor. Mmm . . . while I would love to see you and sit down and frankly talk and hash everything out, and decide what we're going to do—well, this isn't the time to do that either. . . .

That's about all I can think of right now. I'm going to blip off and see if you're available. So—try to be good. Try and stay out of jail. Try and put a little weight on. Stop taking all those pills. Don't give anyone a backrub. And wait. Be patient. I'll come through. Ole Mr. Fix-it will fix it yet. Okay? Give the kids a kiss for me. Bye-bye.

Back again. It appears to be impossible to get through to you today. It's now about twenty minutes to five on a Saturday afternoon and

I'm stretched out on the sofa. The tape recorder is on the coffee table next to me, and I am wondering what are the best things to say to you. . . . If there was any way that I could have reached out and taken your hand and touched you and let you know why you're in the jail, that there is somebody that cares, that there is somebody that isn't going to desert you, that there is somebody that's interested not in anything other than just you, and your children and making sure that you find some degree of happiness. . . .

Just let me get you out of this one. Let me get you on a good, even track and ooohh . . . it's not to say that I wouldn't be interested. I always find you interesting even if you do have some hangups. You need ten pounds. You take too many goofy pills. You have to have your teeth brushed in the morning. Oh, yes, I remember all those cute little things. Yep, the barefoot girl—just rattle on, talk a mile a minute—talk my ear off. I've never listened to anybody as much as I've listened to you. It was delightful.

Sure, I'll always sleep by your unlocked door. I'll do anything you want, within reason. Just remember the thing I taught you: self-preservation is the strongest urge in anybody so, within reason, I'll—within my means—I'll see that you're out to enjoy life. Well, you never know. It's been a funny time. Let me see how much more I have on this tape. Oh, I might talk a little bit more and then I think I'll get this in the mail because I want you to get it the first thing Monday.

Yes, I wonder what you're doing right now besides talking to detectives and lawyers and sitting around wringing your hands and smoking too many cigarettes. You know, you really do smoke too much. Yeah, you ought to slow down. It's time to make a lot of little changes in your life. Well, I'll let you tell me what's wrong with me, too, you know; it's a twoway street, it's not a oneway expressway. Sure, you can tell me what's wrong provided that I can always tell you what's wrong, too. Oh, well.

God, I miss those kids already. Sure, they bug you and they get on your nerves, but they're also pretty cute kids. I couldn't get over how nice Hope was that morning I drove her to school. Of course, K.C.'s a little charmer, he delights everyone, but then children that age are that way. But Keith—I think I could be very fond of him, enjoying sporting things, you know, doing boy-man sort of things, but that morning I drove Hope to school she was a completely different person than when she was throwing things around. It could be a nice relationship . . . hmmm—very nice. I found your family to be very impressive and delightful. I like their mother. Of course, I like the mother the best. Well, I like the mother in a different way, even if you are a grinch at times. Bossy. The very idea of telling me what to do just rubbed me the right way. No, you didn't do anything that really hurt my feelings, or said anything. We got along fine, I thought.

Too bad there wasn't time for more Hamburger Hamlets and had it been a nicer day, go to the beach and riding around. God, I'll never forget that brief twenty minutes up there on the hillside above the ranch—you know, looking out and you sitting on the grass and saying that you were just too weak to walk any further, and I coaxed you into coming up to that next little rock. You didn't know quite what to make of me and all those strange thoughts. Oh, yes, once—once I know that we're on the right track and that everything can be completely trustworthy between the two of us, I'll sit down, start from the beginning, and I'll put the whole thing on a tape and make it available to you. You know, I just—I want to be certain what you've said and how you've said it and what the missing things—I don't want to give any more information than I need to give to get you out of trouble, and I'm definitely not going to put anybody else in jail. I'm not going to put myself in jail, naturally. I'm not going to say, 'Golly, guys, here I am.' Gee, that could be the worst thing. In fact, it would probably hurt you. I can't imagine that my appearance and identity would do you any good, that it would only do you harm. I think we'd be in cells side by side and the newspapers would have a tremendous day.

Oh, God, I'd like to see you right now. Yeah, I know. I'm relaxed and thinking and getting instant replays to you bouncing around and doing that and doing this, sharing my drink and oh, that backrub. I don't think I'll ever forget that. If I thought the massage parlors were half as good as you are, I'd be out in one every day.

Well, it would be nice to do that every day. Get the kids to bed and just kind of relax in front of a fire someplace and have our own time. Oh, probably never will. Probably never will come true. It's one of those things, you know—I'm reminded of a song. 'We almost made it this time, gal.' How did that go? Well, I think you know which one I mean. No, I didn't see anything I didn't like. Oh, so we can't talk this way. You're in trouble. You're worried. You're walking the floor. You're wringing your hands. There's a million people that want to listen to this tape. Forget it. I do suggest that after you listen to this tape once or twice and you've gotten everything out of it you want, that you take your fingers and unwind the tape and put it into the toilet and flush it or burn it or destroy it in some way that no one may ever hear what's on this, because even though I tended to be careful and yet let you know I'm for you, there are things on here that, you know, if they fall into the wrong hands could be very harmful to you. . . .

I like you. I must like you, or I wouldn't be hanging around this area, taking a chance on never leaving. Oh, I know you promised you'd write to me if I ever landed in prison, but I just wonder how long that would last. You don't look to me as if you'd be much of a writing type. No, I don't think you would sit down and write me a letter a day, or a letter a week. No, your life has to go on, but that's neither here nor there. I'm going to say it again: I'm going to say it so that you really believe me and understand:

Hope, I'm not going to leave you in this trouble. I'm not going to rush forward and suddenly present myself to the Beverly Hills police, or the county sheriff up there in the Springville area, or go in and talk to the judge or any of those things. I'm going to—I'm going to stick by you in such a way as to provide you with the information and all the resources of my people so as to get you out of this trouble.

There's no reason for you ever being arrested. You've done nothing. You've committed no crime. You were not involved in anyone's death. You were not involved in actively concealing—I don't think that—I think you realize that you had no opportunity to use the phone to call the authorities, that I'm willing to tell anyone that wants to listen that you were under my control and custody the entire time that we were together from when we left the ranch. You had no opportunity whatsoever to use the phone. You were frightened to death that what happened, happened and you were functioning on the premise of self-preservation. You wanted to do everything that would ensure you and your family complete safety.

So you've played the game fair and square with me up to this point. I'm not too sure what you've told the police. I'm going to ask you. I'm sure that you'll be frank and truthful with me, but since you played it fair and square with me, I'll play it fair and square with you. I'm going to do everything in my power and everything in my financial resources to get you out of trouble. It's the best I can do. It's not the best, it's the least I can do. I think very much of you. I don't know, what more can I say than, hey, hey! I'm going to stay here. I'm going to help you. Okay? That's all there is to it.

There'll be days that I call. There'll be other days that I don't.

Maybe two days will go by, or three days, but whenever I feel that you
need me, or whenever I feel that the world is pressing in and that
something has to be done to alleviate the problems, I'll be in touch.
Right. So that's about all I'm going to put on this tape. Get it in the
mail to you. Bear in mind you're not guilty of a single thing. You didn't
kill anybody, you didn't have anybody killed, that you weren't involved. That you're just a poor innocent woman with three children
that was trying to make the best out of life, and from what I know
of it, a life that hadn't treated you too well.

Well, maybe we can get it straightened out. I certainly know that
I'd love to come home to you. There must be somebody out there
that's just right for you, because I don't see why a sweet young thing
like you isn't married and very happily married and provided with all
the comforts in the world that you need, but that's neither here nor
there. Stiff upper lip.

Stop taking all those pills. Start gaining some weight. You want the
rest of the list? The rest of the list is—become a good housekeeper
by closing the drawers and picking up your clothes. Four is, wait. Five
is, save those backrubs.

Oh, you never know when I just may come up to you and say, 'Hi
there, guy.' I'm sure you wouldn't even recognize me. I was pretty
close to you yesterday. Well, for all you know, I may be an old man
with a bald head and greasy cigar stains out of the corner of my mouth,
and looking like I just left the grocery store where I work, or something.

You know, I've got that chameleon type personality. It changes.
You happened to see one side of me; there are other sides. I can be
any number of things, but I'm safe, standing by, to help you pick up
the pieces. Don't mind anything you ask me to do.

I think a great deal of you, Hope. Okay? Don't play games with the
police, just simply tell them that if they charge you, that you have no
further statements to make, that you will conduct all of your business
through your attorneys; tell your attorneys that you are not going to
make any further statements, you're not going to answer any more
prolonged questions, that you've answered all the statements, all the
questions that you've been asked. Either get on with the nonsense of
bringing you in for charges, or leave you alone and dismiss anything
that's been brought against you to this date. In the meantime, I'll be
scuffling around digging up enough information that will totally clear
you of anything. . . .

Well dear, I'd like to say some tender little things to you, but this isn't the place or the time. Bear it in mind that you must've had some effect to keep a cold-hearted bastard like me around, trying to get you out of the fire. Okay? All good wishes to you. Big kiss. Just for you. Give the kids a kiss. Bye-bye.

Tom Breslin felt an actual shiver as he listened to the tape. He felt he had never heard anything so evil in his life.

At forty-three, with fifteen years of big-city law practice behind him, including a stint as a prosecutor before joining Ned Nelsen's firm, Tom Breslin was not naive. He had talked with killers. But he had never known anything as sinister, as truly frightening as the soft, velvety, insinuating voice on the tape, and the entire affair began to make terrifying sense.

Tom had suspected, almost from the beginning, that the man named Taylor was more than a knight in a white Lincoln who had rescued the maiden. Ned and Gene had agreed with him that Taylor's role at the ranch must have been darker than that. Gene said he had put two and two together soon after Taylor's first call to him, at home. In that call, and in subsequent calls, Gene said the man sounded far too glib. "His answers were too pat, too fast; there were inflections in his voice that gave me a gut feeling he was lying," Gene said.

But when Hope had said nothing more about him, even after she was out on bail and home relatively free, her team was baffled. "She's away from him," Gene had said. "She's free from him. Why continue to take the rap for him?"

They were convinced Hope was afraid, though they were not certain why she was so afraid, after they'd discounted the Mafia angle. "There's no Mafia here," Tom had told Hope. "Anytime somebody's involved with the organization, you can be sure they're not going to tell you." Even after that, Tom had been struck by the depth of her fear, especially after she'd called him that one morning. He could hear K.C. wailing in the background, the older children squabbling, the vacuum cleaning roaring.

"Tom, it's a madhouse here. Do you think it would be all right if my children went outside in the yard and played?"

Now, sitting in Honey's living room, Tom understood. He listened to a man who spoke so soothingly, so comfortingly, the man who wanted to buy Hope a white dress, his voice caressing "the barefoot girl," dripping romance and nostalgia, brilliantly, cruelly playing on her innermost susceptibilities, her most ravenous psychological needs, especially the need for a strong, caring man to solve her life for her: "I'm not far away dear.

I'm going to stay close. . . . Mr. Fix-it will get you through this one. . . .
Hang in, dear. Know that I care for you and know that I respect your
position. . . . You're an awful nice person. . . . There is somebody that
cares . . . there is somebody that's interested not in anything other than
just you. . . . I've never listened to anybody as much as I've listened to
you. . . . I think a great deal of you, Hope. . . . That backrub . . . it would
be nice to do that every day. Get the kids to bed and just kind of relax
in front of a fire someplace and have our own time. . . . 'We almost made
it this time, gal.' . . . Big kiss. Just for you." This tape, thought Breslin,
was not simply a narrative from a marauding killer. This was a love letter
from a man who wanted a woman entirely—body, mind, and soul.

Tom looked at Hope, sitting on the rug, her feet tucked under her, her
head bent forward, her long hair streaming across her face. He could not
tell what she was thinking or feeling. Voices were swirling around the
room—agitated, skeptical, bewildered voices—but Hope seemed not to
hear.

Tom and Ned were busy at their desks early the next morning, when
the call came. Agent Paul Luther of the FBI asked to come over.

"Certainly," Ned said. He called Gene Tinch.

When Paul Luther arrived midmorning, he came directly to the point.
"Do you have a Dan Walker in your case?"

Nobody said anything.

"I understand confidential communications," Luther continued, "but
we're doing some investigating. I ask you again: Do you have a Dan
Walker?"

Tom Breslin took a long breath.

"Well, do *you* have a fellow by the name of Taylor Wright?" Tom
asked.

Paul Luther smiled.

"Yes," he said.

"Yes," Honey said.

"Yes," Van said. "No question about it."

Hope stared at the mug shot of a rumpled, long-haired man with a
certain gleam in his eyes. Other pictures flashed through her mind: hands
in his pockets, gesturing with his pipe. Thick wavy hair, polished boots.
A charming smile. Casual, poised. *My God, this guy's a real number. He
looks like Robert Wagner. He's a ladykiller.* She closed her eyes.

Paul Luther looked at her with sympathy. She was gaunt, with large dark circles under her eyes, hollow-eyed. Paul Luther was talking quietly, but Hope was hearing other voices: *I can't leave you; you could identify me. How could I identify you? I don't even know who you are. I don't know if I can trust you. You can trust me, you can trust me. I would never identify you.*

Hope opened her eyes and looked straight at Paul Luther.

"Yes," she said.

CHAPTER
ELEVEN

Bob swalwell thought he had been angry when he'd heard that Walker had escaped from Illinois Research. He thought he had been angry when, for a while, he wasn't assigned to the case. "It's prison business now," he was told. "Let the Department of Corrections handle it."

But now, five weeks later, Swalwell knew that, angry as he'd been, it couldn't compare with the rage he was feeling, having asked to join the manhunt on the West Coat and being turned down. "It's out of our jurisdiction now," he was told. "Let the state of California handle it."

Swalwell yelled. He pounded on the desk. When he thought of his buddy Gus, still young, his kids still young, shot in the head, in cold blood, and when he thought of the man who had done that to Gus eluding them —all the way across the country—Swalwell felt helpless. And, because he felt helpless, he nearly went out of control. Suddenly he grabbed his desk phone and called a man he knew, a retired FBI agent, to ask him to pull strings. Although Swalwell liked the man, as he talked, Swalwell's voice was ragged and harsh.

For six hours Swalwell waited, chain-smoking, drinking coffee. He was already furious from the frustrations of the past few days. At approximately 12:30 p.m. on Friday, March 2, Officer Kenneth Krzwicki of the

Elk Grove police had thought he'd spotted Walker in a drugstore at the corner of Highway 72 and Arlington Heights Road. Officer Krzwicki had observed the subject enter a bright blue Torino Fastback or Matador, 1973 Illinois license AV 6618, and was last seen heading west on Highway 72. An ISPERN message had been dispatched and again, briefly, Swalwell had thought they had Walker. The manager of the Holiday Inn in Elk Grove—Van Hussen—had said the guest in Room 419 resembled Walker's photograph. The registration card showed that room registered to a Fred Hogencamp, 6901 Columbia Street, University City, Missouri, with the firm of Sinclair-Rush, 6916 Broadway, St. Louis.

When they'd knocked at Room 419, no one answered.

When Swalwell had called the phone number listed on the registration card, Fred Hogencamp's ex-wife confirmed his identity and occupation and the fact that he was on a business trip to Chicago.

And all the while, Swalwell reflected bitterly now, Walker had been running free in the California sunshine, making fools of them all. Fools! Swalwell had learned of Walker's letter from California only after Trooper Rowe had called Marcy Purmal and was told yes, she had received some correspondence and had given it to Mr. Tonsel at the Department of Corrections. When Swalwell called Tonsel and asked about this correspondence, Tonsel had confirmed its existence, adding that FBI agent Baucom had just left Tonsel's office. When Swalwell asked Tonsel what the letters contained, Tonsel told Swalwell he'd have to come down to his office if he wanted that information.

So it was Tuesday, March 6, by the time a furious Swalwell got a copy of Walker's letter with the article about the murder of William T. Ashlock. When he talked to Baucom, the FBI man told Swalwell that a female subject named Hope Masters had been charged with the murder. Baucom said he felt it was very possible that Walker was involved in this murder and, later in the day, Baucom called Swalwell again to report that the parents of Hope Masters had positively identified Walker's photograph and had said they knew him as a man named Taylor.

If they didn't let him go out there now, Swalwell thought, he would simply have to tear the whole damned office apart.

But the okay came. Swalwell packed his weapon and a few things, and made several calls to tell people he was going to California, to get Dan Walker.

"Don't bring him back here," the warden at Joliet said.

On March 6, the FBI issued an All Points Bulletin.

APB
3-6-73

WANTED FEDERAL FUGITIVE   URGENT

Gerald Daniel Walker, also known as Gerald D. Walker, G. Daniel Walker, G. Daniel R. Walker, G. Daniel Wayne Walker, Daniel G. Walker, Daniel Wayne Walker, Richard P. Walker, Hugh C. Dennis, John R. Marcus, Joseph G. Paintner, Robert S. Pietrusiak, Richard Smith, Daniel Stone, Daniel W. Williams, described as white male, date of birth 8/10/31 at Toledo, Ohio, 6' ¼" 186 lbs., brown hair, brown eyes, has the following scars and marks: old gunshot wound right hip, stab wound in abdomen, discoloration center of upper lip, mole above inside corner of right eyebrow, Social Security number 301-24-1357, FBI number 599-125-8. On 2/13/73 Federal warrant was issued at Chicago, Illinois, charging Walker with unlawful flight to avoid confinement. Attempted murder and escape. On 5/12/69 Walker shot an Illinois State Trooper in the head after the trooper had stopped Walker driving a stolen vehicle. Walker was apprehended after a high-speed chase and while serving this sentence escaped on 1/31/73. Since his escape, information has been developed that he was in the Los Angeles area on 2/26/73. When he placed a telephone call to Chicago and also mailed a letter from Los Angeles with a Worldway P.O. Stamp dated 3/1/73 and also a letter postmarked San Francisco dated 3/3/73 in which he indicated he was returning to Los Angeles. Mode of travel unknown. Information has also been developed that Walker attempted to kill another individual in the past by shooting him in the head with a small caliber weapon, but the round bounced off the skull and victim managed to survive. In his letter dated 3/3/73 he indicated that he has already killed an individual since his escape. He is considered to be extremely dangerous and vicious and probably will attempt any means to evade apprehension. He has prior convictions in Florida and Ohio for armed robbery. Subsequent to his escape, he ransacked the residence of a friend, Robert S. Pietrusiak, in Illinois, in which numerous credit cards were taken. It may be possible he is using this alias at the time.

Request all receiving offices place appropriate stops.

Attn CII
Attn LAPD Homicide
Attn LASO Homicide

Attn Tulare County S.O.
Attn California Highway Patrol

"From what this fellow has said to you, do you think he'll shoot, if confronted?" Paul Luther had asked Hope.

"From what he said to me, he'd rather die than go back to jail," Hope replied. "At least, that's what he says, and I think if he thinks he can get away with it, one on one, I think he would shoot."

"How many people do you think we should have?" Luther asked. "Do you think he might try to shoot it out with two or three people?"

"He might," Hope said.

"What about five?"

Hope considered it. "Well, maybe not five."

Thus it was determined that five armed men should be prepared to apprehend G. Daniel Walker. Then that number was tripled.

Gary LePon, the assistant night manager at the Sheraton–Universal Hotel in Hollywood, usually didn't register people, but with the evening cocktail-hour rush—6:46 P.M. on Tuesday, March 6—the place was so busy that Mr. LePon checked the guest in. He noticed that the man was well-dressed and smoked a pipe, and that even after he was given his room key—1102—he stayed around the lobby for an hour or so, relaxed, very much at ease, laughing and chatting with the bellboys and whoever came by. Mr. LePon filed the registration card the man had filled out in his own handwriting: William T. Ashlock, 865 Hyde Park, San Francisco, with a company name, Checkmate. In the space where the form said MAY WE MAKE YOUR NEXT SHERATON HOTEL OR MOTOR INN RESERVATION? YES NO, the man checked NO.

"From now on, everybody is going to know what everybody else knows," Lieutenant Barnes had said, very much as Captain Stoyanoff had said down at LASO. So he had briefed Brown and Parker on his conversation with Ray Clark, Warrant Officer at the Illinois State Prison, who had called Tulare County about two letters that had been received in Chicago, one bearing a Los Angeles postmark, March 1, 1973, the other postmarked San Francisco, March 3, 1973. A clipping enclosed with the earlier letter referred to the death of a William T. Ashlock, found shot to death on a ranch near Springville, in Tulare County, California.

A Tulare deputy had called back to Chicago and transcribed that letter over the phone. Another letter, much shorter, undated and unsigned, was photocopied in Chicago and mailed to California.

Either I am insane or have more guts than sense for, my lovely one, I have just spent an entire day in the company of uniformed and plain-clothes police, the county sheriff, State Police, several district attorneys, and in a crowded courtroom, including the fact that my photograph was taken by reporters outside . . . success! Hopie is out on bond!

I can only assume that my cover is excellent, my manner perfect, and my new identity and character above question . . . there I was, hand never far from my gun and thoughts never much further than from who gets it first, and that famous smile of oh-god-will-these-boobs-never-finish-for-I-am-too-bored-for-words.

Of course, poor Hopie almost blew the scene when I walked into the courtroom for only she knew all the truth about me, and I will give her credit with saying to me within three minutes: "Get your ass out of here! I'll make it! But git!" (Hardly the type to sit around and wonder if I am playing games with her, I suspect, but then she has observed me in a bathing suit and astride a horse and beside a roaring fire—all of which you have missed, therefore, I shall give you the benefit of the doubt).

You must admit that if all does go wrong and back to my cell I go, I will have enough material to write a fair novel, and be ready for your visits. Yes, even with all that goes on around me, I do miss you a bit —but then, our time will come, I am sure, if you keep the faith and remember only that I love you.

Hope had come to like Tom Breslin so much, and to trust him so completely, that in their long working sessions at his office, with the tape recorder on, she was venturing beyond her ranch narrative into her thoughts and background. She told Tom how she had grown up "an ugly duckling," and how, when she'd turned into a "not-so-ugly duckling," she'd lost all her girlfriends in a whirl of jealousy and competition. She had always yearned to be not just somebody's plaything, somebody's baby doll, but somebody who was useful and good, someone who was needed.

Tom knew he was becoming her father confessor, her father figure, so he was not surprised to hear from her one day when they were not scheduled to meet.

"Tom, this is Hopie. Do you think you can take me somewhere without being tailed?"

Tom said he could.

"Then please come over right away," she begged. "I have to talk to you. It's really important." She paused. "It's about Taylor."

Tom said he was on his way. He told Ned he was going to see Hope, and he told his secretary he'd be gone probably all afternoon. When he put on his jacket, he slipped a loaded revolver into the right-hand pocket.

Hope was waiting at the door with her sweater, her sunglasses, and cigarettes. As she closed the front door, Tom could hear the children arguing, the vacuum cleaner roaring again, as Honey's maid attempted to maintain the house in its natural state of grace. Tom grinned at Hope. "Pretty hectic?"

"Oh, God," Hope murmured. She got into the front seat.

"Where to?" Tom asked.

"Let's go to the beach," Hope said.

She said nothing as they drove up the street, turned left on Sunset, and went out the twisting boulevard. Tom glanced at Hope, but she had her head back, her eyes closed.

At the ocean he turned north and drove in the shadow of the cliffs along the Coast Highway. When he parked the car, Hope opened her eyes and looked around.

"We're here," Tom said. Hope got out quickly; he locked the car.

He bought two beers at the snack shop on the road, and they picked their way gingerly down the rocky hillside to the beach. At the water's edge, where the sand was darker brown from the wetness, Hope sat down and pulled her knees up to her chest.

"Do you think anybody can hear us here?" she asked.

Tom looked around the chilly, empty beach. "Nobody can hear us, Hopie," he said gently. He snapped open a beer can and passed it to her. She held it in her hand, not looking at Tom.

"It's Taylor," she said. "When he came back into the bedroom, I knew who he was, Tom. I knew it was Taylor."

"Well, okay, Hopie," Tom said. He smiled. "You know, Gene and Ned and I had a bet, as to which of us you would tell first. I'm glad you told us."

"At first he seemed very wild and very violent," Hope went on. "But he was gentle then." She was not looking at Tom, but at some distant point, straight ahead of her.

"Tom, I was so cold," she said. "I have never been so cold in my life.

When I said I was cold, he covered me with blankets. He covered me with blankets, and I think he probably kept me alive."

The knowledge that Taylor was not Taylor but G. Daniel Walker had its advantages and drawbacks. Certainly it was crucial news; as though to acknowledge its importance, Van—the soul of conscientiousness, whom Hope thought of as Roger Rigid—called his office to say he was staying home the rest of the day.

Not to celebrate, though. If anything, the situation was scarier, now that Taylor was Walker, a federal fugitive who had been imprisoned for attempted murder, with a string of prior convictions, and who was probably guilty, Paul Luther had said, of some unsolved murders, including the murders of two unidentified people whose bodies had been found in a ditch in Omaha, Nebraska, wrapped in blankets, with pillows under their heads. And Walker was not only still at large, not only considered extremely dangerous, but still in the habit of telephoning Hope. Finally, the fact that Taylor was Walker did not alter the ominous fact that Hope was still charged with murder in the first degree.

Paul Luther, a soft-spoken older man, near his retirement from the bureau, seemed to understand. "I can't help you with your case," he told Hope gently, "but I am asking you to help me with mine. You are the only means we have of catching this man. It is important that you keep him on the phone when he calls, try to keep him around. Do you think you can continue to handle this as you have been doing?"

Hope said she would try, and Luther instructed Honey, too. "If your daughter had done anything differently, she would surely have been killed," he said. "You must continue to treat him as the man who rescued your daughter. Flatter his ego. Keep him around, and we will catch him."

Still, Hope's hands shook the next time she took the phone.

"How are you?" Walker asked.

"I'm sick," Hope replied.

"With the flu, or what?"

"With the whole situation."

"Oh, the emotional thing," he said, in an understanding tone.

"The police aren't cooperating," Hope said. "We don't know anything. The only one with it is Gene Tinch. He's straight, and somewhat like you. He's the only guy—"

Walker interrupted. "Other than that, how are you?"

"I feel fine."

"Did you get anything in the mail?"

"Yeah, it came."

"A more detailed one is coming that you can let your attorneys listen to."

"You were wrong about me not writing you," Hope murmured. "I would write to you. I know what it's like to be in jail."

Walker laughed. "I was out of town when I called, but I'm back in the area, in close proximity."

"The only one you can deal with is Gene," Hope said. "He's smart; he reminds me of you." Her voice faltered. "Oh, I'm so scared. I'm going right down the drain."

"Come on, get hold of yourself," Walker said sternly. "The worst they can do is put you in jail."

"I just can't go back to jail," Hope moaned. "Those people hated me. They couldn't wait to get their hands on me."

"Because you're society," Walker explained.

"Right."

"I've got to get off now."

"Will you call again and let me know you're around?" Hope asked.

"Give me a kiss," Walker said. "Love you."

At the Los Angeles International Airport, Detective Robert Swalwell of the Illinois State Police met FBI agent Robert Sage, who drove him into the city. At the Mayfair, where they'd booked him a room—the twelfth floor was practically a police barracks, by now—he met FBI agent Luther, and Detective Kenneth Pollock of the Los Angeles Sheriff's Office. He met Lt. Forrest Barnes, Sgt. Henry Babcock, and Detective Ralph Tucker of Tulare County. He met Gene Parker and Jim Brown, who were back in L.A. again; they were sitting on the edge of the waterbeds, the room being so crowded. Everyone began to talk.

The Tulare men talked about their homicide, William T. Ashlock.

The L.A. men talked about their homicide, Richard Orin Crane.

The FBI men talked about various felonies, traced by various agents, including the fraudulent use of Larry Burbage's American Express card 045-567-1008-500AX on February 17, 1973, in Denver, Colorado. The 1973 Ambassador, yellow, that had been rented at the Hertz agency there had just been recovered at the parking lot of the Beverly Hills Hotel.

Then Swalwell talked. As he talked, he walked up and down, gesturing with his cigarette. The more he talked, the more keyed up Brown and Parker felt, raring to go.

He talked about Robert and Catherine Pietrusiak.

He talked about Taylor Wright.

He talked about Marcy Purmal.

He talked about Gus.

He talked about G. Daniel Walker. "This guy can fit in anywhere he wants to," he said. "He dresses the best, he eats the best, he drives the best. He has got an uncanny ability to lay still. He is very, very smart, and he knows a lot of legal angles. He's a very good listener, and he's very convincing. You can walk up to him and talk to him, and he can convince you he's not the guy you're looking for."

Swalwell talked on, pacing and smoking. Tall and rangy, with his attractively pockmarked face and his blue eyes, he was mesmerizing, and nobody seemed to mind that Swalwell was taking charge. He was a cop's cop. Parker and Brown noticed that he could talk to the FBI agents on their level, but could also talk to the two of them without making them feel like hicks. Jim Brown paid him the ultimate compliment: not badge-heavy.

Plans were made. They would fan out over the city, concentrating on the best hotels, the best bars and restaurants. Through the Intelligence Unit at LASO, Lt. Gary Weins and Sergeant Housner of that office would disseminate the information and photographs of Walker to their Patrol, Metro, and Narcotic units. Walker's face would become familiar to every hotel clerk, every headwaiter, every cocktail waitress in all the right places. Hope Masters's house would be staked out, as well as her mother's house. They would cast a net so wide, so finely woven, that not even G. Daniel Walker would be able to slip through.

There was no time, anymore, even for a sit-down meal, only sandwiches and coffee picked up at a deli and taken into the vehicle. Lunch on the run. There was scarcely any time to enjoy the waterbeds; at 6:30 every morning Parker and Brown were already up and dressed and heading out the door.

As there had been in Chicago, there were false leads, perhaps because they were almost too aware now, too alert. "I see Walker everywhere," Gene Parker told his partner ruefully. "I see him at least fifty times a day." When a dark-haired man wearing a green sweater, acting nervous, driving a cream-colored Mercedes, kept cruising up and down past Honey's house, slowing down at the small park at the corner, then speeding off again, Brown and Parker were very suspicious. Walker was believed, just then, to be driving a Mercedes. But identifying a man in a Mercedes in Honey's neighborhood was so formidable a challenge that the frustration came through in Jim Brown's written report. "Many Mercedes-Benz throughout Beverly Hills, ranging from black, dark blue, dark green, and, of course, all other colors."

But the cream-colored Mercedes kept driving up and down, sometimes swinging around in U-turns and, at one point, seeming to follow Brown and Parker as they patrolled. Since the instructions were that no one— repeat no one—was to attempt to apprehend the suspect, Brown took the license number. When LASO Intelligence traced it to an apartment house in east L.A., the two of them, along with Barnes and Swalwell and two LAPD officers, drove out to the address.

Swalwell was dubious. "This wouldn't be Walker's layout," he said. "It's not fancy enough, and it's too far from the center of things." Still, they approached cautiously. Barnes stayed in the car, at the radio. Inside the building, Parker and Brown stood to one side of the apartment door, the LAPD men on the other side. Swalwell knocked. They heard movement inside, and Swalwell knocked again, loudly. "Coming. *Coming,*" a voice called out. When the tenant opened the door and saw five men with guns drawn, his eyes widened. "My goodness. My *goodness,*" he said. He was wearing a long blue flowered silk robe and cradling a tiny poodle in one arm. When the situation was explained to him, he was very understanding, and invited everyone in for tea.

At eleven o'clock on March 8, Swalwell was notified by Deputy Ted Hoffman of the West Hollywood Night Detective Unit that Robert McRae, a desk clerk at the Holiday Inn at 1755 Highland Avenue in Hollywood, had identified a photo of Walker as being of the person who'd checked in approximately a week and a half before. When Swalwell and a handful of detectives, including Brown and Parker, interviewed Mr. McRae, the clerk accurately described Walker's manner of conversation and dress, and said the man had made many phone calls right after he checked in. When the officers asked Joseph Abdenour, the manager, if they could see his records, he was very cooperative and brought them all out. But in checking all registrations for February and early March, the officers did not recognize any names Walker might have used, or any phone numbers on the call-out slips that would match with Hope Masters's phone number, or with her mother's.

It was Friday, March 9. Parker and Brown had just returned to their room at the Mayfair when Lieutenant Barnes knocked loudly. "Something's going on at Homicide," Barnes told them.

At the Los Angeles Sheriff's Office, Parker, Brown, and Barnes, along with Swalwell, Babcock, and Tucker and a handful of L.A. men, listened as Lt. Joe Antonoff briefed them on his call from Fran Ashlock, who had been notified by Bankamericard that William T. Ashlock's Bankamericard had been presented for use at the London Shop in the Sheraton–Universal Hotel.

Swalwell nodded. A place called the London Shop, in a Sheraton Hotel, sounded very much like Walker, along with the bravado of flaunting the card of a dead man whose name was in all the papers. They raced out into the Friday afternoon traffic on the jammed-up freeway and, when they finally reached the Sheraton, they sifted quickly, quietly through the lobby, the dining room, the bar. Swalwell spoke in a low, urgent voice to Evans Hall, the hotel's security chief, then scanned the guest register: William T. Ashlock, 1102. "See the left-handed slant?" Swalwell said to Parker. "That's Walker."

The Sheraton lobby was swarming with people. Swalwell was told, nervously, that Gov. Ronald Reagan was due to arrive anytime, for a dinner. "Do you think there'll be any shooting?" the Sheraton people asked Swalwell as they approached 1102. He gave them his cool blue gaze. "There might be," he said. "Please get the hell out of here."

Swalwell knocked. There was no answer. He knocked again. He took the passkey Evans Hall had given him and eased it, silently, into the lock. He turned the key, then thrust the door forward with his right knee, opening it in one sudden rush.

There was no one in the room. There was no luggage, no clothing, no personal items except for a can of hair spray in the bathroom.

It was 6:25 P.M.

Michael Moore, the salesman in the London Shop, said the customer had been in around four o'clock, buying a leather jacket. Michael Moore had written up the sale, then told the man he'd have to check on the card and he'd send the coat up to his room. "Fine," the customer had said. He shopped around for a few minutes, then left the shop.

Nine armed officers, along with Evans Hall and James Briscoe, Fran Ashlock's own investigator, roamed through the entire hotel again—the shops and bars, the dining room, the outside and the underground parking areas. The hotel security people put a double lock on the door of 1102, with their guards standing watch on that floor. A little before midnight, Swalwell and the other men gave it up. The room, after all, was empty. Walker was gone.

For a while, Swalwell felt discouraged. Even for a daredevil like Walker, a two-hour miss was a close call, and it seemed likely that Walker might already have made himself scarce in L.A. He was known to like cities—interesting cities—so the word went out to police departments in both directions, San Francisco and San Diego, and Swalwell and Parker headed back to the Mayfair, talking about Walker. All the clothes had been gone from the room; that was a bad sign. But Walker had been calling Hope Masters regularly; he seemed to like talking with her. That was a good sign.

Walker's second tape was left in Hope's mailbox on the Drive. When he called to tell Hope it was there, Gene Tinch alerted the police, but when they got to the house, there was no one around. Van and Gene drove up and got the tape and brought it back to Honey's house.

"This tape may be listened to by her attorney and members of her family to be helpful in the formation of her defense," Walker began, going on to say he was "a non-American national" who had been in the continental United States for "approximately forty-some days." He said he had entered the country illegally, on matters that concerned several foreign governments.

Walker said he had never heard of Hope Masters, had never met Hope Masters, or had any knowledge that Hope Masters existed until he'd had a four-hour lunch with Bill Ashlock on Friday, February 23, when Bill showed him her picture. "Ashlock was really taken with this woman he was dating," Walker observed.

Before they met for lunch, he said, he'd never met Ashlock but had "observed him from a distance and up somewhat close" and had compiled a dossier that included not only Bill's family background—schooling, military, and employment record; salary and taxes paid; his marriage, children, and his separation, but also less vital statistics, such as the fact that when Bill and Fran sold their Winthrop Avenue house, Fran had received $3,668.02 from the sale; Bill had taken the piano, a love seat, a couple of rattan chairs, a coffee table, a dining room set, a tool cabinet and workbench.

Walker said he'd approached Ashlock, in the guise of a free-lance writer, in order to develop "a fast friendship, rather detailed friendship" that would then lead to a friendship with Bill's Checkmate partner, Richard Miller, so that eventually Walker could work with Miller on government projects, making films abroad.

When Bill invited him to the ranch, Walker said he accepted gladly, and drove up—on Saturday. He saw Hope Masters for the first time when she leaned out of the bathroom window, her hair in large curlers.

In the living room, with wine and cheese, Walker found Hope "very gracious; a sophisticated person . . . quite delightful," though it unnerved him, at first, that she couldn't seem to sit still.

Walker described the afternoon in detail—getting the horse, strolling down to the river, Hope kidding him "rather brazenly" about his astrological sign. "She had accepted the identity that I had told her, who I happened to be, and Ashlock was very happy, I was very happy, and I believe that Hope Masters was having a delightful afternoon."

After the trip to the market, where Hope picked up a child with a runny nose, and after buying beer, gin, and vodka, Hope changed clothes and sat in the living room, barefoot, drinking and chatting. "She loved to pull her feet up under her when she was sitting on the sofa. She was a delightful woman to observe. It was obvious that she had a cultured background. . . . I had no problem sitting there talking to Hope, and I somehow got to know her rather well, through her relating various experiences with both her husbands and children, what her life had been somewhat like."

Hope ate very little at dinner, dozed briefly on the sofa, then went into the bedroom. Walker said he'd stayed a little longer, then left the ranch at 11:30 or 11:40 P.M. after arranging to come back Sunday for more pictures. The ranch gate was locked, but he remembered the combination: "thirty-ought-six, like the rifle." On the pathway he saw a young man with long hair and a mustache, wearing ranch clothes, who seemed to belong there, although later he wondered.

When he returned on Sunday morning at 9:45 or 9:50, everything seemed normal as he parked his car. But as he was closing his car door:

"I heard screams from inside the house. The screams were obviously a woman's screams, obviously coming from Hope Masters. So without any hesitation I dashed into the house through the little side rear door that I had entered, that goes through like a mud room and into the kitchen and as I entered the house, everything was obviously the way it had been the night before.

"I dashed into the living room and Ashlock was on the sofa. Half on the sofa and half on the coffee table. He was—his face and upper torso had—was on the cushion part of the sofa where you would normally sit; his legs from the lower thigh to almost the ankle were stretched on the coffee table, and his feet were hanging off the coffee table. . . . There was still the smell of death in that room.

"Hope Masters was still screaming. She was in the front bedroom. . . . I entered the room . . . she was screaming, crying, she was nude.

Her hair was a complete mess. Her hands were bound at the wrist and behind her back, and her ankles were bound. It was impossible to determine from what she was saying what had happened. She was incoherent."

As he untied Hope, Walker noticed that her slacks and underpants were at the foot of the other bed, and the rest of the clothes he remembered her wearing from the night before were in the adjacent bathroom. Walker said Hope "was blurting out the fact that she'd been raped, that somebody had been hired to kill her and her children, and that for some reason, a male person had not killed her."

Walker found no one when he searched the house. "I wasn't certain what had happened. All I know was that Ashlock was dead on the sofa and that Hope Masters was tied up in such a position that she couldn't have tied herself. That there'd been a tremendous tragedy occurred in that home."

He went across the orange grove and knocked on the caretaker's door, and walked up to the barn, but no one was around. Hope Masters was still screaming, so loudly he could hear her from outside, so he went back in to talk with her.

"She told me that she had been awakened in the middle of the night. That there was an intruder. That the man—uh, uh—was tearing the clothes off her. She jumped up out of the bed, went screaming for Bill Ashlock's assistance. When she got to the sofa . . . she proceeded to touch him, and he just kind of rolled away, he fell aside, and when she looked at her arms, she had blood all over her arms. And the man—the intruder —proceeded to tell her that Ashlock was dead and he took her back into the bedroom and proceeded to rape her, and talk, and somewhere in this long conversation that—that took place during the—uh—time that I was away from the ranch, the man alluded to the fact that he had been hired to kill Hope Masters and her two older children."

Walker explained why he hadn't called the police.

"I operate on the basis that I have no contact with domestic police. My identity is not to be known. My intent and purposes within the United States are definitely not to be known, and I'm obviously breaking the laws of the United States of America, and probably in the state of California, in the type of proposal that I was going to make to Richard Miller and William T. Ashlock, and had they accepted, they would have been breaking the laws. My entry into the United States is illegal; I travel under false identity papers. I had material in my possession—documentation, film, tape recordings, photographs—that just simply could not fall into the custody and control of the inspection of any type of authorities."

Although Walker considered Hope's story "rather fantastic," he agreed to drive her back to Los Angeles. But she began screaming that she couldn't pass through the room with the body, and because he was afraid someone would hear, and call the police, "and I would be desperately and hopelessly involved in a situation I was trying to stay out of," he'd placed Bill's body onto a white cotton pad, a sheet, and a bedspread, face down, shrouded the linens around the body, and dragged the bundle across the living room, through the kitchen and into the rear bedroom. Back in the living room, he put another spread over the bloody sofa and changed the pillowcase on the pillow on the sofa—the one Hope had used when she dozed—and put the pillow into the bedroom with the body.

He checked Hope's purse "to make sure there was no weapon," then put her in his car and returned to the house to remove his fingerprints. He picked up the ball of adhesive tape he'd removed from Hope and a couple of other items; using his handkerchief, he wiped the coffee table and doorknobs and latches on the linen cupboard.

As they drove south, Hope gave more details of the night, describing the planned "bloodbath."

They reached the Drive between 4:00 and 4:30 Sunday afternoon, with Hope giving him directions, and found the maid vacuuming, the children out. Hope told a story about a car accident, with Bill staying up north to get the car repaired.

Walker said Hope called her mother and, shortly after, her mother called back. Hope told her about an accident at the ranch.

Even when the children returned, Hope was worried how long she would be safe, for the man who had raped her and killed Bill had warned her not to call the police. Around 6:00, Hope got a phone call. When she hung up she was "very white, very frightened," saying to Walker, "It was him. It was him." The caller had told her he knew she was back, he warned her not to call anyone, and he asked about the stranger who was with her. "Hope was a very frightened girl," Walker declared. "And it was obvious she was in some sort of trouble."

By now, Walker said, he believed her story. "I found the woman the day before to be delightful, sophisticated, gregarious, the type of person you make an easy friendship with and now, in a time of need, I found her to be no less of an intriguing type of person that anyone would have helped."

Walker thought of sending "some of my people" to the ranch to dispose of the body, the sofa, everything. But he stayed the night at her house for two reasons: to protect her and also because, "as long as I was near her, I did have some control over what she was going to do and what she was going to say."

He made a quick trip to the bus stop with the maid, and returned to find Hope in the bedroom with the children, the door locked, "quaking and frightened and somewhat out of her mind." Another call came from the killer, then Hope went to bed, while Walker stayed in the living room, by the balcony door. When he heard "strange noises" outside and went out to investigate, he saw two men walking. Not smoking, not talking, just walking, "apparently interested in Hope Masters' house," until they drifted off into the darkness.

Two more calls came from the killer on Monday, as Walker and Hope were "conferring and talking." When Martha, the young Mexican maid, came back Monday evening, he said he and Hope were sharing his drink.

By Tuesday morning, Walker felt "I could no longer stay with Hope and give her twenty-four-hour, day-to-day protection." Just after he told her he had to leave, the killer phoned to say she could now go down to her mother's, as long as she didn't call anyone, not even about the Chips luncheon, which the caller knew all about.

After he saw her down the hill, Walker said, "I then went my very merry way and proceeded to contact people who were—who were aware what to do and who could be helpful in this situation." He arranged for someone to watch her mother's house. When he called Hope there, "as a matter of concern and courtesy," and heard her so excited and frightened, he drove to the house, met her mother and, later, her father.

Walker didn't like Van. "A very strange man"—in fact, "a complete ass," who seemed more concerned about his ranch foreman than his daughter.

Walker was pretty sure Hope would be arrested. "It's not unusual for the authorities to arrest people," Walker noted. "But I looked on this as probably a blessing in disguise, because I felt the safest place for Hope might be in a jail where no one had access to her."

When Walker left the house and called the police, he first got a recording, then a desk sergeant—"a rather unimaginative nincompoop" who didn't know how to deal with the news of a murder and the request for a plainclothes unit. When the call was transferred, the next man was "about as uneducated and unhelpful as the first." Walker got mad and said he'd call the FBI. Instead, he called the police up north, where again he got someone who couldn't cope; Walker was so mad that when the operator said his three minutes were up, he told her to reverse the charges.

When the police asked his name, he gave Van's name, told them how to find the ranch and how to unlock the gate. Thirty-ought-six: like the rifle.

Walker then explained why he'd stayed around: "I believe I owe a responsibility to Hope Masters. . . .

"I did not know Hope Masters before that Saturday afternoon when I happened to first observe her looking out of the bathroom window with hair curlers in her hair, being passed off as a Beverly Hills socialite.

"I think that if she was just a Beverly Hills socialite, I probably could turn my back on her and let her swim for herself. But she's—she's a very frightened young lady. A mother of three children. She certainly hasn't had an easy life. She's possibly made many mistakes, but one mistake she didn't make: she didn't have anything to do with the death of William T. Ashlock.

"She had nothing to do with me. She didn't know who I was. She is obviously caught up in a situation where she has a husband who wishes to harm her. While the authorities are perhaps slow to use various sources of information, I'm not as slow as that. I do have people at my access who can develop things.

"I have found out, for one thing, that this was not the first attempt on Hope's life. There was an earlier attempt in the fact that an unemployed civil engineer from either the Spokane or Portland area had been hired, or agreeable to—to kill Hope and also kill her two children. Or maybe it was her three children. It's rather confusing when you start talking about these things to various people—who was to be killed and where it was to happen.

"This unemployed civil engineer drove a rather old, light blue Rambler station wagon. He was tall; mustache. He was in the Los Angeles area posing as a millionaire, of all things. . . .

"He went out, supposedly to kill Hope. He instead took the money that had been advanced to him on the premise that he was going to kill these people and wasted it on some nude dancers who work on the Sunset Strip, a Slavic dancer in the Classic Cat and a second dancer, a young redhead, in the Phone Booth. Over a very short period, the unemployed engineer wasted this money with these girls. He was staying in a rather rundown motel on Sunset Boulevard, down in the sleazy part of Sunset. He was staying in Room number 7, if my information is correct.

"The people he had accepted the money from eventually visited him in the motel room. . . . He could not come up with the money, he could not satisfy the contract . . . he was therefore shot once and left in the room. The body has been discovered by the L.A. police. His blue Rambler is parked in a parking lot up on Sunset, adjacent to a place named Gazzari's."

Besides the dead engineer, Walker said, a second person had been given the contract and "for some reason" didn't complete the task. Originally, the contract had initiated in this area, but then it went to Chicago, "to a small chieftain of the juice industry, a person who loans out money for, you know, criminal activities." Walker was reluctant to say more about this person, except that he'd been very helpful in giving Walker information; he seemed to know exactly what had happened at the ranch, and he didn't even seem to mind that Hope hadn't been killed, except he felt she was the only one who could possibly identify the trigger man who had been sent to the ranch.

To assure Walker that he knew what had gone on, this man had given Walker some details, including the fact that the assailant bought a pair of rubber surgical gloves and a roll of adhesive tape, and a third item, in a drugstore in Porterville.

Walker ended by offering to give a detailed statement on Hope's behalf, preferably in Rhodesia, Algeria, Bulgaria, Albania, or Hong Kong, someplace that had no extradition treaty with the United States. He suggested Rhodesia, and he proposed a three-day meeting there, with Hope's lawyers allowed to cross-examine Walker in a controlled situation, where his identity would be concealed from them. He suggested a villa.

"I will do anything to help Hope. If it's a question of her needing money, I will be willing to see that limited sums are provided. I can only say that I know that she's not guilty of anything. If anything, I did more to keep her from notifying the authorities."

Walker took a parting shot at Van, citing "his immature rush" to involve the authorities, and at her lawyers, suggesting that only "a lazy legal staff" would not be familiar with certain forensic tests available, including a nuclear reaction test on human skin that could determine whether that person had fired a gun, or had been close to someone who'd fired a gun, as long as ninety days after a shooting.

Speaking of guns, Walker thought that the murder of Ashlock and the murder of the civil engineer could be linked ballistically with a weapon that had been involved in a longshoreman's death in New York and thereafter shipped to Chicago in a case lot.

"If anyone wants to believe I'm guilty of the crime, that's perfectly all right," Walker said smoothly, even lightly. "I'm not too worried about being apprehended by the domestic authorities and therefore, if it serves

Hope's purpose to have me suspected of the crime, that makes me no difference, one way or the other."

The major surprise in Walker's long narrative was his admission that he had been at the ranch on Saturday. In general, his account coincided with Hope's—except, of course, on the identity of the villain. The people who listened to the tape were particularly interested in his extra statements, which turned out to be both right and wrong.

He was right on the color of the car the dead engineer had been driving. Although the police Miscellaneous Crime Report listed a beige car, Richard Crane's Rambler was not beige. It *was* blue. And it had been recovered in the parking lot by Gazzari's.

But Walker was wrong on the number of the motel room; the body was found in Room 8, not 7. And when he shrugged off the ability of "the domestic authorities," he was also wrong.

Gene Tinch took the tape to the Los Angeles Sheriff's Office, where it was transcribed and copied and passed around. Gene drove up to Tulare County with it, too, and delivered it to the sheriff's office there.

In Porterville, Gene found the drugstore Walker had cited—Cobb's, across from Sears—and he talked with a clerk who remembered a stranger in the store on Saturday, February 24, asking for surgical gloves. But the clerk who had actually handled the sale wasn't in at the time. Gene Tinch relayed the information to the sheriff's office.

When Gene went back to the drugstore, the clerk who had sold the gloves—Juanita White—still wasn't in, and the other clerk, Donna Brookman, said she'd been told by the sheriff's men not to discuss the matter. On a third trip, Mrs. White was working, but she also declined comment.

It wasn't until much later that Hope's people were able to learn what the clerks told the police. Donna Brookman said that on that Saturday, between 1:00 and 3:00 in the afternoon, she'd heard a man ask for "disposable gloves." Juanita White, the only other clerk that day, showed him a pair of regular rubber gloves, fairly thick. "Not those," Donna heard the customer say. "I want disposable ones, because I'm only going to use them one time." When Mrs. White, with Donna's help, found a pair of very thin gloves, surgical gloves, the man seemed satisfied. He bought a roll of adhesive tape, too.

Donna Brookman described the customer as being in his late thirties or early forties, approximately six feet tall, between 170 and 190 pounds, with dark brown, slightly thinning hair, wearing either a dark suit or a sports outfit. He had a professional appearance, Donna said. Both clerks said they remembered the customer because as long as they'd worked at Cobb's, this was the first time anyone had asked for surgical gloves.

When Gene Tinch went back to the drugstore, he was told Mrs. White was away on vacation, nobody knew where, nobody knew how long. Gene was infuriated, and the unease that had simmered between Hope's people and the Tulare people quickly boiled into enmity.

"The only way those turkeys over at the sheriff's even *knew* about the surgical gloves was because I told 'em," Gene fumed. "Then they went over and told the lady who sold the gloves not to talk to me, and to leave town.

"We were cooperating with those guys one thousand percent, giving them information which they took, but they resented it, so they then told us to go to hell."

Besides being shut out at the pharmacy, Gene felt he himself was a quarry for the Tulare forces. Deputy D.A. James Heusdens had accused Gene of impersonating a police officer at a service station in the area where Gene had talked to an attendant, trying to trace Walker's trail. Gene denied it, and showed Heusdens the card he'd shown at the gas station, which identified Gene as LAPD *Retired.* Heusdens was not convinced; Gene was not calmed down, especially when the D.A. then demanded to know why neither Hope nor Honey nor Van had pointed out Walker in the courtroom on the day of her bail hearing, when members of the court staff had later identified him from pictures. Gene insisted that Walker had not been present and that the handsome, well-dressed stranger must have been Hope's stepbrother Michael. Again Heusdens was not persuaded, and the meeting ended in a shouting match. Altogether, relations between the Tulare men and the men whom Hope fondly called "my team" deteriorated so rapidly and so seriously that when Sheriff Bob Wiley offered to assign Gene a deputy to assist him, Gene turned it down. "I don't want your help and I don't need your help," Gene snapped. "Just leave me alone." By Friday, March 9, a full week after Hope's release on bond, when everybody knew that Taylor was Walker, and everybody knew everybody knew, the atmosphere was so strained and suspicious that when Van gave another statement to Gene Parker and Jim Brown, at the Beverly Hills station, with Gene Tinch and Tom Breslin present, the man's true identity was never mentioned. In his fourteen-page statement, Van referred to "Taylor" throughout.

The fact that everybody knew made it harder. It seemed to get harder every time.

"You were out today," Walker said. "And there were two guys with a light tan car lurking around your house."

"They took me to Porterville," Hope explained. "But they'd removed everything up there, like the fact that I'd thrown up. They removed absolutely everything."

"I tried to call you up there because I knew you were there, but they wouldn't put a call through to that number," Walker said.

"It's looking real bad for me at this point," Hope said.

"I've got a surprise," Walker announced.

"Another tape?"

"No, better than that."

"Another item?"

"Right. While you were in custody."

"Well, they're just not buying it," Hope said despondently. "They're not buying anything. They think I'm some sort of a sex freak."

"That's a bummer," Walker said. "And she doesn't even kiss till she brushes her teeth."

In Walker's last phone call, on Saturday, March 10, he asked the question Hope had been expecting, and dreading, since Paul Luther came by. "Have they shown you any pictures?"

Hope tried to evade the question. "They say they found drugs in the house, but we don't have—"

Walker cut in. "Have they shown you any pictures?"

Hope tried again. "Ballistically—" she began.

"Have they shown you any pictures?"

"No," Hope said in a low voice.

"Then they don't realize you don't know who I am."

"I guess so," Hope murmured. "Listen, take care of yourself. I don't want you to get killed on account of me. I don't want anybody to get killed on account of me, anymore!"

"I'm okay," he said cheerfully. "I'll live."

"They have so many people stating that I'm a sex-crazed dope fiend," Hope said despairingly. "We think it's going to be a real long preliminary unless something develops in the meantime."

"I think something will develop," Walker said.

Gene Parker and Jim Brown were in Bob Swalwell's room, sipping brandy and Cokes with their Saturday night reading material, the fifty-one-page transcript of Walker's second tape.

Brown had spoken earlier with Fran Ashlock. She told him she'd received two department store billings for purchases made with Bill's charge cards on Monday, February 26, the Monday after he was murdered. The bill from Robinson's came to $518.70, and from Bullock's, $446.24.

Brown and Parker were just thinking they might knock it off early, get some sleep, when the phone rang.

"Ken Pollock. There's a man registered as Taylor Wright at the Howard Johnson's on Vineland in North Hollywood."

"When?" Swalwell asked quickly.

"Nine thirty-five last night."

"When it was their turn, they sent in eighteen professionals, armed to the teeth," Hope complained later. "When it was my turn, I was supposed to have brought him in by myself, unarmed, with three children."

"That's him," the manager said, looking at the mugshot. Jim Brown always thought the really interesting thing was the name of the manager: Fillmore Pajean Crank.

The Mayfair squad reached North Hollywood in twenty minutes, but the L.A. men were there before that. "He's not in his room, but all his clothes are," Sergeant Reiner said. Swalwell smiled broadly.

Fillmore Crank described the car the man was driving and gave the police the run of his motel, including rooms on the sixth floor, one next to 609—Walker's room—and one across the hall. A broadcast went out to all LAPD units and all LASO units:

> Subject Walker driving Thunderbird brown and gold California 139GFK
> No units are to stop this vehicle Let Walker proceed to his room if possible
> Call in location and time and then rear off

The professionals fanned out over the hotel, in the parking lot, in the sixth floor rooms. Brown and Parker sat in the bar, by the window, staring through a slit in the draperies, looking out into the parking lot. The bar was closed, dark, still, freezing cold.

"Hey, Parker."

"What?"

"Can you tell me what we're doin' here? Who do we think we are, Kojak?"

Two o'clock. Three o'clock. Four. Occasionally a car would pull into the motel lot; both men ached with tension.

"Hey, Brown."

"What?"

"Do you know we could get killed in this thing?"

A silence.

"I know it."

The sky faded from black to metal, then rose, orange, yellow. Parker squinted in the brightness. At eight o'clock, the L.A. men changed shifts. Swalwell and the Tulare men stayed.

Positions were rotated, with some talk of calling it off. Walker must have smelled the trap; he wasn't coming back. Swalwell shook his head. He thought of the clothes—good clothes—in 609. More than that, he had a growl in his gut. "He's coming back," Swalwell said.

Brown and Parker moved up to the sixth floor. Gene eyed the wall-to-wall carpet appreciatively. "Man, that does look good," Gene said, stretching out on his back on the floor. "You snored like a monkey," Brown told him later. At 10:25 A.M., the walkie-talkies crackled, and both men were instantly on their feet.

Aliano and Meyer, LAPD, were transmitting:

"Subject coming in. . . . He is parking the vehicle. . . . He is out. . . . He is locking the vehicle. . . . He's coming in!"

Walker put his key in the door of 609, and the hall came alive. "Freeze!" Swalwell yelled. Walker was pushed into the room, up against a wall. Brown and Parker had him by one arm, Swalwell and Ken Pollock by the other, lifting him off the floor.

"Where is your gun?" Swalwell rasped.

"In my waist. In my waist!"

Swalwell jerked the gun from Walker's waistband and thrust his own gun into Walker's face, almost up his nose. Just for a moment, Parker thought Swalwell was going to pull the trigger; in that moment—a second or two—he saw pure terror in Walker's eyes.

Then Swalwell drew back, and Walker seemed to realize they were the police. Walker smiled.

Swalwell threw Walker's .38, a Colt Cobra Special, blue-black, on the bed. Parker and Brown and Pollock brought him down from his dangling position; Swalwell snapped on the handcuffs and pushed him into a chair. Gene Parker stood over Walker, in the chair, and read him his constitutional rights and the charge, PC 187: homicide, no bail.

Walker kept smiling as the room swarmed with men.

Jim Brown took his wallets. "How much money do you have?"

Walker smiled. "One hundred eighty-six dollars and thirty-three cents."

Jim Brown made a careful count: nine twenty-dollar bills; five singles; three quarters, four dimes, three nickels, three pennies. One hundred eighty-six dollars and thirty-three cents.

The black wallet contained nine of Bill Ashlock's credit cards, his driver's license, his pilot's license, two pictures of his daughters, three pictures of Hope Masters, Bill's library card, a telephone credit card, and two pictures of Sandi.

The brown wallet contained Taylor Wright's credit cards, his Blue Cross card, his Eagle Scout Association card, and a Michigan driver's license with Taylor Wright's name and Walker's photograph.

Suddenly, in the midst of the swarming activity, Swalwell threw himself down on the bed and grinned at Walker. There was no humor in the grin; Parker thought it was kind of scary.

"You no good son of a bitch," Swalwell rasped. "I'm going to sleep good tonight."

Before anybody slept, though, there was a lot to do—searching, photographing, getting Walker behind bars. Brown and Parker sat in the back seat with Walker squeezed tightly between them. Officer Aliano sat in front, driving his own car.

Nobody talked. Walker had a fixed, half-smile on his face. At the North Hollywood station he was booked, then stripped and photographed in the nude, front view. Swalwell got a copy of the picture to take home for Gus.

Even when they all got back to the Mayfair, very late, they didn't sleep right away. Everybody had bought a bottle. They talked about catching Walker.

In many ways, of course, many people caught Walker. Hope's team; secretaries; hotel clerks—a whole string of people had been involved. By keeping him on the telephone, Hope caught Walker. "I could tell it was coming," she told Tom Breslin, "in the last day or two, and I think he knew it, too. His voice was different, toward the end, kind of like, come and get me, here I am. He was like a moth, coming closer and closer around the flame."

In one way, Walker himself caught Walker.

Brown and Parker always insisted Swalwell caught Walker. It was hard to explain, they said, but they felt it, especially early Tuesday morning when they drove him to the airport for an 8:00 A.M. flight to Chicago.

They felt very close to the man. None of them said so in the car, of course; they laughed a lot, especially about the souvenir Swalwell was taking to Gus.

But for a long time afterward, Brown and Parker talked about how Swalwell had caught Walker. Not through any one specific thing, really. Not just because he could describe Walker so well, or because he had given them so much background; not just because Swalwell was so attuned to Walker's habits, his way of thinking. It was harder to explain than that. It was like Swalwell wanted so desperately to catch Walker that he made them all feel that way, and made them know they *would* catch Walker, that there was no way in the world he would get away from them. Which is what had happened, though it was hard to explain, and finally, Parker could only say it in terms of his farm boyhood: "Without Swalwell, we'd have been suckin' hind tit."

PART III

CHAPTER
TWELVE

"WHERE ARE you now?"

"I'm standing out in the hallway where it says AFTER YOU'RE BOOKED, ASK FOR YOUR PHONE CALL."

"Are you in Porterville or Visalia?"

"Visalia."

"Well, Visalia's a lot better than Porterville."

"We'll see. Well, you know where I am, so I'll expect to start getting a letter from time to time."

"You will. When I'm told it's all right."

"I understand that."

"My attorneys apparently can't handle us both. There's a conflict of interest or something."

"Oh, I'm sure they can find somebody else to come in on the case. Work it out to your best interests."

"And to yours."

"I don't have any anymore. I played the game and lost."

"I'll be thinking about you."

"Thanks."

"Take care, and—and I'm sorry this whole thing has happened."

"That's okay. Give the kids a kiss."

"I will."

"Did Gene put somebody in the house with you today?"

"Well, they've been kind of watching me, off and on."

"I suggested they watch you a little more."

"Why? Because of the contract thing?"

"Because of me being here."

"You mean because you're there and you can't watch me?"

"Right."

"Well, I—I'm sure they're providing protection for me here."

"Okay."

"And I appreciate the fact that you stuck this out and did not leave me in such a bad spot. God, it's just bad for everybody."

"I should have cut tail, shouldn't I?"

"I guess you should have."

"But that would have left you high and dry."

"I know."

"Hey, did you brush your teeth?"

"Not yet."

"Oh, and I thought I was going to get a big one."

"I haven't been able to kiss good night, except for the kids, and they don't care."

"Okay, I'm gonna let you go now. Give me a little one?"

Walker made a kissing sound into the phone. Hope made a kissing sound back.

At the North Hollywood station, Walker had refused to say anything, even to give his name. He asked to call his attorney and, at 1:10 Sunday afternoon, he called Van. When no one answered, he called Gene Tinch. Gene drove out to North Hollywood and spent the afternoon with him.

Although Walker looked a little disheveled from the experiences of the day, Gene was impressed. "Articulate, well-educated, and one hell of a con man," Gene reported. Walker seemed very confident, very much in control, almost nonchalant as he talked again of events at the ranch; it seemed to Gene that Walker was virtually confessing to the crime. He insisted that Tom Masters had bought the contract on Hope, that he'd met Tom at the Beverly Hilton to make arrangements. Walker said his instructions had included taking dope to the ranch and strewing it around.

Walker identified the gun that had been taken from him when he was arrested as the gun used to kill Bill Ashlock and Richard Crane and two other people. But he never said he'd used it. He told Gene he'd been in

Vail, Colorado, in Reno and San Francisco, and in general had been "moving around pretty fast," stashing various cars in various places. He especially wanted to know from Gene whether the car with the rifle and the scope had been discovered yet.

Almost as an aside, he said that once, when the police had come to the Sheraton-Universal and knocked at his door, he'd been in the room.

Walker said that when Hope and her family furnished him with an attorney, he would lay the whole story out to the police and clear her.

"If you're going to lay it out, you have to lay it all out, and lay it out straight," Gene told him. "If you don't—if you put fantasy into the story —Hope would be better off if you kept quiet."

Walker asked Gene to ask Hope to write to him.

"How come you let her live?" Gene asked. "The smart thing to do, if you have a contract, would be to kill her and leave, right?"

Walker couldn't seem to explain that.

Because Walker was not in the Thunderbird when he was arrested, the car was impounded until a search warrant could be issued. At 7:30 Monday evening, Judge Armand Arabian of the Los Angeles Municipal Court issued a warrant based on three police affidavits. Detective Ken Pollock signed his affidavit; Gene Parker and Bob Swalwell were orally sworn. Judge Arabian witnessed the search, along with Assistant State's Attorney John Bernardi.

The search and the listing of the items—eleven pages worth—took all evening, until 11:30 P.M. The car was overflowing. Along with pipes and tobacco, matches and towels and soap from various hotels, assorted car keys and hotel room keys, sunglasses, newspapers, magazines—*Penthouse, Madison Avenue, Psychology Today*—road maps, cigars, and jelly beans, there were items of special interest. A four-page typed affidavit, undated and unsigned, matched the affidavit Taylor had read on the tape.

A brown briefcase in the front seat contained Bill Ashlock's W-2 form for 1972, a folder with pictures of Hope Masters, and a statement to Bill Ashlock from Superior Moving and Storage Company. Eight loose pages in the front seat were titled "Extradition in International Law."

A suitcase in the back seat contained several turtleneck sweaters, a ski cap, a pair of red ski gloves, shirts, ties, belts, and a paperback book, *The Day of the Jackal.*

Robert Pietrusiak's gray Smith-Corona electric portable typewriter, his Yashica camera, and a Winchester rifle—thirty-ought-six—with scope, were found in the trunk, along with various Pietrusiak credit cards, Larry

Burbage's business cards, a dictionary, a Panasonic tape recorder, a traveling iron, a pair of field glasses, and two sets of Illinois license plates.

In a brown shaving kit in a brown leather suit bag, the police found shaving gear, a screwdriver, razors, tweezers, a scissors, and, in a brown envelope, a gold ring with the initials W.T.A.

A black-and-red cardboard box in the trunk contained assorted car rental forms and miscellaneous papers, including Mutual of Omaha business cards and a violation notice issued to the yellow Ambassador for parking by a fire hydrant on February 21, 1973.

A garment bag, which Swalwell called "a brown clothes closet," contained new clothes with Bullock's Wilshire labels—a sport coat, a beige suit, and a sport shirt—along with boots, ties, more turtlenecks, another paperback, *Going for Mr. Big,* and one pair of surgical gloves.

Hope weighed seventy-seven pounds when she and her children moved out of her mother's house, at the end of the week, and went home to the Drive. Her hands shook so that she could hardly hold a coffee cup. When Tom Breslin told her that shaking hands could make her look guilty in court, she got a prescription for Stelazine.

Martha had cleaned the house thoroughly before she left, a day or two after Hope went down the hill, Taylor following. Martha had not returned and, almost at once, the house was littered with dirty laundry and empty pizza boxes. Hope didn't have the strength, she told her mother, to drive to the market and push a shopping cart around, then come home and cook and clean, so Honey sent up another young Mexican girl. The new maid didn't drive, though, which meant she couldn't do the marketing, and she didn't speak English, which meant she couldn't control the children. She could pick up around the house, and she could cook, in a very limited sense, so Hope called a small grocery store in Beverly Hills—very expensive, but they delivered—for a huge amount of hamburger and for days everybody ate tacos.

Even with the maid around, and the children clamoring, Hope was scared. When she asked Van to hire a private guard, he refused, and when she asked him to withdraw some of the money that was legally hers, he refused again. "If you use that money now, you'll just come to me for something else later," Van explained. Hope resented his attitude, and when she thought of her mother's three thousand dollar-a-month personal allowance, as she often did, she resented her mother, too. She felt deserted and terribly alone—a cold, empty, desolate feeling that she tried to explain to Tom Breslin.

"Have a friend come stay with you," Tom suggested. "Just be sure it's a girlfriend."

"I don't have any girlfriends," Hope said.

Hope had already talked with her team about her boyfriends. Gene and Ned had taken advantage of the long drive to Springville and back, the day they'd gone up to inspect the ranch, to discuss the matter. She had seen through their discretion. She felt that they were delicately and charmingly pumping her to find out how many men she'd been sleeping with. "You got a right to a normal sex life, Hopie," Gene said, "but we don't want fifty guys walking into court at the last minute." When Hope listed the men—Tom Masters, Michael, Lionel, and Bill—they didn't seem to believe her. "I'm sorry if I haven't lived up to your expectations," Hope had told them. "What can I say? That's it."

Now, when Hope talked with them again, they decided she could have a man stay with her part time.

So Lionel came back to the Drive. He did the marketing and the cooking; he sang old English ballads to the children and, when they'd fallen asleep, he sat with Hope on the sofa, held her in his arms, and told her everything was going to be all right.

At eleven o'clock, when Lionel had to leave, Hope usually went to bed right away, but she almost never slept through the night. She had put Gene Tinch's home phone number on her wall list of numbers, just under the number for the paramedics, and she often called him at 2:00 or 3:00 in the morning even though he could never figure out what she wanted, exactly. Gene came by now and then, sometimes just to talk, to try to keep her spirits up, sometimes with a specific purpose. He had told her to look around her house carefully, as soon as she had settled back in.

"If there's anything that doesn't belong to you, get it together and we'll get it out of there," Gene told her. When she reported an assortment of items, Gene told Paul O'Steen of the LAPD, who came by to pick them up.

Hope had found the calculator and the hot comb Walker had given Keith, men's clothing in extra-large sizes from the suitcase Walker had brought in Monday night, and an unusual item, something she'd never seen before, among the china on the shelf in the living room. It was a small gold chain, a medallion with the initials T.O.W. III, so small it could nestle at the bottom of a teacup.

Hope's notion that Walker's capture would clear her and free her, always a tenuous notion at best, was quickly dispelled, starting with an article in the *Tulare Advance-Register and Times* after Walker's arrest.

"Both are charged with the murder, but officials haven't commented on which of the pair they believe fired a small caliber gun into Ashlock's head." Not even the publication of large portions of Walker's second tape, the tape proclaiming her innocence, seemed to help. When it was mysteriously leaked to the *Los Angeles Herald-Examiner* and carried on the front page under a banner headline, Jim Heusdens, the prosecutor, denounced the leak, and a local paper reported that although sheriff's investigators declined comment on the tapes, they did say "they didn't consider them proof of either defendant's innocence."

Hope had always hated Porterville—"a dumpy, miserable little town" —and since the day Jim Heusdens had argued so vehemently in the justice court that she be held without bail, he had become the epitome of all she disliked. She thought he was biased, ignorant, and provincial, a man with a perpetual sneer and an incurably closed mind. He, in turn, thought she was an arrogant little snip, a jet-set socialite given to drugs and drinking, with a lot of money and a lot of rich friends and, moreover, he thought she was guilty.

With his flamboyant manner and his habit of saying, or shouting, whatever was on his mind (his favorite term for people he disliked was "you weasel"), Jim Heusdens would have been noticed anywhere; in tiny Porterville, he was an immense presence. Blunt and outspoken, he liked telling people off almost as much as he liked being told off. When Jim Brown, who sometimes assisted the D.A. in court, once told him, "You're the most obnoxious man I ever met," Heusdens laughed louder than anybody.

Like so many of the principals in the case, he'd never planned to do what he was doing. He had dropped out of high school in his hometown —Racine, Wisconsin—where his family had already dropped the "von" from the family name, because "von" didn't really mean anything, Heusdens said; his family was "just a bunch of renegades that got run out of Holland, anyway." He enlisted in the navy and, afterward, moved to California to work for an uncle who had a refrigeration supply business in Porterville. For a while he worked as a TV repairman, then he joined the local police force.

At first he'd found it hard to adjust from citizen to cop; he recalled his reluctance, early on, to take a man into custody on Christmas Day. But over the years, as he moved from patrolman to lieutenant, his attitude had shifted. "After seventeen years, hell, I could have locked up my own mother on Christmas Day," Heusdens declared. He opposed the Miranda and Escobedo rulings.

At the time he prosecuted Hope Masters, he was no longer a town cop, of course. In 1969, when his friend George Carter had said, "Let's go to law school," Heusdens had assented, though he said he never knew quite why. He just did. After he passed a college equivalency test, he enrolled at Humphreys, a law school in Fresno. It had been a long grind, just as it had been for Carter—working all day, then making the one hundred fifty-mile roundtrip three nights a week. Heusdens passed the bar on his first try, and went to work in the District Attorney's office, where he was earning $904 a month, less than he'd been making as a policeman.

But he loved it. From his very first prosecution—a drunk driving case down in Pixley—he was caught up in the drama and tension of the courtroom, matching wits and words. He had no use for routine legal work —"the same crap all day long; when you write a will, only the names are different. The courtroom is where it's at!" Heusdens exclaimed. "Unless the evidence is really overwhelming, I finally believe that whoever puts on the best show in a jury trial will win. If you're flat, no color, they won't look at your case. You have to have something to show them. A jury is like people buying a car: they might not buy it, but they'll sure look it over. You have to keep their attention. If I ever think I'm losing their attention, I'll do something to wake them up—maybe kick over my briefcase, knock over a glass of water. I may even let a few tears fall. You have to give an emotional appeal to get an emotional verdict."

However, as much as he loved the courtroom—specifically, prosecuting someone in a courtroom—he had submitted his resignation at the D.A.'s office, when his request for a 5 percent pay increase kept getting turned down. He was headed for private practice; he'd still be in court at times, but on the other side. *The People of the State of California* v. *G. Daniel Walker and Hope Masters* would be his last hurrah.

Heusdens had been involved in the case since shortly after Bill's body was found. He had tried to coax Jim Webb into a late-night polygraph test—"I can get you the best guy from Bakersfield; I can have him here within the hour!"—and, in general, had pursued all possible prosecutorial angles with all possible zeal. Hope had felt the effect of that zeal from the first day she saw him, at the bail hearing, and when she heard that the drugstore clerk had wandered beyond the reach of a subpoena, she asked Tom Breslin whether they couldn't sue Jim Heusdens for malicious prosecution.

Tom said they couldn't. He said there was enough of a thread of rightness laced through the prosecution's case to justify its moves. "They've done everything they can to hinder us," Tom conceded, "but it's legal. Maybe not one hundred percent ethical, but not illegal. With a prosecutor, especially one who's been a cop, everyone's guilty until they prove themselves innocent. So a lot of prosecutors play that game, especially when you're in their playground and not your own."

The playground, of course, was the key. In Los Angeles, in his years on the police force, Gene Tinch had dealt with over two thousand violent deaths, mostly murders, an average of about thirty-five a month. One a day. In Porterville, filing a homicide under Miscellaneous Crime and having it go unreported in the papers was as unthinkable, say, as a preacher handing out drugs at Sunday worship. Tulare County, and especially the Porterville area, was conservative, rural, and fundamentalist, and when Hope walked into the justice court, she walked on truly alien ground. Whether the controlling attitudes—hers, theirs—were perceived accurately or in a distorted way was not really relevant, once they were perceived at all. Hope's team had understood this very early, and was doing what little it could to dilute the atmosphere. Some facts could not be altered—the one and a half divorces, the drinking and the grass at the ranch, her rendezvous there with a still-married man—but she could be instructed to keep her cigarettes out of sight, to wear dresses to court, not pants, and, as a general rule, not to wear anything that wasn't at least ten years old and worth less than twenty dollars. On the day of the bail hearing, Tom Breslin had considered Honey dangerously chic. "If your mother doesn't own a cloth coat," he said to Hope, "tell her to *buy* one!" From the beginning, local newspapers were referring to the ranch house as "luxurious" and "a plush dwelling," and when Jim Heusdens was told that Ned Nelsen was paid more per diem than Heusdens earned in a month, he said he wasn't envious, just more determined to win.

Walker was shackled in handcuffs and leg irons and a waist chain when he was arraigned at the Porterville Justice Court on March 13. Two days later, when Hope and her attorneys drove up, Judge Carter announced that her preliminary hearing and Walker's were being consolidated, at the request of the prosecutor, and thus would be postponed. Hope wore a severe, high-necked black dress, borrowed; no makeup, with her sandy hair pulled back in a tight, Lizzie Borden bun. Tom Breslin looked at her with an appraising glance. "Not *that* plain," he told her. "Nobody would ever believe this guy could be interested in you enough to protect you." So, the next time, she wore a pink wool dress with a round white collar, also borrowed, her hair falling loose but held back from her forehead with a silver clip, and black patent leather Mary Jane shoes. With Max Factor pancake makeup concealing the circles under her eyes, she looked about fifteen.

That was on April 2, the day the white Lincoln Continental was found at the Hyatt House Hotel on Wilshire Boulevard. Bill Ashlock's car had already been found, in the parking garage at the Beverly Hilton Hotel. The ticket issued to the little green Triumph showed it had been parked in the hotel garage since February 28, three weeks. As Hope had said about the Hilton's facilities: "You know it takes forever to park there."

"If you smile, you look callous," Tom Breslin had told her. "If you cry, you look guilty. So just keep a straight face and, above all, don't look at Walker." So when Hope heard the clanking sound in the courtroom, a little way down from her at the counsel table, she gazed straight ahead. Walker smiled at Ned Nelsen. "Did you hear, not the patter of little feet, but the tinkle of little chains?" he asked.

A preliminary hearing was not a trial, Judge Carter explained, but simply that—a hearing of the evidence to determine "probable cause." Probable cause for the arrest, probable cause that Hope, or Walker, had committed the crime. Because defendants are presumed innocent until proven otherwise, there was no need for the defense to present a case; it was the job of the prosecutor to present a case that established probable cause. Privately, Judge Carter felt that most prosecutors did put on a case that established it.

Still, the hearing was very much like a trial; witnesses were sworn in, examined, and cross-examined. Voices were raised in legal and emotional conflict. In a way, the hearing was even more dramatic than a trial; with all spectators excluded, the press excluded, witnesses excluded until it was time for their testimony, and without a jury, only the major figures were present at the curved counsel table in front of the judge's bench. All the drama and the conflict were concentrated.

Gerald Webb said he had seen Walker at the ranch around 1:30 or 2:00 that Saturday afternoon, in a light-colored Lincoln Continental, and that, later on, he had seen the three people—Hope, Walker, and Ashlock—having trouble with the horse.

"What did Mrs. Masters specifically say to Mr. Ashlock at the time she had trouble with the horse?" Jim Heusdens asked.

"Oh, boy," Gerald Webb said. "She asked him to take the horse, to lead the horse."

"Did she ask him, or did she *tell* him?"

Ned Nelsen objected quickly. "Calls for a conclusion. Also leading and suggestive."

Judge Carter agreed, but Jim Heusdens managed to make his point, anyway, as he asked Gerald to describe Hope's "reactions and attitudes toward the deceased."

"She acted frustrated or a little upset, that somebody wasn't helping her with the horse."

"Could you label it?" Heusdens persisted.

"It seemed like she was displeased with Mr. Ashlock," Gerald Webb said, adding that he'd noticed that when she talked to Mr. Walker, "she, like, wanted to make a good impression on him."

The witness tried to explain his inability to identify the man he'd seen at the ranch, whom he now knew as Bill Ashlock, when Detective Flores had taken Gerald to Myers Chapel.

"At that time there was some doubt in my mind because, well, there was other things," Gerald said. "The stuff in the room bothered my eyes extremely, I mean, it was to the point where my eyes were watering real bad before we left. But the general characteristics of the man at the mortuary, as best I could remember, was the man I saw in the Vega at the ranch, yes."

Jay Powell, the public defender for Walker, tried to establish that Gerald's identification of Ashlock now was impossibly tainted by what he'd subsequently heard from his brother and by pictures he'd seen in the papers. He asked Gerald whether he could disregard what he'd subsequently seen and heard.

"You are asking me whether I could just put everything else out of my mind?" Gerald asked in surprise.

"Yes," Powell said.

"Well, that's kind of hard to do," Gerald complained. "It's like saying, 'Don't think of an elephant.' "

"So you can't do it, can you?"

"I can tell you, in all honesty, that other than the mustache, I thought it was the man. But it really threw me, it really did, because when I saw the man he had dark glasses on and when I saw him in the mortuary he did not."

"And when you spoke to Detective Flores, you were trying to speak in all honesty too, weren't you?" Jay Powell asked in an understanding voice.

"Yes sir, I surely was," Gerald Webb declared.

Walker had presented a motion, handwritten on a yellow legal pad, that he be allowed to act as co-counsel in his own defense. Judge Carter considered that motion, and Walker's later motions, as beautifully written, works of legal art, in fact; not just items to be routinely denied, and considered Walker himself intelligent and good-looking. But he had denied Walker's motion, leaving him in the hands of Jay Powell.

Powell was the perfect counterpoint to Jim Heusdens. Where the prosecutor was florid and excitable, Powell was somber, composed, passionless. Heusdens was melodramatic, Powell tight-lipped and precise. Jay Powell wore steel-rimmed glasses, and deviated from his air of scholarly tonelessness in only one respect: every day he came to court wearing a large, floppy Panama hat.

Hope was not supposed to look at Walker, but she could occasionally peek, and she could tell that Walker, always the soul of sartorial elegance and not bad even in jailhouse denim, detested that Panama hat. Perhaps the hat figured in Walker's constant criticism of Jay Powell, throughout the preliminary and beyond. "If Mr. Powell's services are to continue for Walker," Walker wrote to a judge, "they must be brought up to adequate standards. The problem now becomes the court's." He claimed to lack "all confidence and respect" for Powell, labeling Powell's representation of him as "irresponsible, inadequate, and incompetent." There was no more striking example of Jay Powell's imperturbability than his eventual comment, after Walker's consistent, public criticism, even after Walker had filed a malpractice suit against him, that he and Walker had had a good relationship. "We got along fine," Jay Powell said stoically.

Jay Powell was so unassuming that he disliked any mention of his own substantial credentials: a highly rated record at UCLA and a dozen years of legal experience that included a stint in Melvin Belli's office. So Jim Heusdens mentioned it for him. "Jay used to work for Melvin Belli," Jim Heusdens said. "But nobody works for Melvin Belli; they carry his books. And I've never wanted to carry anybody's books."

When Jay Powell visited Walker in jail, Walker told him he'd known Hope Masters for several years, that he'd had her picture in his cell at the Illinois State Prison, and that he'd written to her from prison.

The public defender was struck by Walker's intelligence and poise, his urbane wit. He asked Walker a lot of questions, but not whether he'd killed Bill Ashlock. "I never ask a client, 'Did you do it?' " Jay Powell said. "I don't want to know. It's not important. It has no bearing on my representation of the client; to me, it isn't relevant, and it's better if I don't know. Even if the client said, 'Yes, I did it,' how would I know the client is telling the truth? Maybe the client is just taking the rap for someone else."

Jim Webb testified that when he'd left the ranch to go to work at six o'clock that Saturday morning, only the green Vega was parked at the house.

Heusdens reminded him that in one of his statements, Jim had told Detective Flores that a Lincoln Continental was parked at the house Saturday morning.

"How many statements did you give to Mr. Flores?" the prosecutor demanded.

"Oh, I couldn't say," Jim replied, and when Heusdens whipped out a copy of the first statement Jim had given, in the predawn darkness on February 28, Jim said he didn't recall giving it, at least not the part about a Lincoln Continental on Saturday morning. "The first time I seen the Lincoln was Saturday afternoon when I came home," Jim testified. He said he'd seen both cars, the Lincoln and the Vega, about 9:30 Saturday night and again on Sunday morning early, around 6:00.

But when Jay Powell cross-examined—"Mr. Webb, can you swear that from nine thirty Saturday night until six A.M. Sunday morning, neither the Lincoln nor the Chevrolet Vega were moved?"—Jim Webb said he could not.

Teresa Webb said she'd seen both cars parked at the house Saturday night—she said it was around eleven P.M.—and that on Sunday morning around nine, when she and the children drove by the main house, she'd seen only the green Vega, not the Lincoln.

Hope was only mildly annoyed at the prosecution's prehearing efforts to link her with Jim Webb—"Oh, what a joke," she said coolly. "A duller human being I've never met"—but she was genuinely irked by the testimony of Officer Stien of the Beverly Hills police.

She had never felt comfortable talking to Stien and his partner the night they came to her mother's house to listen to her story. She thought they were both too young to possibly comprehend, and she thought Stien, in particular, looked like a freshman jock at USC. *"Excruciatingly* young," Hope declared. "I wanted to talk to a grown-up person." She still felt that way, as she listened to Stien's testimony about the story Hope had told that evening, a story that he admitted "was not, in effect, a coherent, chronological account of what had occurred at the ranch."

"Did she appear to be upset?" Tom Breslin asked.

"Yes," Stien said.

"Did she appear to be frightened?"

"Yes."

Jim Heusdens picked up on the question. "You say that she appeared frightened. Do you believe she *was* frightened?"

"No," Stien said.

Stien kept saying "supposedly," which made Hope even madder. She was awakened abruptly "by someone trying to force a gun, or something that was supposedly a gun, in her mouth and about her face." "Then, supposedly, she was raped. Then he supposedly got very perverted." Stien said Hope Masters had told him that "this individual" had told her he was hired by a Tom Masters, that "the individual" took pictures of her, put on rubber surgical gloves, and wiped off everything he had possibly touched. He untied her, and they talked till daylight, when he tied her up again and left.

"Did Mrs. Masters make any statement to you about why this person did not kill her?"

"She said to me that this individual stated that he kind of liked her." Jim Heusdens smiled.

Stien said that Hope had said that then "an individual" came to the ranch—"supposedly it was a Taylor or Tyler"—heard her screaming, entered the house, and untied her. At Hope's request, Taylor moved Bill's body and then drove her home, where she received phone calls from "this individual that was up to the ranch prior, and he told her not to say anything, that if she said anything, her life and her immediate family's lives would be in danger."

"Did she tell you why Taylor came up to the ranch?"

Stien said Hope had said Taylor came to take advertising pictures.

"Did she tell you what time Mr. Taylor arrived?"

"I can't recall. I believe it was early in the morning, probably around nine or ten o'clock."

"Did she ever mention Mr. Taylor being up there on Saturday?"

"No," Stien said.

Jim Heusdens leaned across the counsel table and spoke firmly to the witness.

"Did you believe Mrs. Masters's story that she was telling you at the time she was telling it to you?"

"No," Stien said.

At the lunch break, Jay Powell gave Ned Nelsen an envelope with Hope's name on it. Inside, Hope found a cartoon clipped from a newspaper—two little naked kewpie dolls, a boy and a girl, the girl making a fuss, the boy smiling patiently. The caption read: *"LOVE IS . . . taking a stroll while she lets off steam."*

Elisa Arenas smiled at Hope as she told of Hope's trip to the hospital. She said the doctor hadn't said much, because Hope was doing all the talking, and when Hope talked to Arenas, she told her that two men had come to the house and murdered her boyfriend, then both of them, or maybe just one of them, had tied her up and raped her.

"Are you certain she said two men?" Heusdens asked.

"That's right," Elisa Arenas said.

Dr. Wong said he had seen no bruises when he examined Hope, but he had seen two small areas of what appeared to be adhesive tape marks, darkened with dirt.

"Was there anything to confirm that she had been raped?" Jay Powell asked.

"There is no such thing to confirm one way or the other," the doctor asserted.

"Was there any evidence of trauma?"

"There was no evidence of trauma," the doctor said. When asked if he recognized her now, in court, he said he didn't, because in court she was smiling at him, and when he saw her, she was not smiling.

The hearing, which had been planned for two days, stretched into a week, and Judge Carter announced the proceedings would be transferred to City Hall, over on Main Street, because the justice court was needed for other cases. Jim Heusdens pointed out that security at City Hall was very poor—"There are at least six exits"—and requested that, in the new surroundings, Walker's shackles be put back on.

Judge Carter had always been uneasy about the matter of shackles and chains. As a compassionate man, he felt uncomfortable about draping another man in irons, but as a practical man, he felt uncomfortable about the consequences of freeing him entirely. When he'd come to a sort of compromise, and done away with the full machinery of irons, he'd worried about it, and he'd mentioned it to Jay Powell. "I have this feeling, and I hope you have it too, that you should never turn your back on him," Judge Carter told the lawyer. "Do you realize that?"

"I realize it," Jay Powell replied.

When Judge Carter had warned the deputies, too—"Don't get too friendly with him"—they took his advice, especially Allen Pundt, one of the marshals who escorted Walker in and out of the courtroom.

"What did you say your name was?" Walker asked Marshal Pundt one day, in a friendly, conversational tone, as they walked through the narrow corridor to the car that would take Walker back to jail.

"I didn't say," Allen Pundt said crisply.

He didn't say anymore, and Walker shook his head, with a rueful chuckle.

"I never did like quiet cops," Walker said.

Jay Powell objected to Walker being reshackled. He pointed out that three armed deputy sheriffs were watching Walker at all times, "and surely they can shoot faster than he can run." When the hearings moved to City Hall, however, Walker was back in leg irons.

As the preliminary entered its second week, Jim Brown and Gene Parker entered a new phase of their investigation, tracing Walker's trail to other cities, other states. In fact, for two country cops whose official business had never before taken them beyond the rocky boundaries of Tulare County, Brown and Parker were becoming cross-country sleuths, and having themselves a ball.

They had stayed on in Los Angeles for a while, after Walker's arrest, interviewing and reinterviewing, and they'd met Hope Masters for the first time. As members of the prosecution's investigating unit they were not, of course, on her side, but Gene Parker, especially, found her likeable, and Hope liked him. They met under slightly awkward circumstances. In the reception room at her lawyers' offices, Hope thought the two nicely dressed men were some of Tom and Ned's other clients. But when Tom Breslin arrived, it turned out they were detectives, Parker and Brown, come to collect samples of her hair. Everyone filed into a room adjoining Tom's office and just sort of stood around—Hope and Lionel, Tom Breslin, Parker and Brown. Then Tom snipped a piece of hair from her head and dropped it into a manila envelope that Jim Brown held out; the envelope was sealed, dated, and signed, then everybody just sort of stood around some more.

"Well, come on, you guys, there's plenty of hair here," Hope encouraged them, brushing her left arm with her right hand. "See, it's like a wheatfield; it's just hard to see because it's blond." Finally she took the scissors and cut off some arm hair herself. To Gene Parker's great relief, only hair from the arm and head were taken. Jim Brown noted gravely in his report: "No hair samples were taken from Hope's legs as she shaves her legs and none was available."

Parker and Brown talked with Sara Monaco, the receptionist at Dailey & Associates, who identified Walker's picture as being of the man who had taken Bill Ashlock to lunch.

They talked with Hope's neighbor, Mrs. Smith, whose husband had done some business with Tom Masters. She told them Hope was basically a nice person.

They talked with Licha, Hope's weekend maid, who told them that when the stranger who came home with Mrs. Masters that Sunday evening drove Licha to the bus stop, he asked her how to get back to Hope's house.

When they talked with Richard Miller, Bill's Checkmate partner, and a third partner, John Arnold, they learned that Miller had traveled a great deal as a filmmaker, that he had a top security clearance with the Secret Service, and had traveled with the White House staff. Both Miller and Arnold looked at Walker's picture and said they had never seen him before.

Once more, Parker and Brown talked with Sandi, who identified the yellow metal ring with the initials W.T.A., found in Walker's car, as a keepsake she'd bought and given to Bill. She also told the detectives, this time, that just before Bill went to the ranch, he had told her that if she would marry him, he would stop seeing Hope Masters.

They talked with the bartender and with the maitre d' at the Brown Derby, who told them that on Friday, February 23, they had served approximately three hundred lunches, just as they did every day of the week, and they could not possibly identify any pictures.

Sifting through the array of hotel receipts, car rental agreements, room keys, car keys, miscellaneous keys, matches, towels, and soap left in Walker's wake, the detectives found that someone giving the name William T. Ashlock had been registered at the Towne House in San Francisco from March 1 to March 6, and at the Hilton Inn at the San Francisco Airport from March 2 to March 6. Registration forms at the hotels showed the guest had been driving a white 1973 Chevrolet Impala, Nevada license CBK 187. Parker and Brown searched for the car around the Towne House, at Eighth and Market streets, without any luck, and checked in there overnight. Next morning, after driving for what seemed like hours through what seemed like thousands of parked cars at the airport, they spotted the Impala, its windows so dirty by now that all they could see, as they peered in, was a paper bag and an apple on the floor of the back seat. While they waited for Vern Hensley of the crime lab to arrive on a flight from Fresno, Brown took pictures of the car with its inside-joke license: 187 was the penal code section for homicide.

In the trunk of the Impala, they found a brown briefcase initialed W.T.A. containing newspapers, bond typing paper, letterhead paper for "Borough & Carson," and a map of Chicago. A green Samsonite attaché case in the trunk with the name Richard S. Powell was locked; to no one's astonishment, a thin key among the pocketful of keys Jim Brown had carried around for a month fit the attaché case. Under the rubber mat on the floor of the trunk, they found personal checks imprinted Taylor O. Wright III and Patricia Wright.

The green attaché case led Brown and Parker to the insurance salesman who had been robbed at the Hilton in Omaha in February, and that robbery, and a string of robberies at that time, led to a discussion with Omaha authorities of the two unsolved murders there that Paul Luther had described. Two unidentified bodies had been found in a ditch, each with a single bullet hole in the head, each wrapped in a blanket, with a pillow under each head.

Honey cried so much on the witness stand that even Jim Heusdens was momentarily touched. "If you want to recess, you just ask the court for one and they would grant it," he told her.

Honey sniffled. "Thank you," she said with dignity.

Hope's mother related Hope's story of being awakened by an intruder at the ranch, who held a gun in her face, of finding Bill dead, of being raped and tied and then fainting, or passing out, and "at that point Walker arrived. Taylor." Honey told of meeting Taylor at her house on Tuesday—"the Tuesday following this fateful weekend"—the day Hope had come down too, "in a terrible state of shock, and hysterical, and absolutely frantic. Her face was gray." Honey related Taylor's story of his arrival at the ranch on Sunday morning, finding Bill murdered and Hope tied up, moving the body, untying Hope, and driving her home.

"Has your daughter ever told you any story different than this intruder story?" Heusdens asked.

"She has given me a great deal more detail on it," Honey replied. "And she has identified the intruder."

"You say your daughter changed her story?" the prosecutor demanded.

"No, she didn't change her story," Honey insisted. "What she told me was the absolute truth. Hope does not lie."

Honey explained that Hope's story had always been true except that, in the beginning, she had not identified the intruder. After she was released on bail, Honey said, Hope had awakened her one night and said, 'Somebody has to know who he is, because if I'm killed, someone must know who did this horrible thing.' "

"Did she tell you who did this horrible thing?" Heusdens asked.

"Yes. She said Taylor did it."

"By Taylor, does she mean the defendant, Mr. Walker?"

Jay Powell objected on grounds of hearsay, but before the judge could rule, Honey kept talking. "She made me promise not to tell," Honey said, twisting her moist handkerchief in her hands. "She said it was Mr. Taylor. Because we didn't know it was Walker until later, when the FBI brought his picture to us."

"When he came to your house on Tuesday, did you believe him?" Ned Nelsen asked.

"Yes, I did," Honey said.

"Were you frightened?"

"I was scared to death."

One of the most difficult questions put to Honey was why Hope had allowed Walker to take Hope Elizabeth to school.

"She said that he was—she was going to be watched at school," Honey replied, "and that Taylor was going to have her protected, and that she would be watched by his people."

"So Taylor was taking her to school to protect her from someone else?"

"Yes."

"And later you found out that the only person making a threat to your daughter was Mr. Taylor, who is now known as Mr. Walker?"

"Well, I'm not sure if he's the only one. To this day, I don't know," Honey said anxiously. "I wish I did know if he was the only one."

Some of the questions seemed irrelevant at the time.

"Have you ever carried a gun in your purse?" Heusdens asked.

"Never," Honey said firmly.

"You don't own a gun that you have ever carried in your purse?"

"Never."

"You don't own a gun that you have ever carried in your purse?"

"No," Honey said, very emphatically. "I have never carried any kind of firearm at any time in my life in any way."

"Do you know a Mr. Edward Eugene Taylor?" Jay Powell asked.

"I don't recognize the name," Honey replied.

Judge Carter was a kindly man. He even felt compassion for the various attorneys. He knew the tension and pressure they worked under, so he let a lot of things go by that he felt weren't relevant to the case. He knew very well that Honey's testimony was hearsay—double hearsay, really—but he admitted it for two reasons. "One, I wanted to see what the entire picture was. Also, very few women who come before me cry." His sympathy, however, stopped abruptly at Hope's edge of the counsel table. "Mrs. Masters, I would appreciate it if you did not make your head go yes and no," Judge Carter told her, during Honey's testimony.

"I'm sorry," Hope said, in a most uncontrite voice.

"Whether it's involuntary or not, pay more attention to it and desist from it," he went on.

"I will look in the other direction then, okay?" Tom Breslin gave her a definite poke in the side. "I'm sorry," Hope said again. "I don't mean to do it."

Another cartoon came in the relay: Walker to Powell to Breslin to Hope: *"LOVE IS . . . listening to her while she talks and talks and talks."*

"We talked to her briefly during the trip," Sgt. Henry Babcock testified, regarding Hope. "She had been contacted by counsel. I had read her her rights. I could see no real gain by talking to her. She understood her rights, and she would rather talk to her counsel before talking to us. We did chitchat during the trip, though."

Hope was furious and asked Tom at the recess whether she couldn't give testimony about the conversation she remembered in the drive to Tulare, which she recalled as containing threats involving "black dykes," and "lynching." Tom said she couldn't and not to get upset about it.

"Well, okay," Hope said, "but it was the most un-chitchatty, chitchat I ever heard."

Van related Hope's account of the night at the ranch, saying that after she was raped, the intruder was in and out of the room a number of times during the next four to six hours. "He left, on one occasion at the end of this period of time, and did not return."

"Did your daughter tell you what happened after that?" Jim Heusdens asked.

"My daughter told me that, after that, she thinks she blacked out. She awoke when it was daylight. And at that point my daughter stopped talking because Mr. Walker interrupted her and said he would take the story from there."

"Since that day, has your daughter told you any stories that are different from the original story she told you?"

"Yes, she has," Van said. He explained that Hope had told him Walker had arrived at the ranch on Saturday, not Sunday, and that she had described to him the day, up to her going to bed, being awakened with a gun, discovering Bill dead. "She said that she learned, in the course of the post-rape time, that—that the rapist was Walker."

"What did she say about the intruder, when he first came into the room, how could she say who it was?"

"She said that the light was not good enough for her to see who the intruder was, or even to get a good enough look at him to identify him or even to recognize him, and that condition continued until after the rape took place, at which time the conversation between her and the rapist was such that it became clear that it was Walker."

Van said he had learned some details after the visit from the FBI, and he admitted he had known these changed details on March 9, when he gave his second statement to Parker and Brown at the Beverly Hills station.

"Why did you not recite the change of the story that your daughter had told you?" Heusdens demanded.

"Because my daughter had been charged with murder, and I thought it would be inappropriate for me to talk any further about the details of this matter with the police."

Lemars Blount, one of the fishermen the Webb brothers had seen up at the ranch, said that as he and his buddy drove by the big house, that Saturday, heading up to the lake, he saw a girl through the picture window. "They are out of school early," he said, forgetting, for a moment, that it was Saturday. "What's a school kid doing up here this time of day?" He said he saw a small car, like a sports car, a Lincoln, and a third car. He saw a man about five foot ten or five foot eleven, with a mustache and a beard.

Allen Bounds, the second fisherman, said he had seen three cars at the main house that afternoon: a Lincoln, a Vega, and "a small, dark-colored car." He saw a man with a mustache. No beard.

Sometimes the hearing seemed more like an elementary art class than a criminal proceeding. Gerald Webb was surprised, then dismayed, when he was asked to draw pictures of Hope and Bill and Walker, as well as himself and the horse, to establish the placement of people at the time he'd heard Hope make that remark. "Will stick figures do for people?" Gerald asked uncertainly. Ned Nelsen assured him stick figures would be fine.

Virginia Anderson, the court clerk, and William Thompson, bailiff, who had identified Walker as the well-dressed stranger in attendance on the day of Hope's bond hearing, drew the courtroom, the doorway, and the straight-backed benches, indicating where the stranger had been sitting. Mrs. Anderson especially got into the spirit of the occasion and drew the aisle, the railing and the empty jury box, as well.

Finally, another witness drew a purse and a gun.

A woman also named Anderson—Dorothy—said she had been employed as housekeeper at the ranch for about a year, starting in the fall of 1968, and that, one day, when she was at the big house with Honey, counting linens, they were discussing crime, and how people could protect themselves—karate, guard dogs, and things. Mrs. Anderson said Honey had opened her small, bone-colored leather purse and showed her a small gun, saying, "This is my protector."

Mrs. Anderson labored over her drawing, standing at the easel with a large piece of drawing paper. "This is the barrel, here, and then here was a little—kind of a little thing out here, where you pull the trigger."

She drew back, holding the pen, looking disappointed. "That's supposed to be the trigger but, I don't know, I'm not an artist. It may have been a little bigger, and this is the little barrel but, like I say, I'm not an artist, I can't draw at all, I'm just not a draw-er. Do you want me to draw another one?"

Jay Powell, for one, did not. "There is no end to this," he said in annoyance. "Next she could draw the house and then the farm, item for item. Next we will have a picture of the kitchen." So Mrs. Anderson simply drew a handbag and sat down.

"Have you seen a great many handguns like that?" Ned Nelsen asked her.

"No," she said.

"So you are not really sure whether that was a toy or a real gun, are you?"

"I'm sure it was a real gun," Mrs. Anderson said.

She no longer worked at the ranch. She said that when she'd read about the murder in the newspaper, she remembered that incident with Honey, and she'd called the sheriff's office to tell them about it. Mrs. Anderson remembered asking Honey, about the gun, "Do you think it's necessary?" and Honey replied, "You better believe it."

Michael Abbott said he'd known Hope about a year and a half. Jim Heusdens, then, wasted no time.

"And what was your relationship with Mrs. Masters?"

Tom Breslin objected that that was immaterial.

Michael stalled. "At what time are you talking about?"

"Let's put it this way," Heusdens intoned. "Prior to now, what was your relationship with her?"

"From the time I met her?"

"Yes."

"I met her about a year and a half ago and we remained—or became—friends over a period of about three to four to five months. We had dinner a few times, played chess a few times, and became friends."

"Were you ever lovers?"

Hope looked at Michael, and Michael looked at the floor.

"Well, I guess so. Yes," Michael said.

Huesdens went on to suggest that there had been wild parties at the ranch. Michael said he'd never been to a party at the ranch, but that about a year earlier he'd visited the ranch with Hope and her children and two other men.

"What took place?" Heusdens asked.

"We rode horses, and barbecued on Saturday night, and we swam in the river."

"And nothing out of what you consider the ordinary happened on that weekend?"

"It was a fairly normal weekend," Michael replied.

"This was a fairly normal weekend," Heusdens repeated. "You understand, Mr. Abbott, that you are under oath?"

"Yes," Michael said firmly.

Unable to bully the fledgling lawyer into some sort of admission, the veteran prosecutor dropped the subject.

In the hall, Tom Breslin shook hands with Michael, and they chatted. Afterward, Tom told Hope he liked Michael a lot. "How did you ever let him get away?" Tom asked Hope.

Hope shrugged. "I don't know. I guess he just wanted to go."

Martha Padilla talked through an interpreter, Mary Estrada. Martha told about coming home to Hope's house Sunday night, about ten or eleven or twelve o'clock, and seeing the man whom she now saw in the courtroom stretched out in the living room, face down, with no shirt on. About pants, Martha said, "I'm not too sure." "She was massaging him," Martha said. Another time, she said, she saw Mrs. Masters in bed, in Keith's room, and the man was whispering to her.

"Did he appear friendly?" Jim Heusdens asked.

"Friendly, I think," Martha agreed.

"When you saw Mrs. Masters massaging the man's back, did she have a nightgown on?" Jay Powell asked.

"I think she had on pants," Martha said. "I'm not sure."

"Did she have anything else on besides pants?"

"I didn't see."

Walker had brought up his co-counsel motion again, and again it was denied. Jay Powell moved to quash the search warrant—on the grounds that one of the police affidavits was signed and two were not—along with the arrest warrant. Judge Carter denied them, along with Powell's motion to continue the preliminary until a handful of witnesses could be subpoened in Los Angeles, including Tom Masters. The subpoenas had been issued, but apparently were not served.

One subpoena had been served, on Sandi, but while he was talking with her by phone, Jay Powell said, "She cried," telling him that she had four children and a job, no husband and no money. Finding her upset and hysterical, he had excused her as a witness, after her promise to cooperate. "This was done without my client's permission," Powell said. "I went over to the jail this morning and told my client this, and Mr. Walker was most upset with me, and he wishes me to state for the record that he was not consulted prior to excusing her, and that he strongly objects to my conduct in this regard. I state that." Jay Powell turned to Walker. "Is that what you want on the record?"

"Basically," Walker said.

Judge Carter denied the continuance.

The People rested.

Jim Heusdens moved that probable cause had been established and that the defendants be bound over to superior court for trial. Furthermore, he said, based on Hope's father's admission that he hadn't talked openly with the police on March 9, when he gave his second statement, Heusdens felt Van's statement at the bail hearing, when he personally guaranteed Hope's appearance in court, could no longer be relied upon. Heusdens asked that Hope Masters's bail be revoked.

Tom Breslin asked for the charges to be dismissed.

"The only evidence that the court has at this time is the fact that she was going with the victim, there was absolutely no animosity between the two, and the victim was contacted by an individual known as Taylor with this bull story that he's working for the *L.A. Times* and doing an interview. They met for lunch, and following the lunch the victim himself asked if it would be all right if this individual were invited to the ranch.

"There is no showing that Mrs. Masters knew, in any way, Mr. Taylor, before approximately one or two o'clock on Saturday. Now, at the point where Mrs. Masters went to bed, the two individuals—the victim and this Taylor—were in the house. The next thing she knows, Ashlock was killed. She is violated once or more than once, she is tied, she is abused, she is threatened, she was verbally tortured, and she was in absolutely a state of hysteria. But at this point a man is dead, and there is not a scintilla of evidence that Mrs. Masters had any connection with that killing. None!"

Tom Breslin was not flamboyant, but his voice strengthened and rose as he spoke. "Now, to what I consider the second phase of this case. Taylor is, as we all know, an intelligent individual. Having had the interview with Mr. Ashlock, and having listened to the conversation Saturday, he pieces together enough so that when he creates this story of the Mafia contract, he puts enough credence in it that Mrs. Masters finally believes there is a contract. He pinpointed enough facts—her father's heart attack, her mother's burglar alarm key, meeting Tom Masters at the Beverly Hilton —and she recalls that her husband did say he was going to the Beverly Hilton to have a meeting—and the other hit man that was following him.

And she recalled, approximately a week before, she was supposed to go to a certain restaurant, at the last minute changed to a second restaurant.

"All of these things now begin to bring to her mind the realization that there may well be a contract, and of course Taylor is one of the two people involved in that contract. Now, significantly enough, if she is trying to escape a homicide and leave the body there, surely she doesn't leave the car. There is only one reason why the car was left: Taylor couldn't allow her to drive the car home alone, he didn't have enough control at this point. So the car was left, just like a calling card.

"They drive to Los Angeles, and she is not free at any point. Then he finally determines that they are going to find the body anyway, and allows her to go to her mother's.

"But even at the mother's and father's, she is terrified of the intruder, of Taylor, and of the contract, the existence of the contract, and within a short time both her mother and her father are absolutely convinced too, to the point where her father allows Taylor to use his name when he goes to a hotel to make this phone call, because the home line is tapped, and there is somebody in front of the house. He wouldn't even call an attorney for consultation; in his own words, 'That's a hell of a thing to do, to bring a man onto your doorstep and have him shot.' That's how fearful—Taylor had convinced all members of the family that this story was true."

Judge Carter kept his eyes on Tom the entire time. The room was very still.

"Now to the third phase of the case," Tom continued. "That is, Mrs. Masters telling her mother that in fact it was Taylor that performed the rape and it was Taylor who—" Tom paused, very briefly. "Well, she says, 'I can't say he actually pulled the trigger because I wasn't there at the time, but shortly thereafter he was at me.'

"And the question has arisen as to why she didn't contact the authorities herself. But then we have to go into the background of Mr. Taylor. He has escaped from Joliet, is coming to Los Angeles, is possibly connected with a second homicide. At the time he was apprehended he had taken—or he was found with a ring with W.T.A. on it. He was found armed at the time of his arrest. He was found to have a rifle in one of the vehicles he was observed driving. There was property from other individuals, among them Taylor Wright, an extensive amount of property. And even within a short time after this crime occurred, he was using the credit cards of William Ashlock.

"When you leave an institution, you don't have much credit, nor do you have credit cards. And the court can infer as to how they were obtained.

"As far as leaving the scene, or failure to report the incident, I would say that having introduced the statement of Mrs. Masters, and the testimony of her parents, in a legal sense the People are bound by their testimony, unless there is evidence to the contrary. And, going back to the scene of the crime, the People have no evidence that there is any connection between these two individuals.

"And they also haven't shown that she is an accessory. There is no evidence that there was a concerted effort by Mrs. Masters to aid and abet the killing of Bill Ashlock.

"I would submit that the prosecution has failed to establish sufficient evidence to hold Hope Masters to answer for this crime, and urge the court, at this time, to dismiss her."

Jay Powell said that everything Mr. Breslin and Mr. Nelsen had said for their client went double for his.

"The only evidence is that Mr. Walker was present that weekend at the ranch. The only evidence that he personally ever said anything was when he spoke in her parents' home, and stated that he had come to the ranch and rescued Mrs. Masters, and that was the same story that Mrs. Masters was telling, at that time.

"All this other evidence, her changing stories and all the rest, was not evidence against Mr. Walker. The only additional evidence against Mr. Walker is that, when he was arrested, one or two items of Ashlock's personal effects were found on him. At most, that might lead the court to conclude that he may be guilty of some other crime, but certainly not the crime that's charged here.

"I would ask the court to not hold Mr. Walker to answer the charge that is before this court."

Jim Heusdens was mightily annoyed by the argument that the People were bound by the evidence—Hope Masters's statement, and her parents' testimony—without proof to the contrary. "Do we have any proof to the contrary?" he demanded, and answered his own question with a forceful gesture. "First we have witnesses putting Mrs. Masters and Mr. Walker up at the ranch on Saturday afternoon, late, with Mr. Ashlock. We have the car still present at the ranch at six o'clock in the morning, but gone at nine o'clock. After these people have left the ranch, Mr. Ashlock is subsequently found dead, hidden underneath a blanket in a back bedroom —the photographs show that somebody, or something, was moved across that carpet and I don't think it takes too much of an inference to determine what was moved across the rug and into the kitchen.

"We have heard a story from Mrs. Masters: the first story we got was that there was an intruder—she did not know who he was—and that Mr.

Taylor, the hero, came along and rescued her at nine o'clock in the morning. Then, the hero took her home and protected her by the use of a rifle, thirty-ought-six, with a scope, over Sunday and Monday and up until Tuesday.

"She went to her parents' home, and counsel says they were convinced of this great fear. And they *had* fear—that's why they let Mr. Taylor use her father's name on the telephone. But who convinced the parents to believe that Mr. Taylor was the hero who rescued Mrs. Masters?"

Heusdens made a wide wave in Hope's direction. "Who—but Mrs. Masters!

"Then, sometime later, Mrs. Masters changes her story and says, 'No. *Now* I tell you that Mr. Walker was the intruder, *he's* the one who raped me, *he's* the one who did all these things to me, and then she tells *that* story.

"The evidence shows this: that Mr. Walker and Mrs. Masters were present, with Mr. Ashlock, at the ranch on Saturday evening. Then these two people left the ranch, went to Los Angeles, and stayed at Mrs. Masters's home for a period of two days, until *finally*—Mrs. Masters *finally* went to her mother and told her something terrible had happened at the ranch, that Bill Ashlock had been murdered and she had been brutally raped—she brings the supposed murderer, who she says now *is* the murderer, into her mother's home, and then they look to him for protection." The prosecutor shook his head in amazement. "And now we are to believe that Mrs. Masters had nothing to do with it? And that the People are bound with this type of a statement?

"Can the court forget that on Monday evening, when Miss Padilla returned home, Mr. Walker was lying on the floor, and Mrs. Masters was rubbing his back? And *this* was a day after the murder had been committed—*this* was to a man who had just brutally murdered her lover and then had turned around and raped and did all these horrible things to her.

"I think there is more than sufficient evidence to show that Mrs. Masters was a participant in the murder of Mr. Ashlock. There were two people present. But we have more to show than mere presence," Heusdens ended, ominously. "And we respectfully request that they be bound over to the superior court."

Tom Breslin stood up quickly, in a fine Irish temper. "I have *got* to—" he began, then caught himself and nodded toward Carter.

"May I, Your Honor?"

"Yes," Carter said.

"As far as the back rub incident, I would challenge anyone"—Tom waved his arm, encompassing the group—"I would challenge *anyone*, Judge, Mr. Heusdens, Lieutenant Barnes, or anybody else, to be in the situation Mrs. Masters was in at the time, knowing that Taylor had killed Bill Ashlock, and if he said, rub *anything*, any one of us would have done it!"

Jim Heusdens gave a half-smile, half-sneer. "Your Honor, I think maybe Mr. Breslin would, but I don't think—"

"Just a second, counsel, I'm not through," Tom snapped. He went on to explain that he, Breslin, had stopped Van from being totally open with the police, in Van's March 9 statement, because Jim Heusdens had been so hell-bent on prosecuting Hope from the very beginning, that it had made them wary of working with the Tulare cops, except for giving hair samples and answering questions. He disputed the interpretation of the statement Hope had given to Officer Stien and in conclusion, he said, looking not at Heusdens, but at Judge Carter, "The whole purport of my argument is that without any evidence to the contrary, the People are bound. And they are bound by the story of Mrs. Masters! Counsel doesn't seem to understand that. There is absolutely no evidence that she participated in this crime. None! There is not one iota of evidence."

Perhaps what Jay Powell said then, in closing, did not make any difference. Probably not; Judge Carter had listened to two weeks of testimony, some of it damaging to the defendants, and all he had to determine was probable cause, not guilt. Still, it was interesting to speculate how Jay's words must have sounded to a man who wasn't a lawyer, a lay judge whose sense of security could not have been greatly enhanced by the presence of thousand-dollars-a-day attorneys up from L.A. with their elephantskin briefcases, and another mild-mannered but punctilious man from a prestigious law school who had honed his criminal trial skills under the tutelage of Melvin Belli.

Jay Powell told Carter that "this court has no choice" but to dismiss.

A little after 4:00 P.M. on Wednesday, April 18, 1973, Judge Carter chose to order G. Daniel Walker and Hope Masters bound over to superior court to be tried for murder.

CHAPTER
THIRTEEN

TOM MASTERS ALWAYS refused to discuss the case with Hope, both at the time he was implicated and afterward. He declined to be interviewed by Gene Tinch, or to take a polygraph test administered by anyone on Hope's team. Tom maintained a careful distance, communicating mostly through his lawyer, although he did write to Honey and Van, pointing out that he hadn't been able to see K.C. Tom wrote that, before he took legal steps to gain access to K.C., he was writing to try to work something out.

"Honey and Van, certainly this incident has caused a great deal of hardship and strain on your lives, the lives of Hopie's children, and on my own life," Tom wrote. "I'm horrified that you and Hopie could even conceive of the possibilities of my being involved in this case. I've always been very fond of Hopie since our separation and thought that all of us maintained what I considered was a friendly relationship. Hopefully, some day we can all return to some form of normalcy."

Tom's friend Nadine typed the letter for him, and he signed it "Kindest personal regards." Van was impressed with the letter and showed it to Hope. She thought it was a good letter, too. Soon afterward, Tom began coming to see K.C. and to take him places, so Tom was seeing Hope again, too. The incongruity of the situation was so readily absorbed into the habitual incongruities of life on the Drive that when Hope came home from Porterville, trailing so many headlines—DEATH TRIAL ORDERED FOR SOCIALITE—that she couldn't keep track, Tom put his clipping service onto it.

But Tom did talk to the police again, when Gene Parker and Henry Babcock visited him at his office. In that second statement, Tom related again his activities on the weekend Hope and Bill went to the ranch. He said that Hope had asked him to take K.C. on Saturday and Sunday both, and Tom had agreed. When he returned K.C. on Sunday around 6:00 P.M., the child spotted Bill's Triumph in the driveway and began to squeal happily. "Oh, Bill's here, Bill's here!" Tom was interested in the strange car in Hope's driveway. "Who the hell owns the white Continental?" he asked Nadine.

"Who owns the white car?" Tom asked the maid, when he took K.C. inside. Nadine waited in the car.

"A friend of Mrs. Masters," Licha told him.

Tom said he and Nadine had gone to dinner then at El Coyote, a Mexican place on Beverly Boulevard. The next day, Monday, he worked at his office all day, as usual, until 7:30 P.M., when he met a friend for a couple of drinks at the Playboy Club. On the way home he stopped at Schwab's Drugstore for a quick bite and got home early, about 10:30. On Tuesday morning, he and Nadine left early for Mammoth, a long drive, nearly as far as Yosemite, where Tom attended a meeting of the Mammoth Merchants Association, hoping to pick up an account.

He got back to L.A. Wednesday night and on Thursday morning, March 1, was awakened by a call from his business manager, Lou Grant. Lou told Tom he'd just heard on the radio that Hope had been arrested for murder. Tom thought it was a bad practical joke, but when Lou insisted, Tom turned on his own radio. When Tom and Nadine heard it themselves, on the KNX news, Tom went right to his office and stayed there.

"Now Tom, like we've mentioned before, you've been placed in the role of a possible suspect in this, right?" Babcock said.

"Right."

"Would you have any reservations about taking a polygraph, also known as a lie detector test, covering this incident only, nothing to do with your personal life other than this incident we've been talking about?"

"No, I would do it," Tom said. "I have no objections to that."

Hope had no objections to taking one either, at least not after Gene Tinch put his foot down. "We've heard a couple of different stories," he told Tom Breslin. "It's time for a poly. I'm kind of a funny guy; I like to know what I'm doing. If I'm trying to get her off the hook and she's innocent, that's one thing; if I'm trying to get her off the hook and she's guilty, that's another thing, okay?"

Although Gene said a couple of points on the test showed deception patterns, he felt the test confirmed that her second story was true. Tom Breslin attributed the discrepancies to her emotional distress; Hope blamed her deepdown feelings. "When they asked me, 'Do you have any responsibility in the death of Bill Ashlock?' the test went crazy, because I *feel* responsible. I've been *told* I'm responsible. I felt so guilty that I could never take a clean lie detector test."

The issue of her polygraph test never came up in public, nor did anybody else's. As far as she knew, Tom Masters was never tested by the police, nor was the other man who had been asked to take one, Jim Webb. Jim Heusdens finally dismissed the whole matter of lie tests with a sarcastic snort: "If anyone in this damned thing had taken a polygraph, the machine would have burned up."

On April 30, Ned Nelsen and Tom Breslin, on behalf of Hope Masters, and Jay Powell, on behalf of G. Daniel Walker, moved in superior court that the charges against their respective clients be dismissed on grounds of insufficient evidence. Powell also argued that his client had been arrested "illegally and unconstitutionally," and Walker himself presented seven handwritten motions, including a renewed motion that he be appointed co-counsel and that, as co-counsel, he be granted "tools of the trade." Walker cited a 1969 case in which a man named Richardson, accused of shooting a policeman in Long Beach, had been named as his own co-counsel and subsequently provided with a typewriter, a telephone, law books, and a valet-runner to file his motions. Walker said he was willing to waive the valet, but he needed everything else, including a telephone, typewriter, white bond typing paper, carbon paper, envelopes, stamps, and the use of the court's law library. He asked for his money back —$186.33—so he could buy some law books and periodicals that were unavailable in Tulare County, including the most recent volume of the *Criminal Law Reporters,* with its weekly supplement published in Washington, D.C. He said he was a former subscriber. He asked for a battery of tests to be run, including hair examination, tape examination, bullet fragments examination, and fingerprint work. He estimated the cost of these tests would range from $12,469.50 to $40,936.50. He asked for a number of out-of-county subpoenas to be issued to persons in London, Australia, and Dusseldorf, Germany.

Judge Jay R. Ballantyne denied the motions to dismiss, but he ruled that Walker could act as co-counsel and be given the tools of the trade. By the time of the pretrial hearing, when both defendants pleaded not guilty, Walker had another stack of motions prepared, including two that were particularly intriguing. He argued that the Tulare courts had no jurisdiction in the case at all, because it had not been proven that Spring-ville was in Tulare County, and he presented a motion, apparently based on Gerald Webb's problem at Myers Chapel, that "The People have failed to show, in ten volumes of preliminary hearings, that William T. Ashlock is dead." Also by that time—May 14—Walker had been given two cells, one with a picnic table moved in for his work space; and the women trustees in their section of the Visalia jail had made him a quilt.

"I may be a little nuts in my own way, but I'm not violent," Hope had told Tom Breslin, and as the days and weeks passed, deepening into early summer, and the trial was postponed again, her family problems height-ened, and Hope felt she was going more than a little nuts.

During the preliminary, Keith had stayed with Sharon and Bill Pierce, the couple Hope had willed her children to in the note she scribbled in her mother's kitchen. A boy had teased Keith at school—"I hear your mother's a jailbird"—and Keith was getting into fights, so the Pierces had let Keith stay home from school, and Sharon Pierce enrolled Hope in a prayer chain.

Now Keith refused to return to school, and Hope didn't have the strength, or the will, to force him. She had been cut by the cruelty herself; one night, when Michael Abbott took her to dinner to get her mind off things, they'd gone to a restaurant she knew well and felt comfortable in. When the man playing the piano saw her, he played "As Time Goes By," then struck a couple of smashing chords, to get everyone's attention. "How does it feel to be out of the slammer?" he called to Hope across the crowded room.

Honey and Van and Hope quarreled most of the time. Hope resented their telling her what she should have done, what she should have said, and how everything she did and said they would have done and said differently. Hope was bitter about Van's refusal to use his legal influence to help her. When Judge Ballantyne denied the motion to dismiss, Tom and Ned had appealed to the Fifth Appellate Court. When they lost on appeal, Hope's last chance lay in a hearing before the state supreme court. Tom and Ned drew up a long petition for the hearing, citing four reasons: that there was no reasonable or probable cause to believe that the defendant had committed the crime; that there was no evidence to establish that the defendant had committed the crime of murder; that evidence showed that she had been kidnaped by the co-defendant at gunpoint; and that the inconsistencies in her statements did not supply proof of the elements of the crime with which she was charged.

Even for Ned Nelsen, a supreme court hearing was not a cinch to get, and Ned had asked Van to intercede. Specifically, Ned asked Van to ask William French Smith, one of Van's law partners, who was well-connected in Sacramento, to help her get a hearing. When Van refused, Hope screamed. "I'm only asking for a hearing, goddamnit! I'm not asking you to do anything illegal. I'm just asking you to help me." The hearing was not granted.

For a brief time, on the day of the bail hearing—"My daughter is not well. I fear for her"—it had appeared that danger might, at last, have forged stronger links of understanding and affection among the members of the family. But it did not. The emotional rapport momentarily achieved in the justice court had evaporated in the diffused air of Beverly Hills, and Hope and Van had retreated to their customary position, which was, most of the time, an adversary position, too far out of reach for understanding. When Van heard Walker's taped suggestion that Hope's lawyers meet him in Rhodesia, "He hit the ceiling," Hope told Michael angrily. "No *way* is he going to pay to send my attorneys to Rhodesia. And all the while my mother's personal allowance, not including upkeep on her car and lunches at the club, is three thousand a month."

Van did not speak of his own problems to Hope or, if he did, she considered them minimal compared to the pressures on her. But, as early as March 2, when she was still behind bars, when Van and Honey were on their way to Porterville, an interoffice memo had been left on Van's desk, signed by the firm's director of administration. The memo began by expressing sympathy and deep concern for the unfortunate situation involving Van's daughter; then, in a longer paragraph, the director passed along some thoughts that had been expressed to him by several of the partners in the Firm—Van's Firm always referred to itself in caps.

"In view of the prominence of the Firm and of the fact that the media have already identified the Firm by name, and you as a senior partner in the Firm, the manner in which the case is handled, and by whom, has a direct bearing on the reputation, not only of yourself, but also of the Firm. With this in mind, the partners feel that it is your responsibility to the Firm to see to it that the very best lawyer or lawyers available are hired to represent Hope. The partners believe you will agree that your responsibility to the Firm, as its senior lawyer and as a person identifiable (and in fact already identified in the newspapers, etc.) with the Firm, is such as to require that the charges against Hope be handled in the most delicate way, and not turned over to a criminal lawyer who might be competent to handle only ordinary criminal cases."

When he returned to his office and found the memo, Van offered to submit his resignation. His offer was not accepted, but Van traced the "several partners" who had passed along their thoughts, and the episode left a permanent imprint.

Van's own journal reflected a melancholy awareness of the troubled family relationship. On March 15, the day the preliminary hearing was postponed: "Hopie said at lunch that the way I handled things was in some way responsible for her present predicament. I sulked and am still sulking. Seems to me fruitless to go back over things done that cannot now be undone." Another day: "Nothing significant, except that Hopie came by and she and I had a pretty good battle going, re various problems." Van's relief matched Hope's on the Saturday she went back up to the Drive. "I played golf. Honey played cards. Hopie took her car and all three children and went home. *Thank God!*"

Up on the Drive, Keith had become a rebellious truant; Hope Elizabeth was a model student at school but at home would often throw herself on the floor and scream for hours, so long and so loud that neighbors, not just next door but way up and down the block, would call to ask what the matter was. When Hope, rotating between depression and extreme anxiety, finally asked a psychiatrist what the matter was with everybody, he told her he couldn't treat her alone, that everybody's problems—three generations of interwoven problems—were so tight they couldn't be picked apart. On the simplest level, he explained, one child might be manifesting the others' anxieties. He talked about her relationship with Honey and with Van and the preexisting frustrations and resentments. "What this affair has done," Dr. Elstead told Hope, "has been to take everybody's small problems and blow them out of all proportion, magnifying them so that what normally could be settled at home now becomes a job for a doctor." Hope thought that made sense; she managed to transfer five thousand dollars from one of her trust funds and gave it to the psychiatrist in the form of a cashier's check, upfront payment to guarantee a span of treatment for herself and the kids, and when her parents found that out, they were displeased.

One of Hope's resentments stemmed from the attitude she felt Honey and Van displayed, the attitude that they, as much as she, were the victims. Hope had seen the attitude confirmed by the gifts that poured in from the time the news broke—flowers and candy and sympathetic notes, almost exclusively addressed to Honey and Van. "My heart aches for you two darling people. . . ." Honey and Van were invited to dinner, for weekends, to "a place which is secluded and quiet, where you'd need to do nothing but watch the boats go by." Honey shared all the correspondence with Hope, though it might have been better if she had not, especially the note addressed to "Very dear Honey and Van" with an enclosed quotation: "When our children are little, they trod upon our feet; and when they are grown, they trod upon our hearts."

On June 19, a new trial date was set—September 4—to allow time for hearings on Walker's two major motions, one to suppress the evidence accumulated in the wake of his arrest, and the other to quash the arrest warrant itself.

Walker based his motion to suppress on a federal ruling in the Wong Sun case, a judicial concept colorfully referred to as "the fruit of the poisoned tree." Walker spelled it out: "What Begins Ill Can Never Be Anything but Evil and Illegal." Essentially, his argument was that the letter to Marcy, which was the only means the authorities had to link Walker with the Ashlock affair, had been illegally intercepted by the Illinois authorities, and that everything following that illegal act—the identification of Taylor as Walker, his arrest, and the seizure of all the incriminating evidence—was therefore illegal and invalid.

The motion to suppress the arrest warrant was also described: "When a Lie Weaves a Garment of Pure Falsehood, the People Must Shed or Wear It."

In that section, Walker insisted the police had entered and searched Room 609 at Howard Johnson's illegally, before his arrest, and he cited *Stoner v. California,* 1964: "No less than the tenant of a house, or the occupant of a room in a boarding house . . . a guest in a hotel room is entitled to constitutional protection against unreasonable searches and seizures."

In his fifty-two-page motion, Walker poked a good deal of extraneous fun, calling the police "the occupation forces" and noting that an FBI agent had stood by the window for several hours "without even looking under the bed . . . the most common of hiding places down through the years." He scoffed at Jim Brown's inventory of property, which, Walker pointed out, listed a can of shaving cream but no razor—"Would a man have shaving cream and no means to use it?"—and a can of Alberto VO5 hairspray but no comb or brush. "The Court can hardly fail to take judicial notice of Defendant Walker's hair, its length and amount, and draw a reasonable inference it did not attain such length and proportions in custody, therefore, would it be reasonable to assume a man would have nothing to comb or shape his hair with in his room?" Walker listed the clothes he was wearing at the time of his arrest: "one leather coat with hand lacing and three buttons down front; one blue/white checked and/ or pattern shirt with collar, buttons down front, buttons at cuffs, buttons on breast pockets; one white turtleneck sweater with long sleeves; one pair of blue denim bellbottom pants; one white belt with red trim in center around it (in loops on pants); one pair of blue with white trim bikini jockey shorts; one pair of navy blue Supphose to-the-knee socks; one locker key for L.A. International Airport locker concealed in elastic top of sock on right leg; one pair of eight-inch boots with inside zipper, size 10B"—and he pointed out that the police list did not include those clothes. "One must assume from the People's inventory that Walker was arrested nude."

Finally, Walker noted that the search warrant for the Thunderbird was issued on the basis of three police affidavits—one signed, two orally sworn —and that the resulting inventory had not been transcribed and certified by an official court reporter.

All the arguments meshed, of course. If the arrest were illegal, then the warrant would inevitably be defective; if the car keys found in the Thunderbird were illegally seized, then the car that those keys unlocked—the Impala at the San Francisco Airport—was illegally searched, too. Everything, finally, harked back to the letter; once the poisoned tree began to bloom, there was no stopping the proliferation of its fruit.

Jim Heusdens always felt that one person could have stopped the tree from bearing; could, in fact, have chopped it down to a ragged stump. Marcy Purmal could have been subpoenaed at the hearing, to testify under oath that her mail had not been illegally seized and that she had turned Walker's missives over to the Illinois authorities voluntarily, if with some reluctance. Even without Marcy, Jim Heusdens said he would have put up one hell of an argument—for example, on the search of the hotel room business. "How can the search of a hotel room be unlawful when the room is rented unlawfully, on a stolen credit card?" he fumed. "The guy isn't the legal tenant; he's not going to pay the bill. He's just a goddamned trespasser!"

But it didn't matter, then, what Jim Heusdens would have done. He had resigned from the D.A.'s office at the start of the summer and was practicing law on Morton Street in Porterville, just down from the justice court. Another deputy D.A., Joseph Haley, had been put in charge of the action. But that was after Heusdens's triumph at the preliminary and his subsequent spadework in the late spring, when he had joined Gene Parker and Jim Brown on a trip to the Midwest.

Parker and Brown always considered it the high point of their travels, when they stepped off the plane at O'Hare and saw Bob Swalwell in his three-piece dark blue suit, leaning against a wall in the airport terminal, waiting for them. They had an evening together—good food, good wine, and a lot of good cop talk—and the next day the three detectives, with Jim Heusdens, visited Marcy Purmal. Although Marcy's attorney, George Murtagh, had assured them she would cooperate with them, Brown and Parker got the feeling she'd just as soon they hadn't come by.

Marcy said she'd never heard the names Taylor Wright, Larry Burbage, Dick Miller, Richard Crane, Bill Ashlock, or Hope Masters before the investigation began. She said that Walker had never mentioned an advertising agency to her and that, as far as she knew, he never had any connections on the West Coast, though she did seem to remember Walker talking, once, about the TV commercial character, "Captain Crunch," which he said he had created or helped create or something, and she thought Walker might have been sent to California on advertising business, possibly in 1968.

When Marcy was questioned about parties in Walker's hospital room, she said several attorneys had visited him there because they were interested in penal reform, but she couldn't recall any parties. When Marcy was shown a set of photographs, she identified Walker. She identified Hope Masters as the woman whose picture Marcy had received in a letter. She denied knowing Bill Ashlock, except for having heard his name in the letter, but both Brown and Parker noted that Marcy lingered over Bill's photograph with a broad smile on her face.

At the Illinois State Prison, they found thirty cardboard boxes Walker had abandoned.

Jim Brown was not allowed to take his camera inside the prison so he stood on the steps outside and took pictures of the door. Inside, they talked to a number of people, trying to find out if Walker had indeed had Hope Masters's picture when he resided there.

In Aurora, they visited Robert Pietrusiak, who identified, from photographs, many of his stolen items, including his camera, his tape recorder, and a pair of scissors. Robert and Catherine Pietrusiak identified Walker's picture and, in Michigan, so did Taylor Wright.

The low point of their travels came when they found an airline stewardess who identified Walker as one of her Colorado passengers. She remembered him well, because bad weather had delayed takeoff for an hour and a half, and he'd left the plane to get drinks for himself, for the stewardess, and for the woman he was traveling with, whom the stewardess remembered as a beautiful, tall blond. They were never able to identify or locate the woman whom they thought had traveled with Walker to Albuquerque. "Maybe she's just bones out in the desert somewhere by now," Brown told Parker.

Back in Visalia, they discussed Walker's activities with him. He told them they were still missing a car, a Mercedes, and once he told them, with a smile, "You're overkilling your prey." He never identified that woman, though he did give them a lot of tips. "He's teaching us about law, about techniques of interrogation, techniques of investigation, collecting evidence, and preserving evidence, just by our watching him and listening to him," Parker told Brown. "I've learned more from him in a couple of months than I learned in the ten years prior."

Jim Brown, too, found Walker friendly and witty, a most interesting man. Jim was often assigned to escort Walker on his regular visits to the law library, two hours every Monday, Wednesday, and Friday, and when Walker told Jim he liked jelly beans, Jim began bringing in bags of jelly beans for him, usually purple.

Still, Jim was always prepared. He had shot at someone only once in his life, in the middle of a trailer court, ringed by onlookers, when a man he was chasing suddenly whirled and fired three shots at Jim. "The third shot dug dirt out from under my toes," Jim recalled. "But the first two, I didn't know where they went, and those were the ones I worried about. I was lookin' around to see if I'd been hit. Well, he was using a three fifty-seven Magnum, which you can shoot through a car engine with. And if I'd been hit, why man, I'd have *known* it."

After that incident, Jim's dad had laid down the law. "I never wanted you to be a policeman, but you're going to be one, evidently, and if you're going to get into shootouts, you get you a weapon that when you hit a guy, he'll stay down." Jim's dad took away Jim's .38 service weapon and bought him a .357 which Jim, fortunately, had never had to use. But he knew it was there. "I don't want to have to shoot somebody," Jim declared, "but if I have to shoot, I don't want him to get up and shoot back."

Gene felt the same way. One blazing day in late July—Jay Powell's birthday—Gene and six other detectives were assigned to escort Walker to the ranch; he and Jay Powell had been allowed a visit there in preparation for their defense. Two of the detectives carried high-powered rifles;

Gene and the others had their regular service weapons. Gene's hand hovered near the holster the whole time. The gun used to kill Bill Ashlock had not been found; ballistically, there was no match with the gun Walker had when he was arrested. Gene always thought that Walker, following the lead of the Jackal, had welded the gun to the underside of the Lincoln; Gene had heard that when the FBI went over the Lincoln, they found signs that something had been hidden underneath. Still, with Walker, you never knew, and all afternoon, Gene half-expected Walker to suddenly swoop down behind a bush or jump into a gully, grab the gun he'd stashed there, and come out shooting. So Gene stayed ready, and he let Walker know he was ready. "If I see anything in your hand besides paper and a pencil," he told Walker, "you are bought and paid for." Walker just smiled and took copious notes on his yellow legal pad, strolling through the house and around the grounds as though he owned the place.

Gene felt Walker, all summer, was having himself a ball. With his access to a phone, he was making so many calls that Tom Breslin thought it necessary to put it in writing:

> Dear Hopie,
>   If G. Daniel Walker happens to call you, the following, only, will be related by you: 'My attorneys have instructed me not to talk with you. If you have anything to say, please contact my attorneys.' And then, HANG UP!
>   Sincerely,
>   T. P. Breslin

Once Walker called Jim Brown at home, to ask Jim to bring a tape recorder over to the jail because he wanted to confess. When Jim hurried over with the tape machine, Walker smiled. "I confess: I didn't do it."

Some of Walker's calls to Ned Nelsen lasted half an hour, maybe forty-five minutes. "He seemed to think that because they were co-defendants, we were on the same side," Ned recalled. "He'd discuss aspects of the case, ask a lot of questions, but he never made any statements that were incriminating." When the sheriff's office got Walker's phone bill, over five hundred dollars, Walker was limited to two calls a day. Eventually another large bill arrived; Walker had been calling Western Union and sending out a stream of wires. When the sheriff's office explained the situation, Western Union agreed to absorb the cost, and Walker's two calls a day henceforth could be made only to Jay Powell. His letters continued, including long, newsy letters to Ned

Nelsen, bringing Ned up to date on Walker's legal progress. He wrote to Ned about some newly discovered evidence, a medical report indicating that Bill Ashlock had been shot, not in the back of the head, but through the mouth, and he told Ned all about his visit to the ranch. He sent Ned a large envelope, with an enclosure for Hope—Bill's death certificate. William T. Ashlock had been cremated at the Fresno Crematory, under the direction of the people from Myers Chapel. His ashes were scattered at sea.

> Place of Death: Springville.
> County of Death: Tulare
> Length of Stay in County: 3 Days.

Walker's attempt to suppress the evidence was his own, separate motion, with Hope not joining. Items of evidence that would be detrimental to Walker would, of course, be helpful to Hope—the credit cards, the loaded .38, the surgical gloves.

When Van told Hope she could have one lawyer, but not two, to reduce the legal fees, she chose Tom Breslin. Ned Nelsen was older, richer, more or less in a class with her parents; Tom had seen her at her worst, she felt, scared and shaky at the Beverly Hills jail, even more bedraggled that night in Visalia. Tom had become a youngish father figure to her, even a father confessor; it was Tom whom she'd felt the need to talk to most, when they drove out to the beach. So it was Tom Breslin who followed the suppression hearings, day by day, all summer, and who drove north to the Visalia courthouse on the day Judge Ballantyne was to issue his ruling as to whether the evidence would be suppressed.

It was Friday, August 31, 1973, the start of the long Labor Day weekend. The case of *The People of the State of California* v. *G. Daniel Walker and Hope Masters* was to come to trial on Tuesday, September 4.

Tom had not been a bit surprised when Walker moved to suppress the evidence. "That's good jailhouse law," Tom pointed out. "And Walker's a good jailhouse lawyer. In fact, in some ways he's a legal genius." He had talked it over with Ned Nelsen and had made his plans, and he'd talked it over, many times, with the prosecutor, Joe Haley. "If the evidence is suppressed, you've got to appeal the ruling," Tom kept telling Haley. "You can't go to trial without that evidence against Walker. Without that evidence, you don't have a chance to convict Walker." Joe Haley had listened and had agreed that the state needed the evidence. If Judge

Ballantyne ordered it suppressed, Haley said, he would immediately file an appeal.

Although Tom was in court more or less as a concerned spectator, he was the most attentive as Judge Ballantyne swept into the courtroom and read his nine-page decision agreeing with Walker that the letter to Marcy Purmal had been illegally intercepted and that everything stemming from that letter, everything linking him to the Ashlock murder—the search of his room at the Howard Johnson's, his arrest, and the seizure of property both on Walker himself and in the Thunderbird—was illegal. The state had argued that Walker's use of the Taylor Wright credit card was independent information, not linked to the letter, but Judge Ballantyne said that that point "was not adequately developed by the People," and he granted Walker's motion in its entirety. All the evidence was ordered suppressed. The whole lot. None of it, then—not the credit cards, or the clothing, or Bill's yellow metal ring, the gun, the gloves, nothing—could be used as evidence in the prosecution of G. Daniel Walker on a charge of first degree murder. Walker might well be exonerated, then, the coldest, cleverest killer Tom Breslin had ever seen.

Walker smiled when Ballantyne finished reading. Jay Powell smiled. Tom Breslin smiled in relief when Joe Haley stood up to announce that the state would appeal the ruling. Just before court convened that morning at ten o'clock, Tom had reminded the prosecutor, one more time. "Without that evidence, you don't have a chance to convict Walker," Tom had said again. "If Ballantyne rules to suppress, you've got to appeal his ruling."

Judge Ballantyne listened to Haley, nodded, and made a note. He announced that because of the appeal, the trial was automatically postponed for thirty days. He looked over at Tom Breslin.

"Mr. Breslin," Ballantyne said, "you're scheduled for trial the day following this holiday. But with this appeal, of course, we now will have a continuance. You will agree to that continuance?" It did not sound like a question, only a judicial formality. To Tom Breslin, it sounded like trumpets from an angel choir.

"Your Honor," Tom said solemnly, "I cannot agree to a continuance without consulting my client."

"Well then," the judge said, a trifle impatiently, "will you kindly contact your client and ask her to agree to the continuance?"

Tom tried to look suitably grave. "Certainly, Your Honor, I will call my client.

"And I *did* call. I swear I did," Tom insisted later, with a naughty gleam in his eye. "I went over to The Depot and had a martini and then, honest to God, I called Hopie. I let the phone ring at least twice."

Back in court, after lunch, Tom looked even more grave. "I'm sorry, Your Honor, but I cannot reach my client, and I haven't the authority to waive her right to a speedy trial. We are ready for trial, and so we will go to trial as scheduled, on Tuesday."

The prosecutor blinked. Walker and Jay Powell murmured together. The judge looked closely at Tom, who looked right back at him. Then Judge Ballantyne invited Mr. Breslin and Mr. Haley to join him in chambers.

Behind the closed door, Tom tried not to grin as he repeated what he had said in the courtroom. "We're ready for trial, Your Honor. I can't waive my client's right to a speedy trial without her permission. So we'll go to trial. I realize that co-defendant Walker's trial is automatically postponed for thirty days, because of the state's appeal. We will go to trial separately."

It was only too clear to the prosecutor—but a little too late—what was happening . . . what, in fact, had already happened. Still, Tom spelled it out. All the evidence had been suppressed against Walker. Without that evidence, the state had virtually nothing to use against him. As a co-defendant, Hope Masters could claim privilege and could not be forced to testify against him. If Hope's trial went ahead, separately, all the evidence that had been suppressed on Walker's behalf could, and certainly would, be used at her trial. But if all that evidence were made public in her trial, Walker would then have a complete script to follow as he prepared for his own later trial; he would be many steps ahead of the state when he came to trial, if indeed he ever did: so many legal problems would be linked with the use of evidence in her trial, but suppressed in his, on an identical charge, that the unraveling of those problems could take literally years. Beyond all this, Walker could easily claim massive prejudicial publicity against him, as the evidence was disclosed in Hope's trial, and he was likely to slither off the hook entirely.

The fact that it was so clear did not make it less painful to the prosecutor, who stared at Tom.

"Of course," Tom went on, pleasantly, "if the charges against my client were to be dismissed, we would be prepared to cooperate. My client might testify as a prosecution witness."

Haley shook his head. "We can't just dismiss them," he said slowly.

Tom smiled. "Okay then," he said cheerfully. "We'll go to trial on Tuesday."

"Well, how about having her plead guilty to a lesser charge, like not calling the police?" Haley offered reluctantly.

"No thanks," Tom said. "Dismissal."

Judge Ballantyne looked at the prosecutor. "Mr. Haley," he said gently, "as I see it, the thing that will convict Hope Masters is your proof that she knew Mr. Walker before he came to the ranch. Do you have any evidence of that?"

Haley shook his head again. "No, we don't have any evidence of that," he murmured.

"Well then," Ballantyne said briskly, "I don't think you'll get a conviction against her, and I think you're better off getting her cooperation."

Haley made one more try. "I would consider giving her immunity, if she will testify," he said. Again Tom declined. He and Ned had discussed that possibility and had decided that, in the Watergate era, the word "immunity" had a distasteful tang. "No thanks," Tom said. "It has to be a straight-out dismissal." When Haley hesitated, Tom whipped out a copy of Section 1099 of the California Penal Code, which he just happened to have with him, and passed it to the prosecutor to read: "When two or more defendants are included in the same accusatory pleading, the court may, at any time before the defendants have gone into their defense, on the application of the prosecuting attorney, Direct any defendant to be discharged, that he may be a witness for the People."

Tom went one step beyond, then, since he had gone so far already: he said he wanted the dismissal to occur after the trial had begun, after a jury was sworn, and after the first witness had testified. In his legal diggings, Tom had learned that if a defendant were discharged at that point, he —or she—was considered to have already been placed in jeopardy and could never be placed in jeopardy again on that charge, even if he—or she—subsequently confessed.

Judge Ballantyne nodded to Tom. "Well, Mr. Breslin," he commented, "it looks as though you've done your homework on this."

Now Tom tried to look humble. But he *had* done his homework; he had worked hard, and the fact that all his earlier attempts in Hope's case —trying for a change of venue, for a supreme court hearing, trying in any way possible to at least get her case separated from Walker's—had failed, made this sudden victory all the sweeter.

"All right," Haley said finally because, in the end, there was not much else to say. Under the terms of the stipulation that Tom dictated, then, and both attorneys signed, Judge Ballantyne as witness, Hope would agree to a postponement of her trial, along with Walker's postponement, while the state's appeal of his suppression ruling went forward. Only she and her parents, her attorneys, and the prosecution would know that she would not be tried for murder; Walker and Jay Powell would not be told, of course, lest they come up with some legal maneuver to thwart it. When the trial finally began, whenever that was, and the jury was sworn, and the first witness had testified, the charges against her would be formally dropped; the trial would proceed against Walker alone, with Hope Masters as the key witness for the prosecution.

As he drove back to Los Angeles, the signed stipulation in his briefcase, Tom sang along with his car radio. He had not been in such high spirits for months. He felt like Galahad, like a conquering hero; he felt like the Archangel Michael, who had wrestled with the Devil, and won.

Honey wept with joy, and Van was delighted with what they called "the arrangement." But Hope was appalled.

"I just can't testify against him," she moaned. "Don't be mad at me, Tom, because I really appreciate what you've done, I think you're terrific, but I can't testify against him. I promised him I wouldn't. I said I would never, never testify against him, and I swore on the lives of my children! I can't do it, Tom, don't you see?"

In a way, Tom did see. "She promised, and to Hopie, that's it," he told Gene Tinch. "A promise is a promise. That's her flight pattern." But even though he understood, and even admired her for her tenacity, he hollered at her.

"You *have* to do it, Hopie," Tom told her. "You absolutely have to do it! I know you promised, but that kind of promise doesn't count, because it was made under duress. It was not a free, volitional act on your part. It isn't binding." When she still shook her head, Tom pressed on. "Hopie, Hopie, you have to do it. It's your only chance. If you don't go along with this, Hopie, you will have to stand trial and you might"—Tom hesitated, then he went ahead and said it—"you might go to prison, Hopie, maybe for a long, long time."

Hope was so distraught, so confused and upset that she called Reverend Castellanos at All Saints Episcopal Church and asked if she could come over right away. She hadn't been to his church for years, but she didn't know anyone else, she said, to turn to.

She explained her dilemma. "What do you think I should do?" she asked the minister.

"What do you think God would want you to do?" he countered.

"Well, I don't know," Hope said. "I'm having a really hard time figuring out what's right and wrong in this thing. I mean, I promised him, and I meant it when I promised."

"I think God would want you to tell the truth," Reverend Castellanos prompted her. "Without malice, though. Without hatred or feelings of revenge. I think God wants you to tell the truth, as you know the truth to be."

They talked more, then, about what had happened. He tried to link her pain and suffering, her family's suffering, to the suffering of Christ. Crucifixion could happen in many forms, Reverend Castellanos told her, and the troubles in people's lives—sometimes alcoholism, or delinquent children, or incurable illness or, in her case, rape, abuse, murder—had something to do, in fact, a great deal to do, with the troubles inflicted on Christ.

"Did you expect to be treated better than Jesus?" he asked her gently.

Hope thought about that.

"Well, yeah," she said, finally. "I guess I did."

"Okay then," she told Tom. "I'll do it."

"Okay, Hopie," Tom said. "That's good. That's great."

"You know, Tom, I was so cold," she went on, a distant look on her face. "I was just so cold. I have never been so cold in my life. And he put blankets over me. I think he probably kept me alive."

Tom just looked at her. He did not feel so elated, anymore. He still felt he had wrestled with the Devil, but he wasn't so sure he had won.

Visalia was more to Hope's taste than was Porterville. It had a good French restaurant and a glossy shopping mall. Visalia's Lampliter Inn had a more than passable dining room and a handful of private cottages, where Honey and Van were booked; Hope and Gene and Tom had singles in the main building. To Hope, Porterville was battered pickups and farmers in overalls, gaping at her, pointing Instamatics in her face; in Visalia, Van's Cadillac was not out of place. As the county seat, Visalia boasted a convention center, a community college, summer Shakespeare, a country club, and an expensive residential section, Greenacres, where a lot of professionals lived—doctors and lawyers and judges, including Judge Leonard Ginsburg, who became the third, and last, judge to observe the entire cast of characters assembled on one stage when the trial finally began, on November 19.

"Characters" was the appropriate word, Ginsburg felt. When he looked at Van, he saw a man so dignified, so precise, that Judge Ginsburg was convinced Van had seen movies about corporation lawyers when he was a little boy and had vowed to be just like one of them when he grew up. The judge could picture Honey, so thin, so rich, drifting through her perfect living room, wringing her hands in storybook distress. When the entire cast—judge, jury, policemen, attorneys, co-defendants—drove to the ranch so the jury could view the scene of the crime, Judge Ginsburg thought that was like a movie clip, too. "Man and boy, I've been around these mountains all my life," Judge Ginsburg said, "and I've never seen such a picturesque place, in a little valley like that, shut off by the mountains on all sides, with a little crick running through it, and the white frame house set among the orange trees—and Walker strolling around, waving his pipe, as though he owned the place." Altogether, Judge Ginsburg found the trial thoroughly fascinating—an intricate, highly improbable drama in which nobody seemed real, including himself.

Hope liked Judge Ginsburg. She liked the way he looked—bearded, sophisticated, intellectual, "like he came from big bucks, and had gone to school back East." Which came close: Leonard Ginsburg was from San Francisco, a doctor's son, and had gone to Berkeley. Hope also liked the way he handled the question of Walker's chains, which had always bothered her. "It hurts me to see Walker chained," she'd told Tom Breslin, but he'd told her she couldn't say that in court because it would make her look too sympathetic. Jay Powell asked for a removal, now, of all restraints, pointing out that in Walker's many, many court appearances since March, the defendant had never attempted to escape. Joe Haley responded by pointing out that maybe the defendant had never attempted to escape because in most of those appearances, he'd been shackled and chained. "And that's the purpose of the whole thing," Haley said dryly.

Judge Ginsburg listened, then made up his mind. "I question whether the handcuffs and the chain around his belt are necessary," he said. "That is the most conspicuous of the restraints, and I think the leg shackles would accomplish the objective and be reasonably inconspicuous." Although the ankle cuffs were scarcely visible when Walker was sitting or standing, only when he moved around, Judge Ginsburg took pains to explain them to the jury. "This is no evidence whatsoever of anything at all. It has nothing to do with the guilt or innocence of the defendant, and is not to be considered by you in any way whatsoever."

Walker was using the legal materials granted to him earlier very productively. Although bail had been consistently denied him, he now moved again that he be released on bail, based on a recent California ruling, so new it hadn't been published yet, so new even Ginsburg wasn't fully informed on it, either. But Walker knew of it—a superior court ruling only ten days old, dated November 9—which made bail accessible to all defendants, no matter what the charge. Judge Ginsburg checked the *Los Angeles Daily Journal* and agreed that the defendant Walker could be released on bail, which the judge then set at a quarter of a million dollars.

Walker smiled. He looked terrific, in expensive burnished boots, a crisp, new-looking gray suit, pale blue shirt with French cuffs, and a striped tie that looked very familiar to Hope. Walker had had an extensive wardrobe when he was arrested; although those clothes were still in sheriff's custody, they could not be used as evidence against him because of the suppression ruling. At a pretrial hearing, it had been decided he could wear the clothes to court, choosing his outfit each day from a rack wheeled up to his cell by a deputy; he would return them to the sheriff at the end of each court day. In between times, Jay Powell would take them to the drycleaner's.

Hope looked good, too, not nearly so frail and gaunt as she'd looked in the spring. She still wasn't allowed to wear pants, but she'd borrowed two more outfits so that, besides the pink wool dress, she had a plaid coat-dress with brass buttons down the front, and a white wool suit with a white turtleneck sweater and a flowered scarf. She still wore the Mary Jane shoes, with her hair brushed loose and shiny, caught back on top with a barrette. One of the jurors, Ruthe Snelling, thought Walker looked as though he'd stepped from a page in a man's magazine. She thought Hope looked like Goldilocks.

Jury selection took most of a week. The prosecutor asked eighteen questions of prospective jurors—basic questions involving occupation, spouse's occupation, any personal or religious convictions that might keep them from voting guilty. Walker's list ran to one hundred fourteen questions, not nearly so basic. As Walker explained to the panel, some questions were designed "to get down to your inward self." He discussed "the Perry Mason syndrome," their feelings about guns and alcoholic beverages, their feelings about sex-related testimony. "Assuming some loved ones of yours were standing trial in place of the defendants, for the same crime," Walker proposed, "would you feel satisfied with twelve jurors of the same mind as yours to stand in judgment of your loved one?"

Hope would never have picked the jury they ended up with, but she and Tom felt that, under the circumstances, it was only fair to let Walker choose. Walker seemed pleased with the jury, which was two-thirds women, one of them pregnant. When Lois Bollinger, a tall, slender, very attractive blond, asked to be excused because the manager of the music shop where she worked as bookkeeper was sick, the prosecution agreed readily, but Walker said something to Jay Powell, and Mrs. Bollinger was not excused. "She seems to be a fine juror," Jay told the court, "and we would like to keep her."

On the afternoon the jury was sworn, Judge Ginsburg announced the visit to the ranch, with the jury traveling by sheriff's van, Tom Breslin driving Hope over in his car. "I am probably the only one who knows the combination on the outside gate," Tom said, "so I guess you will have to wait for me." Walker smiled. Thirty-ought-six; like the rifle.

Hope knew that Walker would want to take the rocker nearest the fireplace, opposite the sofa, where he'd spent most of that Saturday afternoon, so when he started across the living room, she brushed quickly past him and sat down. He grinned, and moved across the room to the chair by the picture window where he sat casually, puffing at his pipe, winking, and occasionally sticking out his tongue at her as Judge Ginsburg led the jurors through the house counterclockwise, starting with the corner bedroom and bath wing, where there was a momentary crush in the doorway, and proceeding back through the living room, through the kitchen, and into the back bedroom where Bill's body had been found, past a wall plaque with a line from *Poor Richard's Almanac:* MUCH VIRTUE IN HERBS, LITTLE IN MEN.

Hope's annoyance at Walker's antics overcame her dread of returning to the ranch. It seemed infuriating but perfectly natural, somehow, that Walker should be strolling around the property with an entourage, making notes on his clipboard, smiling. Once that afternoon, however, when she looked across the room to the sofa where Bill had sat, his eyes closed, his drink still in his hand, she suddenly began to tremble. One of the reporters who had toured the house and had returned to the living room, to watch Walker and Hope together, noticed Hope's shakiness; the woman stepped over to Hope's side, took her hand, and held it tightly for nearly an hour.

To the world at large, and in the stricter world of the courtroom, it still appeared that Hope Masters was being tried, along with G. Daniel Walker, on a charge of murder. Both stood as the clerk, Ethel Flynn, read the charge:

> The said Hope Masters and G. Daniel Walker are accused by the District Attorney of the County of Tulare, state of California, by the information filed this twenty-seventh day of April A.D. 1973, of the crime of felony, to wit: violation of Section 187 of the California Penal

Code, murder, committed as follows: The said Hope Masters and G.
Daniel Walker, on or about the twenty-fourth day of February A.D.
1973, at the County of Tulare, state of California, and before the filing
of this information, did willfully, feloniously, and with malice aforethought kill William Thomas Ashlock, a human being.

The first witness, Deputy Donald Landers, had nothing enormously
significant to say, but his mere appearance was, of course, significant to
Hope. When he had told, briefly, about getting a phone call at the
Porterville substation on the night of February 27, and had stepped down
from the stand, Judge Ginsburg, who had been alerted to what was
coming, called a recess.

Hope scooted over to Jay Powell and said she had to speak with him.
"Is it all right with your attorney?" Jay asked. Tom nodded, and Hope
and Jay walked into the hallway outside the courtroom. He didn't want
to talk to Hope Masters, but he thought he should listen, and he wrote
notes of their conversation just afterward.

"I am doing this because it's my only way out, Jay," Hope told him.
"I didn't know he was the one until later." Jay wasn't sure whether she
said "know" or "realized," so he wrote both words down. "I have to
testify, but I will try to go easy on him," she added.

"I've already told your attorney that I am going to object to your being
dismissed," Jay said sternly. "And I want you to know that."

"God, I hope you are not successful," Hope groaned.

"I am sure they will dismiss against you either way," Jay Powell said.

"Well, they have to," Hope said. "Haley said they don't have any
evidence against me."

"I know that," Jay said. Later he explained he'd said that so Hope
would talk to him about it. She told him she was still going to testify, and
asked him if he would take some books to the jail. Jay said he would.

"Walker is scowling a lot," Hope told Jay. "He looks like a murderer.
Tell him to smile more, and show his pretty teeth."

When court was reconvened, Joe Haley asked that he be allowed to
make a motion outside the presence of the jury.

"Your Honor, at this time, having made a thorough review of everything before the District Attorney's office and in the hands of the sheriff's department, and weighing that evidence basically circumstantial or
not basically circumstantial we have concerning Mrs. Masters, and
weighing that with the fact that she may—or would—testify for the
prosecution, we feel it best in the interest of the People of the state of

California, because of the comparison of the evidence, that we make a motion to dismiss against Mrs. Masters at this time. This is done subsequent to the first witness being called, and prior to the other witnesses, because we feel it would only be fair to the defendant Walker not to proceed any further with Mrs. Masters being a defendant, because some evidence may be presented—even though it's hearsay as to Walker, it may be evidence that is admissible against Mrs. Masters and we don't wish to—to use an old term—to sandbag Mr. Walker. And so, at this time"—Haley took a long breath—"we make a motion to dismiss this matter as to Mrs. Masters."

Jay Powell stood up. "We object to the motion to dismiss, Your Honor."

Ginsburg looked at Tom Breslin.

"Mr. Breslin, you, of course, have no objections at this point?"

"I have no objections," Tom said.

"All right," Ginsburg said, and the motion was granted.

When the jury filed back in, Ginsburg spoke to them without saying much. "I want to advise the members of the jury that while you were absent from the courtroom, a motion was made by the district attorney to dismiss all charges now pending against the defendant, Hope Masters. This motion was granted by the court, so Mrs. Masters is no longer a defendant in this case, and the case will proceed solely against the defendant, G. Daniel Walker."

The jurors stared at Hope. One older woman with a heavy, lined face, no makeup, seemed to be glaring at her with what seemed to Hope real hatred. Hope stared back at her for a moment until the next witness, Detective Jack Flores, was called, and the trial resumed as though nothing unusual had happened. But Walker passed a large brown envelope to Jay Powell, who pushed it along the table to Tom Breslin. Tom opened it, peered inside, then pressed it closed quickly. It lay at his side the rest of the day, until court was adjourned, when he handed it reluctantly to Hope.

"This is yours," Tom growled. "But for God's sake, don't let anybody see it."

So Hope kept the envelope closed, under her arm, as she walked out of the courthouse into a dazzle of flashbulbs.

"How does it feel? How do you feel now?" reporters were calling to her. She had a typed statement to hand out to the press, and Honey and Van had one of their own, but the reporters seemed more interested in verbal comments. Tom was talking to Bill Bell of the *Los Angeles Herald-*

Examiner. "This is not immunity," Tom told Bell, emphatically. "This is a straight, outright acquittal." Finally Hope gave up trying to pass out her formal statement. "I feel terrific," she said; her snappy line was quoted in most of the daily papers.

In the privacy of her room at the Lampliter, Hope opened the envelope. Walker had written a note, thanking her for "the kind words of advice" relayed to him by Jay Powell although, he wrote, "It will be hard to smile with you gone from the case." He had enclosed a newspaper clipping in which District Attorney Robert Bereman confirmed that his office had considered whether the situation ought to have been reversed, with Walker being offered immunity in exchange for his testimony against Hope. Walker pointed out in his note that obviously he hadn't accepted that deal. "It was generally agreed you should be taken to trial and that I should be granted immunity," he told her. "However, being a stubborn individual, I refused serious consideration and elected to place my fate in the hands of a jury."

There was one other enclosure: a fresh, long-stemmed yellow rose. A thought flashed across Hope's mind, the language of flowers: from somewhere in her Italian past, she remembered that yellow meant betrayal.

Word had gone around that Hope Masters would testify, and the courtroom was jammed. The Visalia courtroom had none of the antique appeal of the justice court; it was modern, fluorescent, with a microphone at the witness stand to underline the impression of being onstage.

Joe Haley's first questions to his witness were intended to establish a moral mood, to dilute the distaste for a married woman running up to the ranch with her lover, leaving a long-suffering husband behind. He brought out that she and Tom Masters were separated, not living together, and that she had filed for divorce.

"Were you and Bill Ashlock just plain friends, or what?"

"Well, we thought of ourselves as married," Hope said primly. "We weren't legally married, but we were going to be legally married as soon as my hearing came up the following week."

"Were you in love with Mr. Ashlock?"

"Yes," Hope said.

With the tone set, Haley led the witness back to that Saturday afternoon when she'd first seen Walker, the man she knew then as Taylor Wright, who Bill said was a reporter from the *Los Angeles Times,* from the bathroom window. "Come on in and have a drink." They sat around and drank. They walked down to the river, where Walker took pictures.

They drove into Springville, where Hope played with the runny-nosed baby. They bought more liquor and, back at the ranch, drank and talked some more. After dinner—filet mignon, wild rice, a salad—Hope got a pillow and lay down on the sofa briefly, then she moved into the corner bedroom.

"Did you go to sleep?"

"Yes, I did."

"Do you recall waking up?"

"I recall being awakened by someone kind of pawing at me and trying to stick a metallic object into my mouth. I was just almost sure it was some kind of weapon."

"Could you see this person as far as features are concerned?"

"It was absolutely black as pitch. I couldn't see anything. I could only feel someone with one hand feeling my body and pushing this thing into my mouth."

"What did you do?"

"I scooted sideways across the second bed toward the door. I went toward the only light in the house, which was the embers glowing from the fireplace."

"Do you know where this other party was as you went into the living room?"

"I—I sensed that he was behind me."

"And did you see Bill?"

"Yes. I saw Bill."

Hope spoke, in a low voice, of running over to the sofa, where Bill sat with his head resting on the back of the sofa, his feet up on the coffee table. She grabbed him and his head wobbled. She was screaming. "Bill, wake up, wake up! Help me! Bill!" Then she heard a voice.

"I heard him very clearly. He said, 'Don't bother with him, he's dead,' in a very cold sort of monotone voice." The person came up behind her, pulled her away from Bill; she heard Bill's body slip and fall.

"You have been saying, 'a person.' Up to this time, did you recognize this person as having seen him before?"

"No, sir."

"Did you recognize the voice?"

"No, sir."

She saw her arms, in the light of the orange embers, dripping blood. She began to vomit. She ran into the bathroom, her clothes being torn off as she ran. In the bathroom she knelt by the toilet; when the person pulled off her pants, she fell flat. She was pulled, but not dragged, into the bedroom, by this person, and thrown down on the bed. She heard a "thunk" when he laid the gun down.

"What happened after he set the gun down?"

"He raped me and he did a lot of things to me, pawed me and talked dirty."

"Were you fully clothed or unclothed?"

"I was unclothed by now."

"Did he restrain you in any way?"

"He put my arms at what would be the top part of my chest, which would be between our two bodies, and then he lay on my arms."

"Let's ask you again: up to this time, did you actually recognize this person?"

"No, sir."

"Do you recall whether he was clothed or not at that particular time?"

"It felt like he had clothing on top, no clothing on the bottom."

"Were you scared?"

"I was terrified, and out of my mind over Bill."

"You say he raped you?"

"Yes. He raped me, and he said, 'Let's just—' He poured out a stream of the worst filth I have ever heard."

"As far as you know, did he reach a climax?"

"I don't know."

"About how long did this—"

"He raped me a couple of times. If he wasn't doing—having intercourse with me, he was pawing and grabbing at me. It seemed to me all one awful thing."

"Then what—what did he do, this person?"

"The only thing he did that I could . . . that made any sense to me that wasn't just a lot of dirt was that he knew or had heard somewhere that I was a real swinger, and he made suggestions about oral sex and anal sex and just all kinds of things. I mean, things I had never even heard of. And I said, 'No, no, no. You know you can do whatever you want to, but I can't do anything, I am just sick, you know, I am just sick.' Then he raped me again."

"Other than this person and Bill, did you during this time see anybody else in the house?"

"I didn't see anybody."

"After the second episode, what took place?"

"He kind of rolled me over to my side and grabbed my hands and feet behind me, and I could hear what sounded to me like adhesive tape coming off a roll, and I felt him taping my wrists and my feet, kind of like you hogtie a calf, together behind me. My legs were brought up behind me to meet my hands and I was on my side."

"Then what happened?"

"Then he left the room and closed the door."

"Did you hear anything?"

"No. I was trying to hear something, hoping that he had—that I would hear him leave, but I didn't. I waited a little while. I had one wrist that was particularly painful with the blood being stopped up, and I began to pick at the tape very, very slowly so as not to make a ripping sound, in case he was there. I picked off, I would say, maybe four or five rounds of tape from this one hand that was hurting me, and then I kept the hand behind me so that if he came in again, he wouldn't know. I thought he would become angry. During this time, and I don't know at what particular point during this time, someone came into the room I couldn't see and did something Bill used to do all the time, put his cheek up next to my face so that his mouth would be by my ear, said very gently, 'I love you,' and went out and closed the door."

"As far as the voice was concerned, did it sound like the same voice that you—"

"I thought for a minute that Bill was alive. I didn't know what or who, and I thought maybe I was hallucinating."

"Then did you stay in the bedroom?"

"Yes. I was alone in there for a long time."

"Did somebody come back into the room?"

"Later on, someone did come in and this time left the doors open from the living room through the connecting wing and into the bedroom. There was no light, but I had a chance for my eyes to adjust to what little light there was in the living room filtering through that doorway."

"And did you recognize this person?"

"Not right away, but after awhile I did."

"About how much time?"

"I don't know. After a little conversation had taken place, I recognized the voice as being Taylor."

"The party you knew as Taylor Wright?"

"Yes."

"And what was that conversation?"

"Well, he came into the room and he came over and uncovered me, whoever, if he had or—or whoever or whatever. I was covered up, underneath I was taped and there were blankets over me, and he came up and he said, 'Well, let's see what's happening to you' or 'What's happening with you?' He pulled back the covers and said, 'Oh, that's cute, you got your arm loose,' or something like that, and I said, 'Well, I wasn't trying to do anything, I just took it off because it was hurting me so much.' He said, 'That's okay,' covered me back up again, and began to talk. And this is where I lose continuity on the conversation."

"When he began to talk, where was he situated in relation to you?"

"He was wandering around the room. Right away, I didn't know it was him."

"When did you realize or recognize in your mind that it was Taylor Wright, or the man identified as Taylor Wright?"

"I don't know, but I know that I did know it was Taylor, because I said to him, 'Please go see if Bill is really dead,' so I sort of had the feeling that someone I knew was there. I was very confused. I said, 'Please go see if Bill is dead.' "

"At this time, did you recognize this person?"

"I knew it was Taylor."

"When you said that about Bill, then what did Mr.—what did the defendant do?"

"He said, 'I have seen him, and he is dead.' "

"What did you say, if anything?"

"I said, 'Why? Why Bill?' "

"Did he say anything?"

"He said, 'Someone wants you dead.' And I said, 'Me? Why me? I have never hurt anybody in my life.' And he said, 'Well, you are going to court next week, aren't you?' I was going to court for my divorce, and I said, 'Yes, but all that's at stake is a couple of hundred dollars. Nobody would do this to somebody for a couple of hundred dollars.' And he said, 'Well, I don't know, I don't know what it's all about, somebody wants you dead, that's all.' "

"What did you say, if anything?"

Hope shook her head.

"Mr. Haley, at this point, I can't tell you what I said when. I know some of the things I said and some of the things he said, but I don't know what I said at that particular moment. I asked who it was that wanted me dead, and at some point he told me my husband, and I said, 'Which one?' "

"Did he reply?"

"He said he couldn't tell me."

"Do you remember any of the other conversation?"

"I remember a *lot* of the conversation," Hope said. "Part of the time he would put on some surgical gloves, and he told me he was wiping off fingerprints he had left during the day, and he would leave the room at those times. After a little while, he came with a washcloth and a towel and he washed my face and hands and dried them, took the tape off me, but warned me that if I did anything, he would kill me."

"This was the defendant, is that correct?"

"This was Mr. Walker, yes."

"Do you remember any other conversation?"

"Yes," Hope said. "Do you want me to just sum it up, because I got it in bits and pieces."

"Yes," Haley said.

Summing up, Hope said that Walker seemed to feel bad about Bill being dead, but he was going to have to kill Hope anyway because she was a potential witness against him. She figured out, from what he said, that her husband had gotten a loan from one of his friends in the Mafia—"or whatever you want to call it"—that her husband and another man had gotten into a hole to The Family for forty-two thousand dollars and had bought an insurance policy on Hope and then put out a contract on her, that a first man had been assigned the job and had been in a restaurant with her the previous weekend but hadn't done the job. "Why did the guy miss you when you left the restaurant last weekend?" Walker wondered, and Hope had replied, "I think because instead of going home, we went to Bill's apartment, which we almost never do."

Hope remembered Walker saying that the first man assigned to the job had been burned, which she later understood meant killed. He told her that when he was nineteen, he had been convicted of murder, then had escaped from prison and had fled to Europe, where he had lived the rest of the time. She remembered a lot of talk about her husband, whom Walker said he had met at the Beverly Hilton. Walker said he preferred killing by poison, or with an ice pick through the ear so it would appear that the victim had had a stroke; he said he had noticed an ice pick in the kitchen when he was in there after dinner, clearing dishes. But her husband had asked for "a bloodbath." Walker told Hope her husband would have the baby all weekend, which Hope never recalled him ever doing before.

Walker seemed to debate with himself about what to do with Hope. "He really felt he ought to kill me, that it was the only sensible thing to do, otherwise I would become a witness against him, and he would rather die than go back to jail." But he said he felt bad about Bill, that it was a terrible, awful thing, that he didn't want to kill me and he didn't know what to do."

"We kept negotiating, back and forth, back and forth, like a judge and a jury," Hope said. "I gave the reasons why I should be left alive, why I was good, why I was useful, why it wouldn't be good to kill me. I promised him that I would never testify against him and swore, on the lives of my children, that I would never testify against him."

Hope's voice dropped. She glanced at Walker, then looked away quickly. He was smiling at her. She felt strange, light-headed. As reluctant as she'd been to testify, she wished, now, that Joe Haley would never stop asking questions; she knew that when he did, it would be time for the cross-examination. Although the court had ruled that either Jay Powell, or defendant Walker, as co-counsel, could examine a witness, and although Jay had handled a few witnesses on cross, Hope had no doubt about who would question her: the man she believed had raped her, terrorized and threatened her, the man who had pressed a cold gun up against her body and murmured, "I love you," the man who had murdered Bill.

It seemed totally unreal, just as the night in the ranch bedroom seemed unreal, crazy scenes from a crazy movie: Bill sitting dead on the sofa, a drink in his hand, the fireplace embers lighting the room; the terror in the blackness, being raped and threatened and caressed with a gun. She had thought she must be imagining it all, trapped in the depths of some monstrous dream. Then daylight had come, and Walker was with her— Taylor was with her—helping her, protecting her, talking and explaining, showing her it all made sense. With Bill gone, Walker had taken care of her. She remembered how, in those two days at her house, she had dreaded a shootout between him and the police. Later, after the visit from Paul Luther of the FBI, she was convinced that, with Walker wanted so badly, any cop would kill her to get to Walker. In any shootout with the police, she had always hoped Walker would win, because she felt that she or the children might accidentally be shot by the police, in their attempt to get Walker. Whereas she knew, absolutely, that Walker would never shoot her, or the children. He would surrender first.

CHAPTER
FOURTEEN

NINETY-EIGHT WITNESSES were called in the case of *The People of the State of California* v. *G. Daniel Walker*, in a trial lasting nearly two months. Some of the faces and some of the voices were familiar, some were new. Along with the usual pointless questions—Dr. Hayes was asked whether the body he had autopsied at Myers Chapel was indeed dead— there were some that seemed unusually pointed: a meteorologist was asked, not merely whether it had rained in Los Angeles on the night of Saturday February 24, 1973, but whether it had rained on the Casa Bella pizza parlor. There were the customary confusions and contradictions: one pathologist testified that Bill Ashlock had been shot in the back of the head, and a radiologist who saw the X rays taken just before the autopsy thought Bill had been shot from the front, into his mouth.

Much of the early testimony echoed the preliminary hearing, although Honey was not permitted to repeat what Hope had told her, since it was hearsay. Still, with Hope out of danger, Honey was in good form, even excellent form. When Jay Powell, referring to notes Honey had made of the phone calls from Walker, asked whether in those calls she had asked him to "stick by" her daughter, Honey looked pained.

"I don't think I would ever use that expression," Honey said.

"I see," Jay murmured.

"I asked him to please come forward, to go to the police," Honey explained.

"But you did not ever ask him to 'stick by' Hope?"

"That doesn't sound like an expression I would use, Mr. Powell." When Jay read to her from the preliminary transcript:

> Q: Did you ask him to stick by Hope?
> A: Yes, I did.

Honey held her ground. " 'Stick by' were your words, not mine. I don't use the expression 'stick by.' Those were your words, weren't they, Mr. Powell?"

Van then was cross-examined by Walker, and the animosity between them charged the courtroom atmosphere. When Van referred to "the correct story" Hope had finally given him, in which she said Taylor had arrived at the ranch on Saturday, not Sunday, Walker sneered noticeably.

"As I understand it, in the first story your daughter gave you, Walker was the hero who rescued her, is that correct?"

"Correct," Van snapped.

"In her second story, Walker was the villain who had assaulted her, is that correct?"

"Correct."

"And you knew the second version of your daughter's story on March the ninth, 1973, when you gave your second statement to the police, is that correct?"

The indignity of being quizzed by the man, the criminal character, who had called him on tape "a pompous ass," rankled Van greatly. "I didn't give a statement to the police," he said coldly. "We had a meeting."

"Did you have a conversation with them?"

"We had a conversation with them," Van answered, with elaborate formality, "and the answer to your question, recognizing it as a conversation, is yes, I did know the second story and no, I did not give it to the police."

"Thank you," Walker said pleasantly.

Among the other veterans of the preliminary, Gerald Webb came back from Hazel Park, Michigan, where he had moved, to identify Walker as the man he'd seen at the ranch that Saturday afternoon. "I don't think I would forget him," Gerald declared. "I really don't."

Jim Webb said again he'd seen two cars at the main house early Sunday morning, around six o'clock: a Vega and a Lincoln, and that Sunday evening, only the Vega remained parked alongside the house. Jim testified that he'd telephoned Honey around 7:30 Tuesday evening, the only call he said he made; he said Van had telephoned him later, around 9:00. Jim said that between those two calls, when he'd gone into the dark house with a flashlight, wearing gloves, and socks over his shoes, the living room draperies were open.

The fishermen returned to tell of seeing three cars at the ranch Saturday afternoon: a Lincoln, a Vega, and a small, dark car. Lee Blount said a man with a beard had spoken to him, thinking Lee worked on the ranch, asking Lee what to do with the horse he was leading. Allen Bounds said that on their second fishing trip to the ranch on Tuesday, when they drove past the main house, the living room drapes were closed.

When Joe Haley said "No further questions," Walker stood up. He nodded politely to the judge, then turned his full gaze on Hope.

The court reporter, Shirley Askins, a brisk, peppy-looking woman with curly gray hair, had noticed how Walker looked at people, even when he'd been questioning jurors. "When he looks at a person, he just gives them his full and entire attention," Shirley said. Walker was looking at Hope with a gaze so intense, so personal, that it could only be called riveting. He had been ordered to remain at the counsel table when he questioned Honey and Hope, not to approach the witness; the distance emphasized the drama.

Hope tried to look steadily back at him. Her head throbbed; all her muscles seemed to tense. Then Walker smiled.

"Mrs. Masters, I'm going to have to ask you a few questions," he said in a sympathetic, understanding tone. "I realize it's probably tiring, and is this the first time you have ever testified in court?"

"Yes," Hope said. She smiled, a tentative, small smile, and relaxed in her chair. Tom Breslin, his eyes glued on Hope too, saw her relax at Walker's soothing approach, and Tom in turn felt himself tense.

"Mrs. Masters, let's go back in your mind to Friday, February the twenty-third, 1973," Walker said softly. "Was Mr. Ashlock living with you at that time?"

"Yes, sir," Hope replied.

Walker smiled. "Let's jump ahead in time now to Saturday, the twenty-fourth. Did you receive any telephone calls at the main ranch house prior to anyone arriving there?"

"Yes."

"And who called?"

Hope was getting annoyed at his smoothness. "You did," she said, a little testily.

Walker led her into the arrival of "the visitor" and the drinking, the snacking, the chatting among the three people, the strolling around the property, the episode with the horse. "Now, Mrs. Masters, when the three of you went down with the horse to take pictures, did you take any pictures at all?"

"You took the pictures."

"I took the pictures," Walker repeated. He smiled. "Did I take many pictures?"

"It seemed like not a whole lot," Hope said. "But quite a few."

"Do you recall what clothing you wore down to have the pictures taken?"

"I wore a beige—gee, I don't know if it's wool, but it's some kind of a knit pants with a small stripe and a matching vest and a pink crepe man-tailored shirt."

"And you changed from this outfit into a different outfit?"

"Because I got wet in the river down there."

"And what did you change into?"

"I'm not sure, but I know I changed my pants. Either I would have changed into some red corduroy pants or some navy blue corduroy pants, because that's all I brought, but I can't remember."

"So I can get this straight in my mind," Walker said kindly, "what, if anything, did you personally take to the ranch with you?"

"I took the outfit I have described, maroonish corduroy pants with a maroon and white striped turtleneck and a maroon and multicolored vest, navy blue corduroy pants with a kind of purply-blue flowered shirt, and a nightgown, and possibly a sweater or a jacket."

"Now, the next day, when you left the ranch, what did you take with you?"

"I know that I had my beige pants, my maroon pants, shirt, and vest. I wore my maroon pants and vest, and I carried my nightgown, my beige pants, and possibly my beige vest."

"So you actually packed before you left the ranch?"

"No," Hope said sharply. "I picked up what was lying on the bed."

Walker held out a photograph, Defendant's Exhibit HH.

"Does that show the bed where the clothing was that you grabbed to take with you on the Sunday before you left to go to Beverly Hills?"

"You know, I was really in such a state, I can't remember where the clothing was," Hope admitted.

"So you are not sure now that it was on that bed?"

"I know it was in the bedroom. I just picked up what I saw in front of me, the clothes that you put on me, and that's all. I think I must have put the clothing in your car. I didn't have very much to carry, because the only thing that ever got home was one pair of pants and one nightie."

"What happened to the rest of it?" Walker asked, with interest.

"I don't know," Hope said. "I think the police took it. The rest of the clothing disappeared in the ranch house, and I don't know where it went to."

"Mrs. Masters, what were you wearing when you went in to take the nap?"

"I'm quite sure that I was still wearing my pink crepe man-tailored shirt. I had probably taken off my vest, and the only pair of pants missing are the navy blue corduroys."

"Do you have the pink crepe top?"

"No, I do not," Hope said.

Walker reminded her of her testimony about vomiting, and finding her arms and hands bloody.

"You were still wearing the pink shirt at that time?"

"I think I had on the shirt, and part of that bloodstain went onto the shirt."

Mr. Haley objected that all this was irrelevant.

"What's the relevancy, Mr. Walker?" Judge Ginsburg asked.

"This witness has said there are clothes missing that she cannot account for," Walker explained. "They are bloodstained. The police inventory does not show any bloodstained clothes being found on the ranch."

"All right," Ginsburg said. "Go ahead and answer."

"Well, I am sure that there are bloodstains on that crepe blouse," Hope said.

"Mrs. Masters, does the sight of bloodstains bother you?" Walker asked gently.

"Yes."

"But if you happened to see those two blouses again, you would be able to recognize your blouse, is that correct?"

"Yes."

Walker smiled, and picked up a paper bag from the counsel table. "Mrs. Masters, we are going to show you what has been marked for identification as Defendant's Exhibit YY and ask you—"

"Is there blood on it?" Hope interrupted.

"—and ask you if you would take the garment out of the bag and look at it."

Hope looked anxiously at the defense table. "Is there blood on it, Jay? I don't want to, if there is blood on it."

"I can't ask any questions," Jay Powell said in a strained voice.

Walker had Powell hold the open bag in front of her. "Is this the blouse you were wearing at the time you touched the body?"

"It looks like my pink blouse, yes."

"Why don't you take it out of the bag?" Walker asked.

"I don't want to," Hope said.

Judge Ginsburg looked at her, then at Walker. "She doesn't have to," he said. So Walker took the blouses out of the bag, a pink blouse and a purply-blue one. Hope knew that if they'd been bloodstained, she'd have heard "oohs" and "aahhs." There were no shocked murmurs in the courtroom, no gasps, because there were no bloodstains or smears on Hope's clothing.

Walker stayed in the third person: "he," "the visitor," "the intruder," and usually Hope did too. It gave a weird, phantasmal air to the colloquy. At any moment, Tom Breslin felt, Hope might break through the illusion to the ugly reality: this man had done these unspeakable things to her.

"When the intruder got you into the bedroom, what did he do?"

"He put his hand around my neck—well, he put me on the bed and cautioned me not to scream."

"Mrs. Masters, how many times were you raped?"

"I believe it was two, but it was kind of an off-again, on-again thing."

"Do you know whether the man reached a climax?"

"No, I don't."

"Mrs. Masters, the intruder, after he raped you, did he stay there in bed with you for any length of time?"

"Kind of got in and out of bed several times. Part of the time when he was making these suggestions to me, he would be standing beside me, and he would be feeling me, and then he would be back in the bed, and he was moving around but always right—right beside me."

"I believe you said the intruder was not dressed from the waist down but he had some sort of garment on, on the top?"

"That's how it seemed to me in the dark."

"Did you sleep at all that night?"

"For a little while."

"Was the intruder in the room while you were asleep?"

Joe Haley jumped up. "I object; it's quite obvious that nobody asleep would know whether somebody else were in the room."

Walker smiled and nodded. "I believe counsel is right. I had not thought of that, Your Honor. I withdraw the question." He turned back to face Hope. "Mrs. Masters, did you see the intruder sleep that night?"

"You mean the person that I am not sure who it was there?"

"Yes."

"Well, I don't know," Hope replied. "You see, it depends on who it was."

At the break, Tom Breslin laid down the law to Hope again, only louder. "You are shading your testimony, damnit!" Tom told her. "You're going too easy on him."

"Well, he's going easy on me," Hope said.

"I don't give a good goddamn about that," Tom said. "Hopie, you have got to be tougher."

It turned out not to be as difficult as she'd expected, when she got back on the stand and Walker took her back home to the Drive.

In the direct examination, the prosecutor had already sketched that period, establishing her constant state of fear. "He would tell me that a certain kind of car would be driving around, watching my house, and he'd leave, and then I would look out and I would see the car, and I was completely convinced that I not only had the Mafia after me but some friends of his that were watching to see that I didn't notify the authorities either, and I would see these cars, or he would tell me, 'Did you see that fellow raking leaves? He is one of my men.' I was under the belief that I was being watched all the time. He would indicate that he knew through his sources what my incoming telephone calls were. He would say, 'You have been very good. You haven't done anything on the phone. If you keep behaving, as long as you behave, I will help you, and everything will be all right.' I was afraid of him, but I was also dependent on him to get me out of this contract situation, so I was feeling two ways. I was afraid to cross him in any way, but I was also feeling that he would help me. He was very kind to me after this incident, and I felt that he was the only person who could change the contract and save the children."

Now, as Walker continued his cross-examination, he brought out that, at some time Sunday evening, she had been alone in her house.

"You left me in the shower," Hope said. Tom Breslin noted that she was referring to Walker in the second person—a good sign.

"Did I have you locked in the shower?"

"No, but you told me, 'You better not get out of the shower.' "

"Did you have your clothes on?"

"No."

"Had I taken your clothes off?"

"No, but you told me to take them off."

"Mrs. Masters, which shower in your house is this?"

"The shower in the master bedroom."

"And adjacent to that shower is your bedroom?"

"Yes."

"Is there a telephone in that bedroom?"

"Yes."

"To your knowledge, was that telephone in working order that evening?"

"I would imagine so," Hope retorted.

Walker smiled. "How did the defendant Walker and your children get along?"

"Very well."

"Did he frighten them?"

"No."

"Mrs. Masters, calling your attention to Monday, February the twenty-sixth, the next morning, who fixed breakfast for the children?"

"You did," Hope said, a little sullenly.

"When Walker returned from taking Keith to the school bus, did he change clothes and go jogging?"

"I don't think so."

"Did he take a shower and shave?"

"Probably. I am sure of that."

"Did you make any attempts to leave the house, take the car keys, his clothes, or anything?"

"No, I didn't."

"Mrs. Masters, when your son Keith returned home, did the defendant Walker go anywhere with Keith?"

"Yes. You and Keith went out."

"When Walker and Keith returned, did Keith have a new jacket?"

"Yes, he did."

"Mrs. Masters, how long was Keith and the defendant Walker away from your home that evening?"

"A couple of hours, I believe. It was a pretty good amount of time."

"You were alone that entire time, with the exception of your other two children?"

"Yes, I was."

"Did you make any telephone calls?"

"I may have called my mother."

"Mrs. Masters, was there a car available for your use that night?"

"No, not that I know of. I didn't know how to drive Bill's car, if it was there, because I can't drive a stick shift. At some later time, there was a car. I don't remember when it came there."

"On Monday night, where did your children sleep?"

"All in my bed, and I told them to lock the door."

"Once the children were in bed, what did you and the defendant Walker do?"

"I sat in the living room, fixed you a drink, rubbed your back, because you were getting mad at me, and watched you sort your suitcases and things."

"What time did you go to bed that evening, Mrs. Masters?"

"About, oh, maybe eleven o'clock."

"Did you join your children in your room?"

"No, there wasn't room for me. I went into my son's room."

"Which bed did you take?"

"The one nearest the door."

"Later that evening, did you see the defendant Walker enter that room?"

"Well, either saw or heard or was vaguely aware of."

"Did he enter your bed?"

"I think he sat down for a little while next to me, and was talking to me, but I was so tired I couldn't stay awake."

"And did the defendant Walker take the other bed?"

"Yes."

"Did you join the defendant Walker in the other bed?"

"No."

Walker suddenly turned formal. "It's your testimony that on Saturday, February twenty-fourth, when the defendant Walker arrived at the ranch, you did not know him, is that correct?"

"Yes."

"It's your testimony that, when you were raped in the southeast bedroom at the River Valley Ranch, the lights were not on, is that correct?"

"Yes.

"It's your testimony that, when your clothes were taken off you, the lights were not on, is that correct?"

"Yes."

Walker smiled.

"Mrs. Masters," he said easily, "isn't it a fact that you have a scar that starts in the pubic hair on the lower abdomen and runs to the right side, which is a Caesarean birth scar?"

"Yes," Hope said shortly.

Joe Haley said this was irrelevant.

"What's the relevancy?" Judge Ginsburg asked.

Walker looked serious. "Your Honor, we are attempting to show that the witness is being deceptive."

"You saw me naked in the morning," Hope said.

"Just a moment, just a moment," Ginsburg said. But Hope continued angrily, "You saw me at the ranch in the morning, you dressed me, and you made me sit naked on the floor while you took a shower. You have seen me naked."

"I don't believe I heard any testimony—" Walker began.

"You know it's true," Hope snapped.

"Would you tell us that story?" Walker asked, sounding amused.

Hope wanted to scream at him. "The story is that you wanted to take a shower," she said tightly. "You got me out of bed and put me on the floor in the bathroom and kept the shower door ajar, and I was not allowed any clothing or even to put a towel around me."

"When was this?"

"That was in the morning."

"Which morning?" Walker still sounded amused.

"The morning after Bill was killed."

"Would that be Sunday morning?"

"Yes."

"Was the defendant Walker nude at that time?"

"When he was in the shower, he was."

"And you'd be able to tell us whether the defendant Walker is circumcised or not, wouldn't you?"

"Oh, Your Honor," Haley protested, "I see no relevancy to this." Neither did the judge.

Walker looked thoughtful. "You say he had a gun in the bathroom, is that correct?"

"Yes."

"Where was the gun?"

"On the window ledge near the shower."

"Mrs. Masters, which way does the shower-room door of that bathroom open?"

"It opens toward the window."

"So that, if the defendant Walker had been in the shower with the gun on the ledge, he couldn't get to the gun, because the door would block the ledge, is that correct?"

"And neither could I," Hope retorted.

"Mrs. Masters," Walker said quietly, "prior to the year 1973, have you ever stayed in a motel with the defendant Walker?"

"No," Hope said.

"Prior to the year 1973, have you ever written to the defendant Walker or sent him any photographs of yourself?"

"No."

"Mrs. Masters, outside of this courtroom, when is the last time you talked privately to the defendant Walker?"

"I think when we talked in the counsel room over there a few days ago. Well, I don't know if that counts. The attorneys were present."

"Do you recall a telephone conversation between yourself and the defendant Walker last Thursday afternoon?"

"That wasn't private—" Hope began. Haley objected, and the jury was sent out while Walker made his offer of proof. Walker explained to the court that when he and Jay Powell had met with Hope and Tom Breslin, looking at a summary of her statement to the D.A., Hope "indicated she could testify any way the defendant wished her to testify; she could remember or forget anything that he elected to have her remember or forget, and at that time, the defendant Walker reminded Mrs. Masters that he only wished her to tell the truth."

"Now do I get to say something?" Hope demanded.

"No," Ginsburg said.

When the jury returned, Walker brought up the out-of-court conference.

"Did you state to the defendant Walker that you could testify or remember or forget whatever he wished you to?" Walker asked Hope.

"That is not the way I put it," Hope protested. "I said on the statement regarding the burning down of the house with Bill's body, or with both bodies, to prevent identification, that I could remember it either way, because you had said it in both ways."

Joe Haley stepped in. "Did he indicate what he meant when he said 'both bodies'?"

"Me," Hope said.

Walker managed to look both sorrowful and righteous. "Mrs. Masters, did the defendant Walker then state to you, 'All we want you to do is to tell the truth'?"

"Yes, he did," Hope said.

Walker smiled. "No further questions," he said.

Jim Heusdens almost came unglued when he heard that the charges against Hope Masters had been dismissed. "They gave her immunity without even knowing what she was going to say!" he exploded to his law partner, Ray Donahue. "Her testimony didn't make a nickel's worth of difference. The evidence she gave, we got anyway." He was never convinced that Hope's separate trial couldn't have been postponed by court order. "That was just a red herring," Heusdens insisted. "Walker would have been tried first because he was the one in custody."

Coming unglued, though, was a minor sensation compared with Heusdens's feelings when he got a call from Robert Bereman, the district attorney. Joe Haley had been taken to the hospital, critically sick with internal bleeding, unable to continue. With such a complicated case— and one that was not going too well for the People, incidentally—it was too late to bring in a new man. Bereman asked Heusdens to return as special prosecutor.

Jim Heusdens discussed it with Ray Donahue. They agreed Heusdens should go back—"We can't just let it flap around"—and they also agreed that if Heusdens were to be paid at the old, unimproved rate—$904 a month—he would make a grand gesture and donate his services.

Thus, on December 10, James Heusdens returned to *The People of the State of California* v. *G. Daniel Walker*. He was paid the special prosecutor's rate, fifteen dollars an hour, which didn't come close to Ned Nelsen's fee, or Tom Breslin's, but the challenge seemed worth it.

There was no more dramatic example of Heusden's taste for that challenge than his handling of certain witnesses. Persons whose testimony he had disparaged at the preliminary, issues he had scorned, now became his valued witnesses, issues to be weighed very seriously indeed. What Walker, in questioning Van, referred to as Hope's "first story" and "second story," Heusdens called the same story, "but told in a different way." When Jay Powell asked Gene Tinch whether he hadn't once identified himself as a police officer to a Tulare gas station attendant—the accusation Heusdens had once hurled at Tinch—Heusdens objected strenuously, and his objection was sustained.

Most poignantly, of course, Heusdens now had Hope Masters in his court. What had once been, for Heusdens, her suspicious intimacy with Walker—the backrubs, the whispering in Keith's bedroom—now became a natural consequence of her fear. When Jay Powell objected to Hope's testimony about several wallets she had seen in the Lincoln, along with Bill's briefcase, on the drive back to L.A., and her quoting Walker's remark that she should look away when he paid for the gas because he didn't want her to see which I.D. he was using, Heusdens made an eloquent plea. "If a person all of a sudden has a dead body at a ranch and is told, 'I can change my identity and be gone, and nobody will believe you,' that certainly would create fear in someone's mind."

When he took over the case, Jim Heusdens was pessimistic. He felt Hope had not been a vigorous witness for the prosecution, and he was afraid that Walker's insinuating charm was mesmerizing the jury. "When you're around Walker, you really don't feel you're dealing with a vicious man," Heusdens explained to his law partner. "I think that's why he escaped, and got away with so much, all along the line. People just do not realize what an evil man he is." Although Heusdens and Tom Breslin had never discussed it, their views on Walker meshed; they knew that evil cloaked in everyday dress was far more deadly than evil undisguised. And Jim Heusdens could see that Walker was beautifully cloaked. "I don't think we'll ever be able to turn this thing around," he told his partner.

But he was determined to give it his best shot, which, for Jim Heusdens, usually meant the most flamboyant shot. Thus, in court, he brandished two pairs of women's underpants, which he said had been enclosed with two of Walker's letters.

When Jay Powell objected, Heusdens turned to him with a sly grin. "I am allowing you to examine them before I show them to the court, Mr. Powell."

Jay winced. "I will let my co-counsel examine them while I am reading something," he said shortly.

The panties were apparently for effect, but the letters, Heusdens maintained, were crucial to the case, along with the testimony of the woman who had received them and who now sat on the witness stand, summoned from two thousand miles away by subpoena—Marcy Purmal.

One juror, whose husband was an army officer, thought Marcy had a military look: wearing a suit, no makeup, strong-looking, businesslike. Marcy did not speak to Walker in the courtroom, nor did he speak to her; Jay Powell cross-examined. But as they watched Marcy watching Walker, some of the jurors felt sure of her feelings toward the man who had courted her, teased her, played with her in the cruel game for which he made all the rules. Marcy typified what Bob Swalwell had always considered Walker's deadliest powers, his ability to manipulate people, especially women. Marcy Purmal and Hope Masters were as unlike in background, in appearance, in style of life as two women could ever be, yet they had things in common. Marcy had met Walker, she said, on November 30, 1972, just about the time Hope met Bill Ashlock. Each woman had known each man for just under three months, before the men were gone from their lives. Then Walker had loomed above them both, the mastermind who did not need to kill in order to damage.

The jury had only a brief look at Marcy before they were sent out while both sides argued the admissability of her testimony. Marcy explained that she'd been assigned by a federal judge to represent Walker in two Illinois lawsuits, one involving prison conditions, one protesting his proposed transfer from Joliet. Marcy's testimony came in shreds, constantly interrupted by Jay Powell's objections on the basis of attorney-client privilege.

"What do you contend in those letters is covered by the attorney-client privilege, Mr. Powell?" Ginsburg asked. When Jay said that to answer that question would in itself violate the privilege, Ginsburg's patience gave out.

"We are not going to play games," he declared. "I am not just going to rule out evidence, Mr. Powell, because you choose to say it is inadmissible. Before I ever came into this case, we had sixty written petitions and innumerable motions, almost all of which were denied. We have had objections to every bit of evidence that has come in, on every possible legal theory, and on inspection, many of the objections are sham, they are irrelevant, and I feel not made in good faith. I have no desire, you may be sure, to impinge on the attorney-client relationship, but I cannot see any grounds at all on which the relationship could be sustained to keep out this evidence at this point." Ginsburg ruled that because the letters did not deal with legal matters on which an attorney was representing a client, no privilege was involved.

Only two letters were under scrutiny—the letter of March 1, telling of Ashlock's murder, and a letter dated February 6, referring to a jewelry salesman. When the jury filed back in, Jim Heusdens exhibited the earlier letter. "Do you recognize this letter?" he asked the witness.

"Yes, I do recognize it," Marcy replied.

"Did it come through the regular course of the mail?"

"Yes, as far as I know."

"Did you give that letter to anyone?"

"Yes," Marcy said. "Through the law enforcement officials in Illinois, through the State's Attorney's office."

Walker's eyes were fixed on Marcy—cold, frightening.

"Who wrote the letter?" Heusdens continued.

"G. Daniel Walker."

In his cross-examination, Powell pointed out that the letter was typed, not handwritten. "Is there something about this letter other than the typing that you can identify as coming from Mr. Walker?" he asked.

"A matter of style," Marcy said. "And certain statements made in the letter that would cause me to know it was written by G. Daniel Walker."

Jay Powell raised a disdainful eyebrow. "Do you have any training or background in literary styles and literature, Miss Purmal?"

"I do a tremendous amount of reading," Marcy replied. "Books."

"Have you independently studied literary styles and compared them?"

"Not making a science of it, certainly," Marcy said coolly.

"Miss Purmal, isn't it true that you receive lots of letters each day?"

"Yes," Marcy agreed. "If you are including matters concerning my cases and office affairs and that sort of thing."

"Do you receive typed letters frequently?"

"I have never counted them," Marcy said.

"I didn't ask you if you had counted them, thank you," Jay Powell said, in elaborate annoyance. "With regard to these typewritten letters that you receive, do you make a study of the literary style of these letters?"

"Well, most of them are not as long as this one," Marcy said evenly. "They are usually very brief, which differentiates them from a letter such as this."

"So, if I understand it," Jay Powell continued, "some letters you receive are long and some are short, is that your testimony?"

"Some letters are longer than others, and some are shorter than others," Marcy said.

For once, Jay Powell's dispassionate composure cracked. He glared at her. "Miss Purmal, isn't it true that you are biased and prejudiced against Mr. Walker?"

Jim Heusdens jumped up. "Your Honor, this could open up a very big problem," he warned. "If she says 'yes,' then the People would go into why she is prejudiced." The question was withdrawn. But when Jay Powell said he would not excuse the witness and wanted her to remain on call, Judge Ginsburg sent the jury out and asked Mr. Powell the reason.

Before Jay answered, Jim Heusdens intervened again. "For the benefit of Miss Purmal, I would ask that the courtroom be cleared," he suggested. The spectators were shooed out, and Jay Powell asked that Marcy, too, be excluded.

"I object, Your Honor," Marcy said angrily. "I'd like to know what's being said. I don't think it's fair to impugn my reputation."

Ginsburg looked at the young woman. "I think Miss Purmal has a right to stay, under the circumstances," he said.

Jay Powell explained that the defense needed Marcy subject to recall because he had seen, on the prosecution's list of witnesses, a man named

Swalwell and a man named Pietrusiak. "If Mr. Pietrusiak were called, he would testify that he was in the hospital at the same time Mr. Walker was, that Miss Purmal would come to Mr. Walker's room at night and visit him almost every night, that she was having an affair with Mr. Walker, that Mr. Walker told her he was having another girl visit him in the daytime and that he liked the other girl better, and Miss Purmal got angry at him, and they had a fight over it."

"Your Honor, I object to all of this," Marcy said furiously.

"Just a moment, Miss Purmal, please," Ginsburg said.

"And Swalwell would testify," Powell went on, "or, I would propose to ask him, that Miss Purmal was taken into custody when she attempted to deliver a large sum of money to Mr. Walker at an airport."

Jim Heusdens could hardly believe what he was hearing, and he was afraid that later no one else would believe it, either. "Your Honor, could I make one comment for the record?" he asked. "I would just like to indicate for the record that this is the *defense* doing this. I think he said any communication with Miss Purmal was privileged, attorney-client privilege."

"I recognize that, Mr. Heusdens," Ginsburg said. He looked at Marcy for a moment. One of Judge Ginsburg's daughters was about to enter law school. "I am not going to permit Miss Purmal to be smeared in this court," Ginsburg said quietly. "This would be a collateral issue, and I'm not going to require her to remain on call for this, Mr. Powell."

"Thank you, Your Honor," Jay said stiffly.

Ginsburg was still looking at Marcy. "You are excused, Miss Purmal. If you feel that you wish to make any kind of a statement, you may do so. I realize you have been under some pressure. But you don't have to. It's up to you."

Jay Powell cut in. "Apparently she's upset by this," he said sarcastically, "and I am sure that she would now apparently deny anything like this."

"All right. The matter is closed," Ginsburg said firmly. So that, ever after, only Marcy knew whether she wished to make a statement because only Marcy knew what there was to say.

Neither Swalwell nor Pietrusiak was called, then, because Walker's status as a prisoner in Illinois, and an escaped prisoner at that, would then be disclosed to the jury. Evidence of a prior conviction was likely to prejudice the jury, Ginsburg ruled. So, with one exception, Jim Heusdens was limited in his witnesses to people who could testify only in connection with the California crime. But that one exception was important to the prosecution, and so was the piece of evidence brought out in connection with his appearance.

Taylor Wright had tentatively identified Walker from a mug shot before any evidence was ordered suppressed, and his credit cards had been used long before March 11, too. He had even identified a voice on a tape, played for him by Parker and Brown, on their spring trip to Chicago, as being the voice of the man who had beaten him and robbed him in a room at the Marriott in Ann Arbor. Nearly everything of Taylor Wright's that had been stolen, that later turned up when Walker was arrested, had been suppressed—the cards, the shaving gear, the clothing. But one piece of evidence had not been suppressed.

The tiny object glittered in Jim Heusdens's upraised hand. He swung it back and forth, for more effect.

"Can you identify that?" Heusdens asked.

"It's mine," Taylor Wright said. "It was given to me for high school graduation."

"Can you tell us what T.O.W. stands for?"

"Taylor Ortho Wright."

The shiny little gold medallion and chain was allowed into evidence, then. Its importance lay, not in its size—it was small enough to nestle at the bottom of a teacup—but in its location. It had been planted far from the poisoned tree.

Tom Masters said he did not know a Gerald Daniel Walker and had never met him.

"Do you see anybody here in the courtroom that you recognize having any business dealings with?" Heusdens asked.

"Not offhand," Tom said.

"Mr. Masters, have you ever hired anyone to kill Bill Ashlock?"

"No, I did not."

"Have you ever hired anybody to kill Hope Masters?"

"No, I didn't."

"Have you ever hired anyone to kill both, or either one of the children of Hope Masters?"

"No, certainly not," Tom said.

Jay Powell questioned for the defense. "Mr. Masters, did you ever borrow money from something called the Mafia or the organization?"

"No," Tom said. "If I did, it wasn't to my knowledge."

"Are you connected with the Mafia or the underworld?"

"Not to my knowledge."

Tom said he had been involved in a business deal with his neighbor and another man in which he had sold them "interest in my business for five thousand dollars and other considerations."

"All right," Powell said. "Is it true that you called your wife 'the second Sharon Tate' and you were obsessed with this?"

"Not that I can recall."

Tom said that on the weekend Hope went to the ranch, he'd arranged to take K.C. on both Saturday and Sunday, at her request. "She didn't want him to stay home alone with the maid both days. I said, 'Fine.'" He said he knew of the pills Hope took, and that the combination of pills and liquor made her "very belligerent, very aloof, very flippy."

"Mr. Masters, what is Hope's reputation for honesty and veracity and truthfulness?" Jay Powell asked sternly.

"Well, I have always found—yes, I think she is basically—or, at least up until the time of that weekend, basically an honest person. Her problem, at least from my standpoint, was always the way she interpreted other people's answers and interpreted events and seemed to amplify situations. You could tell her something one day and three days later she said no, you told her something else. That was the only way it was bothersome to me."

"If the jury doesn't like the way I look, the hell with them," Hope decided. K.C. was sick with an ear infection, and she felt reasonably crummy herself, so when she was recalled to Visalia as a defense witness on December 20, she wore a black body stocking with a very short skirt, black tights, and a rabbit's-fur coat.

When Walker questioned her, it was clear that the tapes she'd made with Tom Breslin, in the early days of the investigation, shortly after she was released on bail, had made the rounds.

"Mrs. Masters, do you recall telling us that in your home on February twenty-sixth that you went into your son's bedroom, you got into one bed, and later the defendant Walker got into the second bed?"

"Yes," Hope replied.

"Do you recall telling us that at no time you entered the second bed with the defendant Walker?"

"Yes, but now I realize I was wrong when I said that, because—"

"You did get into the second bed and cuddle the defendant Walker, isn't that true?"

"If I said that on the tape, I guess I did get into the second bed, but I somehow just lost it," Hope answered. "But I hadn't slept for three days, either."

"But you got into the bed and you cuddled Walker, is that correct?"

"That's what I said on the tape," Hope retorted.

"Did you and Walker have sexual intercourse while you were in that bed?"

"Not that I recall."

"Did you and Walker embrace or kiss?"

"I think I said on the tape that he handled me a lot."

"Do you recall?"

"I don't recall at all."

Walker nodded. "So you wouldn't be able to tell, having been in bed with Walker and having been in bed with the intruder, whether the intruder and Walker were the same person?"

"No," Hope said.

"Isn't it a fact that when you were in bed cuddling with Walker, that he was tender while the intruder was violent?"

"I honestly don't recall it, but I believe that it's true because I heard myself on the tape."

"Do you recall telling Mr. Breslin on the tape that the intruder and Walker were two different people?"

"I don't recall saying that, but if you have a transcript, I will look at it."

Walker asked to play portions of the tapes, but Judge Ginsburg was losing patience. "Ask her whether she made the statements," Ginsburg directed. "If she doesn't remember or if she denies it, then you can play the tapes."

"Mrs. Masters," Walker said, "do you recall telling your attorney on these tapes that when Taylor entered the bedroom at the ranch after you had been raped and after you found Mr. Ashlock's body, that he was definitely different than the man who had raped you and had been the intruder?"

"I may have said something like that, but I can't remember the exact words."

"Was Walker entirely different than the man who raped you?"

"Yes, he seemed to be very different."

"Mrs. Masters, you also told your attorney that you could pinpoint the time you were raped, didn't you?"

"No, I don't believe I did."

"Do you recall telling him that you are a very sound sleeper, it was in the first hour after you had been asleep?"

"I probably said something like that. Since I was so sound asleep, I would have guessed it was during the first part of my sleep, which is when I sleep most deeply."

"Didn't you tell your attorney that when you woke up at six o'clock in the morning, you were in bed with the defendant Walker and that Ashlock's body was in the living room?"

"Probably something like that, yes."

"And isn't it a fact you told your attorney that Walker had gotten in bed with you, wrapped his arms and legs around you, and went to sleep?"

"Yes, maybe not those words, but that's what happened."

"Now, when Walker was in bed with you with his arms and legs wrapped around you, you were both asleep, you both went to sleep, didn't you?"

"Yes, I kind of blacked out there for a while."

"Isn't it a fact that you also told your attorney that Walker didn't arrive back at the ranch until Sunday morning?"

"I don't believe I told my attorney that. I may have said that's what you said."

"When you testified before, you had obviously forgotten that Walker had been in bed with you at the ranch?"

"Nobody gave me a chance to get that in," Hope muttered.

"Mrs. Masters, how many times were you raped at the ranch?"

"Well, I would say two, but altogether, at one time."

"Walker didn't rape you?"

"I don't know," Hope said.

In legal terms, what Jim Heusdens had to do was "rehabilitate" his witness. "Now, Mrs. Masters," he said, "you have lied, so to speak, about a lot of facts of this case at the time you were arrested and what you told your parents and so forth, isn't this true?"

"I only lied about one thing," Hope said firmly. "The identity of the person up at the ranch."

"That was Mr. Walker, is this correct?"

"Yes," Hope said.

"Now, you are not absolutely certain, though, that Mr. Walker was the first one who attacked you?"

"No," Hope said.

Jim Heusdens took a long breath. "At this point, having considered everything and looked at the situation, have you changed your mind as to that?" Jay Powell objected, and Jim Heusdens rephrased. "After reflection, Mrs. Masters, do you feel that the same person who was the intruder is Mr. Walker?"

Jay Powell objected again. "She's had nine months to reflect on it," he complained. "She's testified under oath to it and now, after cross-examination, she is going to change her mind. It's speculative and self-serving."

"Your Honor," Heusdens persisted, "I don't think she's ever had a chance to answer this particular question. Especially after the questioning this morning, there seems to be some ambiguity about this, and we would like to clarify it."

"Go ahead, Mr. Heusdens," Ginsburg said.

The prosecutor turned back to his witness. "After reflection of what had happened on that particular evening, is it your opinion now that Mr. Walker was the intruder?"

Jay Powell objected. "The term 'after reflection' is ambiguous."

"I think that's probably correct," Judge Ginsburg said. "You can ask her what her belief is now."

"What is your belief now as to who the intruder was that night at the ranch?"

"I think it could well have been Mr. Walker," Hope said.

"Didn't you tell Mr. Breslin it *was* Mr. Walker?" Heusdens demanded.

"Yes, I told him that's what I thought," Hope said.

Walker returned for the redirect portion of the questioning.

"Mrs. Masters, did you ever actually see the surgical gloves the defendant Walker had on?"

"I could hear the sound of them, I could feel them on my skin," Hope replied. "They sure seemed to be surgical gloves. I can't recall if I saw them in the daylight."

"So you don't really know if they were surgical gloves?"

"Well, I have had a few babies," Hope snapped. "I know what surgical gloves are like."

"Mrs. Masters, when did you tell your attorney that you thought the intruder was Walker?"

"Within about a week after I got out of jail."

"Do you recall when you made the tapes with Mr. Breslin saying that when Taylor entered the bedroom that he was a different person than the intruder?"

"I believe that I said that he seemed to completely change, or be completely different."

"Do you recall telling Mr. Breslin on the tapes that they were two different people, the intruder and Taylor?"

"I may have said it could have been two different people. There was a great difference."

"And do you remember telling Mr. Breslin on the tape that Taylor was another guy?"

"Acted like," Hope corrected.

In a final flurry of argument about speculation, relevancy, and ambiguity, Jim Heusdens asked one clear question.

"Mrs. Masters, did you shoot Mr. Ashlock?"

"No," Hope said.

Hope and Tom Breslin had coffee in the basement cafeteria of the courthouse, under a sign that read: KITCHEN CLOSED DUE TO ILLNESS—I'M SICK OF COOKING. She had been begging Tom to let her reply to Walker's notes, and Tom had been saying no. Finally she typed out a section from *The Prophet*, about how everybody walks together in a line, and if one stumbles they stumble as a warning for the one behind them, a warning against the stumbling stone, and they also stumble for the one in front of them, who didn't bother to remove the stone; how black and white threads are woven together, inseparable, and thus everybody has some responsibility in everything. Tom gave in, and took it from her to give to Jay to give to Walker. "Well, it's sort of religious, so it's okay," Tom grumbled. "But just this time."

Hope felt strongly that she had a responsibility to Walker, as he had to her. "Walker and I have always been real straight with each other," she told Tom. "We had a brief relationship, but it was very intense, because of the jeopardy we were putting each other in. Each of us was a life-threatening force to the other, and that caused us to establish a kind of rapport. He was depending on me, to do what he told me to do, and I was depending on him. He began to trust me, and he said he would fix things for me, and he did.

"What about that gold chain, Tom? Why do you think he left it on the shelf at my house? He could have thrown it in the trash, or flushed it down the toilet—he could have gotten rid of it in a million different ways. But he didn't do that. He left it where it could be found. Doesn't that say something about Walker, Tom?"

Tom agreed that it said a lot.

CHAPTER
FIFTEEN

"My name is Daniel Walker, more commonly known as G. Daniel Walker. However, I have used approximately ninety names in the past twenty-three years."

The witness smiled. The jurors stared. The prosecutor shifted uneasily in his seat; Jim Heusdens knew that when a defendant admitted something damaging up front, at the very beginning, it often made him seem honest and forthright and thus more believable as he unfolded his story.

It was a long story. Walker said it began in the winter of 1965, when he'd met Hope Stagliano through a dancer on the "Shindig" television show. Between 1965 and 1969, when he came to the West Coast on advertising business, Hope often stayed with him at the Regency Apartment Hotel.

Walker said he had met Bill Ashlock at an ad agency conference in Chicago in 1965, long before Hope and Bill had met, and that in 1969 he'd met her mother, but not her stepfather. He said that on Sunday, January 28, 1973, he had seen Hope and Bill together in Chicago.

"Do you know an attorney named Marthe Purmal?" Jay Powell asked, reading from the list of questions Walker had typed on sheets of onionskin paper.

"Yes," Walker said easily. "Miss Purmal is, has been, and continues to be an attorney of mine, and Miss Purmal was a mistress of mine."

He explained that altogether, he'd had thirty-one attorneys represent-ing him on various matters, and they'd all been subpoenaed to appear before a Cook County Grand Jury on February 5, 1973. He had called various friends around the country, including Hope Masters, looking for a hiding place, and on February 6, Hope had flown into O'Hare Airport, where he met her Braniff flight. When she flew back to Los Angeles on the seventh, he went to Vail for "hiding and skiing," while waiting for someone to gather money that was due him for a liquor license he con-trolled in his wife's name.

He said he was in Vail on the night of February 9 and had not robbed Taylor Wright in Ann Arbor. Back in Chicago on February 10, he planned to meet Marcy Purmal and pick up his money, but when he found she was in police custody, he hid out in a women's restroom at O'Hare for six hours. "I went into one of the little toilets. I took my shoes off and sat in one of them and hoped that no one would realize it was a man's feet next to her," Walker said lightly.

When he got to Los Angeles two weeks later, on Wednesday, February 23, he met Hope and a friend of his, Danielle Gantou, at a Hamburger Hamlet. He arrived at 12:30; Hope was an hour late. The trio moved on to Alfie's, a place on Sunset Strip, where Bill Ashlock joined them after work. Since Bill was living at Hope's, his apartment was available as a hideaway for Walker, who moved his things in that night. The four of them had drinks at the Beverly Hilton and, after dinner, visited two spots on the Strip, the Classic Cat and the Phone Booth. The next day, two airline stewardesses, Monica Jungnickel and Ingrid Kassler, joined Walker and Danielle on an outing to Disneyland. Back in Los Angeles, they met Hope and Bill for dinner at Scandia's, then visited three or four disco-theques. On Friday, Monica and Ingrid left town to go skiing; Hope, Bill, Walker, and Danielle had a long lunch at the Brown Derby.

Early Saturday morning, Walker moved from Bill's apartment to the Holiday Inn and, after breakfast, drove up to the ranch. He said he had two reasons for going: to take pictures for Bill's ad layout—WHAT IF SHE DIES FIRST?—and to explore the possibility of hiding out at the foreman's house, since Jim Webb, he said, was about to be fired.

At the ranch, Bill and Hope and Walker ate and drank and talked about Tom Masters, about a movie Hope had seen in which a girl had a gun shoved into her mouth. They walked down to the river to take pictures. Back at the house, Walker was introduced to two men, Buddy and Lionel. Bill asked Hope for thirty-five dollars to pay Lionel for drugs he'd brought, but since Hope had only fourteen dollars, Bill borrowed the money from Walker.

In the bathroom, while Walker was changing the wet bandage on his infected leg, Hope came in "to play nurse, and when she observed that I had a first-aid kit with Band-Aids, she took a Band-Aid."

"Hope does not wear a brassiere," Walker explained. "The entire time I have known her, she's always worn two Band-Aids in place of a brassiere." He said he rolled the old tape that had been around the Ace bandage on his leg—he'd lost the customary metal clips—into a ball, along with the used Band-Aid, and threw it into the kitchen trash can.

When Lionel and Buddy left, in a little green foreign car, Hope, Bill, and Walker drove into town, where Hope played with a baby at the grocery store. After dinner, which Hope barely touched, she stretched out on the sofa. After a final drink with Bill, Walker left about 8:30 to drive back to Los Angeles, with one stop for gas at a station in Earlimart.

He described his Saturday night in Los Angeles: stopping at the Casa Bella restaurant, with a light rain falling; shopping at a drugstore near the Holiday Inn, where he flirted with a blond woman and took her back to Bill's apartment with him.

On Sunday morning, he took her to her own place, the Hyatt House on Sunset, then went back to the Holiday Inn, where he found a nasty note from Monica, whom he'd been scheduled to meet the night before, written in lipstick on the door. He drove Monica and Ingrid to the airport, then he drove back up to the ranch, stopping to buy gas and coffee, stopping again to buy apples at a fruit stand.

He estimated he got to the ranch about 10:30 Sunday morning. The gate was locked, but he remembered the combination: thirty-ought-six. Up at the house, he saw that Hope's car was gone. Hope was sitting in the orange grove.

"Was she crying?" Jay Powell asked.

"No, she's not a crier," Walker said. He sounded very proud of her.

Hope waved to Walker and ran toward him. He could make no sense of what she was saying, only that she had to get away from that awful, terrible place. Walker wanted a drink, so Hope dashed into the house, through the back door, and returned with a can of beer and a soft drink. They drove in Walker's car up the winding road past the foreman's house and the lower lake, up into the meadow. Hope was annoyed when Walker wanted to take pictures. "You dumb ass, will you stop!" she told him. "Bill is dead."

Walker didn't take her seriously, but he listened, since she was obviously upset.

"Was she crying then?" Jay asked.

"No, Hope is not a crier," Walker repeated. "I don't think I have ever observed Hope cry."

Hope told Walker she had been asleep in the bedroom when she heard a gunshot. She sat up in bed; the light was on. She screamed for Bill. A dark figure with a flashlight appeared in the doorway; she was knocked unconscious. When she came to, she was nude and tied. Through the open bedroom window, she heard two voices: one was Tom Masters's.

She slipped free from her bindings and ran into the living room, where Bill was sitting on the sofa. She thought he was asleep until she shook him and saw that he was bloody, with part of his head missing. She screamed. Someone grabbed her and said, "He can't help you; he's dead."

Hope was taken back into the bedroom and tied again. The person left; again she heard two men talking outside, again she recognized Tom Masters's voice, in a conversation about getting gasoline to burn the house down. She heard a car start up and leave. A man came into the bedroom and proceeded to place his penis into her mouth; when she resisted, he struck her in the stomach and told her she was to be killed "for whoring around and neglecting the children."

Eventually a car drove back up. The voice she recognized as Tom's was complaining that he'd had to drive all the way to Porterville to find an all-night gas station.

Walker said that at this point, as Hope was telling him this story up in the meadow, she contradicted herself by saying she had made arrangements with the man in the bedroom to spare her life. She heard a car go by, in front of the house, and she heard Tom say, "Jesus Christ, let's split, some guy just drove by and he happened to see me."

She heard a scurrying noise, a door slamming, a car pulling away. Eventually she freed herself, got out of bed, dressed, went outside, and sat under the orange trees, which was where Walker found her.

Walker didn't believe her story, which made her angry. But when they drove back down to the house and Walker went in, leaving her in the car, he found Bill's body. He moved the body so no one could see it through the picture window, into the back bedroom, where he placed it on a bed. He gathered the drugs and stashed them in a secret compartment in a cabinet. Neither he nor Hope cleaned the house. She packed her bag and, while Walker carried her things out to his car, she made sandwiches for the trip back to the city.

On the way back, Hope told a new version. She said she and Bill had been sitting on the sofa when a man came up behind the sofa and shot Bill with a long gun. Hope fainted. When she came to, she was in the bedroom, either with or without clothes on, and bound. She told Walker she'd made a deal with the man in the bedroom and had written him two checks made out to cash. She said that Tom Masters had tried to have her killed earlier, one night when she and Bill had gone out to dinner and then, instead of returning to her house, had gone to his apartment. While they listened to music there, Bill got up to close the draperies; a gunshot was heard, and a bullet hit the building above his head. Hope said she and the man she wrote the checks to discussed that incident.

Back in Los Angeles, Hope directed Walker to a house at 1122 Gordon Street, where she visited a man named Taylor, whom she used to date. Walker waited in the car about an hour, until Hope brought Taylor out and introduced the two men. Hope and Walker then drove to Bill's apartment where Walker moved his things out, and Hope carried something out. At Farmer's Market, they bought bread and cold cuts, then went up to the Drive.

Walker took the maid to the bus stop and ordered pizza for the children. He and Hope showered together, then went into her bedroom and had sexual relations. Hope begged him to stay, because he was the only person who could prove she hadn't killed Bill.

So Walker stayed. To make it appear that Bill Ashlock was alive, Walker was to use Bill's credit cards around town. Hope gave him a set of Bill's cards, although Walker already had some, given to him by Bill. Hope left the house in Walker's white Lincoln, saying she was going first to her mother's, then to meet Taylor on Sunset Strip.

Monday morning, Walker jogged and drove Keith to school. He talked on the phone to Honey, who told him that the family had been agreeable to helping him when the police were looking for him, and now that the shoe was on the other foot, it was his responsibility to stick by Hope. Honey told Walker she would try to reach Jim Webb to arrange that the body was not discovered that day.

Hope drove Bill's Triumph to the Beverly Hills Hotel, then, in the Lincoln, she and Walker drove to Bill's apartment, where they looked for his insurance policies and where Hope wished to pick up some personal items—photographs, songbooks, a collage. As they were leaving, they met the postman.

Walker said he did not sit up all night, on the Drive, guarding Hope and her children with a rifle. But he said Hope had produced a rifle of

Bill's—thirty-ought-six—that Walker put into the trunk of the Lincoln. Walker went shopping with Bill's credit cards, first by himself, later with Keith. He took Hope and the younger children to the Hamburger Hamlet for lunch, then to the supermarket, to her stepbrother's house, and to a park. He talked again with Honey, who said she was having difficulty reaching someone at the ranch. Hope and Walker drove down into Hollywood and picked up a yellow and brown car that Hope drove home, Walker following in the Lincoln.

They slept together Monday night. On Tuesday, Walker drove Hope Elizabeth to school, then went shopping again, and rented a room at the Wilshire Hyatt House with Bill's Bankamericard. Hope went down to her mother's house. When he telephoned her there, Hope said Jim Webb had been observed at the house, cleaning up, and wanted to call the police.

Hope and Walker, Honey and Van gathered in the living room and discussed the story Hope was to tell the police: that she had been rescued by a newspaperman, that she'd been told by the killer it was a Mafia job, that she had been taped in such a manner that she couldn't have killed Bill, that the newsman had brought her home and protected her for two or three days.

Walker left to call the police. He said he had not told Hope's parents he was a newspaperman and that both of them already knew who he was. He said none of their court testimony about the story he'd told them on Tuesday was true.

Van called Walker late that night at the Hyatt House to say that Hope had been arrested. Walker went to San Francisco and talked with Honey several times on Wednesday. When she asked him to attend Hope's bond hearing, Walker arranged to fly into Bakersfield, where Gene Tinch picked him up and drove him to the justice court. Walker was disguised: dark glasses, his hair combed differently, a big cigar.

Two days after Hope was released on bail, she and Gene Tinch met Walker at the Hilton in San Francisco, where Walker made a long tape recording to support Hope's story. Later the tape was edited in places, and he made more tapes, between five and twenty altogether. In order to make the entire affair more involved, Gene Tinch found an obscure homicide in the LAPD file, the Crane killing, to substantiate the hired-killer angle, and an elaborate scheme was concocted to lure Tom Masters to a room at the Sheraton-Universal Hotel, where he would be discovered by the police in a room filled with merchandise bought with Bill's credit cards.

Back in Los Angeles, at the end of the week, Gene met Walker again at a cocktail lounge at the International Hotel. They revised the plan involving the frame-up of Tom Masters, but on Sunday, March 11, all the plans collapsed when Walker was arrested at the Howard Johnson's, and charged with killing Bill Ashlock.

"Mr. Walker, did you kill Mr. Ashlock?" Jay Powell asked.

"No, I did not."

"Did Hope tell you at any time that she killed Ashlock?"

"No, she did not."

The jury never seemed to think she had. "I don't think she had malice in her, to kill this man," a juror said later. "And I don't think she led Walker up there to kill." Although the jurors were not enchanted with Mrs. Masters, whose references to "live-in help" and "my girl, my maid" had grated on some ears—one juror got up at 4:00 every morning to drive a school bus around dark country roads before reporting to the courthouse at 9:00—Hope's status was no longer in question. The question was whether the jurors could be convinced of Walker's guilt, for now there began a startling parade of defense witnesses, establishing a line of evidence that seemed to support Walker's itinerary.

Harley Shawn, a service station owner in Earlimart, remembered a man stopping by for gas one night, petting his dog. Mr. Shawn could not positively identify Walker as that man, nor could he specify the exact date. But when a most unlikely defense witness, Jim Brown, was asked about an Arco charge slip that had been taken into police custody, Jim Brown testified that the date on the slip was February 24, 1973. Saturday.

The owner and cook at the Casa Bella restaurant in L.A. identified Walker as the distinguished-looking man who'd bought a deluxe pizza, mostaccioli and sausage, and a draft beer late one night, between 11:15 and 11:30 P.M., nearly closing time. William J. Richardson wasn't sure of the date, but he remembered that it was a good sale for so late on a rainy winter night—$5.30, with 6 percent sales tax—and he brought his cash register tape to court with him, with the date "Saturday 2-24-73" written on the tape. Mr. Richardson said he had definitely seen raindrops on the customer's car, a Lincoln Continental, parked in front, and when John Aldrich, a certified consulting meteorologist, took the stand, he testified that on the night of Saturday, February 24, 1973, traces of rain were reported at the weather station on Van Owen Boulevard, conveniently located just a half mile north of the Casa Bella.

Martha Sindlinger, a clerk at Lee's Drugstore on Hollywood Boulevard, said that Walker was the man who'd come into the store shortly before midnight one night in February.

Robert McRae testified that he'd checked Walker out of the Holiday Inn in Hollywood between six and seven o'clock on Sunday morning, February 25. But he remembered the name as "Tony Tidd." McRae said he remembered that Tennessee Ernie Ford was also checking out that morning, in something of a rush, and he remembered also that Mr. Tidd, or Mr. Walker, had been with two airline stewardesses.

A disabled veteran, Joe Mandrelle, who said he spent a lot of time at a fruit stand in Porterville, identified Walker as the man who'd stopped by the stand around ten o'clock one morning—he wasn't sure just which morning—to buy apples. Mr. Mandrelle remembered telling Mr. Walker, "If you want something really good, those yellow apples are really good."

Walked smiled at his witness. "They were, too," he assured him.

The letter carrier on Bill Ashlock's apartment building route was William Suchman, a man so dignified that he called Ashlock "a client." He identified Walker as the man he'd seen in the hallway of Bill's building on a Monday—perhaps Monday, February 26—along with a woman, who'd been carrying something.

Sandi's testimony left the clear impression that that item might have been a collage, one she'd seen hanging in Bill's apartment when she'd been there with him. Sandi said she'd seen a rifle in Bill's place, too. She said Bill had called her three times during the week before he went to the ranch and that, in one conversation, he had told her he intended to move out of Hope's house. Sandi said they'd made a lunch date for the following Tuesday.

"He told you he was going to break up with Hope?" Jay Powell asked.

"Uh huh," Sandi said, nodding.

"Did Mr. Ashlock tell you that he had told Hope that he was going to break up with her?"

"No," Sandi said. "Bill told me he was. I didn't say he told Hope he was."

Walker was not restricted from approaching any witness except Hope Masters and her mother. So he came up close to the witness, Linda Thornberry, who said she was a waitress in the French Corner dining room at the Hilton Inn at the San Francisco Airport. He looked deeply into her eyes. "Do you see anyone in the courtroom that you have met while being a waitress at that hotel?"

"I see you, the defendant," Linda Thornberry said in a low voice.

She related that she'd served dinner to him, that he'd said his name was William T. Ashlock, but he asked her to call him by the name his friends used, the nickname Dar. That was on Saturday, March 3, the witness said. The next day, Sunday, March 4, she'd seen him sitting with a man and a woman in the Hilton lounge. The man was about six feet, two hundred pounds, medium brown hair, dark suit; he'd told Linda he was a retired police officer. The woman was a slender blond, five foot five or five foot six, her hair pulled back, tired-looking. Linda Thornberry said she had been shown a picture, after that, of Hope Masters. "She looks exactly like the woman I saw in the restaurant," Linda Thornberry said.

Beyond her amazing testimony was an area of pain, which Jim Heusdens probed quickly. "How many dates did you have with Mr. Walker?"

"Three," she said.

"And during those dates, did you become intimate with Mr. Walker?"

"Yes, sir," the witness said softly.

"Did you fall in love with Mr. Walker?"

"I was contemplating it," she replied.

She said she thought she had been in love with the man she called Dar, the man who'd told her he was a war correspondent from Australia, although he said he also had a home in Los Angeles . . . the man who had taken her and her young son out to an ice cream parlor and then had stayed at her apartment . . . the man who had left her on Tuesday, March 6, saying he would be back. He had not come back, though, and when she had called Los Angeles Information to find him, he could not be found, and she had not seen him in more than ten months since then, until she came to court. As Linda talked, even Jim Heusdens felt bad about it, and when he'd established that the restaurant where she'd seen the woman with Walker was a dark room, candle-lit, he had no further questions. So it was Walker who took the knife, then.

"You did pay particular attention to that woman, didn't you?" Walker asked.

"Yes," Linda said.

"Was it because you were personally involved with the defendant?"

Linda looked at him. "It was because I was a little bit jealous," she said.

Jay Powell felt the prison guard was a particularly good witness for the defense. James Wendel, who had worked as a guard at the Illinois State Prison from 1968 to 1973, identified a picture of Hope Masters as the woman whose picture the inmate G. Daniel Walker had had hanging in his cell.

Mr. Wendel said he'd met Walker when the prisoner was first admitted, and had seen him, and the picture, every day for eight or nine months. He said he'd mailed letters for Walker, too—some to a nun, Sister Mavis, some to a woman called C. J., some to a woman named Hope

Masters. The picture he was shown now was not the same picture, he said, but the woman was the same in both pictures. "Definitely one and the same person," the guard declared. He remembered the name because it was not a common name and because when he took Walker and the rest of the unit to shop at the prison commissary on Fridays, sometimes Walker didn't have enough money on account to buy what he wanted. Then Walker would say, "Well, there's always hope."

"What you meant by that, I don't know," Wendel told Walker from the witness stand, "but I have been in the penitentiary business, or the confinement business, long enough to know that when a man makes a remark like that, he's got something behind it. There's a reason for it."

Jim Heusdens scoffed at the witness. "So if Mr. Walker needed more money and said, 'I have none,' was he then talking about the nun, Sister Mavis?"

"He never said he had none," Wendel insisted.

"Did Mrs. Masters ever come to the prison?"

"Not to my knowledge," Wendel said.

Heusdens studied the surprise witness. "Are you not a friend of Mr. Walker's?"

"On an inmate relationship."

"Did you remember all these things from your own recollection, or was it something that Mr. Walker told you about, that refreshed your memory?"

"I have very good recollection," the guard declared.

The testimony was surprising, but even more so was the very appearance of a witness whose testimony revealed Walker's prison career to the jury. Gene Parker speculated that Walker must have felt that the guard's testimony about Walker's friendship with Hope Masters was more important to him than concealing his prior conviction. "I think Walker's just trying to bring Hopie down with him," Parker told Jim Brown.

After the guard's testimony, Walker took the stand again, to explain that he'd been "furloughed" from prison on December 15, 1972, and that he'd been in a hospital when, in January 1973, "I left the state heading west." Furthermore, he said, when he left he'd been comfortably equipped with cash and credit cards of his own—department store cards, telephone credit card, an airline credit card, and a commuter pass on Chicago Northwestern Line, a "class pass."

As though someone had taken a feather pillow, slit open the case, and shaken it heedlessly into the air, Walker's testimony swirled through the courtroom. All Jim Heusdens had to do was catch the feathers.

"You have a witness on the stand who comes along and tells a long story for a day and a half—I think the people have a right to impeach that story at each and every point," he announced to the court, beginning with Walker's labeling Marcy Purmal as "my mistress."

"All the time that Mr. Walker knew her, he was in custody of police authorities, unless the police authorities in Illinois allow Mr. Walker to have a mistress in prison," Heusdens said dryly.

Judge Ginsburg said that while he himself did not understand Walker's gratuitous remark, he felt that matter was irrelevant. Heusdens shifted tactics.

"Mr. Walker, have you ever used the name T. O. Wright?"

"Not that I recall," Walker said.

"Did you hear the witness who testified that you checked into the hotel using the name T. O. Wright?"

"Yes, I heard that witness."

"That witness is not telling the truth? Is that your testimony?"

"No, that's not my testimony," Walker said easily.

Jim Heusdens scowled and waved a hotel registration card in front of his face.

"Well, the question is, did you check into this hotel using the name T. O. Wright?"

Jay Powell objected. "It's argumentative. It's already been asked and answered. He said he didn't recall."

Heusdens shook his head, like an angry dog. "Is this your handwriting?" he demanded.

"It certainly looks like it to me," Walker said casually.

"Now, did you sign that card in the name of T. O. Wright?"

"The name is in T. O. Wright, yes."

Heusdens held up the small, shiny object, so small it could nestle in a teacup.

"Mr. Walker, have you ever seen this before?"

Walker nodded. "Yes, many times."

"Where did you see it?"

"On which occasion?"

"On the first occasion," Heusdens said angrily.

Walker smiled, rather nostalgically. "Hanging over the rather large paunch that my great-grandfather had."

"Is that your great-grandfather's initials?"

"Yes," Walker said. "Taylor Owen Wright the Third of Wellston, Ohio."

Jim Heusdens smiled, then, too, as he swung the chain back and forth.

"Did someone in your family then change your name?" he asked.

"Not that I know of," the witness said. "It was Taylor Owen Walker."

"Taylor Owen *Walker*?" the prosecutor said loudly. He looked at the jurors and raised his eyebrows. "Well, never mind," he said to the witness. At least one feather had been caught.

Gene Tinch tried to capture some more, as he told of his four-hour conversation with Walker on the afternoon of Walker's arrest in Hollywood. He said Walker had talked of taking Bill Ashlock's identification permanently. "He told me he intended leaving the country, writing a letter to Ashlock's place of business, and resigning under the name of Ashlock, and he personally would assume Ashlock's identification and gain employment through the use of his identification and reputation, and he mentioned going to England."

Jay Powell asked Gene whether he'd removed any of Walker's identification from Hope's house. Gene said he had not. "Do you recall removing a passport of Mr. Walker's from Mrs. Masters's home?" Jay asked. "No, I do not," Gene said. He also said that he and Hope had never met with Walker in San Francisco, that he had never met with Walker at the Universal Hotel in Los Angeles, that he had never taken any police reports of murder cases from the LAPD files and furnished them to Walker.

When Gene said there were "probably eight or ten" taped phone conversations between Walker and Hope, Jay told the court that all the defense had been given was a cassette summary of those talks. He said Tom Breslin had told him, "Well, there were a couple of others, but we don't have them. They were erased, and this is all we have." Jay Powell maintained that some of the tapes had been edited; specifically, Walker said that in the tape of his call from the Visalia jail, the portion about the contract and watching Hope and putting somebody in the house had been part of another, earlier tape.

Besides the phone tapes, Walker's long narrative tape was introduced, over defense protests. "It's our position that there are at least five tapes," Powell contended. "I feel that if the court is going to allow one in, without having all five of these tapes, then we are only getting a portion of the story. It's our position that these tapes were made at the direction of former defendant Masters, her father, and her attorneys, and they requested Mr. Walker to make five tapes, different tapes; that when he made one, they would listen to them and he would change them and make other tapes; and the only way the truth is going to come out is to get all of the tapes in."

"You can introduce them if you wish, Mr. Powell," Ginsburg said. "Or you can show that they exist or that they did exist. But that does not, to my mind, affect the admissibility of this particular tape. This particular tape is admissible." And so the tape was played to an attentive jury.

A few more defense witnesses appeared, the significance of their testimony not always readable in the faces of the jurors, who were beginning to chafe at the length of the trial, gone into the new year now, and were beginning to bicker among themselves. Ruthe Snelling and Lois Bollinger, who had become friends in their weeks of enforced togetherness, were particularly aggravated by a fellow juror with what they considered an overbearing, boastful manner. Throughout the trial, that woman had bragged incessantly about her domestic accomplishments: sewed all her own clothes; canned all her own vegetables; made all her own jams and jellies, honey, syrups; even dried her own raisins. One afternoon when she came in from lunch complaining that she hadn't been able to get an omelette, Lois couldn't resist. "Why didn't you lay your own eggs?" Lois asked.

"Don't talk to your roommate. They could use her against you in court," Tom Breslin had warned Hope at the Visalia jail. And Vanessa Guillory now appeared to tell the court that Hope had talked of two men who had burst into the ranch house and attacked her, and that when she was free, she'd run outdoors into the orange grove.

Mary Crane, a doctor's wife who lived between Porterville and Springville, said that on the murder weekend, either Saturday or Sunday afternoon, around 1:30, she'd seen a dark green foreign car pulling into the ranch road as she was driving past with her children. Another man was opening the gate for the man in the car. Mrs. Crane said she didn't see either of those men in the courtroom.

Dolly Hicklin took the stand, but she was not allowed to testify about the murder of her husband by a man named E. E. Taylor. "We are going far afield," Jim Heusdens said, when Mrs. Hicklin appeared. "The only statement we have got is by Mr. Walker saying that he and Mrs. Masters went to the Taylor residence and now, because Mr. Taylor has been convicted of murder, we are to believe that he also killed Mr. Ashlock."

Co-counsel Walker defended Mrs. Hicklin's appearance. "Through this witness, we are going to show that the person who lived at 1122 North Gordon on February 25, 1973, was a man named Edward Eugene Taylor. The People have questioned the fact that the defendant Walker identified the person at that address, that he took Mrs. Masters to see an Edward

Eugene Taylor, and we are now attempting to show that this is the person who lives at that address."

Judge Ginsburg was truly annoyed. "Mr. Walker, if you had someone identify the Brooklyn Bridge, and you had testified that you were at the Brooklyn Bridge on February 25, would the identification of the Brooklyn Bridge prove you were there?"

"Your Honor, I don't think I understand the court's response about the Brooklyn Bridge," Walker said innocently.

"Apparently you don't," Ginsburg snapped. "The objection is sustained, Mr. Walker, on the grounds of lack of relevancy."

Ginsburg was further annoyed when Walker presented a motion asking that the defense be allowed to subpoena a dozen out-of-state witnesses. Among the witnesses Walker wanted was Illinois state trooper Frank Waldrup, whom Walker maintained would testify that on Saturday, February 10, 1973, he'd taken Marcy Purmal in for questioning at O'Hare Airport, after seeing "a large stack of U.S. currency" in her purse, and that, under questioning, Marcy had admitted that her relationship with Walker had been a sexual relationship. Walker also wanted Armond Lee, an elevator operator at the Illinois Research Hospital, brought to Visalia to testify that on the last Sunday of January 1973, when Lee had brought food and drinks to Walker in his hospital room, Lee had seen two visitors; Walker said Armond Lee would identify the man as William T. Ashlock and the woman as Hope Masters. A third witness from Illinois would be James Mager from the Standard station on North LaSalle. Walker told the court that Mager would testify that he had identified Marcy Purmal as the woman who had been with Walker at the station at 2 A.M. on February 5, 1973, and Mager would further testify that Walker had been back at the station the following night, February 6, with another woman; Mager would identify that woman as Hope Masters.

The motion was denied.

Nevertheless, Jim Heusdens was concerned about the impact of Walker's story, especially with the two witnesses, the Holiday Inn clerk and the pizza cook, placing Walker in Los Angeles late Saturday night and early Sunday morning. So on the first weekend in January, Heusdens, Jim Brown, and Gene Parker drove down to L.A. to check out those people and find out what they could. On Saturday afternoon, though it went sorely against his grain, Heusdens met with Hope at her mother's house to discuss what the prosecution might do to strengthen its case.

He didn't like Hope Masters any more than he ever had; he still thought she was snippy and arrogant and probably, in some way, guilty, though that didn't bother him anymore. "It wasn't my duty to judge that case," he explained. "It was my duty to prosecute Walker." He didn't like Honey's decorator living room—"too much crystal and brass crap," Heusdens thought—and he especially didn't like the coffee table, which he thought was much too big. But when he saw Hope's son Keith, just turned thirteen—tall, blond, nicely mannered, and articulate—he liked very much what he saw.

Honey always felt that Keith's appearance in court had a lot to do with his later, long-term problems. "He was given too much responsibility at too early an age," Honey said sadly. "He was the man of the house at a time when he ought to have been just a little boy." It was Keith whom Hope had charged, in her phone call from jail, with taking care of his little brother and sister; it was Keith whom Hope had told, when they drove down the hill to Honey's in the yellow and brown car, that someone was trying to kill them all. Now it was Keith who raised his hand to be sworn in and who perched on the edge of the big witness chair, because Jim Heusdens felt the boy would make the mother's story more credible, to substantiate that she had been very much afraid, and, more than that, to clear her name.

"Did Mr. Walker tell you his name was Taylor?" Heusdens asked the boy.

"Yes," Keith said. "When I came to the house after the basketball game, and he was there with my mother, and I asked him what his name was, and he said 'Taylor.' "

"Had you ever heard your mother mention Mr. Walker's name before?"

"Never," Keith said.

"Now if your mother has a friend—you know, a boyfriend—did your mother always tell you what those boyfriends' names were, and introduce you to them?"

"Yes," Keith said. Lois Bollinger said she was crying inside for the child at that point.

"Keith, before your mother married Mr. Masters, in 1969, did your mother ever leave you for a period of more than one or two days?"

"She couldn't," Keith said, "Because it was just my mother and my sister, and we had no housekeeper and nobody else."

"Now, when you went down to the House of Pies with Mr. Walker, did the waitress ask you where your sister was?"

"I told her that my mother was scared for her to come out of the house," Keith related. "And Mr. Walker told me it wasn't right to talk about family business in front of other people."

Keith said that when his mother came home from the ranch Sunday evening, she seemed kind of quiet. Both she and Mr. Walker told him that Bill had had car trouble and had stayed up at the ranch. Most of the time, then, until they went down to his grandmother's, his mother was in the house—"She was in and out"—and both she and Mr. Walker had told Keith that Mr. Walker was there to guard the house, so nobody could get K.C. Keith said the man had told him he'd stayed up all night, guarding them. On Tuesday, in the car, when Keith asked his mother what was wrong, she'd told him somebody was trying to kill them all. That evening, while he was watching TV in the den, Keith said he'd seen a man pass by the window. He went into the living room to tell the grown-ups, and Mr. Walker told Keith "it was all right, it was just somebody that was protecting the house." After Mr. Walker left, Keith said, he saw his grandfather close all the curtains and turn on the alarm and bring out a lot of guns into the living room. Keith said his mother went away that night, for about four or five days, and when she came back, she never went out anywhere. He and his sister stayed home from school for fifteen days, but they were allowed outside after Mr. Breslin and Gene said it was okay.

When Jay Powell objected, Heusdens said this witness would rebut testimony that had placed Hope in San Francisco eight days after the murder, and Ginsburg allowed the line of questioning.

"She was home every day. You saw her?" Heusdens asked.

"Every day and every night," Keith said firmly.

Walker smiled widely at the witness. "Is it Mister, or Keith, or Super Sport?" he asked jovially.

"Keith," the boy said gravely.

"Do you remember the weekend that you went over to your relatives' house?"

"Yes, I went with my uncle, for a day and a half," Keith said.

"So you weren't there all the time?"

"I wasn't gone eight days," Keith said. "And I know my mother wasn't in San Francisco for eight days."

"Could she have been there for four hours?" Walker asked gently.

"Could have been," Keith said. "But my grandmother and my grandfather would have known it."

Walker paused. "Keith, in 1969, how old were you?"

"Ten or nine," Keith said. "Nine, I think."

"What time was your bedtime?"

"Eight-thirty," Keith said. "I had a strict bedtime."

"So you wouldn't know where your mother happened to be when you were in bed?"

"Yes I would," Keith said stoutly. "Yes I *would*. She would come to my room and cover me up every night."

Walker's smile was sad, as he spoke softly to the boy. "Keith, you love your mother, don't you?"

"Yes," Keith said.

"Wouldn't trade her for anybody in the world, would you?"

"No," Keith said.

Lionel had brought Keith to Visalia. He himself testified briefly that he'd been in London working on a television movie, *Dr. Jekyll and Mr. Hyde,* starring Kirk Douglas, on the weekend of February 24 and 25, 1973, and that he'd been in London from mid-November 1972 until March 12, 1973, except for a twenty-four-hour trip to Los Angeles on February 9 or 10 to pick up a check. On that one quick visit, he said he'd stayed at the Hyatt House. He said he knew Hope's parents but had never been to their ranch, although he'd been told it was in Springville, "wherever that might be. I have no idea."

One of the best things about the legwork Gene Parker and Jim Brown had done in Los Angeles, Gene said, was talking to pretty women, and he was pleased to see Sara Monaco again in court, a state's rebuttal witness, to identify Walker as the man who'd come to Dailey & Associates on Friday, February 23, 1973, to take Bill Ashlock to lunch.

Jay Powell maintained that the witness's identification was invalid because she'd seen newspaper photographs of Walker after that date. In her explanation, Sara proved almost as talkative as Hope. "The pictures that I have seen in the newspaper were not a close picture, they were a distant picture, and I tried to sit down and think of what he looked like when he was sitting in the lobby of where I work, and the way he is sitting there now and what I see, I feel it is the same person," Sara said.

"All right," Jay said wearily.

Sara Monaco said the man had told her his name was Wright Taylor, or Taylor Wright, and he'd said he was there to do a story on Bill Ashlock. When Sara told him Mr. Ashlock was delayed because he was on the phone with his girlfriend, the man was amused, because the story was on Bill's bachelorhood. Sara said that when she told Bill the man was waiting,

Bill had asked her the man's name again; in the lobby, Sara saw them introduce themselves to each other.

Mr. Tony Tidd came down from Markham, Ontario, Canada, to testify that on Saturday night, February 24, 1973, he and his wife had stayed at the Holiday Inn in Los Angeles and had checked out Sunday morning.

The Holiday Inn clerk, Robert McRae, returned to correct his earlier testimony. He said he had not been working the weekend of February 24 and 25 and had not been in the hotel. However, he remembered seeing the defendant, though he didn't know the date; he remembered, from registration slips, the names Kassler, Jungnickel, and Gantou; and he remembered seeing, at some point, Tennessee Ernie Ford.

When Jim Heusdens recalled the Casa Bella owner, the prosecutor pointed out that the California sales tax had been 5 percent in February 1973, not 6 percent. Jay Powell said that Mr. Richardson had simply overcharged Mr. Walker by five cents and there was nothing sinister about a five-cent mistake. Mr. Richardson himself said he could easily have made a mistake like that because he had a cataract on his left eye, and Lois Bollinger said later that she couldn't figure out how, in that case, he could have seen through the restaurant window out into the parking area, so late at night, and noticed raindrops on the customer's Lincoln Continental.

Neither the hotel clerk nor the pizza man was a liar, Heusdens told the jury in his summation, simply people who had seen the defendant at some point and then had been convinced by him that they had seen him that crucial Saturday night.

"He has the whole month of February," Heusdens pointed out. "He puts in a bunch of evidence, a bunch of hotel registration slips with names. He threw in Mr. Tidd—but here comes Mr. Tidd. So he had to find somebody else. I imagine, if we go look, we will find Norman Carter, we will find that he was at the Holiday Inn that night. I don't doubt we will find a Kassler there, and a Jungnickel.

"He has pulled you down a merry path," Heusdens told the jury, "but I think all of you have seen through the man that he is, a man who takes a family, twists them, uses them and then, when he is caught, tells you a twisted story." Heusdens said Walker had used people all his life, especially women, especially Hope Masters.

"Remember Ingrid? Remember Miss Kassler? Remember some of the other people—the maid, the woman up at San Francisco? Remember all these women Mr. Walker has talked about? I think the evidence shows that Mr. Walker thought he could control Hope Masters. I think he believed he could control her, and I think he could do what Mr. Tinch said he was going to do—take Mr. Ashlock's identification and go to England and send a letter back saying 'I resign' and then live in England as Mr. Ashlock.

"Mr. Walker is a planner. He plans things. He knows what he is going to do, and he knows when he wants to do it.

"Now, why did he not kill Hope? Because he thought he could control her! When she first told her story, she didn't tell anybody that Mr. Walker was the killer, and it's probably questionable to you now, what parts of Mrs. Masters's story do you believe—and rightfully so, because, after all, her story was changed on a couple of occasions.

"You have to look at Mr. Walker and say, 'Is Mr. Walker capable of causing enough fear for somebody to do the things that Mrs. Masters did? Is he capable of causing that much fear? Can he convince someone to tell that kind of a story?'

"Mrs. Masters has three children—a two-year-old, a nine-year-old, a thirteen-year-old. She's at a ranch with the defendant. Her boyfriend—who she is going to marry—has been killed. Her three children have been threatened. The defendant is with her for two days. She doesn't even know who he is!

"And sometimes," Heusdens couldn't resist adding, broadly, "sometimes I wonder if even *I* know who he is! Is he Taylor Wright? Is he Larry Burbage? Is he William T. Ashlock? Or is he G. Daniel Walker?

"Now, maybe she went along with the defendant. Maybe she did have intercourse with the defendant. But if those other people can come up here under the influence of the defendant when he's in custody, and commit perjury, what else can Mrs. Masters do, if she was in the condition and in the situation she was placed in?

"All I can tell you"—Heusdens waved his arms dramatically—"is, out of the mouths of babes comes *truth*! Keith took the stand and he told you things that his mother told you. He liked the defendant Walker. The defendant Walker was always nice to him. But that boy knew something was wrong, and he asked his mom, 'What's wrong?' And she said, 'Somebody is trying to kill us all!'

"Now, was Mrs. Masters convinced at that point that somebody was trying to kill them? If Mr. McRae could be convinced, if other people were convinced by the defendant, I think Mrs. Masters could be convinced.

"Now, could Mrs. Masters have been involved in the shooting? Answer: yes. Could she have been the trigger man? The evidence says no. You look at her? You can consider all the facts. And no matter how much anyone can believe she may go to bed with Mr. Walker—she may have done that —but are you convinced that that woman is capable of pulling the trigger and putting a bullet through Mr. Ashlock's head? I don't think so.

"On the other hand, are any of you convinced that Mr. Walker could put a bullet through somebody's head? I am sure Mr. Taylor Wright kind of felt like that on one particular moment in Michigan on February the ninth.

"Mr. Walker said he knew Hope Masters and Mr. Ashlock a long time ago. Miss Monaco, the secretary, was here. After hearing her testimony, do any of you believe that Mr. Walker knew Bill Ashlock?

"Well, he went to Los Angeles, you know. Now, why did he go to Los Angeles?" Heusdens shook his head forcefully.

"Ladies and gentlemen, I can't explain to you a person like Mr. Walker. I can't explain why did he do this? Or why didn't he do that? I won't *try* to explain to you a person like Mr. Walker. The only thing I can explain to you is that Mr. Walker is the type of an individual who for his own purposes—his own desires—would destroy the life of another human being! If Mr. Walker was there—and I think the evidence clearly shows he was there—then only one person who has been in this courtroom was capable of the crime, and only one person in this courtroom committed the crime"—Heusdens swung around and pointed at Walker—"and he is sitting over there at that table, and he is going to wait for you to bring in a verdict, and we ask you to bring back a conviction of murder in the first degree!"

Jay Powell was as cool, as composed as ever, as he summed up the defense case. "We have a most unusual case here," he said quietly, "and I am sure that all of you, for the rest of your lives, will remember it, no matter what the outcome.

"Now, Mrs. Masters has told us that she didn't know Mr. Walker until the weekend of the crime. We have both Mr. Walker's testimony that he knew her for years, and we have the testimony of the ex-lieutenant from the Illinois State Prison, Mr. Wendel. Mr. Heusdens tried to impeach Mr. Wendel by showing that he had a bad reputation among prison guards. Even if he did—and I don't concede that he did—that still doesn't mean he didn't mail letters from the prison from Mr. Walker to Hope Masters. It also does not mean he had never seen her picture before.

"You will recall that Mrs. Masters, the first time around, told us she did not know the intruder. She woke up. She didn't know the intruder.

She did not see him. It was dark. He talked obscene things to her, spoke to her, raped her. Then they had a long conversation in which she finally talked him out of killing her. But she did not recognize his voice, and she did not know him, even though she had several hours with him on Saturday and she had the opportunity to know his voice.

"If he's the killer, why didn't he kill her at the ranch? Why let her live? If she's the only person who can identify him, and he's the killer, why not shoot her as well?

"Remember how Mrs. Masters said there was blood all over her, and there was vomit all over the pink blouse? She said she had never been able to find out what happened to her clothing at the ranch, but she was sure there were bloodstains on that crepe blouse. Then when we took the sack to the witness stand, it was so obvious there was no blood on the blouse, all the buttons were intact, there was no vomit. That caught her in another lie.

"What did she tell her lawyer on those tapes? She said Walker was different from the man that raped her. 'Yes, he seemed to be very different.'

"This woman, pathetic as she may be, or as willful as she may be—that's for you to decide—has lied to us. Maybe she did hallucinate. How much of this did she make up? I don't know. That's for you to decide.

"You will recall also that she told her attorney that the killer-intruder took mug-shot pictures of her with a camera, four or five. Now, the sheriff's office developed the photographs in Walker's camera. If there were mug-shot pictures, as Hope claims, surely they would have been evidence here for you to look at." Jay Powell shook his head, too, not forcefully, as Heusdens had, but in a quiet, bemused way. "It's just another instance of Hope Masters's incredible tale, which they are asking you to believe so they can convict Mr. Walker.

"When they got back to Beverly Hills, why did he stay with her constantly? Did he keep her naked in the shower for a couple of days? No. If we believe she was under such a threat and was so terrified she could do nothing then, why didn't she say to the police on Tuesday night when she was in jail, when she was safe, 'Hey, quick, this guy is the killer.' She didn't say that. Then she was in jail in Tulare County. Did she tell the Tulare County authorities, 'Walker is the killer! Get him!' No. She did nothing.

"She was released on bail. What about the FBI, then? Walker wasn't around, and Mr. Paul Luther was talking to Hope. Why didn't she say, 'Quick, Walker is the killer, go get him!' She didn't say that.

"Now, did Mr. Walker go to Los Angeles on Saturday night? Detective Jim Brown is a very hard-working man, very fine man. He testified that the gas slip to the service station in Earlimart said February 24. Could one think for one minute that Mr. Brown would lie in favor of Mr. Walker?

"Or Mrs. Marvin Crane, who was driving by the ranch entrance. Did Mr. Walker get her to lie? I don't think so. Yet she saw a green, foreign-looking car there. Did Walker get the fishermen to lie? They went by the ranch on Tuesday, and the drapes were open. When they drove out, the drapes were closed. And on Saturday, when the fishermen were there, there was a Lincoln and a Vega and another car—a green foreign car.

"And shall we believe that Mr. Walker has *control* over the weather? Did he arrange the weather so that on Saturday night it would rain at the right time for him? Yet you will remember the weather expert's testimony that the only time it rained at any time back and forth after that Saturday night was between 10:30 and 11:30 that particular Saturday night.

"Ladies and gentlemen," Jay Powell finished, quietly, "you are not trying Mr. Walker for robbery in Ann Arbor, Michigan. You are not trying Mr. Walker for escape in Chicago, Illinois. You are trying Mr. Walker for murder in Tulare County, and I think you will conclude that the People have failed to prove Mr. Walker guilty of murder beyond a reasonable doubt and to a moral certainty. There is no question Mr. Ashlock was murdered up there. But merely because Mr. Walker is the only defendant left in the case, the only person before you, does not mean that you must now find Mr. Walker guilty. We ask that you consider the reasonable doubt instruction carefully, you weigh the evidence, and we ask you to find Mr. Walker not guilty."

In his closing statement to the jury, Jim Heusdens dispensed quickly with a couple of defense points. On Detective Jim Brown and the gas station slip dated February 24: "Mr. Shawn says he works twenty-four to thirty-six hours at a stretch. And the card is dated the twenty-fourth. Okay. When does the twenty-fourth start? It starts at midnight on Friday and goes to midnight on Saturday, so we've got two periods of night, do we not? Mr. Walker had to drive *sometime* to Springville. When did he leave Los Angeles?" On the weatherman: "He said during the month of February it rained sixteen days. Twenty-eight days in February. Sometimes twenty-nine. Over half. It could have been *any* particular night."

Then Heusdens got to the main point. The starting and ending point.

The only point. He leaned toward the jury in a confidential manner, rather chatty.

"I'm not going to tell you that Mrs. Masters is not a pompous little broad. She is. She acted it. She acts kind of smarty.

"But after the charges against her were dismissed, she could have sat on that stand and said, 'I shot Mr. Ashlock myself,' and she would still walk out the door, because the charges were brought, the jury was sworn and at that point, when the charges were dismissed, she could never be brought back in the court again for the charge of murder against Mr. Ashlock. So she did not have to keep this thing going.

"Mr. Powell says, 'Why didn't she tell the police? She had plenty of opportunity to tell them.'

"Now, I ask you ladies on the jury"—Jim Heusdens looked earnestly at each of the women, his gaze lingering especially on the pregnant woman—"I ask you, if you had three children and you were taken off to jail because you were implicated in a crime, would you put the finger on the man who told you not to, and risk your three children's lives?

"You heard the tape Mr. Walker made about 'my people,' 'the organization,' 'the contract.'" Jim Heusdens pounded on the jury rail. "I don't think there is a woman on this jury who would do it! And I don't think Mrs. Masters would do it!

"You heard the tape," he repeated, his voice trembling slightly with tension. "Do you think that was at another person's direction? You heard the ramblings and the goings on. Mr. Walker expected someone to believe that, just as he had Mrs. Masters believing everything, along with her parents. But, ladies and gentlemen, I don't believe Mr. Walker has *you*" —now Heusdens pointed suddenly at the jury—"I don't think he has *you* believing anything other than that he is guilty of murder, in the first degree!"

It was a wonderful, florid speech. One of the jurors wanted to applaud. But beneath the flamboyance, the show for the sake of the show, winning for the sake of winning, Jim Heusdens felt a sense of urgency in this case. As he sank into his chair and pulled out a handkerchief to wipe his steamy face, as the judge was instructing the jury, Heusdens leaned toward his assistant, Jim Brown. "It's important that they don't turn this guy loose," Heusdens muttered.

Judge Ginsburg reminded the jury that a defendant in a criminal action was presumed innocent, until proven guilty, and that in case of reasonable doubt, he was entitled to an acquittal. He told them motive need not be shown, although presence of a motive might tend to establish guilt, as the absence of motive might tend to establish innocence. He not only defined murder—the unlawful killing of a human being, with malice aforethought —he then defined malice—a wish to vex, annoy, or injure another person, or an intent to do a wrongful act.

When he concluded his instructions—meticulous, by the book—he paused, looked steadily at the jury, then continued.

Judge Leonard Ginsburg had considered what he was going to say very, very carefully. In all his years on the bench, he had never before made personal comments to a jury. But neither had he presided at the trial of G. Daniel Walker before. And Walker's jury was two-thirds women.

"At this time, for the purpose of assisting you in deciding this case, I am permitted by the Constitution of California to comment on the evidence and the testimony and credibility of any witness," Ginsburg told the jury.

Neither attorney had ever heard a judge comment before; they stared at him. Walker had a half-smile on his face.

"My comments are intended to be advisory only and are not binding on you," Ginsburg went on. "You should disregard any or all of my comments if they do not agree with your views of the evidence and the credibility of the witnesses.

"It is my opinion that the defendant Walker's testimony contains so many contradictions, improbabilities, and fabrications in material matters that I personally would disregard it entirely and give it no weight whatsoever.

"It is further my opinion that the witnesses produced by the defendant were people of good will but were mistaken in crucial parts of their testimony, such as the dates when certain events took place, and the identities of certain persons.

"It is further my opinion that the circumstantial evidence produced by the plaintiff in this case established that the defendant was the only person present, besides Hope Masters, who was awake, conscious, and had the ability and motive to commit the offense charged, and that he did so for the purpose of taking the credit and the identity of the decedent in connection with the defendant's endeavors to evade capture by the Illinois authorities."

The jury was sent out at 4:03 P.M. on Friday, January 11, told to remain until they reached a unanimous verdict. Over the objections of the woman who dried her own raisins, the foreman was Lois Bollinger, the tall, attractive blond bookkeeper whom Walker had declined to excuse from service when her boss got sick.

At 6:30, when the jury had not announced a verdict, Judge Ginsburg sent them to dinner. Jim Heusdens grabbed a bite with his wife, Gwen, and his son, who had driven over from Porterville for the closing speeches, and his law partner. They discussed the prospects. Heusdens felt Ginsburg's comments had been pretty strong, but with a jury—especially a jury trying G. Daniel Walker—you never could tell. Of the three murder cases Heusdens had prosecuted before Walker, he'd won two, lost one. One of the victims had been stabbed seventeen times, but the jury acquitted, and one of the jurors rushed over and kissed the defendant, right in the center of the courtroom. You never could tell. Walker's jury was two-thirds women, and Heusdens felt that women didn't trust other women. "It's important they don't turn this guy loose," he said again.

Hope opened her eyes, closed them, opened them again, yawned and stretched. She raised her head slightly from the pillow, but the room had no clock, and it was darkened with heavy draperies, so she couldn't even guess the time.

She groaned and fell back onto the pillow, pulling the covers partly over her head. Waking up never seemed to get any easier. As she burrowed in, she remembered she wasn't at home, and she didn't have to get up. She could stay in bed all day, or as long as she liked. It was going to be a wonderful, lazy, restful weekend.

All through the trial Hope had been on twenty-four-hour call. She was still tired and vaguely unwell from the virus she'd had just before Christmas, when she had dressed in her bodysuit and miniskirt to go back to testify. The holidays had been depressing, spent, as usual, in what she called "one of those Christmas-divorce type setups." She took the children to Honey's on Christmas Eve, when Van's children came there; on Christmas Day, his children visited their mother, and Hope had Honey and Van up to the Drive. Lionel went with her to Honey's, but he did not come to Hope's dinner on Christmas Day, when Tom and Nadine were invited. Tom had called Hope just before Christmas. "Am I still invited over this year?" he'd asked. "Well, of course," Hope said. "It's your kid, what the heck."

As January wore on, damp and chilly, she felt she had to get away, and she'd telephoned Heusdens. "Will you need me on Monday? Because if you don't, I'd like to go away for the weekend."

"No, we won't need you on Monday," Heusdens told her.

So Hope and Lionel had come down to La Costa, one of her favorite hotels, where she could lie around the pool, sleep late, watch TV all day, and just hang out in the room, then party all night.

Knowing that she didn't have to get up brought her wide awake. She wriggled out from under the covers and sat on the edge of the bed. She brushed her hair away from her face, lighted a cigarette, and called room service for coffee and juice.

When the knock came, she opened the door, and a smiling waiter pushed in the breakfast cart, adorned with fresh flowers and the morning paper. As he was fussing around, pouring ice water, unfolding the napkins, Hope picked up the paper.

WALKER CONVICTED IN SLAYING OF AD MAN

She did not notice the waiter leave. She stood as though she were frozen, right where she was. She felt alarmed, confused, excited, depressed, sad, and very angry. When Lionel, waking up, said something to her, she snapped at him to leave her alone.

Minutes after they went into the jury room, the jurors had decided that Walker was guilty. There seemed to be no doubt in anybody's mind. But they thought it would look funny if they came right back out and said so, so they talked a while and then took their dinner break, then talked some more. They took one written ballot before returning to the courtroom at 10:00 P.M. to say "We, the jury, find the defendant guilty as charged, murder in the first degree."

After the initial, momentary hush, the courtroom broke into excited conversation and handshaking. Judge Ginsburg thanked the jury, the clerk, the reporter, and the bailiff. He congratulated Jim Heusdens for a performance that he called "unusually brilliant," and he commiserated with Jay Powell "because he has been saddled with a situation that would make any attorney cringe."

Jim Brown was so relieved when he heard the verdict that he folded his arms on the table and just rested his head there for a while. "Boy, that's a relief," he said. "That's a relief."

Three weeks later, in the same courtroom, Jay Powell moved for a new trial.

He argued again that Walker's arrest was illegal, the result of an illegally seized letter, the fruit of the poisoned tree. He said the People had withheld evidence, especially an airline ticket purportedly used by Hope Masters to fly from Illinois to California on February 7, 1973. He argued that the court should have allowed the testimony of Dolly Hicklin, because the murder of her husband had followed the Ashlock pattern: her husband was on vacation, Taylor was an intruder who broke in and shot him in the head. Finally, Jay protested Ginsburg's personal comments, calling it "a directed verdict."

Heusdens defended those comments. "When the testimony is this blatant, this far out, it's the judge's responsibility to make some kind of comment." He reminded the court that Marcy Purmal had testified she gave Walker's letters to the authorities. He said that for Jay Powell to bring up the Hicklin-Ashlock similarities only now, on the day of sentencing, was too late. He said he had never heard of any such airline ticket.

Judge Ginsburg said that in a two-month trial, the court was bound to make a few mistakes, but if he'd made any, he didn't think they were of any consequence. He denied the motion for a new trial.

Jay had one other motion. He asked that the defendant's clothing be returned, along with an undeveloped roll of 35-mm color film taken from the camera found in the Thunderbird. Walker didn't ask for the camera back, Powell assured the court, only the film.

Jim Heusdens argued that the clothing was mostly stolen. He said if the film were given to Walker, and developed, a set of prints ought to be turned over to the sheriff, in case it might be evidence. Jay said it couldn't be evidence; it had been suppressed.

Ginsburg ruled that an attempt should be made to sort out which clothes belonged to Walker and which didn't. He ruled that Walker was entitled to the undeveloped film. He sentenced G. Daniel Walker to life imprisonment.

And so the case of *The People of the State of California* v. *G. Daniel Walker* ended, officially, on the note of confusion and contradiction that had become apparent even before the trial. Whenever the country cops, Brown and Parker, got together, for a long time afterward, they would toss around some of those contradictions and unanswered questions. Down in the city, Hope's team was inclined to do that, too. "The problem is that Walker mixes in one or two percent fact, along with the fiction," Gene Tinch explained, "which is why it's so hard to separate the two."

Were there two cars at the ranch on Saturday, or three?

On Tuesday afternoon, at the ranch, were the living room drapes open or closed?

Why was no bloody or ripped clothing found at the ranch?

How many tapes were made, how many were erased, and why?

Did the rifle with the telescopic sight belong to Bill Ashlock?

Who were Walker's "people"?

Was there an airline ticket in somebody's hands?

What was on the roll of undeveloped film given back to Walker?

Why did Walker say, on tape, that he left the ranch at 11:30 Saturday evening, and in court, 8:30?

Was Walker's involvement with two men who had been college classmates—Taylor Wright and Bill Ashlock—the merest coincidence, or a grudge darkly nurtured for twenty years?

"She's away from him, she's free from him, why continue to take the rap for him?"

EPILOGUE

"FIVE YEARS," Walker had said to Hope, the night before she went down the hill to her mother's house, the night before Bill's body was found, when she and Walker were sitting by the gas-jet fire in her living room, listening to music, sipping wine. "How do you think you will feel about me in five years? If I stay out of trouble for five years, will you marry me?"

"I honestly don't know how I'd feel in five years," Hope had answered, desperately evasive. "I just don't know."

By the spring of 1978, Bob Swalwell was dressed in plainclothes permanently, assigned to the elite unit guarding the governor of Illinois. After Walker's arrest, the men who had so vigorously opposed Swalwell's tracking of the prey welcomed him back to Chicago with a banquet, a colossal cake, and the Superintendent's Award of Merit. His buddy Gus framed the photograph of Walker, taken nude at the North Hollywood station, and hung it in his bathroom.

Marcy Purmal, who had gone to Jamaica for a while, after the trial, then had joined a distinguished private law firm in Chicago and was embarked on a promising career, got a letter from Walker. She considered it a friendly letter, a signal that Walker wanted to strike up a correspondence. Marcy threw it in the wastebasket.

Gene Parker and Jim Brown were each named "Cop of the Year" and received plaques, Jim in 1974, Gene in 1975. Jay Powell was elected district attorney for Tulare County, then moved into private practice, in a modern office with a photograph of Walker, along with Judge Ginsburg's comments, framed and hung on the teakwood wall. When Jim Heusdens ran for D.A. and lost, he blamed the clique in Visalia, who didn't want an attorney from Porterville, across the tracks, running the county. "I'm not a part of that in-group and I wouldn't be in if they let me," Heusdens announced. "It's their loss and my gain, what the hell." But his private practice flourished, and he bought a small ranch outside Porterville, named the 4 Circle Bar for no particular reason. Judge Carter abandoned plans for a law career and moved to a job in traffic court. Judge Ginsburg retired, because he was finding criminal cases routine and boring, mostly involving drugs; although he spent a lot of time in San Francisco, he still lived in Greenacres, in the life-style Hope had instinctively recognized and appreciated; he bought a new Mercedes, burnt-orange.

Both Jay Powell and Jim Heusdens received letters from a New York law firm, with an obscurely worded inquiry about a CIA client. Neither man answered the letter.

In Los Angeles, Gene Tinch often teased Tom Breslin, who had left Ned Nelsen's prosperous office, with the jar containing a million dollars in shredded money, for a job as public defender in a poor section of the city. When Tom declined to discuss why he had traded his paneled office for clipboards and stubby pencils in a clamorous environment where he defended as many as sixty cases at a time, Hope said it was because her case had convinced him the justice system wasn't so just, and the best lawyers ought to work for people who couldn't afford them. "You're Tommy Goodshoes," Gene told Tom, who nodded ruefully. "I *am* Tommy Goodshoes, dammit," Tom said.

Hope was still living on the Drive. Her house was still boisterous with pets and people, noisier than ever, seeming to be always filled with teenagers parading through, rummaging for food, listening to loud rock. Amid the din, Hope was still lonely. Her older boy, Keith, whom she had confided in, seemed to have grown up suddenly; he had graduated from high school and was working as athletic coach at a school for handicapped children. At 18, he had his own friends. Hope still played chess with Michael Abbott once in a while, but much of the time she would shut herself in the bedroom to read or to watch religious talk shows on television.

She still had almost no girlfriends. She saw Phyllis occasionally, but never at Chips gatherings. Although, as a founding member, Hope was in Chips for life, she found the socializing awkward. When she made her first social appearance in public, after the trial, at the annual Colleagues' sale at the Santa Monica Auditorium, she and Phyllis had noticed the sudden silences, the scattering, as they walked among the racks of furs and designer dresses, the excited whisperings. Nancy Reagan wasn't there, but Betty Haldemann was, and a lot of prominent women who knew Hope, but no one seemed to have anything to say to her. "Most of them think I'm guilty," Hope decided. "Maybe not guilty of shooting Bill in the head, but guilty of *something*." Anyway, the Chips didn't have much to do. They didn't serve punch and cookies at Christmastime anymore at the home for unwed mothers, which had been turned into a daycare center. Hope was dropped from the Southwestern Blue Book.

She and her mother stayed in constant touch, in their usual way. Honey was planning to send Hope Elizabeth to boarding school in England; Hope resented her mother's attempt to mold the young girl into the pliant princess Hope herself had refused to become, and she resented Honey's statement that the events of 1973 had had a catastrophic effect on Hope. A year after the trial, FBI agent Paul Luther had called on Honey and Van, for a friendly chat. He said he had always wanted to know what effect random violence had on a family, afterward. Honey told him that Hope had been hardened, toughened, virtually destroyed.

In fact, Hope felt she had survived quite well. In a stab at financial independence from her mother and her ex-husbands, she had taken a real estate course and gotten her license at a fortuitous time in southern California; the subsequent flow of commission checks seemed to have brought her closer, finally, to her stepfather.

Van died of a heart attack one night in the spring of 1978. Soon afterward, his secretary, Mary Bowyer, who had fenced with Walker on the phone the day of Hope's bond hearing, had a long talk with Hope. "She said Van told her I was very competent and he could find no fault with any of my legal paperwork," Hope repeated. "You know," Hope went on, wistfully, "I think Van and I just got off on the wrong foot, in the very beginning. He told Mary he was very proud of me."

Hope had not been to the ranch since 1973. After Van died, when Honey threatened to sell her partnership in the place unless Hope showed some interest, Hope drove up with her children one July weekend. Except that the Webbs had been replaced with a young deputy sheriff and his wife, nothing had changed.

Hope swam in the river. She walked up the ranch road past the lower lake to the high meadow and sat among the wildflowers, in the shadow of Snailhead Mountain, looking down on the house and the orange grove. The children rode Bonnie. Hope slept in the same bed in the corner bedroom she'd slept in five years earlier and found it wasn't scary or traumatic at all. "I felt very peaceful, very content," she said. "Maybe because it's as close as I can ever come to being with Bill."

Back on the Drive, though, Hope locked herself in her bedroom with a stack of Bill's favorite records and cried for four days. In the chaos of the time after his death she had had no chance to grieve. She cried for Bill, she cried for herself, and she cried about Walker. Her thoughts were a mixture of fear and anger and guilt, and even a kind of pride, a feeling she had influenced Walker in a beneficial way. "Walker and I have a very deep, odd thing together," Hope told Tom Breslin. "He told me he was never going to commit another act of violence, and he hasn't. He hasn't harmed a single person.

"I know, I know, he hurt me a lot. But at the same time, he helped me. He stuck around and helped me. He taunted the police with those phone calls, which he knew damned well were being monitored, and he really did make a big effort, for whatever his reasons were, to make it clear that there had been another person at the ranch and that he was still around.

"He promised me, over and over, whenever he phoned, 'I won't leave you.' And he didn't. Tom, at one point, on the phone—do you remember when I said, 'Why are you doing this?' And he said, 'Hey, you take all your life, sometimes it's your turn to give.'

"He said to me, at the ranch, 'I'd rather die than go back to jail.' By hanging around and helping me, he risked going to jail forever. And he *has* gone to jail forever. I know what jail is like now, and the thought of being in jail forever is unbearable. And the only thing he was asking in return was that I write to him. That isn't a hell of a lot to ask. At least to me it isn't.

"What if Walker had left the country, Tom? What if I'd had to stand alone?"

A friend of Hope's saw Walker on television, talking about prison conditions. "He looks terrible," she told Hope. "Can't you do something?"

Hope sent a Mailgram to "G. Daniel Walker, California Prison System," since she didn't know exactly where he was. "Life is hell, how are you?" she started out, and she ended with, "There's always Hope."

Walker wrote back: "Your Mailgram opened unsaid, unvoiced, unadmitted things." They began to correspond—over the objections of her mother, Tom Breslin, Gene Tinch, even her son Keith, who was growing up aware; Keith was angry at what he called his mother's "love letters to that guy."

Hope denied that they were love letters. "I never wrote anything very meaningful," she insisted. She sent jokes, a Star Wars comic book (adressed to "G. Darth Walker"), a packet of romantic greeting cards for him to send to his women friends. She sent him the newspaper obituary when Van died, and Walker sent Honey a condolence card.

Walker sent jokes and clippings, and he sometimes referred to the song she'd played that Monday night on the Drive.

> This time we almost made it, didn't we, girl?
> This time we almost made some sense of it, didn't we, girl?
> This time I had the answer right here in my hand,
> Then I touched it, and it had turned to sand . . .
> This time we almost sang our song in tune, didn't we, girl?
> This time we almost made it to the moon, oh didn't we, girl?
> This time we almost made our poem rhyme,
> Oh didn't we almost make it, this time?

Hope soon became unnerved—Walker seemed to know everything that was going on. He informed Hope that Fran Ashlock had remarried and moved back to the Midwest. Not long after Hope had had lunch with friends at an obscure little restaurant near Farmers Market, Walker wrote to describe that lunch, giving the exact place and time. When Hope Elizabeth got her own phone in her room as a birthday present, Walker called on that phone, even though it had been installed less than twenty-four hours, even though the number was brand-new and unlisted. For months after that call, Keith kept a twelve-inch knife by his bedside.

Hope was even more frightened by little items in Walker's letters. He told her to expect him "to stop by for a martini," and he talked again of going to Rhodesia. When he referred to a book on her living room shelf, *The Other Side of Midnight,* Hope felt he was telling her he'd killed Bill after midnight that Saturday. He talked about crowded visiting days at the prison—"Weekends are murder"—and, most ominously, he informed her that, under a recent ruling, prisoners were now allowed to marry.

So after five years, that question remained. *It's like an unfinished conversation,* Hope thought. *I've really got to settle things. I can't live without wrapping it up.* She couldn't do it by mail. "I have to see his face," she told Tom Breslin. "I've got to feel his vibes."

Early in the morning on his birthday, August 10, Walker telephoned Hope. A week later she flew to Fresno, stayed overnight, and got up before dawn to drive to San Quentin. She stayed with Walker until visiting hours ended. She stayed in Fresno overnight again, and visited him all the next day. Then she came home.

Hope's daughter had taped a new maxim on Honey's refrigerator door:

ONE OF THE MOST IMPORTANT SIGNS OF MATURITY IS THE REALIZATION
AND ACCEPTANCE OF THE FACT THAT NO ONE WILL EVER FULLY
UNDERSTAND

Hope had accepted the fact that no one ever would.

"Everybody thinks Walker let me live for one of two reasons," she said. "Sex, or money. Either we were sexually mad for each other, or my parents paid him off."

Hope's own reason echoed over thirty years, from her days as a lonely, eight-year old boarder at Westlake to the night she'd sat by the fire with Bill at the ranch, talking. "My number one need is to be important to somebody."

And what, finally, was one more irony in the life of the golden California girl with the bad back and the picky appetite, too thin, who lived at the million-dollar address and qualified for food stamps, whose life of apparent status and privilege was as uncertain as the ground beneath her feet?

Hope brushed her long, champagne-colored hair back from her face. She had that look in her smoky green eyes that a man who knew her well called "opaque."

"It never seems to occur to anybody that maybe Walker let me live because he thought I was a good person, a useful person, a valuable human being."

PHOTOGRAPHS

Hope Masters

OPPOSITE: The wedding of Hope and
Tom Masters

Bill Ashlock. BELOW: Bill in
his office with Raquel
Welch, John Gavin, and
Charlton Heston

The ranch

OPPOSITE: Photos Walker took of Hope and
Bill just before Bill's murder, and of
Hope the next day

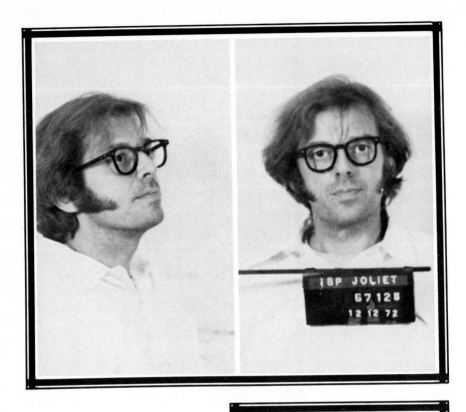

ISP JOLIET
67128
12 12 72

Lock up
your body
for it is
all mine

Taylor Wright

Hope, charged with murder, and her parents at
the Justice Court in Porterville

OPPOSITE, ABOVE: Detective Robert Swalwell,
BELOW: Detectives Jim Brown and
Gene Parker

Walker after his capture

Walker with his legal files at
court in Visalia

At the ranch, November, 1973. Left foreground, Tom and Hope,
Right foreground, Walker and Detective Brown

OPPOSITE, ABOVE: Prosecutor James Huesdens
BELOW: Defense attorney Tom Breslin with
Hope as she arrives to testify against Walker

"What if she dies first?"